In Defense of
Public Opinion Polling

In Defense of
PUBLIC
OPINION
POLLING

Kenneth F. Warren

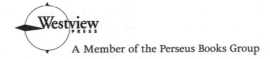

Westview
PRESS

A Member of the Perseus Books Group

Cartoons by Daniel Pearlmutter.

Westview Press books are available at special discounts for bulk purchases in the United States by corporations, institutions, and other organizations. For more information, please contact the Special Markets Department at the Perseus Books Group, 11 Cambridge Center, Cambridge MA 02142, or call (617) 252-5298.

Published in 2002 in the United States of America by Westview Press, 5500 Central Avenue, Boulder, Colorado 80301–2877, and in the United Kingdom by Westview Press, 12 Hid's Copse Road, Cumnor Hill, Oxford OX2 9JJ

Find us on the World Wide Web at www.westviewpress.com

A Cataloging-in-Publication data record for this book is available from the Library of Congress.

ISBN 0-8133-4029-2 (pb.); 0-8133-9793-6 (hc.)

The paper used in this publication meets the requirements of the American National Standard for Permanence of Paper for Printed Library Materials Z39.48–1984.

10   9   8   7   6   5   4   3   2   1

To my loving and understanding wife,

Annette,

and my children,

Heidi, Nicole, Brandon, and Emily,

and all those dedicated and honest public opinion pollsters

Contents

Illustrations

Tables

Cartoons

Preface

This book represents an attempt to place public opinion polling into a proper perspective. It is written for anyone who is genuinely interested in the polling profession, especially for those who have an open mind toward learning about the role public opinion polling really plays in our society, particularly in our politics and media.

Although this book is not designed to be a heavy academic reading, it nonetheless should have significant appeal for college classrooms. I do try to cover most of the important methodological and popular issues in public opinion polling today, yet a special effort has been made to highlight polling topics that have attracted popular attention in the past few years. An attempt has also been made to make the prose light, readable, yet provocative, and, on occasion, even witty. Students should find this style most enjoyable and agree with *Publisher's Weekly* that this book is an "engaging and informative work" or with *Booklist* that "readers interested in politics and social influences will enjoy this book."

Because I address the essential historical, methodological, philosophical, and socio-political questions pertinent to public opinion polling, this book is perfectly suited for courses in opinion polling, survey research, research methods, public opinion, media and communications, political psychology, and even some marketing courses. Since public opinion polling pervades so many fields, professors may also find the book appropriate as a supplemental text in courses in American government, American presidency, presidential elections, electoral behavior, and variety of other courses that cover public opinion polling.

Frankly, as a pollster myself, having polled for the media, local governments, politicians, and a variety of private clients in the St. Louis area, I have become quite concerned about many of the illegitimate charges that have been brought against pollsters. Some of the criticisms of pollsters are, unquestionably, quite legitimate and appropriate, but many are rooted in ignorance and bias and are patently unfair, especially those coming from some politicians, journalists, interest groups, and citizens who hypocritically use and abuse pollsters and their polls to promote their particular agendas. Consequently, another central objective of this book is an attempt to help set the record straight by evaluating the genuine pros and cons of public opinion polling.

The first chapter is a no-holds-barred attack on pollsters which attempts to encapsulate practically all of the various reasons, legitimate or not, for "Why Americans Hate Pollsters." The second chapter is basically a response to these charges made against pollsters, and is appropriately called "In Defense Of Pollsters." Chapter Three deals with the growth of the polling industry from the early years of the straw polls to modern scientific polling. Chapter Four focuses upon the makings of bad polls, while Chapter Five stresses what makes polls good ones. Chapter Six looks at the love-hate relationship journalists have with their use of polls, while Chapter Seven explores the way politicians, often hypocritically, view, use, and misuse polls. In Chapter Eight poll data on the Clinton-Lewinsky affair are examined in great detail to help us understand better how President Clinton managed to "survive" it. Chapter Nine takes a look at the developments of public opinion polling in other countries of the world, particularly emphasizing the positive role polls are starting to play in the increasing number of emerging democracies. In Chapter Ten the pollsters are tested in light of their predictions in the 2000 U.S. presidential, senatorial, and gubernatorial elections. The big question is: how accurate were their election calls? In the last chapter I reflect briefly upon the state of the polling industry, acknowledging the industry's laudable achievements, yet not ignoring its persistent struggles and concerns.

Clearly, many people provided valuable assistance in my writing of this book. I first want to acknowledge Phyllis Forchee, who used her expertise in word processing to assemble this manuscript. John Montre, as Saint Louis University's government documents librarian, taught me how to competently use my computer to retrieve all of the resource materials I needed to write this book. Of course, I want to express appreciation to my cartoonist, Daniel Pearlmutter, who did a superb job on the cartoons for this book. I also want to thank my students who have provided me with valuable feedback. Finally, I want to thank the following for their varied assistance, scholarly insights, and just plain emotional support and encouragement: Don and Julie Marsh, Kevin Horrigan, Leo Wiegman, James Gibson, Steve Puro, Jean Robert Leguey-Feilleux, Tim Lomperis, Cole Campbell, Robert Rosenthal, John Judis, Charles Jaco, John Zogby, Jo Mannies, Chuck Kofron, Clayton Berry, Ellen Carnaghan, Emmanuel Uwalaka, Wynne Moskop, Richard Warren, Verna Warren, Chuck Roberson, Jim Salter, Dick Polman, Bryan Breitung, Katy Schluge, Donna Nonnenkamp, my loving wife Annette, and my dear colleague and friend George Wendel, who tragically died suddenly while I was engaged in the writing of this book.

Kenneth F. Warren
Summer 2002

In Defense of
Public Opinion Polling

Chapter One

◉ ◉ ◉

Why Americans Hate Pollsters

Polling may need a shot in the arm, but it certainly does not rate a
shot in the back. The snipers on all sides are having a field day.
—Archibald M. Crossley, pollster, 1949,
after the pollsters blew the 1948
presidential election predictions[1]

Let me be frank. I am a pollster and it sometimes seems that everyone hates me, or at least what I do for a living. Over the course of a few decades I have served as a political analyst for television and radio stations in the United States and abroad; done talk radio; taught political polling as a professor of political science at St. Louis University; testified often as a pollster in state and federal courts; and given many guest talks to educational institutions (high schools and universities), professional groups, and civic organizations. Overall, the message that has been conveyed back to me has been loud, clear, and persistent. An enormous percentage of Americans hate pollsters and their irritating, pervasive, "stupid" polls.

At least my extensive research for this book has convinced me that I have not become simply paranoid, although driving behind cars with bumper stickers reading "Lie To Pollsters," "Nobody Has Polled Me," or "Pollsters Are Witch Doctors" has not helped to alleviate any paranoia that I may have. It appears that the attacks on pollsters and their polls come from all sorts of people for a large variety of reasons. Most journalists, especially the columnists and editorial writers, really love to trash pollsters, even though their news departments, somewhat ironically, use and rely on them heavily. The prominent columnist William Safire, who is highly critical of pollsters, argues that pollsters are often mistaken and their polls warp politics;[2] journalist Daniel Greenberg contends that pollsters damage the electoral process through the "voodoo output of polling";[3] while another journalist, Steve Neal, refers to pollsters and politicians as "partners in slime."[4]

Of course, the editorial cartoonists have great fun taking potshots at pollsters. In fact, spotting a positive editorial cartoon on pollsters is about as rare as spotting Dan Quayle spelling *potato* correctly. As Herbert Asher notes in his book *Polling and the Public*, "The nation's political cartoonists, many of whom are syndicated in newspapers that themselves conduct polls, have had a field day attacking the polls."[5] Asher even cites a 1987 study in which 61% of the comics and cartoons depicted polls negatively. (Note: This does not mean that the remaining 39% treated polls positively.) Without the benefit of a follow-up study, my guess would be, given the fact that I have almost never seen a positive comic or cartoon on pollsters and polls, that the negative percentage has increased.[6]

Politicians also love to throw stones at pollsters. But, just like journalists, the irony is that politicians rely extensively on pollsters for their political survival. Actually, as expected, politicians don't seem to mind the polls when polls favor them or the positions that they support, but when the polls show them in an unfavorable light or fail to provide statistical support to their position on the issues, they are quick to blast the pollsters and their polls. For example, reacting to his feeble showing in the polls among Republican contenders for the presidential nomination in the 2000 presidential race, Dan Quayle, in frustration, charged that Republicans were making a "colossal mistake" in placing polls before principle while stampeding to the George W. Bush camp.[7] Still plummeting in the polls two weeks later, Quayle said, "These polls are totally irrelevant right now."[8]

People who call in to talk shows, send letters to the editor, write commentary articles, or who speak out at all sorts of public gatherings make clear that they are not fond of pollsters. It does appear that attacks on pollsters come from those of all political persuasions, although at least a cursory examination of the complaints indicates that conservatives are somewhat more likely to ream pollsters than are liberals, probably because often pollsters are linked to the so-called liberal media. For example, Casey Meyers of St. Joseph, Missouri, responding to the controversy surrounding Juanita Broaddrick's rape allegation against President Clinton, wrote to *The Wall Street Journal*: "Like many, I have always believed that most of the political polls are manipulated to achieve desired results. Certainly, the Broaddrick poll lacked any pretense of objectivity. . . . This confirms my suspicion that liberal pollsters were attempting to protect Mr. Clinton, discredit Broaddrick and stifle any action on this ugly matter."[9]

My experience has been that even judges, reflecting the suspicious and cynical attitude of countless Americans, tend to look at poll data with disfavor. In *State of Missouri v. Dennis N. Rabbit*, Circuit Judge Henry Autry, in light of pretrial publicity poll data presented by me for a change of venue motion by the defense, wrote: "The only evidence that he [Rabbit] asserts . . . is the dubious statistical data presented by the testimony of Dr. Warren."[10] Rejecting polling data as "dubious" is easy for judges because it is, in many respects, politically correct to do so since poll data are so unpopular with many Americans.

This case is mentioned here to make a larger point that needs to be understood if the theme of this book is to be appreciated. Judge Autry called the polling data "dubious" without any discussion as to why. Well, critics of polls from all backgrounds and with various agendas do the same thing because they can easily get away with it. Why? Because all poll data are inherently dubious, or according to a dictionary definition of "dubious," they are "fraught with uncertainty or doubt" or "questionable."[11] It must be understood that it is the inherent dubious character of poll data that makes attacking pollsters and their polls so attractive. Even the most accurate polls are dubious in nature because they all are contaminated by various forms of bias, design problems, and technical flaws. However, as will be discussed at length in Chapter 2, all of these problems that make poll data suspect or dubious do not necessarily mean that poll results are inaccurate. In the words of Humphrey Taylor, chairman of the polling firm Louis Harris and Associates, Inc.: "I re-word Winston Churchill's famous remarks about democracy and say, 'Polls are the worst way of measuring public opinion and public behavior, or predicting elections—except for all others.'"[12]

Although pollsters and their proponents can talk about the accuracy of polls, it is nonetheless true that pollsters have angered and frustrated many Americans, as well as many elsewhere in the world, as we shall see in Chapter 9 when the focus turns to "Polling in Other Countries." The focus in this chapter, however, is on the many criticisms Americans have of pollsters and their polls, whether the criticisms are legitimate or not. Possibly, the theme of this chapter is summarized best by a column that appeared in *The Houston Chronicle* entitled, "Why Do I Hate Opinion Polls? Let Me Count The Ways."[13]

POLLS ARE UN-AMERICAN

Many Americans dislike, distrust, and even hate polls for a large number of reasons. Many of those reasons, as we shall see, have been articulated and made painfully clear in feedback to pollsters and to those who use and tout their polls. However, there seems to prevail among the American public a deeply embedded attitude toward pollsters that somehow their polls are simply un-American. That is, numerous Americans just seem to feel that pollsters have come on to the American scene and assaulted traditional American customs, institutions, and values. To many, pollsters, not just in politics but in business, entertainment, sports, and just about everywhere else, have taken over and corrupted our American way of life. It seems that no institution, no issue position, no candidate for public office, no public official, no television or radio personality, no celebrity can survive, at least in the same manner, unless they have sufficient support in the public opinion polls.

So, just how do polls appear so un-American? Take, for example, the old American notion that our country was founded and built by "rugged individuals," people of integrity who fought for what was right, not just for what was popular. Whether more fantasy than real, many Americans like to think that back in the "old days" our political and business leaders bit the bullet and made tough decisions based on principle, not on the basis of poll data. In those days, as the thinking goes, our great leaders consulted their "inner spirit" and trusted their instincts, and were guided by a righteous value system when they made their decisions, certainly not by poll numbers.

But the prevalent feeling is that things have changed for the worse and now our country is run by pollsters and their followers, not by leaders with principle and integrity. As Allan Rivlin commented in *The National Journal*, "We are a poll-driven nation. Every night of the week, Americans answer questions about politics and policy for scores of opinion surveys. Poll statistics accompany news coverage, political commentators throw them around like water balloons, and policymakers use them to support favored approaches and undercut opposing ideas. In all, we treat public opinion surveys as if they were precise scientific instruments. . . . Actually, public opinion surveys are like bulldozers at an archeological excavation."[14]

Once more, the American people have become aware that some of these pollsters, as well as their clients, seem to be scoundrels with very questionable morals and integrity. Consider, for instance, Dick Morris, who became the driving force behind the Clinton administration as Clinton's pollster and spin doctor. Morris is credited with getting Clinton to endure as president by convincing him to abandon his commitment to any principle and unpopular programs (e.g., health care reform) and instead "follow the polls, spin your way out of trouble and win the next news cycle, whatever the long-term effect."[15] Of course, Morris had to leave the Clinton administration abruptly when it was revealed that he loved frequenting prostitutes as much as he loved giving Clinton advice. But as a *Wall Street Journal* editorial made vivid, reflecting the sentiments of many Americans, Clinton's obsession with polls reveals "a cautionary tale for all modern politicians: Spend too much time following the polls and you simply forget how to lead, especially when it matters."[16]

As felt by many Americans, the dominance of the new "poll culture" has had the impact of discouraging various noble ideas and worthwhile ventures, although not very popular, while encouraging and even killing ideas and projects that have less genuine merit and worth, yet are popular in the opinion polls. Of course, the legendary American public opinion philosopher Walter Lippmann noted often in his works that what is popular is often not a good idea. He maintained that public policy decisions should be rooted in sound principles and reasoning, not popular will.[17]

In the eyes of many Americans, because the new "poll culture" has been largely responsible for crushing traditional American beliefs and practices, it has along the way been partly responsible for eroding and undermining some fundamental constitutional ideals, minorities and minority viewpoints, and even whole subcultures as well. For example, because public opinion polls have shown that the public favors tough law and order measures, in recent years our state legislatures and Congress have toughened laws to almost a silly extent in some areas, criminalized and federalized more offenses as crimes (irritating many federal judges who say they can't handle all the new cases), eroded due process protections for the accused so prosecutions can be made easier, implemented questionable mandatory sentences that have angered many judges by severely reducing their judicial discretion in sentencing, and, in states where the death sentence is legal, encouraged state officials to execute inmates at a record rate because the death sentence is so popular in the opinion polls (even when it is clearly appropriate, governors, knowing the popularity of the death sentence, almost never dare to take the political risk of commuting the sentence). Lack of sensitivity by the general public to certain other fundamental constitutional rights and protections, especially pertaining to First Amendment freedoms and Fourth and Fifth Amendment privacy protections, has caused public officials to permit these freedoms and protections to be undermined by dubious new laws and sometimes outrageous court decisions. Legislators and judges cannot resist being somewhat influenced by the "statistical precision" and tyranny of the poll numbers, even though they may often condemn them.

Minorities and entire subcultures in the United States have for decades now felt the almost tyrannical force of public opinion polls. Because there seems to be something magic about majority opinion (that 51% plus), it is often difficult for minority opinion to be given much weight. Of course, this becomes even more true as support for the position slips in the polls. Consequently, minority opinion, as expressed by African Americans, Hispanics, gays and lesbians, divorced fathers, and the like, receives inadequate representation and respect in American society because the poll numbers are simply not there for them. But not only have minority interests been deemphasized and devalued because of the dominance of opinion polls, whole American subcultures have lost out as well. Ask any southerner about the impact opinion polls have had on southern customs and values. It is difficult for southern customs and values to survive the pressures of national public opinion polls that generate poll data that overall reject so mightily so many of the customs and values of the South. It seems that public opinion polling tends to have a rather un-American "mainstreaming effect" by grossly overemphasizing majority will and opinion at the expense of minority viewpoints and rights.

But maybe what bothers Americans the most about the new "poll culture" is that they feel left out. As the popular bumper sticker reads, "Nobody Polled Me." In frustration, Harry DeWese wrote: "I have never been polled by anybody. Not 'CNN,' *Time, Newsweek, USA Today*—nary any national media pollster or political party pollster has called me. Hey, I'm in the phone book. I've even got an e-mail address. . . . The pollsters can damn sure find me!"[18]

Of course, as will be discussed in Chapter 5, the statistical odds of a person being called by a pollster, particularly a national pollster, are very low, but the average citizen does not understand this and certainly cannot understand how 500 to 1500 respondents, a typical number in a national poll, can represent accurately national public opinion. But citizens understand one thing—they were not interviewed—and in their minds, the poll numbers certainly do not speak for them.

The problem is that they really feel left out of the debate. They resent the elitist community of politicians and their spinmeisters, including the pollsters, who make decisions while apparently ignoring them. Frustrated Americans hate pollsters because poll numbers tend to assume this authoritative, scientific persona that appears to command enormous respect among the "elitist" decisionmakers who rely heavily on this "authoritative" poll data to make all sorts of decisions that the disenfranchised general public is forced to accept. Political party elites, for example, determine what candidates they will support or not support based on the poll numbers. In fact, many partisans have become disillusioned with their parties in recent years, asserting that their parties have abandoned some core party principles just because these principles played poorly in the polls. Meanwhile, politicians, as mentioned, are fearful of backing any issues that aren't popular in the polls. Americans are also frustrated with the way poll numbers have determined what they can watch on television since ratings determine what is shown. Numerous educators and social critics have commented recently that the obsession with poll numbers or only with what's popular has had the unfortunate impact of lowering American standards, corrupting America's youth, and generally "dumbing down" Americans. They rest their case by pointing to such mindless, sex-crazed, crude, and tasteless television and radio shows as *Melrose Place,* Howard Stern, and Jerry Springer.

It seems that even the "sacred" institution of American football has not escaped the nefarious reach of the pollsters. One irate Nebraska Cornhusker fan lashed out at the poll that ranked Penn State's Nittany Lions over Nebraska, claiming that the poll voters were hypocritical: "Considering the Nittany Lion schedule is 51 times easier than the Husker schedule, poll voters revel in hypocrisy."[19] Sports polls even anger the sportswriters. One sports columnist, Bryan Burwell, argued that a bowl game for the national collegiate football title had been corrupted by the pollsters.

He wrote bitterly: "If you think for a minute that this little party in the desert was for a legitimate national title, you're really fooling yourself, because even if the game were decided on the field, it was set up by bogus polls and biased pollsters."[20]

Because of what they see as the "tyranny of polls," some Americans have just had enough! A few years ago Arnold J. Oliver captured this feeling in a newspaper piece entitled "End the Pollsters' Tyranny—Don't Play Along."[21] Focusing on the negative aspects of polling for political life, Oliver argued that "too often it [polling] has been perverted to trivialize public life, to turn Americans against one another and to make of us the objects, rather than the subjects, of politics." Oliver would like the government to regulate public opinion polling in America, but because of the polling industry's enormous power and the legal obstacles to governmental regulation of polling, he concludes that "there is little immediate hope for government regulation." But he warns, "It's time to wake up. . . . In the short run, only the people themselves can end the tyranny. Do yourself and the nation a favor; when the pollsters call, don't play along."[22]

POLLS ARE ILLEGAL, IF NOT EVEN UNCONSTITUTIONAL

Arnold Oliver made the astute observation that various political and legal obstacles would inevitably prevent the government from regulating or even banning public opinion polling, but this does not mean that certain zealous public officials, over the years, have not tried to pass antipolling legislation and win lawsuits against pollsters and their clients. Realizing that ultimately it would be virtually impossible to restrict or ban polling under the free speech and press guarantees of our Constitution's First Amendment, public officials, inspired by outraged citizens and encouraged by the prospects of getting the pollsters and the "unpopular" media at the same time, focused their sights on exit polling. Exit polls, which are discussed at length in Chapter 5, appeared to be easy targets because exit interviews must only be conducted very near voting places on election day as voters leave the voting sites. Consequently, eager governmental officials believed that they could pass legislation and administrative rules, as well as successfully defend these laws and rules in court, by arguing essentially that exit interviewing must be banned or severely restricted because it is disruptive to the voting process.

Television projections of election contests have irked many public officials, political candidates, and citizens for at least four decades now. The late Senator Barry Goldwater (R-Arizona), aggravated over the networks' early projections in the 1960 presidential election, introduced a bill soon after the election that would prohibit any radio broadcasts of presidential election returns and projections until the day after election day. Early network projections, based mostly on inferences from early returns, of Goldwater's lopsided loss to Lyndon Johnson in 1964 and George McGovern's devastating defeat by Richard Nixon in 1972 inspired several Senate bills to be introduced during those years to muffle early calls of presidential races.[23] Simultaneously, local TV and radio stations were also feeling the pressure from state officials for projecting winners before the polls had closed on election day.

But it was the networks' use of sophisticated exit poll methodology in the 1980 presidential election that really caused an uproar against their projections and their exit pollsters. Further refinements in exit polling techniques and rapid advancements in technology, especially computer hardware and software, allowed networks to make astoundingly accurate projections on state races and the presidential election before a single vote had actually been counted. Not being able to resist employing the new darling of the media, exit polling, the networks stunned election watchers and voters by calling Ronald Reagan the winner over President Jimmy Carter almost three hours before the polling places closed on the West Coast or before tens of millions of voters got home from work. Upset citizens, angry politicians, and some political scientists claimed that the "inappropriate" early call of Reagan's victory caused many citizens not to vote, thus changing the outcome of certain close elections on the West Coast. Two Democratic U.S.

congressmen, Al Ullman of Oregon and James Corman of California, specifically blamed their razor-thin losses on the networks' early prediction. According to electoral studies at the University of California at Berkeley, the early call decreased voter turnout in California by more than 2%.[24]

What impact the networks' early projection in the 1980 presidential race really had on election returns on the West Coast is still debated, but there is no question that decisions by the networks to use their exit polls to call the 1980 presidential election before the polls closed on the West Coast infuriated many and caused the politically influential in our society to take legislative and legal action against pollsters and their media sponsors.

In the state of Washington, Secretary of State Ralph Munro was successful in getting the state legislature to approve a law banning exit polling within 300 feet of voting places, holding that exit interviewing unconstitutionally interferes with the right of voters to vote in a peaceful manner. Since making exit poll interviewers stand at least 300 feet from a voting site (i.e., the length of a football field) effectively prevents any exit poll from being conducted at the site, the media (ABC, CBS, NBC, and a few major newspapers, including *The New York Times*) immediately challenged the law.[25] Although the state won an initial battle in federal court in 1984, which prevented exit polling in Washington in the 1984 presidential election, the ban was eventually ruled unconstitutional by the United States Court of Appeals for the Ninth Circuit in 1988. In upholding a 1985 Federal District Court decision, the Appeals Court held that the ban on exit polling was unconstitutional because it violated the U.S. Constitution's freedom of speech protection. Specifically, the court reasoned that trying to prohibit speech just because such speech (i.e., projections) might influence voters is unconstitutional. In the court's words: "A general interest in insulating voters from outside influences is insufficient to justify speech regulation."[26] Additionally, the court noted that exit poll data are used for purposes other than just projections and, as a practical matter, the ban would not achieve its intended goal since election predictions are based on exit poll findings and projections from other states, particularly the eastern states.[27]

The fact is, however, that if enough states did pass laws effectively banning exit poling, the Ninth Circuit Court's argument that the ban would not work because exit polls were conducted in other states would fall short. The reality is that at one time over half the states were considering passing laws that would have had the impact of "killing" exit polls, and some states did pass such laws. If just a few key states with large electoral votes passed such bans and had them upheld in federal court, exit poll projections for presidential elections would have been virtually impossible to make.

But the quest to make exit polling illegal in the United States has failed. Federal courts have struck down all other attempts by states as well. The media are free, therefore, to legally make calls on presidential races at, say, 2:00 P.M., Eastern Standard Time, if they wish (and actually the networks could make them accurately, if they wanted), but the networks have voluntarily agreed not to project a winner in the presidential election until after the polls are closed on the West Coast, and for state races, not until the polls are closed in their respective states. In reality, however, the networks have only upheld the "letter" of their voluntary agreement, not the "spirit" of their agreement. Also, I must admit that I have always wondered what voters in Alaska and Hawaii think of this agreement since, if early projections adversely affect election outcomes on the West Coast, would such projections not have the same adverse effect on elections in Alaska and Hawaii? Are Alaska and Hawaii second-class states in the eyes of the networks?

The litigious craze to stop exit polling has passed, but by the mid-1990s another type of polling emerged to raise the hair on the back of the necks of numerous candidates and voters. These polls are called "push polls." Push polls, which are critiqued in Chapter 4, are really not legitimate polls at all because their primary purpose is not to sample voter opinion but to influence an election outcome by "pushing" voters in a certain direction by asking questions that unethically distort the position or image of opposition candidates and issues. In such "polls" more voters are contacted than needed for a valid sample in a legitimate poll because the objective is to influence as many voters as possible, not to conduct an actual poll.

Without doubt, these "polls" have a very seedy character, which unfortunately helps to give legitimate pollsters an undeserved bad reputation. However, legally they have been hard to stop because of our Constitution's free speech protection. Obviously, what the Ninth Circuit Court of Appeals said about attempts to restrict or ban exit polling would most likely apply to efforts to restrict "push polls" as well: "A general interest in insulating voters from outside influences is insufficient to justify speech regulation."[28] Nonetheless, because of the heightened resentment toward pollsters conducting these kinds of "polls," some futile legal attempts have been made to restrict push polling. For example, in Wisconsin the State Election Board in 1996 passed a rule aimed at holding accountable those who conduct push polls (the Election Board called them "suppression polls" because the board believed that such polls suppress or discourage voting by "turning off" the voters on candidates and politics in general). Election Board Executive Director Kevin Kennedy explained that the rule required any organization conducting "suppression" interviews to disclose during the interview who had paid for the poll. Failure to disclose who paid for the poll could be punished by a fine of up to $500 per call.[29]

Finally, it seems that the last thing some Americans want is for pollsters to be given the responsibility for conducting the U.S. Census. To many Americans, this is a matter of integrity. As Dan Miller of *USA Today* wrote: "Fairness requires the American people to cast their votes one by one on Election Day, and so, too, must the Census be an actual count to protect its integrity."[30]

The debate over whether an actual count must be taken or a survey could be used to provide a census count developed into a hot political issue in the late 1990s. The Republicans favored an actual count, whereas Democrats favored polling because actual counts in the past had omitted so many difficult to reach and count Americans (e.g., the homeless and lower-income and transient people, especially poor minorities in the inner cities) and those less affluent Americans who were most likely to vote for Democratic candidates. Proponents of an actual count insisted that Article I, Section 2 of the Constitution requires an "actual enumeration" of the U.S.

population each decade. Proponents of polling contended that an accurate count is required, not literally an enumerated count, and that modern statistical sampling techniques can provide a more accurate census count than an actual count that fails to include millions of Americans. Even Republicans have acknowledged that the actual count approach undercounted Americans by about eight million people in 1990, but they have recommended better counting methods to include those who have been left out of the count.[31] Nonetheless, skeptics doubted that pollsters could do the job any better and the dispute ended up in federal court.

In February 1999, the U.S. Supreme Court did not actually rule that polling for the 2000 census was unconstitutional, but in effect the Court said as much by holding that the Constitution requires an "actual enumeration" when conducting the census, conveying the clear message that census polling is unacceptable. During this debate the polling profession took some jabs from those who dislike pollsters, but the Supreme Court seemed to base its decision on the point of law (i.e., the Constitution seems to require an actual enumeration), not on whether they felt that pollsters could competently do the job.

POLLS ARE UNDEMOCRATIC

Pollsters have been the targets of frequent and emotional attacks by Americans who charge that polling is not only un-American and sometimes unlawful, but very damaging to our democratic institutions and practices as well. Although a plethora of allegations have been made to substantiate the claim that polling is basically an antidemocratic practice, the most prevalent complaints by protesters have been that public opinion pollsters have been allowed to emerge as a major, yet illegitimate, force in American society and that their "revered" polls, embraced by our society's "movers and shakers," serve unfairly and undemocratically to (1) sway, contaminate, and bias public opinion; (2) influence public policy decisionmaking; and (3) disrupt campaigns and election outcomes.

Often Americans lash out at the pollsters and resort to calling them unflattering names for reasons similar to why so many foreigners like to call the U.S. president insulting names. Both are powerful and influential and, therefore, predictably resented and feared. In a letter to the editor of *The Boston Globe*, a frustrated citizen, Jennie Dunkley, contended that she has been painfully watching "Congress and our judicial system slowly abdicate their responsibilities to the fourth estate and the amorphous polling industry."[32]

In a column entitled "Polls Shatter Creativity, Fun in Politics," appearing in the *St. Petersburg Times*, columnist Martin Dyckman blamed the pollsters for ruining democracy, referring to public opinion pollsters as "a plague of locusts."[33] Annoyed by how opinion polls unduly pressure politicians into altering their policy positions, he quipped: "When the obituary of American democracy is written, campaign finance corruption will be only the first chapter. Polling will be Chapter 2."

Not denying the dominance of pollsters in American politics, David Moore, Gallup Poll executive and a person certainly in a position to know about the role polls play in America, stated in his book *The Superpollsters* that polls "influence perceptions, attitudes, and decisions at every level of our society."[34] Moore adds that polls have the ability to contaminate and sway public opinion and ultimately have a major impact on determining public policy outcomes, like it or not. This is so, he maintains, because "Polling dictates virtually every aspect of election campaigns, from fund raising to electoral strategy to news coverage. And, after our representatives are elected, polling profoundly shapes the political context in which they make public policy."

Poll observers acknowledge that surveying public opinion can be useful in democratic decisionmaking, but they assert that the American people are fed up with how their opinions are frequently misunderstood and misused, often intentionally, to bolster some party's or interest group's policy position and political agenda. Public opinion scholars tend to defend this citizen complaint, raising the point that the dynamics of public opinion are very complex and well nigh impossible to decipher definitively.

Such scholars contend that reliance on simple poll numbers can distort the true public opinion picture because such reliance ignores many complex factors that contribute to opinion formation and frequent and sometimes dramatic opinion change on the issues. In his book *Polling and the Public*, Herbert Asher concludes that "public opinion is not synonymous with the results of public opinion polls, yet today the two are treated as though they are identical."[35] Americans, critical of how opinion polls are often used by their leaders, stress that conducting and interpreting public opinion polls is not synonymous with democracy either.

Those frustrated with the influence of the polling industry today also point out that even assuming public leaders try to interpret and employ poll data correctly to make wise democratic decisions, the odds are great that they will fail since public opinion polling is normally incapable of capturing the true public opinion picture on issues, especially the more complex ones. This is in part because even the best pollsters ask only a few relatively easy-to-ask-and-answer questions, failing to ask many more substantive and essential questions, especially ones that are harder to ask and answer. Various pollsters frequently appear to get very different answers to similar and sometimes almost identical questions. Why? Experts contend that this is because some event may cause answers to change dramatically; simple word changes in the question may elicit very different results; answer categories may elicit different responses; question placement in the questionnaire may also cause respondents to answer differently, and so forth.

In an article for *The Sarasota Times-Picayune* called "Polls' Words Can Sway Answers," Chris Adams provides a good example of how even "minor" changes in a survey question can cause dramatically different poll results, thus confusing even the most sincere policymaker trying to understand the public opinion. To the poll question "Who should have the primary role in providing health insurance to all Americans and controlling health costs?" 60% said the government, while 34% answered the private sector. Yet, just a month later another major polling company received a very different response when it asked: "If it came down to a choice, who would you more confidently entrust the management of the American health-care system: the private insurance industry or the federal government?" This time only 33% answered the government, while 52% said the private sector.[36] Any experienced pollster will tell you that words are very powerful and in context will convey something very different to respondents.

We can only speculate here why the wording of two questions generated such different results. However, critics of pollsters use such examples to make their argument that not only do all the conflicting poll data confuse citizens and politicians alike, but that pollsters and their clients all too often purposely word their questions to seek the results that they want. They hold that the impact of all of this is obvious. Everyone is confused, including the citizenry, the media, and our democratic leaders who might be trying in good faith to understand all the confusing poll data. But to Chris Adams, undoubtedly representing the view of many Americans, "some pollsters capitalize on [this] confusion to produce poll results that will help their causes,"[37] yet undermine democracy.

In "Polls Provide the Numbers, But the Truth Is Hard to Figure," Norman Solomon drives home the point that polls distort public opinion and sway the electorate because the structure of the questionnaire provides only limited choices to questions. He cites scholar Herbert Schiller, who claims that polling most often serves as "a choice-restricting mechanism. . . because ordinary polls reduce, and sometimes eliminate entirely, the. . . true spectrum of possible options."[38] This is no doubt true because one of the most common complaints by those being interviewed is that there was "no choice to fit my answer." Worse, critics such as Schiller conclude that the "guided" choices in polls are much more likely to serve special interests than the interests of democracy: "Those who dominate governmental decision-making and private economic activity are the main supports of the pollsters. The vital needs of these groups determine, intentionally or not, the parameters within which polls are formulated."

In the frank piece "Do You Trust Polls or Not? (Or Are You Undecided?)," Allan Rivlin, a vice president at the well-known Democratic polling firm of Peter D. Hart, stresses that poll data cannot serve democratic decisionmaking if we try to compare apples and oranges. Poll data can only be understood in context. "Context is everything," he exclaims. For example, he says that it is difficult to compare the favorability ratings of President Bill Clinton with House Speaker J. Dennis Hastert because Clinton is well known but Hastert is not. "For more meaning," he notes, "we can compare Hastert's results to those of other House Speakers, and we can track Clinton's measures throughout his presidency."[39] Rivlin is also quick to point out that it is foolish to rely on public opinion to solve difficult public policy questions confronting our democracy, especially questions that even stump our democratic leaders. Rivlin contends that the public does a good job sending general messages to our governmental leaders to "stop this," "do that," or "fix this," but that Americans are not capable through public opinion polls of guiding democratic decisionmaking by "weighing trade-offs and selecting specific policy options. With complex issues such as how to fix Social Security, the public cannot give an answer until the problem is defined, but defining the problem usually biases the results." Rivlin and others express concern and dismay with pollsters who insist on asking the public to give their opinions on issues that they know practically nothing about. Scholars assert that such useless polling can only irritate respondents and confuse policymakers but certainly not serve democracy well. They ask, for example, how helpful can public opinion be on NATO or U.S. policy toward Yugoslavia when few Americans really know where Yugoslavia is?[40]

The public is not as dumb as some pollsters must think. Common sense would suggest that the American people must wonder why pollsters pressure them to answer questions on complex policy issues that they should not be expected to know much, if anything, about. After all, Americans are generally aware that we have a representative democracy, not a direct democracy. Consequently, the attitude of most Americans must be, "Don't ask us, what do we know about, say, foreign policy, we carpenters, dentists, social workers, farmers, doctors, engineers, secretaries, etc. . . . We elected you to look into it and figure it out." Herbert Asher notes that radical critics of polls hold that polls "are simply a sop to the citizenry, that they give people a false sense of being influential when in reality political power is held and exercised by a few elites who may or may not act in the public interest."[41] However, there is reason to believe that most Americans are not fooled by pollsters into believing that their opinions are really influential since numerous behavioral studies in political efficacy (efficacy is a person's perception about his or her ability to influence the governing process) reveal that only a minority of Americans believe that they are truly influential and can have any significant impact on politics and democratic decisionmaking.[42] Although some Americans do hold an unrealistic perception of their influence in our political system, most Americans seem to have a fairly realistic view of their limited impact on politics and specific public policy choices by democratic decisionmakers. In fact, public opinion research, if you can trust me to cite a poll after all of this, reveals that Americans in the past few decades, especially since the Watergate scandal, have developed more distrust and cynicism toward politicians, government, and certain other American institutions. William Flanigan and Nancy Zingale show, for example, that "trust in government" has declined from a high of about 75% in 1963 to a low of around 27% in 1994. In turn, "positive political efficacy" has dropped from a high of 72% in 1960 to 44% by 1996. That is, in 1960, 72% of the respondents answered "Disagree" to the question, "People like me don't have any say about what government does," while in 1996 only 44% "Disagreed."[43]

In a *Congressional Quarterly* article in the early 1990s, Ronald Elving may have put his finger on a consequence of polling that may disturb the American people the most about the polling industry. Namely, that polls, but particularly the poll numbers, have an enormous effect on practically all aspects of political campaigns and, thus, election outcomes.[44] Critics contend that possibly nothing may impact democratic government more than something that adversely affects the way Americans choose their democratic leaders. Elving mentions that the old adage was, "Whom the gods would destroy, they first show favor." But today, the modern corollary should be, Elving asserts, "Whom the gods would destroy, they first show favorable poll results." Candidates who are showing poorly in early polls often tell their supporters that "These polls mean nothing!" The irony is that they may mean nothing in the sense that poll numbers can change dramatically as the campaign season progresses, but as any astute political observer or politician knows, the hard reality is that the poll numbers mean a whole lot! Just ask Lamar Alexander, Dan Quayle, Elizabeth Dole, and others who dropped out of the 2000 presidential race because their poll numbers were "too low," thus making the launching of viable campaigns virtually impossible.

Before the era of the "plague of pollsters" that now invades every campaign season, candidates had time to develop their campaigns and the luxury of being able to advance issues that they truly endorsed. Unfortunately, the realities of modern campaign politics do not afford candidates or would-be candidates that luxury. The reasons are simple. If those seeking the presidency or any other major public office[45] cannot demonstrate that they have support in the polls, they will be unable to assemble and/or maintain a campaign staff, attract money (the lifeblood of campaigns), get and hold the critical attention of the media, or gain the necessary support from interest groups and their "political party." What happened to Alexander, Quayle, and Dole after, in a sense, a "meaningless" and truly unrepresentative straw poll in Iowa during the summer of 1999 provides an "ugly" example of what dismal showings in the polls, especially relative to other candidates, can do to a candidate's campaign. In the straw poll, Dole received 14%, Alexander 6%, and Quayle 4%, but George W. Bush finished first with a whopping 31%. Alexander acknowledged the writing on the wall immediately and announced his early withdrawal. Quayle and Dole, however, tried desperately to hang on by trying to put a positive spin on their dismal numbers in the straw poll. But the inevitable was right around the corner. Supporters started to lose confidence and eventually found themselves drifting to other campaigns, especially jumping on Bush's seemingly unbeatable "bandwagon." Simultaneously, of course, interest-group backing evaporated, money for the campaign war chest dried up, and the media collectively pronounced the campaigns "dead on arrival."

Tragically, these Iowa straw poll results were largely responsible for the demise of these candidates even though Iowa is a very unrepresentative microcosm of our nation's electorate as a whole and only a total of 23,685 people voted (out of over 100 million who vote in the presidential election). This seems like small potatoes out of a U.S. voting population of approximately 190 million voters.

Many Americans recognize this scenario as a democratic tragedy and they are furious that the tyrannical power of polls has led to the destruction of American political campaigns. An emotional editorial appearing in *Nation's Business* addressed this phenomenon during the 1996 presidential campaign, noting in particular that predictions by pollsters can even convince citizens that the winner will be Clinton, so what is the sense of turning out to vote. The editorial read: "If you listen to the pollsters and pundits, you might think that the 1996 presidential election has been decided. They see the actual voting on November 5 as merely a confirmation of their prescience. The danger in their scenario is the possibility that many voters might accept it as inevitable and, as a result, neglect to cast ballots."[46]

Poll statistics may alter American elections and ultimately long-term American politics far more than the public is aware because ongoing and pervasive poll numbers constantly and even subliminally influence choices by candidates, potential candidates, elected officeholders, interest groups, journalists, and others, often before the American people are aware of it. Let me make this point through a personal experience. Minority Leader Richard Gephardt (D-Missouri) had flirted with the idea of running for president in 2000. Gephardt has always been quite popular on Capitol Hill among congressional Democrats and many interest groups and it appeared that he had a decent chance of winning his party's nomination and possibly the presidency. In a phone conversation with him, on November 5, 1998, two days after the Democrats surprisingly upset the Republicans in the off-year congressional election, I asked him if he were going to run for president, especially considering, as I pointed out, how many IOU's he could bank on from House and Senate Democrats because of his leadership position and the fact that he had unselfishly raised so much money for the campaigns of many fellow Capitol Hill Democrats. With a sigh, Gephardt's general response was that, given Gore's enormous name recognition and his strong showing in the polls relative to his own, it would just be too hard to try to defeat Gore for his party's nomination. And, of course, as a loyal Democrat, Gephardt felt that an effort by him to capture the nomination would be just too disruptive to the Democratic Party. The point is that Gephardt was influenced by poll numbers, among other considerations, way back in 1998, about two years before the November 2000 election. He made a decision that really changed the course and content of the 2000 presidential campaign, involving issues, strategies, and outcomes, and yet only a few even knew Gephardt had contemplated so deeply a possible run.[47]

Voter turnout in the United States has declined dramatically since it reached its modern high in the 1960 presidential election at around 63%. The 1996 presidential election, as well as the 1988 presidential election, failed to attract even 50% of the electorate to the polls, while the 2000 presidential election turnout was estimated at just over 50%.[48] Political observers cite many factors to help explain this decline in voter turnout (e.g., the Twenty-Sixth Amendment, which lowered the voting age in national elections to 18 years old, and voter apathy and alienation "caused" by scandals such as "Watergate," "Irangate," and "Lewinskygate"), but some critics and Americans apparently still think the dynamics of polling should receive most of the blame.

Regardless of the precise impact polls may have on American campaigns and elections, antagonists charge that polling has become practically a tyrannical force in American society, eroding the free exchange of ideas that gives democracy its very life. Jeremy Rabkin, a renowned constitutional and democratic scholar, believes that to save our democracy we must carefully debate the issues and "rise above the quick calculations of lawyers and pollsters."[49] Holly Idelson, in her article "From Every Poll, Several Opinions," argues that to preserve the integrity of our democracy our leaders must follow the wisdom of the eighteenth-century British political philosopher Edmund Burke, who believed that "political leaders must act according to their best judgment."[50] Unfortunately, she writes, our political leaders are afraid to act contrary to the poll numbers, even when they should, because of the potential political consequences of appearing to defy public opinion. To bolster her point, she notes somewhat humorously that during President George H. W. Bush's administration the "Secretary of State, James Baker, III, assured Congress that the administration would not run its policy by poll numbers, but seconds later he alluded to a poll indicating public support for the administration's course." Martin Dyckman feels that polls sabotage democracy because their numbers insidiously "kill new ideas in the cradle." To Dyckman, polls promote tyranny by majority opinion that crushes minority viewpoints that need to be heard in a healthy democracy. As a result of the enormous influence of polls, he concludes: "Where American politics used to be a crucible of change, it now commands conformity."[51] Ironically, long before public opinion polling emerged on the American scene, the legendary French statesman and philosopher Alexis de Tocqueville, in *Democracy in America*, warned Americans about the dangers to a democratic society that unwisely promotes conformity of ideas over idea diversity.[52]

POLLS INVADE OUR PRIVACY

In an editorial appearing in the *St. Petersburg Times*, citing a recent *Wall Street Journal* poll, the point was made that in the twenty-first century Americans will fear the loss of personal privacy more than anything else, even terrorist attacks. The editorial commented: "It's no wonder people are spooked. In an information age, where personal data is a valuable commodity and powerful computers make storing, referencing, and selling that data a matter of a few keystrokes, we know our privacy is slipping away."[53] In a recent book entitled *The End of Privacy*, Charles Sykes contends that the battle to preserve personal privacy will be the fiercest battle fought during this new Information Age. Sykes acknowledges that privacy advocates have circled their wagons, but so far they have not been winning the battles.[54] On the issue of privacy, as with so many issues discussed thus far, the pollsters once again have become one of the chief targets of a disgruntled public—a public frantically looking for someone or something to blame for their diminished privacy. In this Information Age, pollsters emerge as the choice culprit because, after all, pollsters are the most blatant data gatherers. Call them what you want (e.g., survey researchers, market researchers, data collectors, medical record data compilers, consumer information data collectors, census takers, behavioral survey researchers), they are all pollsters of sorts gathering and storing various forms of information for a variety of reasons about the American public. We call this the Information Age because information is being collected and stockpiled as never before. Every business and nonprofit, educational, religious, professional, community, and governmental organization seems to have an insatiable thirst for information about us.

The public seems to be fed up with the barrage of pollsters invading their privacy. Genie Dickerson, in an "Op-Ed" piece in *The New York Times*, articulated many of the consumer complaints: "Polls take up my time. The calls interrupt me, whatever I'm doing. What right does Gallup or whoever have to something of mine that he intends to turn around and sell to parties and publications?"[55] Once more, she comments, the people calling may not be who they say they are. It may be downright dangerous to give answers to some of the questions they are asking about my private life. In her words: "Some questions are too personal, or even dangerous, to answer—like the bank questions. I've also been asked the number of people in my household, whether I have a dog and a gun, and my total household income."

Dickerson has raised a question that has, frankly, always intrigued me about polling. That is, why do respondents place so much trust in the person at the other end of the line? The scary truth is that by the time the interviewer finishes answering the questions, especially the personal demographical questions at the end of the questionnaire, the interviewer, if the respondent thinks about it, has the kind of personal information that could easily place that respondent at risk. For instance, the interviewer could know, as the result of rather "stock" survey questions, (1) where the person lives (can be obtained through a "reverse" telephone-address directory since the interviewer obviously already has at least the respondent's telephone number); (2) the person's sex; (3) whether the person lives at home; (4) how long it takes to commute from work; (5) family income; (6) age; (7) marital status; (8) occupation; (9) place of employment; (10) political party preference; (11) religion; and (12) depending on the nature of the particular poll, a lot more personal information—enough key information to build a rather comprehensive profile of the person. To top it off, often respondents allow their privacy to be invaded by answering questions about very intimate subjects, such as a person's sex life. As Deborah Burke, chief of operations at the polling firm Zogby International, exclaimed: "We recently did a survey about sex and the city, and they were like, 'Yeah, I'll talk to you about that.'"[56] Some Americans abhor pollsters and simply hang up on them because they don't want to have their privacy invaded by interviewers asking the most personal questions about their lives. However, the polling business is flourishing because, obviously, a lot of people are telling "everything" to pollsters. For the sake of these very cooperative and trusting Americans, they better hope that the interviewers at the other end of the line are really legitimate pollsters. Fortunately, it seems that virtually all of them are.

But many Americans have learned to distrust and condemn pollsters because pollsters commonly say or imply very strongly to respondents that their answers will be held in strictest confidence, yet oftentimes this turns out to be a flat lie. When respondents are first contacted by phone, typically the interviewer, in order to get the interview, will tell the respondent that they were randomly selected from a telephone data base; their name is not attached to their numbers; their answers will be held in confidence; and that the personal answers to the demographical questions will be used only to compare their responses to others who responded to the survey. This sends a very positive message to respondents and helps to make them feel comfortable with responding to the survey questions. Respondents get the message that they cannot really be identified and they enjoy double protection anyway since, even if they could be identified, at least their answers will be held in total confidence.

Technically and legally, of course, everything said to the respondents may very well be true. The problem, however, is that too often it is only technically true. It is correct that their telephone numbers were selected randomly from a data base and that the telephone numbers used by interviewers normally do not have attached the names and addresses of the people being called. However, most data bases used by polling companies (e.g., Select Phone) include a complete listing, so the polling companies do have the name and address of everyone they interview. Obviously, then, respondents can be easily identified and many times they are. Sometimes survey researchers want to identify certain respondents because they may want to conduct follow-up interviews. Other times they might want to make additional money by selling their lists and respondents' answers to other companies, especially those wanting to sell something to these people. But you might say that this would violate the promise of anonymity and confidentiality, but this is not necessarily the case. Respondents are usually not told that they cannot be identified per se, this is just implied by telling them that, say, "Your telephone number was selected randomly and your telephone number is not attached to your name." They were not told that the original data base includes their name, address, and telephone number, and that, if the need arises, their telephone number can be joined again with their name and address. Upholding the terms of confidentiality does not present a problem either as long as others obtaining the data agree to hold their responses in confidence. Of course, this means that your answers could be given or sold to numerous organizations for a variety of purposes, yet they could all agree to hold your answers in confidence. Ironically, this could mean that you could be called dozens of times by different organizations and, if you got suspicious and asked one of the callers, "Where did you get my name?" the caller could easily uphold the conditions of confidentiality by not telling you. "I'm sorry, but we cannot give out that information."

No doubt Americans are becoming more sophisticated and beginning to realize just how some pollsters are exploiting them by violating their privacy. Many Americans are now, fortunately or unfortunately, refusing to cooperate with pollsters, and their numerous astute critics are exposing the nasty tricks of pollsters and the potential risks of responding to interviews. For example, Arnold Oliver advised citizens in *The Houston Chronicle*, "It's time to wake up. . . . In the short run, only the people themselves can end the tyranny. Do yourself and the nation a favor; when the pollsters call, don't play along."[57] Genie Dickerson's position is: "Blame me, if you wish, for the poor showing of conservatives in opinion polls. I refuse to respond to telephone polls."[58] And Max Frankel's take on this situation is this: "That telephone pollster called, naturally, in the middle of dinner. He asked what kind of car I dreamed of owning next. Fortunately, I was annoyed. 'Do you get paid for asking that?' 'Yes, sir.' 'Well, then, how much will I get for my answer?' 'Why nothing, sir. We have selected you so that we can learn how to serve you better.'" Frankel asserts that at that point he immediately invented a doctrine that he has used ever since to deal with pollsters: "No pay, no say."[59]

Frankel's "No pay, no say" doctrine, which he promoted in an article in *The New York Times*, is worthy of a little more attention. His doctrine is rooted in the basic assumption that information has value just like any property does. He notes: "Knowing that my answers would be sold not only to the inquiring auto maker but also to raffle mongers, credit-card usurers, catalogue peddlers and countless junk mailers, I decided that information about me, like anything created by me, is valuable property. You want my business, let's deal."[60] He claims that the simple truth in the Age of Information is that Information Is Property, so just "Let the lawyers work out the details." So much money is made by these "infomaniacs" or pollsters that certainly, he reasons, they must recognize the value of this "intellectual property" and be willing to pay. Does not the violation of personal privacy have a price?

Frankel contends that a sticky problem emerges under his "No pay, no say" doctrine because, he reasons, "I can say 'no pay, no say' to a pollster, but I have no clear legal right to stop the phone company from selling my name and address to merchandisers. How, then, will I stop computers from routinely merging and merchandising my medical and credit records?"[61] To him, Internet polls and the use of personal information in cyberspace will present greater and greater horror for those who cherish privacy. Citing Anne Wells Branscomb's "Who Owns Information: From Privacy to Public Access," Frankel credits her with concluding that today's information rights are rooted in the 1700s and they simply will not do for the twenty-first century. He asserts: "The principles underlying the First Amendment and our copyright, patent, and privacy laws no longer suffice to define which information deserves to be private property—and when it should be sacrificed to social or technological priorities." He submits that Branscomb is absolutely right when she concludes that our legislators and judges must begin to treat personal information, in her words, "as an asset with legal attributes, not unlike real estate or personal possessions."[62] What alarms Frankel, as well as millions of polled Americans, is that we spend countless billions on developing technologies to help pollsters collect, store, process, and distribute information on Americans, but we spend next to nothing trying to understand the economics of information and on developing institutional and legal safeguards to protect us from having our personal privacy exploited by pollsters.

Polling by telephone presents some serious problems for privacy advocates, but the tidal wave of the near future appears almost certain to be in Internet polling. At present, Internet polling is in its infancy and many pollsters, methodologists, and organizations are afraid to put much stock in the results of Internet polls because such polls employ very questionable sampling techniques that do not generate representative samples. In fact, most sampling experts hold that they are not sure what Internet polls represent at all except that they certainly do not represent a fair cross section of the American people. According to Tod Johnson, CEO of NPD Group, Inc., a successful market research company, "Internet users differ demographically, behaviorally, and psychologically from the general population. Saying that we can generalize about this audience without making adjustments flies in the face of all sampling theories."[63] Uncomfortable with on-line sampling at this point in time, Johnson says: "I wouldn't tell clients to buy a huge plant or make big strategy decisions based on on-line research. I would still tell them to use a more traditional technique."

However, because of many advantages of Internet polling, methodologists will be working hard to make those necessary "adjustments" (most of the adjustments will be done through a technique known as "weighting"). In *Marketing News TM*, Dana James informs his readers that "the Internet rapidly is becoming a favorite in the market researcher's collection of tools because it's cheaper, faster, and easier than surveys done in malls, by mail, or over the telephone. They can conduct wide-open, anybody-can-answer polls; opt-in, invitation-only surveys; password-protected research sites and forums; and Internet-based panels." James stresses that the speed, convenience, and low cost of Internet polls make them inevitably irresistible to the polling industry's clients. He notes that it used to cost a fortune and take maybe weeks to complete a survey, but now the new Internet pollsters can go on-line and complete a poll in twenty minutes.[64]

But already consumers have developed a love-hate attitude toward "e-commerce" on the Internet. This is because in many respects it is convenient to use the Internet to surf and to purchase items, but the costs to the consumer's privacy may be way too high. In "On the Web You Have No Secrets," Roberta Furger asserts that, for busy people like herself, using the Internet to catch the news, conduct research, or purchase something is like "a dream come true."[65] But lately, Furger adds, "I've been balking at the asking price. You see, the cost for all this convenience is my privacy—my right to buy what I want, when I want, or visit whichever Web sites I want without someone collecting personal data about me or tracking my mouse clicks. And, as much as I value my time, I value my privacy even more." She notes further, "I'm not alone, either. Anyone who's spent time on-line has experienced some assault on his or her privacy: junk mail solicitations following a Web site visit; cookies dumped into the hard drive, or demands for detailed personal information in return for browsing a site."[66]

Going to a store to buy something, especially if the consumer pays cash, will involve virtually no invasion of one's privacy. Even a credit card user will not have to answer a bunch of personal questions to make a purchase, although originally the consumer had to have answered some questions to obtain the credit card. However, once securing the credit card the consumer can use it freely for years to shop and withdraw money without being pestered with invasive personal questions. Not so on the Web! Browsing often involves responding to seemingly endless "poll" questions, while purchasing something always involves providing personal information. Of course, it is only reasonable that some personal information needs to be supplied, especially in making a purchase, but many Internet users are soured by Web page sites that require or at least pressure users to fill out relatively long questionnaires containing seemingly endless and unnecessary personal questions.

Americans are not only annoyed about having to provide information about their private lives as a condition to using a Web page, but they have become very unhappy over how their polled personal data have been used by those controlling those Web pages. Dana James contends that protecting a person's privacy on the Internet has become an enormous problem because the personal information retrieved through Internet surveys can be used to invade a person's privacy in a way never possible before the Internet. He exclaims: "Most of the general on-line population recognizes, to some extent, the ability for Internet experts to use such arcane technology as Internet Protocol addresses to 'find' them in cyberspace and, in a worst-case scenario, gain access to information about them and to potentially sensitive 'information' stored in their computers." Respondents may be spammed[67] by firms contacting them with a survey or may be spammed if a firm uses or distributes their e-mail addresses after the survey is completed to sell products.[68]

Poll data collected through Internet polls can be used by profiteers and interest groups of all kinds to bombard consumers with regular junk mail, e-mail, and annoying telephone calls. This can prove very disruptive and irritating, but at least not dangerous. When your privacy is invaded through Internet polls, your real worry is that Internet "crackers" (i.e., criminal hackers) will access your personal information to commit criminal acts against you (e.g., drain your bank account, trade your stocks, burglarize your home, or worse). Most businesses assure their customers that this can't happen, but informed Americans know that the personal information demanded by businesses and other organizations in their surveys can in fact be accessed by crackers "armed with only the most rudimentary skills."[69] In an article entitled "Can Hackers Be Stopped," Brendan Koerner, Doug Pasternak, and David Kaplan reveal that in one year crackers hacked their way into Ameritech, Bell South, Packard Bell, and the White House, making a laughable mockery of their security systems. They note that an FBI Computer Security Institute survey disclosed that 163 organizations said that they lost a combined total of about $124 million due to crackers. In another survey by the Computer Security Institute and the FBI's Computer Intrusion Squad of leading corporations and governmental agencies, 30% confessed that their computer files had been accessed by outsiders in the past year, while 55% reported illegal access to computer data by insiders. Koerner, Pasternak, and Kaplan stressed that this represents only the tip of the iceberg because "huge losses often go unreported, as most corporate victims want to avoid bad publicity."[70] Consequently, they note: "The stakes for consumers are also getting higher, as banking records, monetary transactions, and personal data rapidly become little more than 1's and 0's zipping through the Internet. Credit card numbers, the lifeblood of e-commerce, are particularly ripe for pilfering. Last August, two members of Hacking for Girlies made off with 1,749 credit card numbers."[71]

Have concerns for privacy caused Americans to avoid responding to telephone and Internet polls? At least to some extent, the answer seems to be "Yes." Not only have incensed Americans started to sue pollsters and their clients over invasions of their privacy that have led to personal losses, but a significant number of Americans, worried about having their privacy "milked," have refused to respond to those surveys that are required when entering a Web page or buying a product or service. According to Furger, even the pollsters "who gather our personal info are getting the message. In a survey of top executives of high-tech firms conducted by the Information Technology Association of America and Ernst and Young, 60 percent of respondents said they thought lack of privacy protections was the number one factor inhibiting the growth of e-commerce."[72]

Regarding phone polls, pollsters claim that it is getting harder and harder to get interviews because so many Americans are fed up with interviewers trying to invade their privacy. Busy Americans, especially in large cities and particularly in cities on the East Coast such as New York, often have little "private time" and, therefore, regard intrusions by pollsters at, say, dinnertime as meddlesome and flat-out rude. Consequently, polling firms claim that their interviewers are treated rather uncouthly by potential respondents who do not hesitate to tell the interviewer to "Get a life" or "Get a real job" or much worse. David Johnson, president of the polling company Conquest Communications, acknowledges that when they have tried to conduct interviews "we've been told exactly where to put the phone—and a number of them have offered to help put it there."[73] Regardless of whether this boorishness is warranted, the reality is that polling firms are reporting that completing interviews is becoming increasingly challenging because not only is the rejection rate well over 50% in most phone surveys, but it is becoming very difficult to even reach a live person since many Americans, protecting their privacy, are screening their calls with answering machines or services. John Zogby, president of the prestigious New York polling firm Zogby International, claims that in New York City it takes an average of approximately twelve calls to reach a live person, and an average of about five tries nationwide. He explains: "There are huge amounts of unlisted numbers, and it's a telephone culture that screens phone calls."[74]

POLLS ARE FLAWED AND INACCURATE

Still another reason why millions of Americans are turned off by polls is because they claim they are so riddled with methodological errors that they end up being grossly inaccurate and, therefore, next to worthless. My personal experience as a pollster has been that many Americans tend to react to polls the same way they relate to their sports teams and athletes. That is, they appear to remember the worst blunders and dwell upon them. In sports, fans cannot help but remember the time their team lost because of that costly errant throw in the ninth inning; that last-second blocked field goal; that crucial missed shot at the buzzer; or that fatal interception in the end zone. With polls, Americans tend to focus on the mistakes by pollsters, especially those that caused pollsters to make the wrong predictions in major election contests. For example, what serious Boston Red Sox fan can forget the time Bill Buckner let an easy ground ball roll through his legs to cost the Red Sox the 1986 World Series against the New York Mets? Or what older American, who has even casually followed politics, can forget the 1948 presidential race when so many pollsters erroneously predicted that Thomas Dewey would defeat Harry Truman, underscored by one of the most embarrassing journalistic blunders headlined in the *Chicago Tribune*, "Dewey Defeats Truman"?

Whether or not it is true that polls are commonly flawed and inaccurate, a popular perception exists that polls are routinely off the mark because they are burdened by all sorts of methodological problems and consequential errors. To borrow an irresistible quote from the London newspaper *The Guardian:* "Predictions Made By Pollsters Are Famously Inaccurate."[75]

Polling cynic Arnold Oliver opines that political polls "have two things in common. They are far less accurate than has been claimed, and the information that they reveal, even when accurate, is regularly misused."[76] Even the popular television celebrity Andy Rooney of CBS's *60 Minutes* cannot resist questioning the accuracy of polls. He exclaims, "We are all suspicious of polls. We don't trust them. We don't like to believe that we're so predictable that pollsters can tell what we think by interviewing 800 strangers."[77] Rooney said he would like to test the pollsters by having each pollster ask the exact same question. "This," he asserted, "would be a way of testing their accuracy. Their polling should produce identical figures, and my bet is that it would not."

Citizens, politicians, and critics complain constantly how methodologically unsound polling has led to poll results that are blatantly wrong. Typical of the emotional attacks on polls is a charge lodged against *The Columbus Dispatch* by Bill Moss, a Democratic candidate for mayor of Columbus, Ohio, in 1995. Moss lashed out at *The Columbus Dispatch* claiming that poll results published in their newspaper have been wrong in the past and continue to be, thus distorting election results. He contended that the newspaper's poll was not very scientific and failed to reflect the gains made by him with the voters during his campaign: "Our daily newspaper wants the people of Columbus to believe that Lashutka has a huge lead over Bill Moss, and nothing has changed between last March and August."[78] He concluded his attack by exclaiming: "They have to know the poll influences people's thinking, and that some will be discouraged from going to the polls when they're told the race is over."

In *The New York Times,* Clifford Levy was quick to point out the mistakes of some pollsters, who apparently failed to accurately predict the extent to which challenger Charles Schumer would win over Senator Alfonse D'Amato in New York's Senate race in 1998. Levy held that most polls showed a few weeks before the election that Schumer was in a virtual dead heat with D'Amato, leading D'Amato by only a percent or two, yet Schumer ended up winning the race by about 9 percentage points. Levy seemed to take delight in reflecting on some of the possible reasons for the faulty poll predictions. He began by focusing on some of the stock excuses voiced by pollsters when they blow a prediction. He mentioned that some pollsters felt that Schumer must have made significant gains over the last weekend before the election after most pollsters stopped polling. Other pollsters confessed that they failed to anticipate that most of the undecided voters would vote for Schumer, while still others maintained that they employed faulty weighting because they based their weighting on the midterm 1994 election in which there was "last minute" switching to the Republican candidates.[79]

Levy's analysis of polling errors and the pollsters' faulty assumptions about voting behavior helps to fortify the attitude of countless Americans, who already distrust pollsters, that polls are too flawed to be taken seriously. Indeed, much of the public appears to follow the advice of poll antagonist Genie Dickerson: "I do my part by taking opinion poll results with a grain of salt. Others might do the same."[80] Levy used selected quotations from Lee Miringoff, head of the Marist Institute for Public Opinion, and John Zogby to make these pollsters look ridiculous in trying to explain why their polls failed to accurately predict Schumer's decisive victory. Levy wrote that Zogby attempted to explain away his errant prediction by holding that "he had fallen victim to his belief that the turnout would be higher upstate, where Republicans dominate, and lower in New York City, a Democratic stronghold."[81] He quoted Zogby as saying, "I just went with history. I assumed a good Republican get-out-the-vote operation." Levy quoted Miringoff as saying something that cast possibly greater doubt on the ability of pollsters to conduct polls "scientifically" and make accurate predictions. In explaining why the Marist Poll was off on the Schumer race, he said: "You can't measure who is going to make a surge for get-out-the-vote." Specifically focusing on why his last poll showed Schumer with only a four-percentage-point lead, Miringoff said: "You are shooting at a moving target. If the Republicans had spent $30 million on the get-out-the-vote effort, you can take the polls and put them in the shredder."[82]

No wonder millions of Americans don't like or trust pollsters or their polls, judging from these comments by Miringoff and Zogby. These pollsters, at least in the context of these few quotes, don't seem to trust their own polls. Consider the implication of Miringoff's flip comment that poll results might as well be put in the shredder if a party spends "X" amount of money on a get-out-the-vote campaign. Are polls so unreliable that what a party spends on this or that or how much money a candidate raises or how a candidate conducts his or her campaign can render them inaccurate? Are not monies spent on get-out-the-vote drives by one party normally offset by rather predictable amounts spent by the other party? Do you think it would be comforting for Americans to learn, wanting to believe in the accuracy of polls, that what the Republicans spend on a get-out-the-vote campaign could totally destroy the validity of a poll, as Miringoff suggests? Are poll watchers comforted any more by Miringoff's remark that pollsters are just "shooting at moving targets" when they take polls? Does this insight by Miringoff not suggest to people that what pollsters find in their polls may shift dramatically from day to day during the campaign? And what can observers of polls make of Zogby's comments that he fell victim to certain assumptions about Republican upstate turnout and Democratic New York City turnout and Republican get-out-the-vote operations? How much stock could Americans place in poll predictions if poll prediction accuracy must depend so much on getting all of the assumptions correct? The point here is simply that Americans already see all sorts of problems with polls and this is why so many Americans resent the power and influence these "inaccurate" polls seem to have in our society. One would think that these comments by Miringoff and Zogby, although most likely not representing their true position on the potential corruptibility of their polls by outside influences, would cause Americans to question the accuracy of polls even more.

It is easy for the public to question the accuracy of polls, as John Watson did in a letter to the editor in *USA Today*, "since all polls are flawed."[83] Unquestionably, Watson is right. All polls are flawed. There is no such thing as a methodologically perfect poll! The list of possible methodological shortcomings in polls could prove endless. In fact, any attempt by me to comprehensively cover the flaws in polls would prove futile since readers could always think of more. I am particularly sensitive to the potential flaws in polls because I have had to defend my pretrial publicity polls, used in criminal cases (mostly murder cases), in court. Let me say frankly that it is absolutely impossible to comfortably defend polls under cross-examination because opposing counsel, with their experts, can ask endless questions as to whether you accounted for this or that. Under such circumstances, the pollster is placed in the position of defending not just his or her poll, but the practice of polling in general.

Lawyers in court can draw from a huge arsenal of potential methodological hazards in polls to try to bolster their argument that pollsters produce only inaccurate and useless polls. Understanding that the list is virtually boundless, let's look at some of the most common flaws Americans see in polls. Possibly the most prevalent complaint is that polls are inaccurate because pollsters contaminate polling with all sorts of biases. For example, regarding political polls, conservatives claim that Democratic pollsters conduct polls to favor their Democratic clients, whereas liberals contend that Republican pollsters tinker with their polls to benefit their Republican clients. This has always been a fact of political life, as Kathleen Frankovic conveys. For example, she notes, "Harry Truman called George Gallup a 'Republican pollster' when he and other public pollsters said Truman was trailing. The Dole campaign decried 'Democratic bias' in polls and poll-takers when the GOP candidate was running far behind."[84] Reporter Godfrey Sperling says that he wonders too about the validity of polls conducted by "partisan-connected" pollsters "when a pollster's findings seem to be putting a surprising glow of promise on the future of one of their clients."[85] Of course, bias in polls is not unique to political polls. Americans probably instinctively distrust market surveys used to promote some company's service or product because they often reek with blatant bias. Any intelligent consumer would be justifiably suspicious of company claims that boast, for instance, "that a university poll showed that beer drinkers preferred our beer by a margin of four to one," or "that in a survey of dentists our toothpaste was recommended over other brands by 77% of the dentists."

However, interest-group-oriented biases are not the only kind of biases that bother Americans about pollsters. Survey results can be affected, sometimes dramatically, by various methodological techniques used by pollsters. Astute Americans are aware of many of these "technical biases" that can cause polls to be inaccurate. The key to accurate poll results is drawing a sample that is truly representative, that is, that reflects a fair cross section of the population universe being surveyed. If the sample used in the poll is not representative of the population universe (e.g., the entire voting population in the United States), then valid inferences could not be made from the sample about the population universe as a whole. But the fact is, as many critics are quick to point out, some polls underrepresent or overrepresent various population groups, thus biasing the poll's statistics. Some critics claim that the "dirty little secret" in polling today that undermines the representative character of polls is the "no response" problem.[86] Falling response rates, as discussed earlier, are a "terrible problem" for pollsters according to Everett Ladd, late director of the Roper Center.[87] Low response rates (e.g., 20%) can throw off the accuracy of a poll, especially if we assume that those who can't be reached or those who refuse to respond have different opinions on things than those who do respond.

As noted earlier in another context, many Americans don't put much stock in polls because they feel that so many polls are way off because people are polled on things that they know absolutely nothing about. William Flanigan and Nancy Zingale, two electoral behavior scholars, hold that a poll question that asks respondents to simply "agree" or "disagree" with a policy choice "seriously exaggerates the number of people who hold views on political issues. People can easily say 'agree' or 'disagree' in response to a question, even if they know nothing about the topic."[88]

Plenty of Americans are particularly peeved at pollsters who imply that their poll numbers take on an aura of scientific accuracy or mathematical precision just because they interviewed a magic number of people, say 600, that allows them to claim that their poll numbers are accurate within an error margin of plus or minus 4% at 95% confidence. This was another complaint voiced by the citizen poll critic John Watson, quoted earlier. "Too often," he contends, "opinion researchers hide behind stated sampling error or margin of error to suggest accuracy."[89] Concerned citizens such as Watson should be disturbed by any pollster who suggests that error margins and confidence limits per se have anything substantive to do with accuracy. Naturally, error margins and confidence limits only make statistical sense if the random sample was drawn properly and all other orthodox polling procedures were followed. Of course, in reality, as hard as professional pollsters may try, it is practically impossible to uphold "by-the-book" approved polling techniques every step of the way. Contamination will inevitably creep in at each and every polling stage (e.g., when drawing and obtaining the sample; when drafting the questions and ordering the questions on the questionnaire; during the interviewing since different interviewers, because they are human, cannot help but elicit different responses; during the coding and entry of data; and while interpreting the data and reporting the results). Even the very best pollsters can only try to limit the extent of the contamination so the poll, despite its flaws, will still "satisfice" (i.e., be "valid enough").[90]

One final comment about error margins. Astute observers of public opinion polls also understand that normally the stated error margin applies only to the whole sample (e.g., the 600 interviewed), not to subsamples. That is, the error margin for the entire sample of 600 is ±4%, but it is ±11% for, say, a subsample of 100 African Americans. A personal experience helps to convey how silly it is to make inferences from very small subsamples. The Associated Press interviewed me immediately after Senator "Kit" Bond won reelection in Missouri to the U.S. Senate in 1998. Since Bond, a Republican, had made an extra effort to gain black support and his opponent, Jay Nixon, had said and done a few things to alienate some African American voters, an interesting question emerged: What percent of the black vote did Bond receive? The Associated Press told me that Bond had received 34% of the black vote and then asked me to comment. My immediate response was that this can't be right because Republican candidates in Missouri just do not win such high voter support from the African American community. However, Jim Salter, the AP reporter, insisted that this is what the exit poll showed. I then asked him how many voters were interviewed statewide and how many were black. He told me about one thousand total and fifty to sixty blacks. I said only fifty-plus blacks! I stressed that no one can make a valid inference from only 50 or so black voters since the error margin would be in the range of ±20–22%. This veteran reporter understood this and later the AP, in light of actual results, revised downward its estimate of the African American voter support for Bond.[91]

In sum, opinion polls may suffer from an enormous number of problems that can cause them to be grossly inaccurate. Erroneous poll results can prove to be more than just worthless, for their distortion of the real state of public opinion can cause much grief for those who are affected adversely by the poll's numbers. The American people have a right, as well as an obligation, to question the methods of pollsters and to do what they can to expose bad polls.[92]

POLLS ARE VERY ACCURATE AND MOST INTIMIDATING

In the last section, Andy Rooney was quoted as saying, "We're all suspicious of polls. We don't trust them."[93] But, undoubtedly, Rooney is wrong. Obviously, millions of Americans don't trust polls because they think that they are so fallacious, but it is also clear that countless Americans believe that they are amazingly accurate—so veracious, in fact, that they are intimidated by them. As ironic as it may seem, there is overwhelming evidence to substantiate the contention that many Americans are intimidated by polls because they know that most of them are so accurate that they have achieved an elevated status in American society because of this accuracy.

Every day we see in the media testimony to the perceived accuracy of polls and, consequently, our society's broader reliance upon them. As each year passes, despite the poll bashers, polls have evidently gained more acceptance in America as more and more Americans, while still intimidated by their use, nonetheless feel that they cannot but defer to their overall precision. As Michael Kagay and Janet Elder acknowledged: "After nearly 60 years of modern opinion polling, pollsters have shown that 1,000 carefully chosen Americans can speak for the country, that the answers they give will be the same as if every American could be polled—plus or minus three percentage points."[94] Wow! Talk about intimidating!

Possibly American politicians are the most visible hypocrites in our society when it comes to their attitudes toward public opinion polls. When running for office, they are constantly bashing the pollsters if they don't like what the pollsters' numbers reveal about them. But while complaining about these "awful" pollsters and

For all your crimes against humanity

their "dubious" poll data, they rely heavily on their own pollsters, paying them "big bucks" to steer their own political campaigns. Even heavy-weight columnist William Safire, who is not exactly in love with pollsters, acknowledges this hypocrisy: "Relying on poll numbers as they denounce reliance on pollsters, establishment politicians, and the Boys on the Bus have leapfrogged primary elections to decide—nearly a year-and-a-half before Election Day—that the contest is between George the Dubyah and Albert the Gee."[95] However, when it comes to citing and using polls, we all seem to be hypocrites. That is, we use polls when convenient to help substantiate our claims and justify our behavior, while we are quick to condemn them as foolish and inaccurate when we hear others use them to advance positions and actions that we oppose. Of course, U.S. companies spend billions of dollars each year on polls to promote their businesses, yet abruptly denounce their competition's surveys as flawed and bogus.

Those Americans who are not disingenuous understand that reputable polling firms have established a solid track record over the last few decades. They might not like the results, but "down deep" most Americans know that the results of the vast majority of polls are pretty accurate and, yes, often quite intimidating. Naturally, Americans are intimidated by pollsters who tell you who is going to win a particular political race weeks before election day before a single vote has been cast, especially when they know that the pollsters' predictions will most likely be right. It is particularly discomforting to Americans to hear that their candidate is predicted to lose.

On March 6, 2001, I conducted an exit poll for the *St. Louis Post-Dispatch* on the mayoral race in St. Louis. My poll showed that Francis Slay would win by about a 12% margin, as he did. Nonetheless, as I made clear on KMOX radio on election night, it was unsettling to learn that a boisterous victory party was taking place at Slay's headquarters on the basis of my exit-poll projections alone, since no actual vote count had been released by the election board. How intimidating the exit-poll-based victory party must have seemed to the losing candidates and their supporters.

Like many voters, Safire is intimidated and annoyed with the "Boys on the Bus" and others driven by the poll numbers. Yet even Safire is not saying the polls are wrong, he is just saying that people should not be so intimidated by the predictions to ignore the political realities that might cause the projections made a year and a half before election day to be wrong. He asserts: "How wrong they may be. One of the anointed may make a terrible gaffe under stress or lose his voice or suffer an unexpected malady."[96] Safire maintains that poll figures intimidate politicians and political journalists so much that our election process has suffered as a result. Not only do poll numbers determine who will indeed be around to debate, but it changes the content of the debate itself since politicians, frightened by pushing something not popular in the polls, feel secure in promoting only motherhood and apple pie and "cool" images. Reacting to this development in our polity, he laments: "What's bad is that it fuzzes up legitimate debate about ideology and leaves the electorate with a choice between personalities and campaign styles."

Kathleen Frankovic, director of polling at CBS News, contends that in recent years the polls, particularly media polls, have had a greater impact on the political process. Politicians have reacted and attacked pollsters, placing the pollsters "under greater stress."[97] Yet politicians defending their programs and candidates trying to win their election contests have become intimidated and stressed out by poll figures because they know that the public probably more often puts more faith in the poll numbers than in what the politicians have to say. Frankovic states: "Clearly, candidates feel they have to combat negative poll results because polling has succeeded in gaining a reputation for providing accurate and accepted measures of public opinion—more unbiased than attack ads, more believable than campaign speeches."

James Bennet finds it somewhat ironic that journalists love to berate politicians for giving in to the pollsters when journalists most often are intimidated by pollsters' numbers, too.[98] Journalists routinely rely on polls to give credibility to their stories. They often work poll statistics into their stories, as if to suggest that their stories would fall short unless they can cite a poll percentage to substantiate what is being said. As a pollster, I can tell you that I have been called frequently by journalists asking me if I could give them a poll statistic to help them strengthen a story. The following Associated Press lead paragraph to a story serves as a typical example of the media's routine reliance on poll data: "The Social Security retirement age is rising—to 67 from 65—and Americans will begin to feel the effects next year. The changes have been in the law for 16 years, but pollsters say most people have no idea they take effect in months."[99] As Bennet observes, "Journalists can be pretty snide about the tendency among politicians to dance with the polls, but news organizations often do the same."[100] The fact is that electronic and print journalists depend heavily on poll data. Few journalists are bold enough to ignore the latest polls before they air or publish their stories. Polls have gained such respect among many Americans for their accuracy that reporters and editorialists simply cannot risk their credibility by broadcasting or printing stories that fly in the face of some poll statistics. Imagine a network story airing just minutes after the network disclosed their own latest poll results that contradict the story's chief points or a newspaper report appearing beside, say, Gallup Poll statistics that blatantly undermine the story's validity. Consequently, typical news organizations subscribe to poll data services so their journalists always have on tap the latest poll information.

The fact that polls play such a prominent role in American society, especially because reputable polls tend to be so accurate, will remain a constant sore spot for Americans in the foreseeable future. Although millions of Americans may cry "Out damn spot," the increasing refinement and accuracy of polls guarantee that they will play an even more important role in American politics, business, and social life in the years to come. Undoubtedly, as polls become even more accurate and pervasive, they will become even more intimidating to Americans. Curse these mighty polls, but they will continue to flourish because so many American citizens and workers, while controlled and intimidated by them, nonetheless seem to be torturously addicted to them.

Chapter Two

◙ ◙ ◙

In Defense of Pollsters

Polls are the worst way of measuring public opinion and public behavior, or predicting elections—except for all others.
—Humphrey Taylor,
Chairman of Louis Harris & Associates, Inc., 1998[1]

All right now, in the first chapter we had great fun attacking pollsters and their polls from all fronts. And certainly it was healthy to get all of our frustrations off our chests by telling pollsters what we think of their polls. Some of the jabs were most unfair, but we enjoyed it anyway. But for those readers who cheered this assault on, this chapter does not promise to be much fun. I am just thankful that those of you who took such delight in reading the first chapter have gotten by the second chapter's title and are still reading. The theme of this chapter is probably best expressed by Humphrey Taylor's quote in the chapter's epigraph, although I would edit out "or of predicting elections" to give polls a broader application: "Polls are the worst way of measuring public opinion and public behavior . . . except for all others."[2]

When hurling grenades at pollsters, this must be kept in mind. Yes, we can criticize polls for all of their flaws, and they have many, but the bottom line is that pollsters still measure public opinion better than any competitor. I would defy the pollsters' antagonists to tell us how public opinion can be tapped any better than through polls. But the critics might say, "That is not the question. The question is whether public opinion polls should play such a dominant role in American society."

However, my answer is this. Not only do public opinion polls measure public opinion very adequately, better than any other method, but overall these polls serve American society quite well, especially American democracy, businesses, and consumers. Pollsters are not nefarious predators who prey on the American fabric. Pollsters are, excluding the always-present rotten apples, business professionals who try to uphold professional standards and ethics while dedicating themselves to doing the best possible job. In polling, that means trying to employ the best procedures practical to produce the most accurate polls. In truth, if pollsters perform their jobs badly (e.g., make false election predictions), they suffer more than other professionals who make mistakes in their jobs because pollsters' errors are "out there" for everyone to mercilessly jump on. Pollsters' "public" errors can suddenly doom their careers.

Many opponents of polls do admit to their overall accuracy, but then turn around and blame the pollsters for how their polls are misused. But can pollsters be blamed fairly for how others use their polls? To a limited extent, yes, but in most cases, no. Actually, the sciences have always been plagued with this intellectual question. That is, can we or should we hold scientists responsible for how their inventions and discoveries are eventually used? For example, should we hold Vladimir Kosma Zworykin, the inventor of television, responsible for our children watching "too much" television today? Can we blame those responsible for inventing the automobile for deadly car crashes and city smog? Analogously, can we hold pollsters responsible for the way some of their polls are misused by politicians, businesses, and the media? Probably not!

In this chapter the polling profession is defended. Many of the charges made against pollsters and their polls in the first chapter are scrutinized and dismissed as not entirely unfounded, but weak and unconvincing. Overall, I perceive pollsters to be professionals with integrity and I defend polls as quite accurate and in the democratic mainstream. Polls are also defended as useful, helping us to record and interpret history, understand the present, and plan for the future. Yes, some polls (e.g., entertainment polls) are not justified as being methodologically sound, yet depending on their use are accepted as simply provocative, interesting "fun" polls. However, I will stress that polls should never be accepted at face value. They should all be scrutinized in the context of their intended purpose and role that they play in our society. This means that we should not get upset with those methodologically flawed "fun" polls since they are not promoted as representative or accurate, but only as curiously entertaining and amusing.

MOST POLLSTERS ARE PROFESSIONALS WITH INTEGRITY

The vast majority of pollsters try hard to uphold professional and ethical standards, not only because they want to, but because they must to survive. After all, most polling firms are in business for the long term, and polling companies would not be able to survive for long in a very competitive market if they gained a reputation for conducting unprofessional and sleazy surveys. Respectable clients would refuse to hire them, professional associations such as the American Association of Public Opinion Research would condemn them, the media would publicize their bad conduct, and the informed public would reject the firms and their polls as trash.

This does not mean that there are not some "bad apples" within the polling community trying to make some short-term quick cash. As John Robinson and Robert Meadow acknowledge in their book *Polls Apart*, there are always some unscrupulous pollsters who are willing to throw away standards and principles for a price. These pollsters are known as "hired guns" who are willing to conduct "loaded" polls for clients who simply want pollsters to give them the "desired results." Robinson and Meadow assert that these "hired guns" are "commissioned by a client expressly to establish a point of view. In order to get the desired results, these polls are often conducted with blatant disregard for proper procedures."[3]

The temptations to cast aside professional standards and ethics are evidently sometimes too great to resist for some pollsters and their clients. Such pollsters, especially those who are misguided and not well established in the field, may be tempted to work for "important" political, business, or interest group clients who are willing to pay "big bucks" for certain poll results. In politics, for example, doors open more easily when candidates can pass around poll results that show they are strong and their opponents are weak. This will allow these candidates to raise more money, attract more backers, obtain more easily free "in-kind" donations such as free catering and banquet rooms, catch the serious attention of the media, and so forth. In business, obviously more positive poll numbers on a business's products or services will, at least in the short run, allow the business to attract more customers. Of course, interest groups have been notorious for using biased polls to promote their causes, although many of their polls are conducted "in-house" or by those who really are interest group supporters and not true pollsters at all. The best that can be said about these polls is that they are usually so blatantly slanted that no perceptive person would place any stock in them. The media normally reject them and the neutral "movers and shakers" roll their eyes. Nonetheless, the minority of pollsters who engage in sleazy polling practices help to give legitimate and reputable pollsters an unwarranted bad name. And, as the title for Chapter 4 makes evident, "Reputable Pollsters Hate Bad Polls" whether the polls' methodology is shoddy or the polls are just plain slimy.

To guard against unprofessional and unethical polling practices by polling firms, professional societies and associations have been created to promulgate professional standards and ethics to guide the polling profession. Reputable polling firms, many of them being members of these professional societies and associations, make every reasonable effort to comply with these professional standards and ethical principles. Those polling companies that insist on violating these standards and ethics are condemned not only by the professional associations but also by those polling firms that are upholding these standards and ethics. The media, other concerned organizations, and the public at large may also on occasion cite the standards set by these professional survey research associations to condemn dishonest or shoddy polling practices. For example, in a letter to *The Washington Post*, Francis Kissling, president of Catholics for a Free Choice, wrote:

> Catholics for a Free Choice was delighted that *The Post* reported the findings of our national poll. . . . But one thing troubles us. While our poll was conducted and the results released in a manner conforming with the customary professional standards required by scrupulous polling surveys, another poll cited in the story was given the same credence as ours even though no supporting documentation was cited.

Kissling elaborated further:

> The release of our survey was accompanied by all pertinent supporting documentation. Every question in the poll was included in our announcement. The cross tabulations were made available. And of course, the methodology was described. We even had a representative from KRC Research and Consulting, that national firm that conducted the poll, attend our press conference to answer any questions about the survey itself.

Kissling continued to attack the other poll released by the National Conference of Catholic Bishops, charging that

> the NCCB has provided no similar data to justify the statistic it provided *The Post*. We are left to wonder about the bishops' poll. What was the sample size? What other questions were asked? Who conducted the poll? When? Where? And most important, why was there no attempt to explain why this statistic (claiming that 82 percent of "church-going Catholics" oppose abortion except in limited circumstances) differs so markedly from dozens of independent

polls conducted on this subject? If we are expected to take the NCCB figures seriously, we need to know the whole story.

Finally, emphasizing that the NCCB released "no supporting data and only a few selected polls," Kissling condemned *The Washington Post* for printing selected poll findings. "If the bishops' poll was meant to be private, then none of the results should be quoted in news stories. If it was meant to be public, then let's see the whole poll."[4]

Francis Kissling's letter is given much space here because he did an admirable job condemning the reporting of a dubious poll. He listed the reasons why the Catholics for a Free Choice poll was one that complied with professional polling standards and why the National Conference of Catholic Bishops' poll did not. The reasons he cited do, in fact, reflect many of the professional standards for survey research and the proper reporting of polls endorsed by the American Association of Public Opinion Research and related associations. Kissling was also right to expose this flawed poll and to condemn the quoting of it by *The Washington Post*. This is one way of informing the public about bad polls and the irresponsible reporting of them. After all, it is unfair for those who pay considerable amounts of money for professionally conducted polls to have their polls given the same weight as poorly conducted polls that fail to meet even minimal ethical and professional survey research standards.

Professional polling associations such as the Council of American Survey Research Organizations and the American Association of Public Opinion Research, as well as professional societies associated with the polling profession such as the American Association of Political Consultants and the American Statistical Association, maintain that probably the best way to promote ethics and standards in the polling industry is to promulgate professional standards and ethics, make them known, condemn those pollsters who fail to comply, and enforce compliance with professional standards as much as possible.[5] In *What Is a Survey?* published by the American Statistical Association, it is held that "the quality of a survey is best judged not by its size, scope, or prominence, but by how much attention is given to dealing with the many important problems that can arise,"[6] that is, that can occur in each phase of the polling process from the conceptualization to the reporting stage.

The American Association of Public Opinion Research has developed professional standards and ethics for pollsters that are known as "Best Practices for Survey and Public Opinion Research," which reputable polling firms try to uphold.[7]

1. Have specific goals for the survey.
2. Consider alternatives to using a survey to collect information.
3. Select samples that well represent the population to be studied.
4. Use designs that balance costs with errors.
5. Take great care in matching question wording to the concepts being measured and the population studied.
6. Pretest questionnaires and procedures to identify problems prior to the survey.
7. Train interviewers carefully on interviewing techniques and the subject matter of the survey.
8. Construct quality checks for each stage of the survey.
9. Maximize cooperation or response rates within the limits of ethical treatment of human subjects.
10. Use statistical analytic and reporting techniques appropriate to the data collected.
11. Carefully develop and fulfill pledges of confidentiality given to respondents.
12. Disclose all methods of the survey to permit evaluation and replication.

The American Association of Public Opinion Research also promotes professional standards and ethics in the polling industry by publishing survey practices that the AAPOR condemns. The "Survey Practices That AAPOR Condemns" are listed below. AAPOR, joined by the Research Industry Coalition and the National Council on Public Polls, prefaces this list by stating: "In no case are the following practices deemed legitimate or acceptable elements of professionally conducted research":[8]

1. Requiring a monetary payment or soliciting monetary contributions from members of the public as part of a research process.
2. Offering products or services for sale, or using participant contacts as a means of generating sales leads.
3. Revealing the identity of individual respondents to a survey or participants in a research process without their permission.
4. Representing the results of a 900-number or other type of self-selected "poll" as if they were the outcome of legitimate research.
5. Conducting a so-called "push poll," a telemarketing technique in which telephone calls are used to canvass potential voters, feeding them false or misleading "information" about a candidate under the pretense of taking a poll to see how this "information" affects voter preferences.

However, despite AAPOR's efforts to monitor the polling industry through the promulgation and publication of "Best" and "Condemned" survey research practices, critics have charged for a long time that such efforts have not been completely successful in eliminating unethical and unprofessional polling. Unfortunately, some unscrupulous pollsters seem to be content in ignoring professional standards and ethics. AAPOR acknowledges, for instance, what skeptics Charles Turner and Elizabeth Martin noted back in 1984, that "existing standards for the conduct and reporting of surveys appear to have a limited impact on survey practice."[9] AAPOR today agrees that this observation by Turner and Martin is still quite true.[10] Consequently, AAPOR and other professional associations monitoring the industry have started to play a more aggressive role to stop those unscrupulous pollsters who have no problems "thumbing their noses" at the polling community's professional standards and ethics. These societies feel that it is critical to rid the industry of bad pollsters because, as the Standards Committee for AAPOR holds, unprofessional and unethical polls (e.g., "push polls") "can easily be confused with real polls, they damage the reputation of legitimate polling, thereby discouraging the public from participating in legitimate survey research."[11] To its credit, AAPOR is not just talking about the problem. AAPOR members are angry over how damaging these corrupt polls are to the legitimate polling industry and are serious about exposing and punishing pollsters who continue to conduct such polls. For example, to identify those who conduct sleazy "push polls," AAPOR set up a "hot line" so they could be notified if "push polls" are spotted. AAPOR publicized: "If you are a 'respondent' in a 'push poll' or otherwise become aware of one, please collect as much information about the situation as possible and call the President of AAPOR, Michael Kagay (212/556-3888), or . . . ."[12]

POLLS HELP PROMOTE DEMOCRACY

A lot was said in Chapter 1 about how polls serve to undermine our democratic institutions and practices. However, poll advocates contend that there are many more persuasive arguments that can be advanced to justify the position that public opinion polling is well within the democratic mainstream. These proponents claim that the use of public opinion polls in American society helps to preserve and promote our democratic system of government. More poignantly, they contend that, if we carefully analyze and weigh the advantages and disadvantages of public opinion polling for our democracy, we will see that the pros far outweigh the cons.

To this day probably no scholar has given a more visceral, emphatic, rational, or persuasive defense of the virtues of public opinion polling for American democracy than George Gallup, the "father" of American public opinion polling. Gallup, whose name is synonymous with polls, was totally convinced that public opinion polling could make modern democracy in America better. In his 1940 book *The Pulse of Democracy*, Gallup and his coauthor Saul Rae argued that political polling was essentially the very lifeblood of democracy in modern American society. Upholding an anti-elitist perspective, Gallup and Rae maintained that polling was necessary to prevent elitist interests from dominating American political decisionmaking. They asserted: "Shall the common people be free to express their basic needs and purposes, or shall they be dominated by a small ruling clique."[13] To Gallup and Rae, the existing system was dominated philosophically by the Progressive Era's thinkers, such as Walter Lippmann, who believed that American government should be left to those who know how to run the country, namely, the elite, not to ordinary citizens who know little about governance. While Lippmann placed very little faith in the virtues of public opinion,[14] Gallup and Rae felt that our political leaders had to know, understand, and be guided by public opinion if a genuine American democracy was to endure.

Gallup and Rae were particularly critical of the journalists of their day who they felt did much more to promote elitist opinion in newspapers, magazines, and on the radio than the viewpoints of ordinary citizens. To Gallup and Rae, this advancement of elitist ideals was undermining American democracy. So what was the remedy? They held that public opinion polling was the answer, increasingly so as more sophisticated techniques were being developed to measure public opinion more precisely. They contended that the health of democracy depended on "building machinery for directly approaching the mass of the people and hearing what they have to say."[15] Of course, polling provided the means to reach people "scientifically" and ask them what they thought about this and that, about this policy or that policy, about this approach or that approach, and so on. To Gallup and Rae, a democracy in touch with its people required getting feedback from its citizenry, not just on election day, but during the long time between elections. In fact, they even argued that poll results provide more timely and specific information about public policy issues than elections because elections are too infrequent and suggest nothing specific about issues.[16] That is, who knows why candidate X won over candidate Y, especially if public opinion polls are not used to help tell you why?

Rae and Gallup believed that as polls became more reliable and, thus, more influential, the less likely our society's elites would be able to dominate political decisionmaking in America. They reasoned that elites would not be able to pretend to speak for the people to get what they selfishly desire if opinion polls show that what they are pushing has little support with the people.[17] Of course, this turned out to be a very prophetic insight because today our socioeconomic and political elites may try to shape public opinion, but they rarely decide to ignore the poll numbers. In fact, as we saw in Chapter 1, polling critics argue that our leaders have become slaves to polls, too afraid to make decisions that contradict what the polls show.

Gallup and Rae also asserted that public opinion polling helps to limit the impact of propaganda in American society because opinion pollsters discover and publicize the "truth" about the level of support that various issues and interest groups enjoy. For example, they found that only 3.8% of the American people supported the Townsend Pension Plan, despite the fact that the Townsend Clubs had managed to get politicians to do "political somersaults" over the plan. They also claimed that poll data caused unions to back off supporting sit-down strikes after learning how unpopular this tactic was with the public.[18] In short, Gallup and Rae believed that polls provided a great service to democracy by exposing falsehoods and propaganda about ideas, policy proposals, programs, political leaders, interest groups, and the like. Yet skeptical critics felt, as some still do today, that powerful pollsters and their intimidating polls may emerge as the new technological elite, simply replacing the old, traditional power elite.

These two polling pioneers understood this concern, but felt that most of the fears were unfounded and rooted in the old "tyranny by the majority" theme launched by Alexis de Tocqueville over a hundred years earlier. They also contended that some of the criticism from the elites was self-serving because these elites stood to lose the most if their feeble support should be exposed. In summarizing Gallup and Rae's position, propaganda scholar J. Michael Sproule noted that they felt deeply that "polls served as antidote for 'mobocracy' and demagoguery because, by accurately reflecting public sentiment, polls invariably exposed the pretensions of self-appointed local Caesars. No wonder the politicians and interest-group leaders, who desired that 'polls should do their propaganda for them,' became outraged when their shallow support was exposed."[19] Sensitive to the charges that the use of opinion polls in American society could be politically risky, Gallup and Rae pointed out that a checks and balances system would apply to polling. First, competition among numerous polling firms would keep pollsters honest since polls out of line with other polls would need to be explained. Second, skepticism toward polls would ensure that critical eyes would always be focused on them. Third, the credibility of polls would ultimately rest with their ability to accurately predict election results. And fourth, polls should be scrutinized in the context of who conducted and sponsored the polls so that possible biases could be explored.[20]

The debate over what role public opinion polls should play in a democratic society, if any, centers essentially on what sort of democratic system different people favor. Generally, those who believe that polls undermine American democracy contend that our political leaders, once elected, should not have to consult public opinion, but should be able to make decisions on the basis of what they think is best. If the people don't like what they have done, they can boot them out on the next election day. This form of representative democracy is probably best expressed in the thinking of the conservative British philosopher Edmund Burke, as noted in Chapter 1; but we can also go way back to Plato to gain support for this viewpoint. Plato took a dim view of democratic government, stressing basically that democracy demands more from the people than they are capable of delivering. To Plato, only an elite few were capable of focusing on important matters of state, given the limited experience and knowledge of most people and the fact that "only a very exceptional nature could turn out a good man. . . . A democracy tramples all such notions underfoot; with a magnificent indifference to the sort of life a man has led before he enters politics, it will promote to honour anyone who merely calls himself the people's friend. . . . These then, and such as these, are the features of democracy, an agreeable form of anarchy with plenty of variety and an equality of a peculiar kind for equals and unequals alike."[21]

Oh, how elites throughout history have hated to be thrown into the same pile with ordinary people! Gallup recognized this, and that is why he knew the elites would condemn the virtues of public opinion polling for democracy. He and others who believe that polls can serve democracy well reject the elitist view that the public is incapable of participating more directly in the governing process. Gallup, for instance, builds more upon the political thinking of Plato's student Aristotle, to justify the importance of public opinion polling. Both have problems with "extreme" representative democracy because there is ultimately no guarantee that elected officials will understand or even try to understand the wishes of the people, and attempt to sincerely represent them. In addition, they both maintain that the "collective wisdom" of the people is far superior to the individual judgments of elected leaders. Thus, to Aristotle and Gallup, it is essential to a healthy and responsive democracy that public opinion plays a fundamental role. Aristotle's famous passage from *The Politics* sums up his position, but also certainly captures the spirit of Gallup's thinking on public opinion:

> It is possible that the many, no one of whom taken singly is a good man, may yet taken all together be better than the few, not individually but collectively, in the same way that a feast to which all contribute is better than one given at one man's expense. For where there are many people, each has some share of goodness and intelligence, and when these are brought together, they become as it were one multiple man with many pairs of feet and hands and many minds. So too in regard to character and the powers of perception. That is why the general public is a better judge of works of music and poetry; some judge some parts, some others, but their joint pronouncement is a verdict upon the whole. And it is this assembling in one what was before separate that gives the good man his superiority over any individual many from the masses.[22]

In a recent poll, 70% of the American people said that polls are good for democracy because "polls work in the public interest."[23]

Naturally, the late George Gallup would say it is to be expected in a true democracy that the people would want to be heard. To Gallup and Rae, this is because democracy "is a process of constant thought and action on the part of the citizen."[24] This does not mean that direct democracy should replace indirect or representative democracy. But it does mean, Gallup and Rae argue, that our elected leaders should use public opinion poll data to help them make democratic decisions, that is, those decisions that at least take into consideration the opinions of the people that they represent.[25]

In sum, proponents of public opinion polling today, reflecting the basic views of Gallup, believe that opinion polls can strengthen American democracy by:

1. allowing ordinary citizens a chance to meaningfully participate in the governing process;
2. permitting elected leaders to review and evaluate the constant flow of public opinion poll data;
3. making policy preferences and preferred courses of action known to governmental decisionmakers;
4. promoting the truly popular ideas and leaders and exposing those unpopular ideas and leaders;
5. dispelling misperceptions about public opinion that are disingenuously advanced by unscrupulous politicians and special interest groups;
6. revealing valuable insights on how different people with various demographical characteristics (e.g., race, age, sex, marital status, educational level, party affiliation, occupation, family income, domicile) feel about different issues, candidates, leaders, etc.;
7. disclosing overall a sense of how citizens develop opinions and attitudes and ideologies;
8. probing beyond the superficial through in-depth polls to discover deeper and more complex answers to public opinion questions and problems; and
9. becoming even more valuable to our democratic system as the sophistication and technical accuracy of opinion polls improve over time.

PROFESSIONAL POLLSTERS PROVIDE
AMAZINGLY ACCURATE DATA

In Chapter 1, a polemical argument was presented denouncing polls as inaccurate measurements of public opinion. However, virtually all who attack polls for their inaccuracies are citizens, columnists, partisans, or special interests who actually know very little about the polling profession or who may know better, but claim disingenuously that polls are "pernicious voodoo"[26] to promote their own agenda. The truth is that those who understand the polling business the best (e.g., methodologists, scholars, and practitioners from various fields who carefully follow and use polls) realize that polls are not perfect, but they know that professional pollsters today produce polls that are overall pretty accurate and reliable. For example, presidential scholar Stephen Wayne in his book *The Road to the White House*, like so many scholars, relies on poll data to develop certain points. Partly to justify his use of polls, he includes in his book's appendix a section on "Why Polls Tend To Be Accurate and How They Are Conducted." He concludes that the "main reason polls have become increasingly accurate is the improvement in sampling procedures."[27] Another presidential scholar, James Pfiffner, in *The Modern Presidency* exclaims: "Modern public polling techniques have become much more sophisticated in the second half of the Twentieth Century."[28] George Edwards and Stephen Wayne, in *Presidential Leadership*, admit that "early polls did not accurately forecast the results. The most notable gaffes occurred in 1936 and 1948, when major surveys predicted that Alfred M. Landon and Thomas E. Dewey, respectively, would win." However, Edwards and Wayne went on to stress that "the principal errors in these surveys were that their selection of people to be interviewed was not random and that they concluded polling too early before Election Day. These problems have been corrected with the consequence that public opinion surveys are more accurate."[29]

As noted in the last section, George Gallup believed that public opinion polling would never survive as a profession unless, among other things, pollsters could consistently and accurately predict election results. Clearly, Gallup was correct because elections provide a unique opportunity for pollsters to show off their talents or lack thereof. As a pollster myself, I can say that nothing is more nerve wracking for pollsters than election day, because on election day their predictions are put to a very public test and their credibility, reputations, and even their careers are placed in jeopardy. One must realize that the accuracy of the vast majority of polls that are conducted for clients (e.g., market surveys, citizen polls, planning surveys) can never be checked out for their precision (e.g., that 74% of the respondents favor brand A over brand B, or that 66% of the city's residents prefer building a swimming pool instead of a hockey rink). Therefore, those who pay hefty sums of money for poll data do so because they have become convinced by the long track record of polls that polls will provide them with information that is accurate enough to allow them to use it for their purposes (e.g., selling product A instead of product B, or building a municipal swimming pool instead of an ice rink).

Fortunately for the polling industry, the record shows that pollsters have been able to predict election outcomes accurately, sometimes with truly amazing precision, and this is why decisionmakers trust polls and are willing to spend billions of dollars on pollsters every year. Yes, of course, pollsters have had their bad days and have made some infamous calls, but as Warren Mitofsky found in analyzing predictions of presidential elections by major polling firms going back to 1948, the pollsters' predictions have improved over time and have mostly been very close to the money, if not right on the money. In commenting on predictions for the 1996 presidential contest, he noted that "the 1996 polls were unanimously correct in predicting that Clinton would win by a safe margin. Unlike those storied exemplars of polling frailty, earlier occasions for embarrassment and consternation, polling in the 1996 election could be judged a clear-cut success."[30]

Similarly, in scrutinizing the 1998 Senate and House election contests, Jennifer Hickey found that, although some pollsters missed the mark, predictions were "relatively accurate."[31] Ironically, Hickey's analysis of ten media polls in New York's U.S. Senate race led her to conclude that practically all of the pollsters came fairly close to predicting that Democratic Representative Charles Schumer would defeat Republican Senator Alfonse D'Amato. I say ironically because, if you recall from Chapter 1, journalist Clifford Levy tried to make it sound as if pollsters had blown their calls on this race, but in fact the pollsters had tracked Schumer closing in on D'Amato, catching him, and then opening up a lead just before election day.[32] The only criticism that can be made is that some pollsters presumably underestimated slightly Schumer's victory margin, although most of these polls were pretty much right on the mark if we allow for the polls' usual 3–4% error margins. Also, in fairness to these media pollsters, their polls would very likely have been even more accurate if they were allowed to poll right up until election day with their last polls being conducted the night before the election.

However, as a pollster with media clients myself, I should point out that pollsters are rarely given this luxury by media clients. This is because the media generally require the polls to be completed about five days before the election so that they can have the poll data to do their stories. The electronic media need the data for their pre-election stories and to organize for election night coverage (i.e., news directors plan their coverage, including reporter assignments and air-time allotments, around who is going to likely win or lose); magazine editors want the poll statistics so final poll predictions and related stories will arrive in their readers' mailboxes on Monday before the election; while newspaper editors need the poll data for their expanded Sunday, Monday, and Tuesday election stories with their headline predictions. The problem for pollsters is that modest electoral shifts can occur during those last five days before the election when candidates are blitzing the airwaves with ads and many of the undecided voters are finally making up their minds. In New York's 1998 U.S. Senate race, how could pollsters track Schumer's late surge if media pollsters (the most visible pollsters) had to have their final polls completed, say, the Thursday before Tuesday's election? The point is that election predictions would be even more accurate if pollsters could poll right up to the night before the election, even though this would be unacceptable to the pollsters' media clients.

Okay, enough chatter in defense of the accuracy of polls. Let's look at the actual record of major pollsters in predicting certain election results. We will start by looking at how well these prominent polling firms did in predicting presidential results since 1948. Table 2.1 shows the final poll predictions compared to the actual election results for presidential elections from 1948 to 1996. There are many hotly debated methods for calculating the statistical error of the predictions,[33] but simple mathematical calculations and common sense accomplish my objective of conveying the message that the pollsters have become quite accurate over the past few decades in forecasting the outcomes of presidential elections. First, let's give Table 2.1 a cursory look. It is no big news to learn that the pollsters were way off the target in 1948 during polling's infancy.

Both Gallup and Roper predicted that Dewey would win. The Roper Poll was clearly way off, while Gallup and Crossley missed the call, but they were not as far off as many think, considering the normal ±3–4% error margins. For example, Gallup has Dewey winning with 49.5%, but with a ±4% error margin, this would mean that Dewey could win with as much as 53.5% of the vote or lose with as little as 45.5%. Dewey won 45.1% of the vote, not that far beyond the low limit of the error margin. Truman won the election with 49.6% of the vote, yet the high end of the error margin for Gallup puts Truman at 48.5%, again not that bad for the pioneer pollster.

Clearly, since 1948 the major polling firms have posted a fairly decent track record. Gallup improved his performance in 1952, predicting Eisenhower's victory with 51% of the vote, although he still underestimated Eisenhower's actual vote by 4.1%, just outside the tolerable error margin. But practice makes perfect—or at least close to perfect. Starting with 1956, Gallup has had an impressive record with his predictions, extending only once just beyond his demanding ±3% error margin, and that was in 1980 when an abnormally high percentage of undecided voters just days before the election made it difficult for pollsters to make very

TABLE 2.1   Final Pre-Election Polls vs. Results, 1948-1996 (in percent)

Year	Candidates	Gallup Poll	Roper (1948–1976) CBS/NYT (1988, 1992) NBC (1996) Polls	Crossley (1948) Harris (1964–1996) Polls	Actual Result
1948	Truman	44.5	37.1	44.9	49.6
	Dewey	49.5	52.2	49.6	45.1
	Others	6.0	4.3	5.7	5.3
1952	Eisenhower	51.0			55.1
	Stevenson	49.0			44.4
1956	Eisenhower	59.5	60.0		57.4
	Stevenson	40.5	38.0		42.0
1960	Kennedy	51	49		49.7
	Nixon	49	51		49.5
1964	Johnson	64		64	61.1
	Goldwater	36		36	38.5
1968	Nixon	43		41	43.4
	Humphrey	42		45	42.7
	Wallace	15		14	13.4
1972	Nixon	62		61	60.7
	McGovern	38		39	37.5
1976	Carter	48	51	46	50.1
	Ford	49	47	45	48.0
	Others	3	2	3	1.9
	Undecided			6	
1980	Reagan	47		46	50.7
	Carter	44		41	41.0
	Anderson	8		10	6.6
	Others				
	Undecided	1		3	1.7
1984	Reagan	59		56	59.0
	Mondale	41		44	41.0
	Others/Undecided				
1988	Bush	53	48	51	53.4
	Dukakis	42	40	47	45.6
	Others/Undecided	5	12	2	1.0
1992	Clinton	44	44	44	43.0
	Bush	37	35	38	37.5
	Perot	14	15	17	18.9
	Others/Undecided		6		
1996	Clinton	52	49	51	49.2
	Dole	41	37	39	40.8
	Perot	7	9	9	8.5

SOURCES: Based on data presented by George C. Edwards III and Stephen J. Wayne in *Presidential Leadership: Politics and Policy Making*, 3rd and 5th eds. (New York: St. Martin's Press, 1994 and 1999), pp. 78 and 83, respectively; and a speech by Archibald Crossley reprinted in *The Polls and Public Opinion*, edited by Norman C. Meier and Harold W. Saunders (New York: Henry Holt and Co., 1949), pp. 61–62.

accurate predictions. Still, Gallup was only off by the actual win- ·
ning percentage for Reagan by 3.7%. In 1968, 1984, 1988, and
1992, Gallup's predictions were amazingly accurate in forecasting
the winner's winning percentage, being off only 0.4%, 0%, 0.4%,
and 1%, respectively. Imagine a pollster being able to employ a
methodology so sound that he could be that accurate! When
people bash pollsters, they almost never mention these near-per-
fect calls. If we look at Gallup's record for the eleven presidential
elections beginning in 1956, we see that his predictions were only
outside the ±3% error margin once, and that his average error for
predicting the winner was a laudable 1.6%.

Table 2.1 discloses that the Harris Poll has also been quite accurate since starting to make presidential contest predictions in
1964, but its record has not been as remarkable as the Gallup Poll.
In nine presidential election calls, the Harris Poll has been outside
of the ±3% margin of error only twice, in 1976 and 1980. In these
nine elections, the poll's average error has still been a respectable
2.5%. The Roper Poll (1956–1976), the CBS/New York Times Poll
(1988 and 1992), and the NBC Poll (1996) have together been outside the standard error margin only in 1988. For the six presidential elections polled, their average error was 1.8%, but this error is
inflated by the CBS/NYT poll's big miss in 1988, when the prediction was 5.4% off Bush's actual victory percentage. Excluding that
one call in 1988, the average error for the other five elections was
just 1.1% and only 0.7% for the 1960, 1976, 1992, and 1996 elections (Table 2.2).

Using a more elaborate statistical formula for measuring prediction error in presidential election forecasting, Warren Mitofsky
calculated the average error for pollsters from 1956 to 1996. His
examination, which included a total of 42 poll predictions, led him
to find almost the identical average error as my analysis. While I
found an average prediction error of 1.97%, he discovered an average error of 1.92% (Table 2.3).

Experts acknowledge that poll predictions for state and local
races are normally not as accurate as for presidential election forecasts, but state predictions are still reasonably accurate. In Mitofsky's comprehensive analysis of presidential election forecasts, he

TABLE 2.2   Average Pre-Election Presidential Poll Prediction Error, 1956–1960
             (in percent)

Year	Winning Candidate	Gallup Poll	Roper CBS/NYT, NBC Polls	Harris Poll
1956	Eisenhower	2.1	2.6	
1960	Kennedy	1.3	0.7	
1964	Johnson	2.9		2.9
1968	Nixon	4.0		2.4
1972	Nixon	1.3		0.3
1976	Carter	2.1	0.9	4.1
1980	Reagan	3.7		4.7
1984	Reagan	0.0		3.0
1988	Bush	0.4	5.4	2.4
1992	Clinton	1.0	1.0	1.0
1996	Clinton	0.2	1.8	2.8
	Average error	1.6	1.8	2.5
	Combined average error: 1.97			

SOURCES: Roper poll (1956–1976), CBS/NYT poll (1988–1992), and NBC poll (1996).

TABLE 2.3   Mitofsky's Calculated Average Presidential Poll Prediction Error,
             1956–1996

Presidential Election Year	Number of Polls	Number of Candidates	Average Error (%)
1956	1	2	1.8
1960	1	2	1.0
1964	2	2	2.7
1968	2	3	1.3
1972	3	2	2.0
1976	3	3	1.5
1980	4	3	3.0
1984	6	2	2.4
1988	5	2	1.5
1992	6	3	2.2
1996	9	3	1.7
Average error: 1.92%			

SOURCE: This table is adapted from Warren J. Mitofsky's calculations in "Was 1996 a Worse Year for Polls Than 1948?"
Public Opinion Quarterly 62 (summer 1998): 230–249, Table 4. To figure the error, he used "Method 3,"
which he explains in the text.

compared presidential predictions with state polls forecasting presidential outcomes, as well as U.S. Senate results. He acknowledged that state polls are very numerous, appear frequently in the local media, and are rarely conducted by the same pollsters who conduct the national polls.[34] He did not say it, but state and local polls are commonly done by pollsters, such as myself, who work with a much more limited budget than the national and even international polling firms. Money isn't everything, of course, but pollsters with big budgets can afford to do certain things that smaller polling firms can't afford (e.g., use more expensive computers and software and verify data entry more elaborately), possibly causing average prediction error to be at least slightly lower.

Table 2.4 shows how well state pollsters did in predicting results in presidential and U.S. Senate races. Mason-Dixon, a polling organization that conducts polls for the local media throughout the United States, did over half of the polls. As Mitofsky notes, Mason-Dixon's calls were overall somewhat better than those of the other polling firms. Collectively, of the 55 state polls predicting the presidential outcomes within the states, 15% practically hit the bull's-eye, 62% were within a 3% error margin, and 20% were way off the mark with their predictions falling beyond 6% error. The predictions were less accurate for the state races, with 47% being within the 3% error margin, yet 26% of the calls exceeded 6% error. Actually, the record for these state predictions is fairly good, especially if we spin the forecasts to stress that 80% of the presidential calls were within 6% error, while 74% of the state predictions for U.S. Senate were within 6%. The problem is that the public expects or even seems to demand more precision.

Talk about demands for near perfection! There are always those who blast the exit pollsters for their predictions, yet exit polls, especially network exit polls, have established a very impressive record. In 1996, the network exit poll pool projected the wrong winner in the U.S. Senate race in New Hampshire, although the error was corrected a few hours later. Incredibly, this was the only error made by the network exit poll pool in approximately 500 calls since this collaborative pool started in 1990.[35] One blunder in about 500 predictions means that the networks' exit poll has a

TABLE 2.4   Prediction Error in State Polls, 1996

Error of Margin Between Leading Candidates (%)	Number of Presidential Races	% in Range	Number of Senate Races	% in Range
10+	2	4	6	12
7–9	9	16	7	14
4–6	10	18	13	27
1–3	26	47	22	45
<1	8	15	1	2
Total	55	100	49	100

SOURCE: This table is adapted from Warren J. Mitofsky's calculations in "Was 1996 a Worse Year for Polls Than 1948?" *Public Opinion Quarterly* 62 (summer 1998): 230–249, Table 6.

"batting average" of .998. Nonetheless, it seems that exit poll critics remember only the New Hampshire gaffe! Give the pollsters some credit for a bravo performance!

However, the networks, relying on their exit poll data, made a disastrous mistake in the 2000 presidential election when they declared that Al Gore had won Florida, and were then forced to retract this call when actual vote tallies in Florida placed its 25 crucial electoral votes in doubt. This blunder, which may replace 1948 as the pollster's worst nightmare, is discussed in Chapters 10 and 11.

POLLS HELP US TO RECORD AND INTERPRET HISTORY

Historians crave knowledge about what happened in the past. It is inconceivable that historians would ignore looking at poll data from the distant past to help them interpret historical events, if poll data in fact existed. For polls disclose fascinating information and insights into what was going on in the past. This is the main reason why polls have grown in popularity, especially with the media because journalists know that, despite the poll bashers, people in general love to ponder poll results. This is true because polls help satisfy an instinctive curiosity that humans seem to have, that is, polls tell us what others think about all sorts of things. Such curiosity starts in childhood. What does mommy think of this, what does daddy think of that, and do my friends like me? As we grow older, we want to know more of what others think about virtually everything from entertainers and movies to politicians and their ideas and programs. Social psychologists acknowledge that we want to know what others think about things so we can fit in. On one level, we all take cues from opinion surveys so we can conform to social norms and mainstream thinking. The promotion of radical ideas may cost the average person some friends or loss of membership in a club; a politician may lose the upcoming election; or a business may suffer the loss of clients and profits.

Scholars understand the appeal and value of polls. No measurement can record the feelings of people during a moment in history better than public opinion polls. Presidential scholar James Pfiffner, after acknowledging the unique ability of modern polling to measure public opinion accurately, adds that "by examining these polls historically we can try to understand the waxing and waning popularity of presidents."[36] Polls, for example, gave us enlightening insights into the rise and fall and rise and fall again of Richard Nixon during the course of his on-again-off-again political career—from his rise to national prominence as President Eisenhower's VP after his famous and successful "Checkers speech" to his loss to John Kennedy in the 1960 presidential race to his losing bid to become governor of California in 1962 to his dramatic political comeback that allowed him to win the presidency in 1968 and 1972 to the Watergate scandal that eventually forced him to resign the presidency in disgrace. The opinion pollsters were there to track the public's opinion toward Nixon every step of the way. Political historians, political scientists, and the American people in general understand Nixon's career more today in part because of the insights the polls have given us. The historical poll data, for instance, show us what people originally liked about him, what certain groups always disliked about him, what public sentiment allowed him to win the presidency in 1968 and win big in 1972, and what caused him to fall from over 70% public approval ratings in the polls right after his State of the Union speech in January of 1973 to support low in the 20s in August of 1974 when he resigned. Pollsters were able to measure what contributed to his rise and fall with the American people with great precision. As he fell during the Watergate scandal, for example, the polls traced his demise as he lost more and more support from Nixon-Democrats, Independents, Republicans, labor, business groups, professional associations, churches, and, most of all, with the American citizenry.

Without polls, it would be futile for historians and other scholars to try to examine or explain certain things about the past— why a politician won or lost an election, or attitudes toward governmental policies. For example, in a book largely rooted in poll data, William Flanigan and Nancy Zingale employ poll data to explain American attitudes toward domestic policy from 1973 to 1996 regarding governmental spending.[37] By relying on poll data over nearly a quarter of a century, they are able to graph the changing attitudes of Americans toward spending in areas such as health care, welfare, and the environment. Just a glance at their graphs provides readers with valuable statistical data on how support for these areas has changed over the years. In one graph, Flanigan and Zingale are able to show "Attitudes Toward Cutting Spending Versus Increasing Services" by various demographical traits, including region of country, race, ethnicity, religion, and educational level. Only poll data can accurately provide such fascinating and valuable information. But public opinion polls do not focus on just politics. Since the dawn of public opinion polling, pollsters have tapped the opinion of Americans on about every conceivable subject from favorite entertainers, to the ice cream they like, to sexual preferences. Some of these polls are just plain silly, but the legitimate polls conducted on all sorts of subjects have recorded valuable, historical information about the changing American culture; these polls will be archived and examined by historians as they look back on American history.

Still not convinced about the historical value of polls? Can you imagine how much better we would understand our past if pollsters had been there to accurately tap public opinion on the different personalities, events, and issues of the day? The one thing that polls do very well is to dispel false impressions and expose myths. Assuming we could look at poll data going way back in history, we could learn the truth about historical figures and their times, destroying misperceptions about these people and the events of their day. Yes, some of our legendary heroes and much celebrated events might suffer as a result, but wouldn't it be nice to know how the Greeks regarded Plato? Did he command a lot of respect, or was he an unpopular nerd? Would Julius Caesar have won high job approval ratings? Did the British people really support King George II's war against American independence? What did the French actually think when Napoleon pronounced himself Emperor of France? Was George Washington as admired and as popular as Americans are led to believe? What popular support existed for the Civil War among Northerners in 1860? And, what percentage of the German people supported Adolf Hitler's rise to power in Germany during the 1930s? The answers to these questions and related questions would provide historians with insights that would no doubt alter their interpretations of historical figures and events.

Would people in past times have been better off if pollsters were around to conduct polls? This is a very intriguing and provocative question. Without thinking, those who hate polls would not hesitate to answer with a resounding "No!" But if George Gallup was right in his contention that elitist leaders hate polls because polls disclose the real feelings of the people, thus preventing these elites from pretending to speak for the people, the answer would be "Yes!" Many tyrants in world history have taken power and have ruled ruthlessly, often asserting that their tough rule has the support of the people. It is very doubtful that such leaders could govern with any credibility if public opinion polls existed to contradict their claims. As Machiavelli noted in *The Prince*, leaders cannot survive without the support of others, nor can leaders endure if the vast majority of people condemn their governance. At least to me, the existence of public opinion polls would have had a positive impact on world history because the very unpopular, whether in politics or elsewhere, would have had a more difficult time surviving because vital high-level support would tend to vanish if it became obvious that public support was lacking. Even the thinking of tyrants would have been tempered by poll results showing virtually no public support for their contemplated actions, if for no other reason than their own self-preservation.

Just look at the situation today regarding the acceptance of polls in different countries. Truly democratic nations such as the United States have no real problems with the use of polls. However, as we shall see in Chapter 9, nondemocratic countries like China or struggling democracies like Yugoslavia have problems with polls because their experiments with polls have proved somewhat disruptive to governance, especially when the opinion polls disclosed that the vast majority of the people were highly critical of the leaders and their policies.

POLLS HELP US UNDERSTAND THE PRESENT

We are all people in the same boat. Each day presents new challenges to us. We all rely on any information that may be useful in helping us to understand and successfully handle these new challenges. Although we sometimes express hostility toward polls, just as we display anger and frustration toward computers and software, we nonetheless rely on them to help us gain the information we need or desire as we negotiate our way through life. Actually, polls generate data that can be very helpful to us as we try to comprehend and manage the social, economic, and political forces in our lives.

Social psychologists tell us that humans are "social animals" and seem, instinctively, to try to conform to popular or group norms to win social acceptance.[38] Of course, polls tell us what others think about all sorts of things. If we keep even a casual eye on the polls, we can gain the necessary information we need in order to "fit in." Naturally, there are those "nonconformists" who don't seem to care about what others think. But actually these "nonconformists" also want to know what others in their circles feel so they can be accepted in their "nonconformist" groups or movements. Social psychologists have found that there are very few true loners who do not seek social acceptance in any group. They have also stressed that the typical person fears social ostracism more than about anything else.[39]

Think about how polls help us to "fit in," to seem "normal," or to act in a "politically correct" manner. People may be applauded and respected for their individuality and creativity to an extent, but those who stray too far from generally accepted social norms are considered improperly socialized and are inevitably rejected or even punished by society. So polls can tell us about majority and minority opinion on social phenomena and, thereby, provide us with valuable information that can help us make wise social choices. For example, knowing what is commonly accepted by mainstream society and minority groups can prevent us from saying something that is so rude or insensitive or so socially unacceptable that we will have to pay the social consequences. Years ago, CBS's sports guru Jimmy the Greek made a "politically incorrect" statement regarding African American football players and was fired as a result. Later, Marge Schott, the owner of baseball's Cincinnati Reds, made a reference to Adolf Hitler that also was not socially acceptable, causing her to not only be ostracized and sanctioned by baseball's power structure, but also condemned by millions of Americans.[40]

One might say that you do not need polls to prevent such socially unacceptable behavior. Of course, this is true since the socialization process has taken place in societies for thousands of years without the benefit of polls. Social norms have been taught rather successfully to children and others entering a society by parents, teachers, community and religious leaders, peers, and a common body of literature. Nonetheless, a plausible argument can be made that polls do a solid job in our busy and impersonal modern society surveying public opinion on just about everything, while the communications network does a fine job circulating the poll results to the people. Consequently, astute people can learn rather easily and efficiently what's in, what's out, what's acceptable, what's unacceptable, what's good, and what's bad. More than we may think, we trust and use this poll information every day to help us make choices, even though some of these decisions involve very minor matters. Survey data might help us dress and act properly and say the appropriate things in a job interview or at a social gathering. Of course, politicians, sales people, and others who absolutely depend on social acceptance for their personal and career success know that they positively cannot afford to offend people by acting or saying something that will cause them to be rejected. For example, virtually all major politicians study poll data because their career success depends on them saying the right things to certain people and groups, appearing to embrace their values and goals, and overall convincing them that they are "one of them." We also rely on consumer polls to help us decide what movies to see, where to dine, what vacation spots are best, what music CDs to buy, what fashions are in, and what actors and actresses are hot.

Various economic surveys, combined with consumer and other informational polls, can help us sharpen our understanding of the nation's economic condition, allowing us to make wiser financial decisions in our lives—decisions that may help us to keep more money in our wallets today and prudently secure our financial futures for ourselves and our families. In specialized areas, pollsters not only poll the general public, but commonly poll experts such as economists, business executives, bankers, investors, financial planners, educators, and other experts in their fields who can help give us the insights we need into complex economic matters to enable us to make much better choices regarding educational needs, career paths, living locations, market investments, health and retirement plans, "big ticket" purchases such as cars and appliances, and so forth. Even famed economists such as the Fed's czar, Alan Greenspan, regularly consult important economic surveys of business and financial leaders, as well as key economic indicators, before making critical monetary decisions regarding interest rates. Before increasing or decreasing interest rates, Greenspan would need to know, for example, what percentage of the American people intend to make major purchases in the next six months or what percentage of corporate heads anticipate increased or decreased sales.

Of course, polls help us follow and understand political life better. For most Americans, politics is quite confusing. We have frequent elections, especially on the state and local levels, involving numerous candidates and many complex ballot issues. Our political institutions, history, customs, and events may also prove quite confusing. Before public opinion polling became prevalent, responsible voters would have to spend considerable time asking others what they thought about various candidates and issues and follow the news quite carefully. But without reliable and representative polling, it was impossible for citizens to really find out what candidates and issues were truly popular or unpopular with the people and why. Again, George Gallup and Saul Rae, in *The Pulse of Democracy,* contended vehemently that polls can provide a very valuable service to democracy by exposing bad candidates and bad ideas and thereby preventing them from being advanced in our society. Polls typically go beyond just asking respondents who and what they like, to why they support or do not support certain politicians, institutions, policies, and ideas. The Aristotelian "collective wisdom" displayed in poll data can then be used to help citizens make up their minds about various political phenomena.

It is unfair for critics to say that polls yield only meaningless, superficial nonsense. Poll results can provide very comprehensive public opinion information about politics, as any major political candidate knows. For example, by studying poll data, citizens can find out not only who is popular, but what groups are supporting candidates X, Y, and Z and why, and to what extent. Today's poll data can also be placed in a historical perspective to give it more meaning. For example, poll followers knew that Bob Dole's 1996 presidential campaign was in big trouble from the start because his level of support among traditional Republican voters (e.g., the religious right, bankers, veterans) was significantly lower than it was for winning Republican presidential candidates in the past. Did the polls of 1996 help us to better understand the presidential election that year? Of course they did. Overall, pollsters did an admirable job in accurately tracking the presidential campaign from the campaign hype before the Iowa Caucus and New Hampshire Primary through the caucus and primary season, through the Republican and Democratic national conventions, and through the fall campaign to election day. The pollsters' findings provided enlightening information during the course of the campaign that helped us all understand why Bill Clinton was going to win and why Bob Dole was going to lose. Because of what we had learned from the pollsters, we all understood on election day why Dole lost.

MANY WHO PLAN USE POLLS

Reasonable people don't just "wing it," they plan. We at least casually plan our days and more carefully plan for our futures. Governments, at least responsible ones, plan before they spend thousands or millions or even billions of tax dollars on public projects and programs. Businesses also plan before they set forth on costly and uncertain new business ventures. In fact, planning is so basic and important to decisionmaking that universities offer special degree programs in planning. Let's face it, only careless or reckless people would risk wasting time and resources, to say nothing of their reputations, pursuing goals without planning. Clearly, careful planning can detect unanticipated consequences and prevent disastrous quests.

So what does all of this have to do with polls? The answer is obvious. Polls are frequently an integral part of the planning process. Of course, most of us in our personal lives do not hire pollsters to help us with our planning, yet in fact many of us or our advisors (e.g., financial planners) do use various forms of survey data to aid us in planning (e.g., consumer polls to help us with our major purchases, and other polls to help us select the best universities, investment opportunities, and retirement and health plans). However, governments and businesses do spend millions of dollars each year to help them develop sensible plans. I realize that many Americans simply think that our governmental bureaucrats recklessly throw our tax dollars "out the window" on ill-fated, unneeded projects and programs. But the truth is, according to an endless list of public opinion polls, that the vast majority of Americans support these projects and programs,[41] and governments at the national, state, and local levels normally plan carefully before they spend tax dollars.

Cities and counties across the United States collectively spend billions of tax dollars each year on roads, bridges, highways, sidewalks, sewer systems, police and fire protection, parks and recreation, education, public transportation, health care, poverty and elderly programs, new city halls, recycling centers, and on and on. Virtually everyday we see evidence of poll use by local governmental planners. For example, one story in *The Los Angeles Times* begins: "Nearly 60% of Orange County's business leaders are opposed to an international airport at the former El Toro Marine Corps Air Station, according to a survey commissioned by Irvine."[42] As a pollster who has done many polls for local governments, I must say that the local officials, especially the elected ones, become concerned and nervous over spending tax dollars on proposed projects and programs. Consequently, they like to commission pollsters to find out how their citizenry feel about their proposed plans. The last thing most mayors or city council members want is to be thrown out of office because they pursued a project that the residents did not want. Therefore, to feel more comfortable and secure, local officials like to act democratically and ask their citizens what they think about proposed actions before they act.

Citizen surveys on proposed projects can actually be quite comprehensive and, therefore, very helpful in the planning stage. Let's say a city plans to build a new municipal swimming pool complex. Typically, the city would hire a pollster to conduct a relatively comprehensive citizen survey to find out exactly what kind of swimming pool facility they want and how much they are willing to pay for it. Specifically, this citizen poll would tell city planners: (1) whether the residents even want a new swimming pool; (2) where on the priority list the proposed new pool stands (i.e., would residents rather have a new ice rink or new recycling center instead); (3) do they prefer just a traditional swimming pool or a more elaborate aqua center; (4) if an aqua center, what it should include (e.g., water slides, children's wading pools); (5) where in the city it should be built; (6) how much residents are willing to spend on it; (7) what sort of user fees should be charged; and (8) other related information. Because demographical questions would also be asked (e.g., sex, age, number of children in the household, residence location), city planners would gain valuable perspectives on what different groups of residents favor or oppose regarding the proposed pool. With such comprehensive opinions from residents, city officials could feel confident in building the kind of swimming pool complex their residents really favor. These resident polls also make for good public relations since officials can always cite resident opinion to justify their democratically sanctioned actions. The results of these surveys are almost always published in the city's local newspaper with a headline such as "73% of Community Residents Favor Building New Aqua Center."

States frequently use polls to plan for major projects and programs involving new highways, water resources, conservation, and human resources. States also employ polls in planning cooperative, regional projects and programs (e.g., dams, transit systems, pollution and disease control projects/programs). The feds in Washington also seek public approval for most of their proposals. In fact, as noted in Chapter 1, some critics believe that Washington politicians rely on polls too much in making their decisions. This may be true, but it still would not be wise or very democratic for our president and/or our legislators to defy public opinion on various public policy matters and spend billions of tax dollars on things that the majority of Americans say they emphatically don't want. Fortunately, our leaders at all governmental levels do frequently rely on polls in the planning process, thus taking into consideration public opinion. Consequently, most implemented public projects and programs do have the approval of the American people.

Businesses, although not democratic institutions, cannot afford to ignore public opinion either, so they also rely on polls to help them make their business decisions. "Know your market or go broke getting to know your market" is a motto no business can afford to ignore whether the business is a neighborhood pizza restaurant or a large car manufacturer. Any successful business knows that you can't survive by trying to sell consumers something that they don't want. Consequently, market surveys are commonly used by all sorts of businesses to find out what their customers like or do not like. Even the tables at the local pizza place may have those short, unsophisticated, yet still somewhat useful polls asking customers how they liked the food and service. Of course, car companies survey their customers by asking them how they like their new cars. Before building a store (e.g., Nieman Marcus) in a particular area, business planners would want to know whether enough of the "right" people will patronize the store so the store can realize their projected profit goals. In sum, businesses use polls to gain the information they need to make intelligent planning decisions involving economic forecasts, projected consumer purchases, market trends, consumer buying habits, and site and relocation feasibility.

POLLS CAN BE INTERESTING, PROVOCATIVE, AND JUST PLAIN FUN

Admittedly, there are many "fun" polls out there that are simply ridiculous. These polls seem to appear everywhere, in our newspapers and magazines, on radio and television, as well as on the Internet. Only if we hide our heads in the sand could we escape them. Often the subject of these polls are silly and bizarre, and most seem to be conducted for mere amusement. They are also as unsound as the old Ford Edsel. No attempt is made to follow any established and approved polling procedures. Clearly, such polls are representative of nothing. In particular, these polls are unrepresentative because no effort is made to select respondents randomly. In fact, in most cases respondents select themselves and they are permitted to vote as often as they wish, for example, by repeatedly calling a 900 number and registering their opinion, voting over and over again at a Web site, or filling out and submitting the same questionnaire countless times. Also, since normally there are no controls over the respondents or responses, individu-

We have found the charges against you to be unsubstantiated

als or interest groups can significantly distort the results by organizing people (e.g., fans of movie stars or supporters of political candidates) so that hundreds or even thousands of, say, fans call in or log-on to vote countless times for a particular TV star or show. For instance, it was amusing to notice that in freevote.com's poll of top TV programs, *60 Minutes*, one of the top-rated shows on television, received only 12 votes, or about 0% of the total vote, yet *Buffy the Vampire Slayer* got 3085 votes, or 11.4% of the total vote. Mike Wallace would certainly wince at this!

But are these bad polls? From a methodological standpoint, of course they are. However, from an entertainment perspective they provide amusement and no sensible person would take them seriously. Even the people behind these polls don't take them seriously, nor do they feel compelled to defend these indefensible polls as methodologically sound. Even the pollsters' usual critics, who are quick to denounce the legitimate pollsters for even their most minor errors, seem to "chill out" and accept these fun polls for their "light" informational and entertainment value.

Come on now, don't women want to know who is the sexiest man alive? Well, according to achiev.com, it is Harrison Ford. And aren't we men dying to know who is the sexiest woman in the world? Of course, Kate Winslet is. Well, she wouldn't get my vote, but then I shouldn't complain because I failed to cast my opinion at 100sw.com. Oh, but I didn't miss the opportunity to vote for my favorite *Baywatch* star at cgi.dreamscape.com/throb/baywatch. I just love these polls because we all can learn so much from them. I particularly like peeking at my daughter's *Cosmopolitan* to read the results of their "Passion Poll" because, after all, who can resist finding out the poll results to the question, "Would you rather marry your soul mate or a billionaire?" Well, since countless women read this magazine, I don't think "us men" would have to wait for the next issue to find out the answer to this one! And if this sort of information is not enough, I can discover from these polls just about anything I want about the cities I may visit. I can find out, for example, where is the best place to dine, what are the best hot spots, where are the best bike trails, and even the best place to "people-watch." If you are going to Chicago, I can tell you already, as a result of checking out the poll data at metromix.com, that the Lake Shore path is the preferred bike path and the Navy Pier is the best place for people-watching. See you there.

So let's all lighten up and enjoy these polls. They cause no real harm, although they may sadden momentarily the hopefuls who lost out in the sexiest men and sexiest women alive polls. These are just fun polls and they are not advertised as anything more. They provide us with that "vital" information and they bring smiles, something America needs more of.

Chapter Three

□ □ □

The Giant Polling Industry

We in the field of public opinion research know that this work of ours
is destined to grow and to become more important every year. . . .
There is resistance . . . but . . . a whole army of critics can't stop it.
—George H. Gallup, 1949[1]

Much to the dismay of those over the years who have cursed the pollsters and wished for their undignified demise, the pollsters have not only survived, but they have flourished like those frightening killer bees, becoming more pervasive and mighty with each passing year. Today, the polling industry is not only a dominant force in the United States, but the industry is booming as well in many other parts of the world, especially in Western Europe, Australia, and Canada. A new frontier is even developing for the polling industry in those areas of the world once ruled by totalitarian governments. As those old totalitarian regimes crumble, giving way to the influence of Western politics and practices, the polling industry has crept in. In America, it seems that clients cannot spend enough money on pollsters. This demand has caused the number of polling firms to increase dramatically, about doubling since 1980. Political candidates have really fallen in love with the pollsters. In the 1968 election, candidates spent about $6 million on roughly 1200 polls, but by 1980, political hopefuls paid about

$20 million for close to 2000 polls, while today it is estimated that candidates spend well over $100 million during the political season for, literally, countless polls.[2]

However, the amount of money spent on political polls is only peanuts to the polling industry, as it amounts to roughly 5% of the industry's total annual revenue of around $5 billion. Many polling firms like to do some polls for highly visible political clients because conducting polls for these high-profile politicians (e.g., candidates for governor, U.S. Congress, or even president) can prove extremely valuable in promoting the name recognition and image of the polling companies, not to mention placing these firms in a much better position to secure lucrative polling jobs from government contractors in the future. In fact, the real reason the polling industry has grown by leaps and bounds in recent decades is because pollsters are performing many more polls for the government, the academic community, corporations, unions, special-interest groups, and, possibly most of all, the media.[3] Parenthetically, because media polling has become so pervasive and its impact on American society so profound, I devote an entire chapter to it (Chapter 6).

Political science professor Robert Shapiro notes that private clients, especially corporations wanting market research, have always been the chief clients of pollsters, even though "high-powered political work has always served as a blaring advertisement for other clients."[4] Shapiro claims that nonpolitical jobs have always been the bread-and-butter work for pollsters, but he stresses that today this is even more true.[5] There are many reasons why pollsters would rather work for nonpolitical clients, but probably the main reason is that the tumultuous, tense, frantic, do-or-die, client-absorbing ambiance of a campaign organization or even an elected official's administration cannot be tolerated for very long by most pollsters who know that the money is better and the pace is much more enjoyable when polling for nonpolitical clients who do not insist that their polls be done by "yesterday." Of course, overall, political clients do not make the best business investments either, since most political candidates ultimately lose, unless they are incumbent U.S. legislators, and most elected executives (e.g.,

Raking in the money

the president, governors, big-city mayors) serve only a relatively short time, not only because of term limits but also because their highly visible public positions tend to make them quite vulnerable at the ballot box.

The point is that the polling industry has become so successful that many pollsters have the luxury of picking their clients. In some respects, polling has become a very visible and glamorous profession. Many pollsters have been thrust into the limelight so often that they have become household names, nearly reaching celebrity status. Pollsters have become the "go-to" people for many clients because of their unique skills and inside knowledge of fascinating and often very crucial poll data. Of course, politicians rely on pollsters to guide their campaigns, administrations, or their votes as legislators, while the media tap them for their valuable insights into today's news and tomorrow's stories. Pollsters are routinely interviewed by newspaper and magazine reporters and regularly appear on the radio news and talk radio shows, television news, and most of all on political talk shows on television, especially cable TV, not only locally and nationally, but sometimes internationally on networks such as CNN. Not missing a beat, pollsters have also made their presence well known on the Internet.

However, with all this fame, fortune, and power comes a new responsibility for pollsters. Over a half century ago, Julian Woodward, the partner of the famous pollster Elmo Roper, prophetically saw the day when pollsters would inherit so much power and responsibility, but he worried about whether pollsters would act as responsibly as they should, especially since he did not believe, as did George Gallup, that the competitive arena of polling could ensure that the pollsters would necessarily serve the public interest. Perceiving polls as a future "public utility," he held that pollsters "must conduct themselves in such a way as to justify the responsibilities which will increasingly be theirs and to deserve the respect with which the public will regard them."[6]

THE POLLING INDUSTRY'S EARLY STRUGGLES FOR FAME, FORTUNE, AND RESPECT

As the new millennium began, the polling industry, despite some minor setbacks from occasional blown calls and the usual attacks on the industry by its detractors, is overall a well-established and respected industry on a remarkably prosperous roll. But clearly, it has not always been that way. Let's take a look back to the early years of polling when it was more commonplace for people to laugh at the pollsters' outrageous blunders than to praise their impressive accomplishments.

Sophisticated scientific polling is a modern phenomenon, but attempts to conduct unscientific polling in America go back to the early years of our republic. Maybe our government was the first to use informal surveys when they polled farmers to help government bureaucrats make projections on the year's agricultural production. Of course, as David Moore acknowledges in *The Super-pollsters*, "Pre-election polling is a time-honored sport in this country."[7] Polling has always aroused curiosity, so the media have always been partial to polls. Hoping to increase newspaper or magazine sales, the early print media used polls to "scoop" the competition, using its exclusive poll data to provide unique insights into election contests. *The Harrisburg Pennsylvanian* in 1824 published the first presidential "straw" poll, predicting that Andrew Jackson would defeat John Quincy Adams by a huge margin.[8] Jackson did win the popular vote that year by a modest margin, but he failed to win a required majority in the Electoral College, thus forcing the election decision to be decided in the U.S. House of Representatives. By orchestrating and benefiting from scandalous quid pro quo politicking in the House, Adams eventually managed to get the House to pick him.

Unscientific and unreliable straw polls were used sporadically throughout the 1800s by politicians, journalists, and the government, gaining in popularity as the century drew to a close. But despite their growing use, mostly because of their almost irresistible, intriguing numbers, everyone who relied on them normally got "burned," for these polls were so methodologically flawed that their results were virtually guaranteed to be grossly inaccurate and unreliable. Naturally, on occasion a straw poll would hit its mark, but as the popular joke goes, even a broken 24-hour clock has got to be right once a day. As the years passed and America began to give way to the momentum of scientism, the demand for scientific precision increased and, consequently, unscientific straw polls, especially in academic circles, became seriously discredited and were viewed mostly as a "joke." Business decisions to employ straw polls became very risky, especially for the media, because reputations were ultimately linked to the reliability of the commissioned straw polls. But businesses could also lose more than their reputations by employing these straw polls, as grossly inaccurate market surveys could cause them "to lose their shirts." Obviously, pollsters could never win true acceptance and build a reputable industry unless polls gained a reputation for accuracy and reliability.

Thus began the quest for methodologically sound polling techniques that could produce accurate polls. By the late 1920s and early 1930s, a few serious and dedicated pollsters were committed to developing more systematic and even "scientific" methods that could produce accurate, reliable, and, ultimately, respected and trusted polls. These almost evangelical pollsters were deeply committed to making the polling profession scientific because they believed that methodologically sound polling practices were needed to preserve and promote democracy. The accurate measurement of public opinion, these pioneers held, could promote the good health of American democracy by making known to everyone how the American people felt about various public issues, elected leaders, and their government. Jean Converse, a scholar on the origins of public opinion polling in America, depicted the attitude of these new pollsters: "Pollsters saw themselves as innovators who would defend a democratic faith with new methods of conveying the popular will. They saw their role as providing a continuous measurement of public opinion which would supplement and strengthen the normal operations of representative government and protect it from the domination of lobbyists and special interests."[9]

According to a strong consensus of scholars who have written about the development of scientific polling in America, the crusade by these adamant prodemocracy pollsters should not be dismissed as simply poppycock. Given the era, these pollsters, such as Archibald Crossley, Elmo Roper, and especially George Gallup, were convinced that American democracy was seriously threatened by undemocratic leaders who purposely misrepresented true American public opinion to promote their own selfish and ruthless agendas. For instance, public opinion scholars Carroll Glynn, Susan Herbst, Garrett O'Keefe, and Robert Shapiro emphasize that what motivated these pollsters cannot be understood outside of the context of their times. They note that: "One reason opinion polling became so popular in America is because George Gallup and others were so concerned with the way dictators—like Adolf Hitler—attempted to speak for the people instead of letting them express their own opinions. In the mid-Twentieth Century, after two bloody world wars and the rise of multiple totalitarian regimes, polling seemed like a very democratic way to communicate public opinion. The rise of surveys was, in part, a reaction to the menace of dictatorship."[10]

But the hope of using public opinion polls to help save democracy in America could not become a reality, these pollsters realized, unless polling methods were dramatically improved. Although other pollsters sought to make polling more scientific, unquestionably it was George Gallup who led the charge. After experimenting with various polling techniques, by the 1936 presidential election Gallup was convinced that the only way to make polls accurate was to make certain that the sample population used to make inferences about the total population universe be reasonably representative of that total population. Today, this only seems to make common sense, but in the 1930s it constituted a giant conceptual breakthrough in the thinking about polling.

To prove that scientific polling techniques were superior to straw polling, Gallup set out in 1936 to challenge the undisputed leader in straw polls, *The Literary Digest*. To promote sales, the *Digest* in 1916 started to conduct elaborate straw polls. Over the years, it mailed millions of ballot cards to people, asking them for their candidate preferences. The basic methodological assumption of those running *The Literary Digest* poll seemed to be: the more polled, the greater the accuracy, almost regardless of who is polled. Consequently, every presidential year the *Digest* mailed out so many million ballots that by 1932 it is estimated that, at enormous expense, it had sent out over 350 million ballots![11] Even though the *Digest*'s straw polls had quite accurately predicted the winners of the 1928 and 1932 presidential elections, Gallup was not impressed. This young upstart claimed boldly and quite arrogantly that the *Digest*'s methodology was fatally flawed and that it was about to run out of luck. While those at *The Literary Digest* bragged incessantly about their poll's accuracy, Gallup predicted that if the *Digest* continued to send ballots chiefly to those who own telephones and automobiles, its 1936 presidential prediction would grossly underestimate lower socioeconomic voters, thus biasing the poll against President Roosevelt, the Democratic candidate, who would likely draw the most electoral support from those less affluent voters. Gallup wrote in 1936: "If *The Literary Digest* were conducting a poll at the present time, the actual figures would be in the neighborhood of 44 per cent for Roosevelt and 56 percent for Landon."[12] Gallup's comments infuriated Wilfred Funk, president and editor of *The Literary Digest*, who replied angrily: "We've been through many poll battles. We've been baffled by the gales of claims and counterclaims. But never before has anyone foretold what our poll was going to show before it even started!" Sarcastically, he countered Gallup's challenge, warning "our fine statistical friend" that the *Digest* plans to continue "with those old-fashioned methods that have produced correct forecasts exactly one hundred per cent of the time."[13]

Of course, as David Moore notes, Funk's rebuttal "was neither modest nor accurate, since in previous elections the *Digest* had incorrectly predicted the winner in several states. But the claim had an element of truth: in no election had the *Digest* incorrectly predicted the overall national winner."[14] However, as Gallup predicted, *The Literary Digest* was in fact about to run out of luck. Based on two and a quarter million ballots in all forty-eight states, on October 31, 1936, the *Digest* published its ill-fated prediction that Alf Landon would win the presidential race with 57% of the Republican and Democratic vote. Most embarrassing to the *Digest* was the fact that this was only one percentage point more than what Gallup predicted their poll would forecast fourteen weeks earlier. Gallup, employing a new experimental scientific polling technique called "quota sampling," interviewed only a tiny fraction of the number that the *Digest* did, yet sought a representative sample by trying to include a proportionate percentage of people in various and key socioeconomic strata. Gallup predicted that FDR would win with 54% of the two-party vote. Of course, President Roosevelt did win by a landslide, capturing 61% of the two-party vote.

Gallup and scientific polling were deemed the victors over *The Literary Digest* and straw polling. Gallup did miss the call by seven percentage points, yet he at least picked FDR to win, something the public tends to remember more than the percentage point margin. The *Digest* was humiliated not only by predicting the wrong winner, but by predicting that FDR would receive only 42% of the two-party vote, missing Roosevelt's percentage by a whopping 19%—wildly off the mark even for a straw poll. Within a year *The Literary Digest*, its credibility and, consequently, its subscription list devastated by its grand polling gaffe, went "belly up."[15] Gallup and the other scientific pollsters, on the other hand, were inspired by their victory and were getting ready to launch the development of a huge polling industry.

THE POLLING INDUSTRY'S MATURATION YEARS: 1937–1972

Riding the wave of confidence and arrogance preceding the 1936 presidential election and after receiving much praise for their lucky yet accurate 1928 and 1932 predictions, *The Literary Digest's* editors exclaimed proudly: "All we can say in answer to the loud applause is this: 'When better polls are built, *The Digest* will build them.'"[16] But they were as wrong about this as they were about the 1936 presidential election outcome. The *Digest's* outrageously inaccurate call in 1936 discredited not only the *Digest*, but the validity and credibility of straw polls forever. Ever since 1936, straw polls have been synonymous with unscientific polling, so it would be those new scientific pollsters such as George Gallup, Archibald Crossley, Elmo Roper, and eventually "newcomers" like Mervin Field and Lou Harris, capitalizing on the death of *The Literary Digest*, who would inherit the responsibility of building a reputable polling profession and industry.

Even though Gallup's prediction of the 1936 presidential race was much more accurate than the *Digest's* dismal call, his projection was still not that close. In fact, his prediction was quite inaccurate by today's standards. Although Gallup was delighted that he had discredited straw polling and *The Literary Digest*, he knew that his forecast of the 1936 outcome was not that accurate either. He understood that much had to be done to improve the accuracy and reliability of polls so that the polling profession could flourish. The irony is that George Gallup, in retrospect, became possibly as pig-headed and stubborn as those at the *Digest* in clinging to a flawed polling methodology. Gallup did experiment for a while with various polling techniques, but he eventually became convinced that quota sampling was the best way to sample and represent American public opinion.

But just as the straw poll methods of *The Literary Digest* were ill-fated, so was Gallup's quota sampling. Yes, quota sampling proved to be a better method for obtaining a more accurate representative sample than totally unscientific straw poll methods, yet, as Gallup's competition maintained, it had some serious methodological problems too. The most serious problem was this. Basically, quota sampling requires the survey researcher to stratify the population universe (i.e., the target population to be interviewed) into socioeconomic and political strata that supposedly reflect or mirror it very accurately. For example, typically in those days, Gallup and other pollsters employing the quota sampling method would stratify the population by age, sex, income, profession, and region of country. Of course, this approach made perfect sense in theory as long as the various strata and specific stratum selected were truly reflective of the population universe as a whole. But this approach posed a serious problem because its fundamental assumption was that the pollster could actually determine the percentage of people in each stratum (e.g., the true percentage of people in the upper-income, middle-income, and lower-income categories). In practice, this proved to be impossible, so ultimately the quota sampling pollsters such as Gallup had to guesstimate the actual proportion of people in specific strata. However, in truth, guessing was not going to work over time since the quota sampling approach required that a certain percentage of respondents (i.e., quota) had to be interviewed from each stratum (e.g., interview 56% men and 44% women). Naturally, if the assumed proportions were wrong, so would be the poll. In fact, Gallup's quota sampling technique caused him to consistently underrepresent voters in the lower socioeconomic stratum. Consequently, his predictions normally underestimated the Democratic Party vote strength in elections. If you will recall, Gallup predicted in 1936 that FDR would win reelection with 54% of the two-party vote, yet Roosevelt actually got 61%.[17]

Based on "confessions" of former Gallup interviewers of that period, we know now that his interviewers even failed to interview the "right" people in the selected stratum because they were often simply too inconvenient to interview. That is, interviewers would select people who were easier to interview, often going to parks, construction sites, and houses that looked "friendly," favoring people who were outside and "interviewer ready" rather than choosing respondents on a random basis. Eventually, the fact that Gallup's interviewers employed grossly nonrandom techniques in choosing respondents became the chief target of criticism by social scientists.[18]

Gallup's stubborn refusal to abandon quota sampling for a better scientific polling method eventually proved disastrous for him in 1948, seriously harming his image and tarnishing the reputation of the polling industry until its remarkable triumph and comeback in 1960. As discussed in Chapter 2, 1948 was a very bad year for pollsters, particularly George Gallup. It was not that the Gallup Poll was the most off-target in wrongly predicting Thomas Dewey to win the presidential election, because it was not. Others, especially the Roper Poll, were way off. The Roper Poll missed the Truman victory margin by a staggering 12.4%. Gallup underestimated Truman's vote strength by 5.3%, while Crossley was the closest, being off by 4.7%. However, Gallup was the leading name in scientific polling at the time. He had won respect for his accurate calls over the years. People had come to believe him, when he argued amid the growing criticisms of quota sampling, that such sampling was the superior approach. Ironically, Gallup's 1948 prediction in the presidential race was closer than his prediction in 1936, when he was off by 7%. But this did not seem to matter because Gallup, as well as the other two prominent pollsters, Roper and Crossley, predicted the wrong winner. To reiterate what I said earlier, people tend to remember best who the pollsters predicted would win, especially when banner newspaper and magazine headlines so boldly publicized their predictions. How could the American people forget how wrong the pollsters were? In fact, as I have previously pointed out, older Americans still remember and chuckle at how wrong the pollsters were in 1948. Even Wilfred

Funk, the former editor of *The Literary Digest*, and by 1948 a successful book publisher, was able to have the "last" laugh and utter gloatfully: "I do not want to be malicious, but I get a good chuckle out of this."[19]

The immediate post-1948 election years proved difficult and humiliating for those pollsters who were determined to build a respectable polling industry. The academic community was especially critical of pollsters, attacking in particular the validity of quota sampling. The prestigious Social Science Research Council established a committee to investigate the pollsters' methods, trying to determine why their predictions were so wrong. Even Congress, particularly disturbed that the pollsters consistently overestimated the Republican vote, conducted a congressional investigation into the pollsters' record, with some legislators calling for the regulation of the polling industry.

Gallup and the other pollsters tried in vain to explain why they were wrong, citing excuses that you still hear pollsters using today. Remember, as noted previously, the excuses Zogby and other pollsters used to try to explain why they had underestimated the vote strength of Democratic challenger Representative Charles Schumer in the 1998 Senate race in New York? For instance, "last minute" polls should have been conducted to detect the "sudden" shifts of voters from one candidate to the other, and undecided voters were not allocated properly. Gallup and his fellow pollsters actually cited these same excuses for why they underestimated the Democratic vote in the 1948 election.[20]

Unfortunately, excuses never really work. People are not happy with excuses, only results. In 1948, George Gallup had failed the acid test he set for himself and the polling industry. As David Moore explained: "Whatever the explanations, and no matter how persuasive they might be to the academics and experts investigating the debate, the aura of invincibility created by the 'scientific' polls had been wiped away. Gallup had argued that elections provided the acid test for polling techniques, and the incontrovertible fact was they had failed that acid test."[21]

It must be stressed that the polling industry would not be accepted and their polls used generally in politics or in business until the pollsters passed consistently that crucial acid test. Sure, companies still used pollsters to conduct their market studies, but even in business circles eyebrows would be raised when it was suggested that major market decisions should be made based on dubious poll data. Pollsters were still looking for respect. Frequently, the stamp of approval for new developments in products, technologies, and methodologies came from the academic community. But professors in their ivory towers were very reluctant to accept these new "scientific" pollsters. In fact, university professors, most of them in the social sciences, were very suspicious of pollsters, not only because they too often were off target on their election calls, but because the early pollsters were too commercially oriented. As Albert Cantril pointed out, "Suspicions abounded in academic circles that commercial agendas would subvert the independence of research and redefine norms of intellectual and methodological rigor."[22] Simply put, social scientists felt that these commercial pollsters were more interested in making money than in developing sophisticated, "academically pure" survey research methods. So, in the post-1948 election era, the challenge for pollsters was to win back the confidence of the American people and the respect of the academics by refining their polling methods and demonstrating that their new techniques were reliable.

Although Gallup, Roper, Crossley, and other pollsters accepted this challenge, it was a new name, Lou Harris, who would enthusiastically take the polling industry's baton during the 1950s and 1960s and carry it to new, laudable heights. Harris actually started in the political polling business working for Elmo Roper in the late 1940s, heading Roper's political polling unit for a few years. While with Roper, Harris took time off to write a major book that analyzed election outcomes based on public opinion polling data. This book, *Is There a Republican Majority? Political Trends, 1952–1956*, was the first of its kind, winning great praise in general, but especially within the academic community. In fact, two very prestigious social scientists, Paul Lazarsfeld of Columbia University and Samuel Stouffer of Harvard University, actually gave the gifted Harris $10,000 from their research monies to sponsor Harris's book writing. Upon its publication, they praised it, emphasizing that

Harris did a solid job underscoring the analytical merits of public opinion polls for election analysis.[23]

With his book's success and a passion for polling, Harris abruptly left Roper in 1956 and formed Louis Harris and Associates, reportedly angering Roper for life because Harris took with him three of Roper's lucrative clients.[24] Harris was devoutly committed to improving polling techniques and producing quality polls, yet ironically he did not like and even feared using the new computer technologies. Moore explains: "Harris himself resisted the encroaching computer technology. On his desk was a huge slide rule, at least a yard long, prominently displayed for any visitor to see. It was part of the Lou Harris mystique, the image of old-fashioned quality he wanted to project. Theodore White had first described Harris using the slide rule to tote up the numbers for Kennedy in the 1960 campaign. And in the mid-1980s, Harris still professed to use the slide rule instead of a calculator."[25]

This might seem literally incredible to people today to think that Harris built a reputation for accurate polling while failing to take full advantage of the new computer technologies, especially when the newly established survey research centers at universities were quickly embracing computers. However, Harris knew that what really made polls accurate were not computers (i.e., "garbage in, garbage out"), but the methodological rigor of the survey itself (i.e., properly constructed questionnaires, properly drawn random samples, professionally conducted interviews, and the like). Make no mistake about it, Harris was right. Computers are analogous to nailing guns, they help make the job go faster, but they do not guarantee a better product. Harris did have a reputation for detail. I learned much about public opinion polling from Duane Hill, my mentor at Colorado State University in the 1960s. Hill learned his polling directly from the master, Lou Harris, whom he even traveled with during some of Harris's polling field trips. Hill taught me that Harris was a stickler for detail, insisting, for example, that every tedious step in the sampling and interviewing process must be followed meticulously to help ensure a quality poll. The truth is that typically those having to follow these tedious steps would respond in frustration, "Oh, why do we have to take so much time doing it this way? What difference does it make?" To purists such as Harris and Hill, following such tedious steps made all the difference!

But such attention to detail and pride in his work paid off. Between 1956 and 1963, Harris polled for literally hundreds of political campaigns, many of them involving major political candidates running for governor, U.S. Senate, U.S. president, and even prime minister. His work was impressive and his success rate was extraordinary. Of course, Lou Harris attracted the attention of U.S. Senator John Kennedy when he was running for president in 1960. Harris was hired by Kennedy to poll for his presidential campaign, making Harris the first pollster ever hired by a presidential candidate. Harris conducted numerous polls for Kennedy throughout the primaries and up to election day, helping Kennedy fine-tune his campaign strategy from week to week. On election eve, Harris predicted that Kennedy would edge out Nixon to capture the presidency.[26] When the vote was in, Kennedy had done just that.

Harris's more scientific polling, based on probability (random) sampling techniques, had brought public opinion polling to a higher and more trustworthy level. In election after election, Harris made predictions that were consistently close to the actual results, bringing a new respect to the Harris Poll and the polling profession. In 1964, he missed the call on Lyndon Johnson's winning percentage by only 2.9%; in 1968, he underestimated Nixon's winning percentage by just 2.3%; and in 1972 he hit the bullseye, being off by a mere 0.3%.[27] Other pollsters, by the 1960s and early 1970s, were making quite accurate predictions also, especially in the Gallup organization, using random sampling methods and immensely improved survey research techniques. The scientific pollsters had finally won the distinction that they had sought for so long. The industry had entered a new age where suddenly there was a great demand for their amazingly accurate polls, a demand that at first outstripped the supply. The proud polling industry of the early 1970s was about to boom.

THE POLLING INDUSTRY'S
MODERN ERA: 1973–PRESENT

By the early 1970s, it seemed that there was nothing that could stop the dramatic growth of the polling industry. People from all sorts of professions and interest groups realized that they could use accurate poll data in various ways to promote their causes. Businesses, politicians, the media, universities, think tanks, labor organizations, religious groups, governments, and countless special interests on the local, national, and international levels now sought valuable information from poll data to help achieve their goals. At first, however, the polling industry's enviable problem was that there were not enough qualified pollsters to meet the enormous demand. Contrary to a popular but erroneously held notion, it takes a lot of training and hands-on experience to become a competent pollster. Virtually all universities taught a certain number of courses in inferential statistics, survey research design, survey research methods, and other related courses, yet the courses were not normally assembled in a common, sensible polling program. The bottom line was that students who had taken a few such courses, often taught in different departments with no common polling thread and normally no actual field experience in public opinion polling, could not be expected to really know how to conduct polls.[28] Sure, there were a few good programs for students wanting to learn how to become public opinion pollsters, most notably the Survey Research Center at the University of Michigan, but such programs were a real rarity. Consequently, in the 1970s qualified pollsters were hard to find, but as the years passed, better educational opportunities developed at universities for those wanting to learn the polling trade, while many of the new pollsters left established polling companies to form their own polling agencies. Eventually, the supply seemed to have met the demand, although I still feel that there is at least a slight shortage of qualified pollsters today, especially in local communities where there are specific survey research demands.[29]

Today's modern polling industry is characterized by three major trends: (1) rapidly changing advanced technologies used to collect, process, and analyze poll data; (2) the mind-boggling proliferation of poll data and access to it; and (3) crucial new challenges to pollsters. Reputable polling firms today employ polling methods that have survived the tests of time and the scrutiny of critics. Public opinion polling has improved as it has evolved. Old, unscientific and unreliable sampling procedures have been replaced by new, relatively sound methods. No longer do serious pollsters employ totally nonrandom sampling procedures to select those to be interviewed. Legitimate polling firms no longer mail out questionnaires to nonrandom and "uncontrolled" respondents. Awkward, expensive, and problematic door-to-door interviewing has been virtually replaced by more reliable modern sampling and interviewing procedures.

Statistically speaking, almost all reliable public opinion polling is now done through phone interviews. During the late 1960s and throughout the 1970s, phone interviewing started to replace door-to-door interviewing at a rapid pace. It was virtually impossible for pollsters to resist switching to phone interviews because there were so many advantages to conducting public opinion interviews by phone. By the 1970s it was estimated that over 90% of the American people could be reached by phone, making phone interviewing for the first time in American history quite feasible. Also, survey researchers argued that the viable percentage was even higher for "with it" Americans (i.e., those who had phones were found to be more likely to participate, more likely to vote, etc.), justifying the use of phone interviewing even more because, conversely, it was held that the small percentage who could not be reached by phone would, for example, not be likely voters or "active" consumers anyway. Actually, as a generalization, this reasoning has basis in fact, as electoral behavior scholars and market researchers have found.[30] But phone interviewing was also enticing because samples could be drawn randomly from convenient phone listings, and phone interviews were many times cheaper than door-to-door interviewing. Phone interviewers could also execute necessary "call-backs" much easier than door-to-door interviewers, and they could be supervised more easily than door-to-door interviewers who were "off in the field" somewhere.

New Technologies to Collect, Process, and Analyze Poll Data

In the past decade phone interviewing has been almost revolutionized by new computer and software technologies. Many polling firms today, especially the large polling companies, use what is called CATI (Computer Assisted Telephone Interviewing). CATI systems dial the random phone numbers for the interviewer and display the questionnaire on the computer screen. The interviewer works directly from the screen, recording answers into the computer as the respondent answers, greatly reducing the time it takes to complete specific interviews and the entire poll. Another polling technique being used is called CATS, standing for Completely Automated Telephone Surveying. In this experimental approach, a preprogrammed interview is used and the respondent communicates with an automated voice (sometimes a familiar, local television anchor hired to record the questions), using the telephone's key pad to respond. Although fiercely defended by its creator, Jay Leve, president of Hypotenuse, Inc., this represents technology gone crazy.[31] The approach is plagued by a myriad of problems that are self-evident.

Telephone polling has been assisted greatly by the development of enormous electronic telephone data bases (e.g., Select Phone) that are updated regularly and have in them virtually all business and residential phone numbers in the United States on convenient CD-ROM disks. Pollsters can use these disks to select a random sample of just residential phone numbers in any part of the United States, say, all residential numbers in the state of Missouri or a specific county in Missouri, or even a city, by adjusting the data base for smaller areas using zip codes. With a statistical software program designed to randomize numbers in a data base (e.g., SPSS, the Statistical Package for the Social Sciences), pollsters can generate a random sample of numbers in just a few minutes, while in the "old days" it took pollsters endless hours or even days to select a random sample from awkward, error-ridden, often incomplete, dated nonelectronic multiple sources (e.g., telephone books, utility listings, voter registration lists). In fact, many times it was even difficult to obtain some of these lists because of legal concerns over privacy rights, causing in-house attorneys for, say, a utility company to balk at giving a pollster the list of the utility's customers. Evidently, these phone data base companies have resolved, or worked around, these privacy rights problems, but probably not to the complete satisfaction of those being polled.

However, the irony is that just as it was becoming really easy, convenient, and methodologically superior to conduct phone interviews, a serious and annoying problem was mounting for phone interviewers because of the growing popularity of another new technology, phone answering machines. As noted in Chapter 1, phone machines are routinely used to screen calls, allowing people to not pick up when they hear unwanted calls. Of course, this is a great convenience for people, but it frankly has been a disastrous development for pollsters because it has caused their "no response" rate to skyrocket, helping to contaminate the theoretical purity of the random sample. How much it has actually biased poll results is hotly debated. Since the interviewer can simply go on to another randomly selected number on his/her list, some argue that phone machines just cause inconvenience and escalate the cost of conducting polls. Others, however, hold that it erodes the randomness of the sample and causes bias since those who have answering machines, or at least use them to avoid interviewers, may answer the questions differently. Some research suggests that the bias caused by answering machine "no response" is not significant since it has not been demonstrated that people who use answering machines to avoid interviewers answer any differently than those who don't.[32]

Nonetheless, answering machines have at least caused pollsters serious inconveniences and annoying extra costs, and when combined with the concern over the "no response" bias problem due to other difficulties associated with reaching residents by phone (working, traveling, lack of telephones in student dorms, retirement homes, etc.) have caused some pollsters at the dawn of the new millennium to experiment with Internet polling. Gordon Black, chairman and CEO of Harris Block International, Ltd., and George Terhanian, director of Internet Research at Harris Block, exclaim that: "Telephone polls, on the whole, have proved to be remarkably accurate predictors of vote behavior—the gold standard of all polling research. Telephone polls are also far less expensive to conduct than door-to-door interviews, the method they have largely replaced."[33] However, they acknowledged that the refusal rate problem has become very serious, commonly exceeding 40% of total households, while "unreachable respondents" due to answering machines and other reasons can account for another 30% of the survey sample. Consequently, Block and Terhanian assert that they have really been forced to experiment with Internet sampling. As experienced professional pollsters, they understand why their colleagues in the polling industry are quite skeptical about the promise of Internet polling, especially since it is impossible to employ random sampling—the accepted standard of the industry—because no central directory of Internet users exists. Consequently, they know that Internet polling will be hard to sell because "virtually every social scientist in America was educated on the power of random sampling."[34] To social scientists and traditional pollsters, Internet polling is regarded as "convenience polling." This means that such polling will be ridiculed by academics and "legitimate" pollsters until Internet polling can meet the old acid test established by George Gallup in the 1930s: being able to predict accurately election results.

Block and Terhanian feel confident that Internet polling can eventually pass this test. These new pioneers are determined to make Internet polling reliable by tapping the opinions of millions of Internet users by developing sophisticated weighting processes to reflect accurately the opinions of the American people as a whole.[35] Ironically, abandoning random sampling for another form of "quota sampling" will force these new Internet pollsters to struggle with the same sort of sampling and representativeness problems that eventually embarrassed Gallup, Crossley, and Roper

over fifty years ago. Wish them luck! It is for this compelling reason that I place Internet polling at this time in the "bad poll" category, which is discussed in the next chapter. Nonetheless, Internet
polling in the long run, as more and more people become Internet
users (today about one-third of the U.S. population are Internet
users, although estimates vary enormously depending on the
source), promises to be the new hope of the polling industry. Just
as pollsters eventually abandoned door-to-door interviewing in
the 1960s and 1970s for phone polls, as phones became so commonplace in American homes, Internet polls may become the new
"gold standard" within a few decades, if not in the next decade
given the rapid proliferation of Internet users. Pollsters and their
clients will not be able to resist the obvious advantages of Internet
polling, particularly the ability to complete polls very quickly and
at lower costs, "which is why Terhanian is confident that the question is when, not if, the Internet will replace the phone as the pollster's tool of choice."[36]

The modern era in public opinion polling is also characterized
by crunching numbers so fast that it seems almost unbelievable
unless you actually watch the instantaneous results appear on the
computer's monitor just seconds after "OK" is clicked to allow the
processing to begin. No longer are large, awkward, expensive, and
often "unavailable" mainframe computers needed to process vast
amounts of public opinion data. Electronic data entry long ago replaced the old "IBM" punch cards that were fed to mainframes
(anyone under 37 years old has probably never handled such a
card or even knows what a counter-sorter or key punch machine
is). Nowadays, incredibly speedy, small, convenient PCs, very af-
fordable to most Americans, have replaced the mainframe computers for the typical polling firm. Of course, the laughable irony today is that pollsters must wait much longer for the printouts of
their processed polling data than for the actual processing of the
data, since even the average PC can crunch the numbers (i.e., tabulate the results of the survey's raw numbers) in just seconds.

Data analysis, as contrasted to the mere running or processing of
the data, has been aided enormously by quite sophisticated software programs that allow pollsters to run all sorts of statistical

tests on their raw poll data, from simple frequencies and percentages to chi-square measures of association to simple regression and multiple regression analysis. As Brian Tringali notes, new computer technologies allow poll data to be crunched at phenomenal speeds: "That has turned the use of advanced statistical methods like multiple regression from rare to routine."[37] Modern software programs (the most popular being SPSS and SAS, or Statistical Analysis System) are becoming more and more sophisticated with each passing day, not only permitting pollsters to subject their data to elaborate statistical tests, but allowing them to display their results in beautiful, aesthetically pleasing, and pedagogically helpful color graphics from simple line graphs to "exploded" pie graphs to three-dimensional, overlapping bar graphs. It must be understood, however, that these new computer and software technologies do not necessarily make polls more accurate and reliable. As noted before, fast computers and sophisticated statistical programs cannot cure a bad poll. In fact, fast computers can actually only serve to produce the results of a poorly designed poll more quickly, while the application of advanced software will ultimately make more glaring to all how bad an ill-designed poll really is. However, in the hands of competent pollsters who conduct sound polls, sophisticated computer software enables them to analyze their poll data on a higher level, thus allowing them to gain better insights into what their polls are actually showing.

Mind-Boggling Proliferation of Poll Data and Access

Possibly nothing is more noticeable in polling's modern era than the staggering proliferation of public opinion poll data and the easy access to it. Just a few years ago, most poll data were considered a very valuable, expensive commodity. Now, poll data are virtually everywhere and anyone can obtain recent polls or archival poll data at no cost or at very little cost. ABC, CBS, CNN, and NBC all have Web sites where their reputable poll data can be retrieved with a few clicks of the mouse. This is also true for most print media, although getting poll data from their archives tends to be rather expensive because they usually charge for retrieval.

But for public opinion junkies, there are services that provide virtually all the poll data from major and minor polling sources (companies, universities, the media) on virtually anything for nothing or very modest fees, although they tend to feature poll data on political institutions and candidates. Some of the best poll data sources are pollingreport.com, gallup.com, harrispollonline.com, maritzameripoll.com, and, my favorite, nationaljournal.com. Although poll data are available in all sorts of publications (e.g., *National Journal*, *The Polling Report*, *Congressional Quarterly*, *The New York Times*), and hard copies of voluminous poll data may sometimes be tidy and convenient, overall obtaining poll data from the numerous, quality on-line sources seems to make the most sense since you can scan and then print out only what you want.

Crucial New Challenges to Pollsters

Today's modern polling industry faces a variety of new challenges. One challenge stems from what we have just discussed. The polling industry has been successful in producing huge mounds of poll data, yet a problem exists in separating the "gold" from the "garbage." Literally, for everyone, including professional pollsters, the mind-boggling production of poll data has proved overwhelming. Frankly, we are swamped with poll data and it can become difficult to tell the "good stuff" from the "bad stuff." This presents a real challenge because many polls today are not generated by legitimate pollsters, but rather by interest groups and others interested primarily in promoting their own agendas or innocently producing just "fun" polls. For proof, just go on the Internet and search "polls" and you will see instantly what I mean. For every legitimate poll such as an ABC, CNN, Pew, Zogby, or Gallup poll, you will see countless methodologically "diabolical" polls such as the "Supermodel Net Poll," "Nutcases of the WWW Survey," "E-Poll," "Open Poll," and "The Great Breast Vote."

With so many polls, the real danger is that the solid poll data produced by reputable pollsters will be lost in the mounds of bad polls. Therefore, responsible Americans have the obligation to learn something about the makings of sound polls and to recognize those polling firms who produce them, while those polling professionals have an obligation to uphold the highest standards for public opinion polling.[38]

The polling industry today is prosperous, expansionary, powerful, and fairly prestigious. However, the industry must meet its new challenges by not abusing its new, prominent position in American society. Professional pollsters must promote the integrity of their industry by: (1) relentlessly insisting on methodological excellence in their polls; (2) more specifically, not sacrificing obvious quality in polling for tempting, faster, "convenience" polling; (3) refusing to conduct unethical and sleazy polls for their clients such as "push polls"; (4) not using their polls to manipulate and undermine the nation's political institutions and system; and (5) making certain that they do not use their polls or their presence on media interview shows to intentionally and disingenuously deceive and manipulate the public.

Unfortunately, not all professional pollsters have handled these challenges very well. Of course, if too many industry professionals abandon fundamental standards and abuse their power, the polling industry will attract the wrath of critics and American citizens like never before and it will cease to function as an influential and reputable industry. Fortunately, however, as we shall see in Chapter 4, "Reputable Pollsters Hate Bad Polls," and there are still plenty of reputable pollsters left.

Chapter Four

Reputable Pollsters Hate Bad Polls

Public opinion pollsters are people who count the grains of sand in your bird cage and then try to tell you how much sand there is on the beach.

—Fred Allen, American comedian (1894–1951)[1]

As columnist William Safire is delighted to stress, "[As] elections demonstrate, a poll is an educated guess and not a hard count. A sampling is not an enumeration. Often pollsters are mistaken."[2] Of course, this is true, but the flip side of this is that, as elections demonstrate, a sound poll is a very good educated guess based on scientific sampling and can reflect quite accurately the actual hard count. Often pollsters are not mistaken. My point is simply that there are good and bad polls. Good polls represent reasonable, reliable guesses, whereas bad polls constitute wild, unreliable guesses. But the reality is that reputable pollsters hate bad polls, and seek to eliminate them because they can really ruin the image of the profession and eventually destroy the polling industry.

Bad polls are not just bad because they have crippling methodological flaws; they are bad because they distort public opinion and are a genuine disservice to people who rely on them. Because of this, it would be much better to have no poll than one that grossly misrepresents public opinion on something, just like it would be much better for people who count on a weather forecast to hear no forecast than to base important plans on a bad one. Too many inaccurate weather forecasts will cause people to laugh at and distrust the weather forecasters, and likewise too many bad polls will cause the American people to laugh at and distrust the pollsters. The polling industry cannot afford for this to happen. Consequently, as noted in Chapter 2, the industry has formed various professional societies to promote standards and ethics. However, despite sincere efforts by members of the polling industry to promote these standards and ethics, it is apparent that there are those who refuse to employ basic methodological standards or polling ethics when conducting their polls. Of course, many of the people responsible for these bad polls are not really professional pollsters at all, but those who find it profitable to use polls to promote their selfish or even dishonest ends (e.g., interest groups who conduct intentionally biased polls because they believe that the end justifies the means, or TV news directors who conduct "call-in" polls to boost their news ratings—"Stay tuned, results at ten").

The main purpose of this chapter is to make consumers aware of the bad polls "out there" and to make it very clear why they are in fact bad polls. Herbert Asher acknowledges the importance of this: "If citizens are able to recognize unscientific polls and their associated deficiencies (as well as the shortcomings of scientific polls), then they are less likely to be misled by the results of such surveys."[3] Two basic kinds of bad polls are discussed. The first kind I categorize as "polls that really 'stink.'" These polls are so flawed methodologically, if not ethically, that they are hopeless as polls. That is, they stand virtually no chance (remember, a broken 24-hour clock is accurate once a day) of accurately measuring public opinion on anything. These blatantly bad polls need to be exposed so consumers can immediately recognize them and summarily dismiss them as quickly as they would stinky fish. I call the second grouping "ill-fated bad polls." These polls are normally conducted by well-intentioned survey researchers, yet they are ill-fated because they involve some very serious methodological flaws that ruin their ability to accurately measure public opinion. Let's look at both of these poll types.

BAD POLLS: POLLS THAT REALLY "STINK"

The polls discussed in this section are so bad they "stink." In fact, they are so obviously bad that it certainly would not take a "rocket scientist" or some methodological wizard to spot them, but just an ordinary person taking a little time to think about them and employing a touch of common sense. These polls are: (1) straw polls; (2) "street-corner" or shopping mall polls; (3) media "call-in" polls; (4) biased interest-group polls; (5) "push" polls; and (6) Internet polls. I will focus on the major problems with these polls, since space does not permit the examination of all of their methodological shortcomings.

Straw Polls

Straw polls refer generically to any kind of poll in which there is no real effort to follow any "scientific" polling procedures. I place the word scientific in quotation marks because there are those who would argue that no polls are really scientific. In fact, even as a pollster, I think it is a stretch to contend that any poll can be truly scientific from a philosophy of science perspective, given the contamination that creeps into even the best "scientific" polls. Allan Rivlin, a pollster himself at the polling firm of Peter D. Hart and Associates, is honest enough to acknowledge this reality too. He says "flat out" that "polling is not a science." He goes on to say, "Pollsters use instruments of scientific quantification—but these are a distraction." Among other problems, he adds that "surveys are composed entirely of words. Words set the context for every question, and words ask and answer every question."[4] So, even though polls appear to be scientifically precise because of the numbers and percentages attached to their results (e.g., 61% of the respondents support aid to China), questionnaires contain subjective words (all words are subjective) that by themselves reduce polling to less than a pure science. Having said this, I can now continue in good conscience to distinguish between straw polls and scientific polls, and I will drop the quotation marks around scientific for the sake of convenience and readability.

Make no mistake about it, although there is no such thing as a purely scientific poll, straw polls are patently inferior to scientific polls because straw pollsters simply fail to follow sound methodological procedures when seeking to measure public opinion. As noted in Chapter 3, in the 1800s and early 1900s newspapers and magazines such as *The Harrisburg Pennsylvanian, Chicago Tribune, The Sheboygan Press, Buffalo Courier Express, Cincinnati Enquirer, The New York Herald, Harper's Monthly,* and *The Literary Digest* used straw polls to predict election outcomes. They conducted these polls mostly by sending their reporters out to "ask around" or to take straw votes to see how particular candidates were doing. They also sent out "straw ballots" to nonrandomly selected people and asked people to send them back, or they asked their subscribers to return "ballots" printed in their newspapers and magazines. Of course, even when *The Literary Digest* received thousands of mailbags full of millions of straw votes in 1936, the *Digest's* prediction of the presidential election results that year was way off because their sample grossly misrepresented the American electorate by ignorantly excluding lower-income voters, who were most likely to support FDR.

But such straw polls are also flawed because they let the respondents determine who is going to respond to the survey, thus causing gross response bias. As Herbert Asher makes clear: "But even with hundreds or thousands of replies, these 'straw polls' are usually not representative simply because people who voluntarily choose to participate are likely to differ in important ways from the general population."[5] However, it is even worse than this because straw pollsters are infamous for only approaching certain groups when conducting their polls (e.g., those who owned cars or telephones during the 1930s or those who have Internet service today or those who can be found conveniently at a shopping mall), systematically excluding groups who may hold very different opinions. Therefore, straw poll results are usually very inaccurate, not only because straw sampling methods exclude certain socioeconomic groups or those with different behavior patterns (e.g., those who don't shop at malls), but because they allow respondents even in the included groups to easily exclude themselves from participating in the poll (e.g., subscribers who choose not to send back the straw ballot or poll questions). In a nutshell, straw polls are destined to be inaccurate because they violate the basic canon of scientific polling by using an unrepresentative sample—a sample that fails to represent a fair cross section of the population universe being surveyed.

Although George Gallup and other scientific pollsters built their careers on discrediting straw polls starting in the 1930s, straw polls are still being conducted today. Despite their almost complete worthlessness for accurately measuring public opinion, evidently their sponsors see something of value in them because we see various kinds of straw polls everywhere. We still see people being surveyed on street corners and in shopping malls, while restaurants, hotels, and car dealers continue to use straw polls to survey their customers. Those in political parties still love to conduct absurdly biased straw polls of a candidate's supporters to show, duh!, that the candidate has support among his or her supporters. Newspapers and magazines still employ straw polls to survey their readers, evidently for the purpose of increasing their readership, and television and radio stations can't resist using embarrassing "call-in" polls (usually very embarrassing to the serious journalists who must read their results), which are clearly used to boost their ratings among, obviously, the "unsophisticated" viewer/listener market. Of course, countless straw polls have appeared recently on the Internet.

Street Corner and Shopping Mall Polls

We have probably all witnessed or even participated in a common type of straw poll in which interviewers approach convenient "walk-by" traffic. I call these "street corner" or "shopping mall" polls, even though such surveying is conducted just about anywhere there are easy-to-access "walk-by" people. Of course, these classic straw polls are usually bad for many reasons (i.e., those conducting these grossly unscientific polls are not likely to care about question placement bias, filter questions, word bias, and other weaknesses), but they are most condemned by serious pollsters for being outrageously unrepresentative. And to reiterate, since representativeness is the key to sound polling, the absence of representativeness makes these polls necessarily wretched ones.

As with other straw polls, there is no real attempt to make these street corner or shopping mall polls representative. These polls are strictly unscientific convenience polls, which blatantly sacrifice basic survey research standards for easy interviewing. Let's face it, they are also quite inexpensive to administer, making their low cost their greatest attraction. In sharp contrast, in scientific polling the costs associated with obtaining and using a representative sample for interviewing normally run quite high (e.g., costs of computers, large data bases, complex software programs). Naturally, the price tag for any poll is always an important consideration to any client, but price should never become the determining factor. Obviously, a cheap, nonscientific poll does not end up to be a bargain when the poll's results are totally unrepresentative nonsense.

Specifically, street corner or shopping mall polls are usually grossly unrepresentative and, therefore, unreliable because the people that interviewers tend to conveniently interview are very unlikely to reflect a random, fair cross section of the whole target population of the poll (e.g., consumers, voters, teenagers). In fact, the problem with getting representative respondents by convenience interviewing is what got George Gallup into trouble with poll predictions in the 1940s, causing him to abandon the approach. As David Moore points out about Gallup's interviewing, "by the mid-1940s, statisticians recognized that interviewers could very easily bias the results by the way they were allowed to select respondents. By going to parks and work construction sites, interviewers would slant their selection toward people who were outside and available, rather than those who were at home. Even when they went to homes, interviewers would select houses that seemed most friendly, or where people were outside. In general, when they had discretion in choosing respondents, they would choose people with whom they were most comfortable, rather than give every person an equal chance of being selected, and that was the key to the statisticians' objections: interviewers selected their respondents in a non-random fashion."[6]

In their marketing textbook, Michael Solomon and Elnora Stuart focus on the modern equivalent of going to parks and other convenient public places, such as shopping malls. They note that this contemporary equivalent is still plagued by the same old problems of unrepresentativeness. "However, because only certain groups of the population frequently shop at malls, a mall-intercept study does not provide the researcher with a representative sample unless the population of interest is mall shoppers."[7]

Ironically, such a mall survey may not even be representative of mall shoppers. Why? For openers, to even begin to get a representative sample of mall shoppers the interviewers would have to devote equal time to interviewing at different areas of the mall (e.g., entrances). Otherwise, the poll would be biased by the mall locations selected by the interviewers. For example, if they stood close to women's clothing stores, they would naturally tend to get those more interested in women's clothing; if they interviewed by candy stores, they may very likely interview people more interested in eating candy than shopping; or, if they stood by the mall's movie theater entrance, they would likely attract younger people going to the movies. Interviewers would also have to make sure that they interviewed at all different times during the week or else their poll results would be biased by a time problem. Clearly, for example, working men and women at day jobs shop at different times than do nighttime workers or those who do not "work" at a regular job.

In addition, the personalities of people can affect refusal rates, and refusal rates have always posed a serious problem to pollsters. To obtain a fair, random sample of even mall shoppers, beyond what I have already mentioned, interviewers would have to question a fair cross section of different personality types—in reality, an impossible job. The fact is that some people are more likely to grant interviews than others, as experienced pollsters can attest. For example, those who are more extroverted, secure, confident, fairly well to well educated, affluent, nonminority, women, and

Type B personalities (i.e., not in a rush or too busy) are more likely to give an interview than those who are more introverted, insecure, lack confidence, poorly educated, less affluent, minority, men, and Type A personalities (i.e., "always" in a rush or too busy to, say, be interviewed). This "personality problem" exists to some extent for all types of polling, but it is particularly pronounced in street corner or mall surveys because it is just too easy for people to refuse to be interviewed by looking away and walking on.

Media "Call-in" Polls

Radio and television stations have used silly call-in polls since about the mid-1980s. Call-in polls are utterly ridiculous as polls because virtually everything is wrong with them. In fact, scholar and poll critic Herbert Asher refers to them as "pseudo-polls."[8] These polls are totally unrepresentative because opinions can only be recorded if a respondent pays 50–90 cents to call a 900 number advertised by the station, obviously eliminating most potential respondents who do not want to take the time to make the call or who don't want to spend their money on such nonsense. Also, no one really knows who is actually making the calls and there is normally no effort to stop the same people from making numerous calls.

But as TV and radio critic Tim Cuprisin claims, the stations don't actually care about polling methods or poll results because radio and TV call-in polls are really run for their promotional value. In reviewing the absurdities of the Miss America Pageant call-in poll in 1995, Cuprisin concluded: "Bottom line: the poll really wasn't designed to test what the viewers want. It was hype for the 75th anniversary of the pageant."[9]

Another reason why many call-in polls cannot be representative is because often very few people actually call in, especially to local stations. Let me give a true but pathetically humorous example from personal experience. One evening Bill Davis, a sports anchor at KTVI-TV in St. Louis, where I was then employed as their political analyst and pollster, saw me at a St.

We only had three call-ins on our sports show

Louis Blues hockey game. He came over to me and mentioned that he had had a problem with a sports call-in poll. (I had nothing to do with the poll.) He said they had announced a call-in poll during the five o'clock news with the results to be given during the evening newscast. So, I asked essentially, "What was the problem?" He said with a sigh, "Only three called in." "So what did you do?" I inquired. He responded, "What could we do, we presented the results saying 67% said "yes" while 33% said "no." Admittedly, receiving only three calls is unusually low, but local stations commonly and unabashedly present poll results in percentages with only very low numbers (e.g., 20–80 respondents) supporting these percentages. Remember, stations using call-in polls are only interested in them for their promotional benefits, such as getting listeners or viewers to tune them in later for the results. Out of curiosity, the next time a local TV or radio station presents the results of a call-in poll, contact the station and ask how many people actually responded to the poll. The truth will probably embarrass them.

Still another problem with call-in polls is that the questions are almost always absurdly simplistic, normally requiring only "yes" or "no" or "for" or "against" answers. Typical examples would be: "Should we bomb Serbia?" or "Do you think O. J. Simpson is guilty?" or "Should Drew Bledsoe start at quarterback this Sunday?" Filter questions are almost never, if ever, asked to "filter out" those who know absolutely nothing about the substance of the question, and no follow-up questions can be asked to gain more insights into the simple "yes" or "no" answers since respondents are simply asked to call one 900 number to answer "yes" or another 900 number to answer "no."

Finally, evidence suggests that those who call talk radio shows and respond to call-in polls are not very representative of the American public. According to a study by Andrew Kohut, talk radio and at least call-in radio poll callers tend to be men who are more conservative, more Republican, more educated, and wealthier than those in American society as a whole.[10] And from my experience doing numerous talk radio shows with occasional call-in polls in St. Louis, callers also tend to be suburbanites and white, often calling from their car phones, which only adds to the Republican image described by Kohut.

Biased Interest-Group Polls

On occasion interest groups commission pollsters to conduct polls, or they might do polls with in-house staff. Interest groups sometimes seek honest and reliable data and, if they do, they usually hire reputable polling firms. In fact, sometimes groups may have the technical expertise and resources to do the poll in-house, allowing them to save on outside polling costs, yet they choose to hire professional firms because they do not want people, particularly their detractors, charging that their poll is intentionally biased and "junk."

However, the public should be aware that probably the majority of interest groups, possibly the vast majority, do not conduct polls to obtain objective, reliable data, but rather seek intentionally biased or slanted poll data that they think will help promote their particular agendas. Political parties and candidates, activist political groups such as pro-life and pro-choice organizations, equal-rights groups such as the National Organization for Women, consumer groups such as Common Cause, environmental activists such as Greenpeace, special interests such as the National Rifle Association, and the large number of labor, business, professional, and religious organizations all have special causes that they want to advance. Unfortunately, these interest groups feel too often that they can push their agendas by using biased polls to "prove" that their cause is justified and that they have significant and enthusiastic public support.

Typically, interest group polls are filled with biased or loaded questions, but most often respondents don't seem to notice or care because the respondents usually share the same biases because they normally are members or supporters of the group conducting the survey. For example, Democrats and Republicans will be mailed surveys from the Democratic National Committee and Republican National Committee, respectively, especially if they have ever donated money or services to these parties, and Planned Parenthood members would be the most likely people to be asked to participate in a Planned Parenthood survey. So, for openers, no attempt is made to obtain objective opinions based on a randomly selected representative sample; rather, these polls are actively fishing for biased opinions guaranteed to please the sponsoring interest group. But if this isn't enough, a cover letter is almost always attached that is designed to influence strongly the respondent's answers to the survey. And if this still isn't enough, the wording in the questions almost guarantees that the respondent will answer the questions in a certain way.

Let's take a look at a typical biased interest-group poll, one sent out to Planned Parenthood supporters.[11] The cover letter starts out "Dear Friend" and goes on to explain that the "survey contains questions concerning a wide range of related issues—sexuality education—birth control—abortion . . . religious extremist violence and other threats to freedom of choice." After noting that they "desperately need your financial support to aid our efforts to fight back against the seemingly endless attack today on reproductive freedom," they make clear that "the struggle we face with anti-choice fanatics is truly life-threatening." Consequently, the letter concludes: "Your input to this survey can be a major weapon in our battle to preserve reproductive freedom in this nation." Then the slanted questions begin. One loaded question reads: "Do you support FDA approval of mifepristone (also known as RU-486) and other safe, effective, non-surgical methods to end pregnancies?" How can any respondent say "no" considering not only that the respondents are Planned Parenthood supporters and the forceful cover letter, but also the loaded wording "other *safe, effective, non-surgical methods*" that is designed to elicit a predetermined response?

It is difficult to believe that such flawed polls could ever be given any serious attention by "outsiders," thus one would think that they could not be effectively used by lobbyists to influence policymakers. In reality, it appears that these interest group polls are designed to stroke supporters by conveying to them that their opinions really count, even though the truth is that their money is valued much more than their predictable opinions, which is why a convenient contribution form is usually attached to the end of the questionnaire, as it was in the Planned Parenthood survey. The final kicker is that, as critics note, very often no one even bothers to tabulate the results of these interest group polls because, in the final analysis, who cares?[12]

"Push" Polls

The noted columnist David Broder once wrote in disgust: "Every time you think that the political campaign operatives have hit bottom and can't find anything sneakier and more underhanded to do, they prove you wrong." However, in 1994 he went on to say, "Last week, I was introduced to something far sneakier. It is known as the 'push poll.' "[13] Broder was, of course, right. Push polls are really sleazy polls condemned in no uncertain terms by AAPOR and every other professional society for pollsters, yet the use of push polls, as Broder notes, has spread like a terrible plague, becoming the "real stealth weapon" in too many political campaigns.[14]

Push polls are actually not legitimate polls at all since they are really designed to "push" voters away from a candidate's opponent into the camp of the candidate responsible for the "push poll." These polls are not used to measure voter opinion. Here is how a typical, dirty push poll works. Your phone rings and an anonymous "interviewer" says that he/she is taking a survey and wants to know whether you favor Joe Blow or Suzie Q for, say, governor. If you say you favor Joe Blow for governor or are "undecided," and the "interviewer" is working for Suzie Q's campaign, you will then hear the "push" question such as: "If I told you that Joe Blow is a Mafia-connected drug addict who has been indicted and undergone repeated drug treatment, would you support Joe Blow for governor?"[15] Push polls may include several "push" questions, but they inevitably conclude with a question, after the targeted candidate has been thoroughly "trashed," that essentially asks whether the voter would vote for, to take our example, Joe Blow. What is implicitly being asked is: "Given all the *negative* things that I have told you about Joe Blow, do you *still* plan to vote for him?"

Of course, after hearing such trash about a candidate, many naive voters may actually switch their candidate preference during the interview, ending up supporting the candidate who is behind this nasty but effective push poll. Unless push polls are exposed in a campaign (and if they are they can backfire on the candidate responsible for them), they can be effective in smearing a candidate and destroying his or her candidacy. With distorted "poll" data that inflates the strength of the candidate using the push poll, this politician can now boast of his/her strength "in the polls" to raise more money for the campaign. For example, about a year and a half before the 2001 mayoral race in St. Louis, challenger Francis Slay's pollster conducted a push poll to be used in part to show that incumbent Mayor Clarence Harmon was vulnerable, thus placing Slay in a better position to raise crucial early money. The push poll, although more subtle than some, nonetheless unfairly associates Mayor Harmon with many negatives while simultaneously asking voters to rate Harmon's job performance. The "push" question reads: "Is St. Louis Mayor Clarence Harmon doing the best job he can as Mayor? Or is he a nice but indecisive person who has failed to come up with a plan as the city continues to lose population and its neighborhoods decline?"[16]

Those who resort to sleazy push polls have also used phone banks to call many thousands of voters with the sole intention of smearing their candidate's opponent, not to honestly collect any poll data. In fact, this is one sure way to detect a push poll, because a legitimate pollster's sample size normally runs between 500 and 600 people (giving the pollster a respectable error margin of ±4.5% at 95% confidence), although pollsters may interview somewhat more or less. This is not to say that a particular push poll may only include, say, 500–600 voters, because the priority objective may be to obtain "good poll numbers" to aid fund-raising, not to maximize smearing.

In an editorial, *The Boston Herald* criticized the ignoble practice of "push polling," along with a variation called "suppression polling." "Suppression polls" trash an opponent before his or her supporters with the specific objective of discouraging these supporters from voting. Very appropriately, the editorialists said this about such slimy polls: "Not only is it sleazy, it poisons the well for legitimate polling, by candidates and by news organizations. Who'll give an honest answer if he thinks there's a chance the caller is a trickster?"[17] As the editorial recommended, legislation should be passed to at least require interviewers to disclose to respondents the sponsor of all polls, just as campaign literature normally has to state, for example, "Paid for by citizens for Suzie Q." Mandatory disclosure would promote accountability in polling. Today, unfortunately, such sleazy polling still thrives, as made clear by the complaints about the use of "push polling" in the 2000 presidential race.[18]

Internet Polls

Internet polls may be the wave of the future, as some observers of Internet polling speculate, but at this point they command little respect in the polling community because these polls are riddled with crippling problems. Murray Edelman, president of the American Association for Public Opinion Research and director of the Voter News Service, an exit poll organization, calls Internet polls "pseudo polls." He says posted polls on the Internet tend to attract only certain types of people who "like to fill out surveys and have a lot of time on their hands." Edelman stresses that the poll information generated from Internet surveys "isn't representative of anything. Who would buy it, who would want it?"[19] In discussing the value of Internet polls, the cofounder of InterSurvey, Douglas Rivers, puts it bluntly: "Their polling information is worthless."[20] In a humorous spirit, *New York Times* columnist Gail Collins cited Internet polling to try to place the worth of the Iowa caucuses into proper perspective: "The Iowa caucuses are about as good a barometer of what the public thinks as the *Time* Internet poll that named Elvis the Person of the Century."[21]

Some acknowledge the many problems that plague Internet polling, but they are confident that some day Internet polls can be made accurate and reliable and will win acceptance in the mainstream polling industry. Kurt Ehrenberg, an Internet pioneer experimenting with Internet polls, accepts the widespread criticisms of such polling: "It's not a perfect system. We're not saying that it is."[22] Nonetheless, he contends that it is just a matter of time before the methodological problems in Internet polls are overcome. Anna Greenberg, an opinion researcher and assistant professor at Harvard's Kennedy School, agrees, stating emphatically: "I do think it is the wave of the future." However, there are others who see no promise in Internet polls, given the methodological problems that are inherent in them and that are unlikely to ever be resolved. As *Boston Globe* writer Anne Kornblut reports: "Questions about the long-term use of such polls are troubling to some, given the history of Internet polls."[23]

Serious methodological flaws in Internet polls conducted to date have rendered them "cute" at best, according to some observers, and certainly not accurate. For example, Kurt Ehrenberg conducted an experimental Internet poll through politics.com for the 2000 New Hampshire presidential primary. Although the impressive number of 8000 people responded, his poll results were way, way off. He had George W. Bush in the Republican primary winning with 29% of the vote, and John McCain trailing badly with only 12%.[24] Of course, McCain won a convincing primary victory, defeating Bush 49% to 30%. The politics.com poll also predicted that Bill Bradley in the Democratic primary would easily defeat Al Gore, 21% to 10%, although when the votes were counted Gore beat Bradley 50% to 46%.

So why was the politics.com poll so far off? Although some Internet polls are better than others, they all suffer from very serious defects that compel me to categorize them as "bad" polls. The chief problem is that they are conducted on the Internet, which provides a very poor data base for pollsters. The current reality is that the vast majority of people don't use the Internet. That is, about two-thirds of the American people are not on-line, and those who are on-line "are heavily skewed toward a young, upper-class group."[25] Another devastating sampling flaw is that the respondents self-select themselves to participate in the polls. As *Washington Post* reporter Sarah Schafer found, this means that those responding to Internet polls will most likely be "the most vocal people . . . , leaving out the more silent but no less important sector of the population."[26] For example, snowboarders were angry over an aspen.com poll that led to a ban on snowboarders on Ajax Mountain. Critics charged that the Internet poll was extremely biased in favor of older, traditional skiers, not the younger snowboarders. Larry Madden, a snowboard rights advocate, argued: "The survey has a bias to it. aspen.com is read by people who go to Aspen and, by self-selection, don't snowboard."[27]

Ironically, Internet pollsters have exacerbated the problem while trying to increase their data bases and samples for their polls by offering ill-advised incentives. For instance, Harris Poll Online, possibly the industry leader in Internet polling, further contaminates the representative character of their respondents by dangling incentives. Harris Poll Online notifies Internet users that they may become poll participants by "entering a sweepstakes sponsored by MatchLogic"[28] and can "win one of ten $500 cash prizes, simply by completing the survey."[29]

In sum, Internet polls must overcome many serious methodological hurdles before they can be considered sound. However, the worst problem is that Internet pollsters must abandon reliable random sampling techniques for far inferior and unreliable "quota sampling," and this makes no sense. Some proponents of Internet polling contend that eventually sophisticated weighting techniques can make such polling reliable. However, the truth is that Internet pollsters would have to make the inherently unrepresentative "quota sampling" work, a sampling method that failed dismally and embarrassed pollsters such as George Gallup and Elmo Roper over fifty years ago when they blew the call in predicting that Dewey would easily defeat Truman.

ILL-FATED BAD POLLS

The following polls are not flagrantly bad polls like the dismal ones just discussed. In fact, all the doomed polls discussed in this section were initially accepted by the polling industry for their apparent methodological soundness and promise. However, as time passed, flaws in these polls attracted mounting criticisms from survey research methodologists and even from the pollsters' clients. Today, personal or "door-to-door," mail, and focus group "polls" are still used somewhat, but they are viewed with great suspicion. The Nielsen polls, which produce your television program ratings, have come under severe attack by critics and TV managers for well over a decade now, but the Nielsen ratings persist because, as is often said, "Nielsen is the only game in town."

Personal or Door-to-Door Polls

George Gallup made personal or door-to-door polls famous during
the 1930s and 1940s. At first door-to-door interviewing seemed to
be an appropriate "scientific" response to the old-fashioned,
grossly unrepresentative mail-in surveys made infamous by *The
Literary Digest's* atrocious 1936 presidential prediction. After
Gallup's "accurate" prediction of FDR's victory in 1936, systematic
"door-to-door" field interviewing became the hot new scientific
way to interview people.

Door-to-door interviewing seemed far superior to past straw poll
methods for several reasons. The major advantage of personal interviews is that they ostensibly allow the pollster to select the
"right" respondents to be interviewed, ideally permitting the pollster to obtain a representative sample—the key ingredient in any
good poll. Typically, interviewers are required to interview a certain percentage of different types of people (e.g., by age, sex, religion, income) from various predetermined areas (e.g., region of
country, as well as urban, suburban, or rural), which will supposedly mirror the same proportions in the targeted survey population. This is called quota sampling. Another advantage is that during the personal interview the interviewer can control the
interviewing process, making certain that all questions are answered thoroughly, especially difficult questions that may require
probing to obtain a complete response. Door-to-door interviews
are also better suited for longer surveys, especially when the respondent is asked to react to visuals (e.g., candidate pictures,
packaging of products), and when it may be very helpful for interviewers to establish some personal rapport with respondents to get
through complex and challenging questionnaires.

However, it soon became very clear, except for those who insisted on wearing blinders, that the cons of door-to-door interviews far outweighed the pros. In the first place, pollsters were
only fooling themselves in thinking that quota sampling could
work in practice. That is, not only could they not know the exact
demographics so they could pick a representative sample that actually reflected the proper demographical proportions, but it was

naive to think that the interviewer could actually manage to interview the precise people needed to fill each quota. For example, former Gallup field interviewers tell horror stories about being panicked toward the end of the week when they knew it was going to be impossible to get the people they needed to fulfill their assigned quotas. Buck Buchanan, one of Gallup's interviewers, recalled how impossible it was to fill the quotas: "When we got to the end of the week, we did our best to fill the quotas. We would do 'spot' surveys. We'd drive down the streets trying to spot the one person who would fit the specific quota requirements we had left. We did our best. But, of course, sometimes we had to fudge the age a little bit, or the income. It couldn't be helped."[30] Buchanan also recounts that it was impossible to interview "quota-selected" respondents who "had an attitude." He recalls that one farmer had a particularly hostile attitude, responding: "That ain't none of your business!" When he probed, allegedly an advantage of personal interviews, the farmer raised his shotgun and offered this unhelpful response: "Now, you git! And don't come around here asking who I'm going to vote for! Git."[31] (Given his fierce independence, Buchanan must have figured he was a Republican and checked that he favored the Republican candidates.)

Actually, this is not entirely a joke. Because of the sensitivity or personal nature of some questions, door-to-door interviewers, because they were placed in face-to-face situations, have admitted that they sometimes guessed or fudged responses. For instance, Buchanan noted that he never asked respondents their age or sometimes their income because it was too personal, too taboo, and particularly awkward in face-to-face interviews.[32] Buchanan was not unique as an interviewer. In fact, critics list problems with interviewers as being a major source of bias in personal interviews, causing significant contamination of the poll data. Despite efforts to train interviewers to conduct interviews in a neutral fashion, interviewers are all different (e.g., some are men, some are women, some are black, some are white, some are good-looking, some are not, some are young, some are old, some are well-spoken, some are not), with different personalities and body language and employing various techniques as interviewers. There has never been any realistic way to supervise interviewers in the field either, leaving interviewers with enormous discretion to conduct interviews the way they want. As Chava Frankfort-Nachmias and David Nach-mias note in *Research Methods in the Social Sciences*, "The very flexibility that is the interviewer's chief advantage leaves room for the interviewer's personal influence and bias. . . . Although inter-viewers are instructed to remain objective and to avoid communi-cating personal views, they nevertheless often give cues that may influence respondents' answers."[33]

Still other methodological and practical problems doomed door-to-door interviews. The obvious lack of anonymity, critics claim, intimidates a significant percentage of respondents, causing them to not answer questions candidly. Of course, tracking down hard-to-find respondents (e.g., transient people, people behind "secu-rity screens," students, mobile professionals) and trying to inter-view people in high-crime areas pose additional problems for pollsters and their interviewers. Beyond all of these methodologi-cal and practical problems, however, the escalating costs of door-to-door interviews, especially in light of a not-so-hot track record for polls based on personal interviews, doomed these polls. By 1980, who would want to pay around $40.00 per personal inter-view or about $24,000 total for just interview costs (i.e., $40.00 $\times$ 600 interviews = $24,000), especially when critics felt these polls were fatally flawed and grossly inaccurate anyway?

Mail Surveys

In the history of polling the quality of mail surveys has been mixed, but their "scientific" quality has never been good. In the prescientific polling era, as noted in Chapter 3, newspapers and magazines (the most famous or infamous being *The Literary Digest*) either sent out mail questionnaires to their subscribers and tabu-lated the small percentage that were returned or they printed questionnaires in their publications and expected readers to fill out the usually short and simple polls and send them in. Only an unimpressive percentage of readers did so. On occasion, some publishers would expand their survey base by sending out questionnaires to those other than just their readers (e.g., to those who owned cars and/or telephones), but still there was no serious attempt in these early mail surveys to obtain a representative sample. Consequently, these mail polls proved inaccurate and just plain "ugly."

However, the scientific pollsters from the mid-1930s on tried to make mail polls more scientific and, thus, more reliable by drawing representative samples based on quota or random sampling techniques. But it soon became apparent that even if questionnaires were sent to representative people, this did not guarantee that the questionnaires that were returned were representative. In fact, for numerous and mostly obvious reasons, they were not.

The assumption that questionnaires can be sent to representative respondents is a far-fetched assumption anyway, because the source lists used as sample frames are almost never truly representative of the general population that the pollsters seek to survey. Such lists (e.g., voter registration, utility, car registration, welfare, and various license and membership lists) are notorious for being quite outdated and filled with inaccuracies, although naturally some lists are more reliable than others.

Another serious problem with mail polls is that the survey researcher has no control over the interview situation. Therefore, there is no guarantee that the targeted people actually filled out the questionnaire. They might have given it to another person to complete or sought help in filling out the questionnaire. Also, despite follow-up efforts such as reminder postcards to help maximize returns on mail surveys, only certain personality types under particular circumstances will most likely complete and return the questionnaires, thus severely biasing the mail poll. In fact, critics of mail surveys argue that the very low response rate in mail surveys (response rates vary greatly depending on the surveyed sample, but response usually runs between 10 and 20%, but may easily drop below 10%) makes it literally impossible to obtain a representative sample. Frankfort-Nachmias and Nachmias stress that those "who use mail questionnaires must always face the problem of how to estimate the effect the non-respondents may have on their findings. The non-respondents are usually quite different from those who answer the questionnaire. Often they are the poorly educated who may have problems understanding the questions, the elderly who are unable to respond, or the more mobile who cannot be located. Consequently, the group of respondents is not likely to constitute the representative group originally defined by the investigators, and this will undoubtedly introduce bias into the study."[34]

In addition to the representativeness problem, mail surveys present still other problems. Complex polls are difficult to conduct by mail, so questionnaires are usually kept simple, although there are examples of very long and tedious questionnaires sent to unique groups (e.g., doctors, judges, and other professionals). Probing is also difficult on mail questionnaires and respondents could bias their answers by looking ahead in the questionnaire or even filling out the questions out of order when the questions are designed to be answered in sequence.

Yet mail surveys have a few advantages. The absence of interviewers may eliminate interviewer bias, and the lack of interviewers also gives respondents "felt" anonymity that may encourage more frank answers, especially involving personal and sensitive questions. For example, mail questionnaires have normally been used in surveys on human sexual behavior. However, low costs of mail surveys have over the years been the greatest attraction of such surveys, although the low costs may be somewhat more apparent than real since administrative, stationery, printing, and postage costs can be considerable, especially if self-addressed, stamped envelopes are included in the mailings, as well as follow-up mailings to increase the response rate. In any event, regardless of the perceived low costs of mail surveys, mail polls end up being no real bargain since pollsters who use them get what they pay for—unrepresentative, bad poll data.

Focus Groups

I know you thought we were discussing only bad polls in this chapter, so why are focus groups being covered? The reason is simple. I have run many focus groups and I have always been amazed at how many of my clients erroneously want to equate focus groups with polls. But focus groups are radically different from polls and they should not ever be conceptualized as "mini" polls. Focus groups are qualitative research endeavors, whereas polls are quantitative research projects. The people who participate in focus groups, typically numbering from 10 to 16 participants, do not constitute a random sample of anything and really represent nothing and no one but themselves. On the other hand, the hundreds of respondents who participate in a legitimate poll constitute a randomly selected sample and are quite representative of the population universe as a whole.

After conducting focus groups over the years, I cannot tell you how many of my clients have come up to me and told me how valuable they thought the focus group was, noting that the opinions expressed were "so enlightening" and "so representative." On occasion, even the people responsible for running focus groups, who should know better, have momentarily lost sight of the unrepresentative character of these groups and commented on how "telling" and "representative" the participants and their responses were. Actually, others in my profession have noticed the same thing. For example, Brian Tringali, a Republican pollster with the Tarrance Group, acknowledged that the danger with focus groups is "that some will try to apply their findings to the population as a whole." He then stressed: "No matter how many focus groups are conducted, they can never precisely represent public opinion—a fact that some in our business seem to have forgotten."[35]

Focus groups were popular for a while many decades ago, but during the 1950s their popularity declined mostly because they were attacked harshly by critics, especially by methodologists and sociologists, as largely a waste of time because of their unrepresentative nature. Frankly, many scholars looked at focus groups as unproductive "bull sessions," especially during an era when social scientists were putting their faith and energies behind developing reliable, quantitative measures (e.g., public opinion polls). Focus groups continued to be used to a limited extent between the mid-1950s and late 1980s, especially by market researchers, but since the late 1980s focus groups have gained a new popularity. Ironically, evidence suggests that focus groups have regained their popularity because many people are "sick and tired" of looking at mounds of poll numbers. Paraphrasing what Mike Brown, city administrator of Kirkwood, Missouri, and one of my clients, said to me a few years back: "I really like focus groups. I can see real people say real things and they can elaborate on what they think. Polls just give me 'endless numbers' and I get tired of just looking at cold numbers."

Brown reflects the thinking of many today. In one sense, focus groups are refreshing because a small group of real, live people are brought together for a few hours to discuss (i.e., focus on) a specific topic. A focus group moderator leads an exploratory discussion in which, it is hoped, valuable insights can be gained. Often focus groups are used to provide further understanding of poll data. That is, a follow-up focus group could be assembled to provide additional insights into some of the responses obtained in the survey. The chief advantage of focus groups is that they allow for extensive probing, so certain issues can be clarified. In focus groups, people can also be shown things and asked to react to them. For example, often ad agencies show political or market commercials to focus group participants to get their reactions so they can avoid running expensive yet ineffective ads. However, Richard Warren, former ad executive who has had considerable experience with market surveys and focus groups, stresses that the two should never be confused since market surveys and focus groups are two "completely different animals with two very different objectives. . . . Market surveys can give you the representative numbers, while focus groups can give you ideas that maybe you have never thought of before." But, Warren adds, "It would be a total misuse and misunderstanding of a focus group to think that what is said in them is representative because such opinions are simply not 'projectable.'"[36]

Focus groups have their supporters, but to reiterate, focus groups are not polls. In fact, they are very bad substitutes for polls because they are in no way representative of any population as a whole. Actually, opinions expressed at focus groups can be counterproductive if misused by clients, especially if clients (e.g., city administrators) treat unrepresentative opinion as representative opinion and act on it. This could cause, say, city officials to implement something that most people in their city do not want. When interpreting responses in focus groups, analysts must always keep in mind these questions: Who does this person or who do these people really speak for? How representative is this person's or this group's opinion? Have participants responded honestly and frankly or have they been influenced by "group think,"[37] or a natural tendency to uphold acceptable "community standards," or to say things that are "politically correct"?[38]

The Nielsen Ratings

The Nielsen ratings are a big deal in America because network television and especially local television stations "live or die" by Nielsen's ratings of the programs that they air, particularly during the four "sweeps" periods in February, May, July, and November. The ratings are critically important because they determine how much the networks and local stations can charge advertisers. But they also determine whether specific programs are continued or canceled and whether, say, particular news anchors get the ax. In other words, a lot rides on these ratings.

Unfortunately, the Nielsen ratings are included in this chapter on bad polls because Nielsen's survey procedures suffer from all sorts of methodological inadequacies, calling into question just how reliable they are. In the 1990s, media scholar J. Ronald Milavsky, in a *Public Opinion Quarterly* article, concluded that the Nielsen survey procedures have "severe faults" that cast "considerable doubt on the system's ability to reflect data that is projectable to national television viewing behavior."[39] Don Aucoin, a *Boston Globe* writer who investigated Nielsen's methodologies in light of a rating's blunder in Boston in October of 1999, concluded that "there are persistent questions about Nielsen's accuracy, methodology, and ability to keep up with an expanding TV universe."[40] Aucoin had reported on the rating's gaffe when *Judging*

Amy, a CBS drama airing on Boston's CBS affiliate station, WBZ-TV, received a viewership rating of 72,000 households even though the program wasn't really airing because a fiber-optic cable glitch had wiped out the show for twenty minutes. But how is such a rating possible? Did people in 72,000 homes just sit around their TV and watch a blank screen for twenty minutes, only thinking that the show was quite dull?

If we look into the methods employed by Nielsen Media Research, we can understand how this happened, but not why it should happen. Nielsen's basic way of polling who is watching what is through "viewing meters," which by 1999 were in 44 markets, including about 61% of television viewers in America. They work like this: When the TV is turned on, the meter automatically records the time and the station. The data collected are transferred automatically each night through telephone lines to Nielsen's computers and instantly tabulated, and then the ratings are forwarded to Nielsen's subscribers. The obvious problem, however, is that the meters only measure the television sets that are turned on the stations that they are tuned to, not whether people are actually watching. To paraphrase what Jeff Allen, news director of ABC's affiliate station in St. Louis, told me: "This means that if people left the TV room for any reason (e.g., went to the store, bathroom, kitchen, or to walk the dog or left the TV on to discourage burglars while away from home), Nielsen's meters would nonetheless include these absent people as viewers, distorting the true ratings."[41] Of course, another problem with this viewer meter approach is that the meters do not survey who or how many people in the household are watching a program. I see this as a major methodological defect.

In response to advertisers who really want to know who is watching so they can target their ads to the right people, in 1986 Nielsen began to place "people meters" in a relatively small number of selected households. The people meter is attached to the TV with green and red lights. Each family member is assigned a light, with additional lights for guests. When the TV is turned on, blinking red lights appear, but the red lights go off and green lights come on as members of the family or guests push a button to log in, indicating that they are watching. People are supposed to push their button every time they come and go or switch stations for more than a few seconds.

As you can imagine, this highly interactive approach has attracted many skeptics who charge that it is highly unlikely that people will responsibly keep pushing their buttons.[42] In fact, Clarence Jones, in "TV Ratings—How They Know Who's Watching," asserts: "People Meters are subject to cheating, too. One member of the household can log in absent family members."[43]

Nielsen also uses "diary households" to find out who is watching what, but this approach raises glaring problems. Those assigned diaries are supposed to record what program is being viewed and who is watching every fifteen minutes when the TV is on. "But," as Jones contends, "diary-keeping is a real chore, and there has always been a concern that some families aren't very precise."[44] The fact is that Nielsen's "people meters" and "diary households" call for interactive approaches to polling that defy common sense, especially considering that most of us can't remember to turn off the lights. Remember from our discussion on personal interviews that such interviewing presented serious reliability problems because field interviewers could not be feasibly supervised, thus creating too many opportunities for errors and fudging. To me, common sense would dictate that Nielsen would have even greater problems with errors and fudging in his use of people meters and household diaries because any real supervision would be impossible. Additionally, the poll data Nielsen is collecting are more tedious, comprehensive, and time-consuming than the typical data sought in a field interview.

However, probably the worst methodological problem with the Nielsen ratings is that the samples are just not representative of American television viewers as a whole. Critics, including methodologists and television executives, charge that "the Nielsens are skewed toward some demographics and away from others. For example, the placement of 'People Meters' (usually in middle-class and higher-educated homes) and those who have the most time to fill out Nielsen diaries (the elderly) can skew the demographics. . . . Even worse, Nielsen ratings don't count TV viewing in bars and college dorms, among other places, which the industry says can affect the demographics of sports and late-night programming."[45] Don Aucoin's research in Boston led him to the same finding. He reports that Nielsen makes no attempt to measure millions of viewers who watch TV in "college dorms, bars, and health clubs. Boston has the highest concentration of college students of any city in the country—roughly 140,000 students—yet their viewing habits are not reflected in the ratings."[46]

Ed Goldman, general manager of WBZ-TV in Boston, offers a succinct summary: "The system was designed 50 years ago. . . . The methodology is very limited and way outdated."[47] More specifically, as critics point out, the Nielsen methodology was developed when people watched only three or four channels, but now people have VCRs and remote controls and can instantly surf more than a hundred channels; they can even watch more than one program at once with picture-in-picture technology.[48] In fairness to Nielsen Media Research, developing survey methods that can accurately measure television-viewing behavior, especially in light of rapid technological advances, poses a real challenge, but thus far the Nielsen system has not met this challenge. Consequently, the Nielsen ratings are suspect.

Chapter Five

But There Are Plenty of Good Polls

They [exit polls] are the most useful analytic tool developed in my working life . . .
—David Broder, syndicated columnist, 1987[1]

In the last chapter the focus was on bad polls and what makes them so disreputable. In this chapter our attention turns to good polls and specifically what makes them so laudable. Probably nothing is more rewarding for a pollster than to pass the acid test for polling as developed by George Gallup over sixty years ago; that is, to make election predictions and have those predictions consistently hit their mark. Of course, pollsters cannot do this by luck, they have to know what they are doing. When professional pollsters make election predictions, they "sweat bullets" waiting for the election returns because they have put their professional reputations on the line. Fortunately, for them, most times projections by reputable polling firms are reasonably on target, often astoundingly so, because these firms have worked diligently to refine their survey research procedures to make their polls accurate. Pollsters responsible for the ABC News/*Washington Post*, CNN/Gallup/*USA Today*, CNN/*Time*, Fox News/Opinion Dynamics, Gallup, NBC News/*Wall Street Journal*, *Newsweek*, Pew Research Center, Yankelovich Partners, and Zogby International polls, to name only a few, have over the years conducted sound polls and built impressive track records. Although these pollsters may not follow identical polling procedures (e.g., pollsters may use different wording, apply different weighting, interview a few more or less respondents), they obtain the accurate results they do because they adhere to basic, professional standards and ethics in their survey research. In fact, frequently these pollsters make strikingly similar election predictions, attesting to the fundamental similarity in their survey techniques.

In this chapter I have two major objectives. First, I want to present an overview of the basic ingredients that go into all good polls. However, I have no intention of going into elaborate, tedious detail because this is not a survey research methodology book. There are plenty of excellent such books on the market. Second, I want to conclude this chapter by discussing phone polls and exit polls because, despite some shortcomings that they may have, these polls provide the best examples of polling excellence today. Phone polls and exit polls have proved more accurate and reliable than other polling methods because they normally incorporate the best polling practices.

BASIC INGREDIENTS OF GOOD POLLS

Adherence to Professional Standards and Ethics

The Research Industry Coalition aptly notes: "Properly conducted, research has great value to its sponsors and to the public, as citizens and consumers. The value rests, in the end, on the intelligence, creativity and technical skills of research practitioners and, most critically, on their integrity and ethical standards."[2] So what does this mean in the everyday practice of a professional pollster? It means that reputable pollsters can never entertain abandoning professional standards and ethics for short-term convenience or profit, even though it may be tempting at times. Good polls are never the consequence of compromises to ethical principles and professional survey research standards. In the long run, such compromises will inevitably expose the pollster and doom his or her career. The following is a summary of "best practices" codes of conduct promoted by virtually every professional research and polling society, including the American Association for Public Opinion Research, the American Association of Political Consultants, the National Council on Public Polls, and the Research Industry Coalition.

Honor the Polling Profession with Each Polling Job. Reputable pollsters understand that every time they conduct a poll, they represent, at least in a small way, the polling profession. So pollsters must be fair and principled in their business dealings. They should only conduct polls for which they have the technical expertise, resources, and time so that quality polls can be completed on schedule. Polling contracts should be awarded on the basis of merit and open bidding, not given in secret negotiations behind closed doors involving "sweetheart" financial deals. Clients should never be deceived about the qualifications, academic credentials, and experience of those working for the polling firm. Pollsters need to respect the rights of their clients' access to the poll data that they bought and to protect the confidentiality of their clients' business. Pollsters also must recognize that clients have a right to validate the survey research commissioned as well as encourage professional analysis of the research findings and methods. To promote the polling industry, pollsters have an obligation to expose bad polls and defend those polls that are attacked unjustifiably.

Conduct Polls in a Professional Manner from Start to Finish. Most of this chapter is devoted to looking at the specific ingredients of good polling, so it is necessary to note here that good polls require in general that pollsters apply professional rigor from the beginning to the end of their survey research. This requires that a well-defined research design and strategy be developed. The research objective should be honest and stated clearly. Polling procedures should be orderly and logically contribute to the fulfillment of the survey's goals. Poll data should be carefully collected to minimize error, contamination, and bias. Pollsters need to make sure that they use samples that are truly representative of the population they seek to study so valid inferences can be made about the entire population universe from the sample. Careful attention must also be given to questionnaire design, the interviewing process, coding and raw data entry, data processing, and analysis. Double checking of procedures helps to ensure the quality of polls, although it is understood that no poll is perfect because of the inevitability of honest errors. But clearly, meticulous attention to details in polling can reduce error to very tolerable limits.

Treat the Public with Utmost Respect.   Public opinion polls are obviously supposed to represent what the public is thinking. Consequently, pollsters have the general obligation of making certain that their survey procedures are designed to accurately and honestly reflect true public opinion. The manipulation of public opinion poll data for selfish purposes shows a blatant disrespect for the people who participated in the survey. Pollsters should never waste the time of respondents, pressure or embarrass them, or not respect their right to refuse to participate in the research. Polling firms must also do everything to protect the privacy rights of respondents, especially making certain that answers to questions are kept anonymous even when outsiders seek to verify and disclose survey data. The collection of unnecessary information on respondents (names, addresses) should be avoided to guarantee the anonymity of the respondents, understanding of course that a confidential, random audit of some respondents may be required to verify that the interviews in fact were conducted (names and addresses still need not be used or disclosed), because it is common for an auditor to call and ask, for example: "Did the oldest male in this household respond to a poll regarding . . . ?" The disclosure of respondents should only be done when the respondent permits it. Finally, pollsters should never show disrespect to the public by conducting phony polls, that is, "polls designed to solicit money, sell something, or influence a person's thinking (i.e., through sleazy push polls), but not to honestly collect data."

Make Certain That Poll Results Are Reported Responsibly.
Pollsters may do an excellent job conducting the poll and analyzing
the data, but we all know that the results of any study can be distorted, manipulated, or just falsely reported. Consequently, pollsters
must *try* to see that their results are reported fairly and accurately.
Actually, in practice this is an impossible task because pollsters cannot totally control all of those who may use or report on their released data. More about this later, but ideally pollsters have an obligation to present their poll results in a complete, fair, unbiased, and
clear manner to their clients, as well as to the media and public if it
is appropriate. Full and honest disclosure of the results means that
pollsters need to report all relevant findings, whether the findings
are favorable or unfavorable. Factual findings should not be confused with any subjective interpretations or conclusions the pollsters may make. Conclusions, of course, must be logically rooted in
the quantitative findings. Without giving away any trade secrets,
the survey research methodology should be disclosed in relative detail (e.g., how the sample was drawn, how many were interviewed,
what statistical tests were applied) so their clients and others may
understand how the results were derived. Pollsters should also explain and disclose anything else that may help with the evaluation
of the quality, worth, or relevance of the poll data.

A Well-Developed, Intelligent, Yet Doable
Survey Research Design

Good polls do not just happen; they are the product of carefully
developed survey research designs. Research designs are intended
to present an overview of the survey research project, noting general goals and more specific research objectives while charting the
methodological course and answering any client concerns. In fact,
many of the items that are addressed in the survey research design
are normally included in the polling firm–client contract.

So what goes into a solid survey research design? Before conducting a poll, pollsters must know what they are doing. They

need to know what their client wants to get out of the poll. What are specific objectives? Whom shall be interviewed? How many should be interviewed? Are the polling goals and objectives within the client's budget? Is the poll doable from a financial, technical, and organizational point of view? Given what the client wants to pay for the poll, can the polling firm make a fair profit? What sort of precision (i.e., error margin) does the client want? Are there other methods, besides survey research, that are better for attaining the client's research goals? Are focus groups going to be used in conjunction with the poll? Are follow-up polls needed to satisfy the research objectives? How are the poll results to be used? Who will see the poll—only the client? The media? The general public? Will the polling agency be working closely with advertisers, the media, marketing people, campaign staffs, and others? Is the poll sensitive? For whom? Are there going to be any particular or unusual obstacles to overcome to complete this poll? What are the politics surrounding this poll (e.g., Who wants it done? Who opposes it? Is there in-fighting among the client's people over what questions should be asked?). Obviously, those responsible for the research design must address many questions and resolve many survey research problems. But as Chava Frankfort-Nachmias and David Nachmias assert, "The research design is the 'blueprint' that enables the investigator to come up with solutions to these problems. It is a logical model of proof that guides the investigator in the various stages of the research."[3]

Not all of the questions that need to be answered and the problems that need to be resolved are difficult. Obviously, an experienced, competent pollster knows the ropes, has the resources to do the job, can submit a competent bid, can meet the poll's deadline, can handle the client's "office politics," and can skillfully employ the survey research techniques necessary to conduct a good poll. Nonetheless, all polling jobs are somewhat unique with novel research goals presenting different challenges. Clearly, each poll's general goal and specific objectives are unique and must be given careful consideration in the survey research design. At least implicit in every poll are the hypotheses to be tested. For instance, say a city is hiring a pollster to find out whether residents would approve of the city's proposal to build a new recreation center. Obviously, the hypothesis to be tested is: Will city residents approve the city's proposed new recreation center? Related or subhypotheses (questions) might be: Do residents prefer an elaborate aqua center over a traditional swimming pool? Do they want a hockey rink included in the new recreation complex? How much are they willing to pay for the new recreation center? Pollsters, in planning their survey, must make certain that their poll will answer such questions.

A Carefully Drawn and Used Representative Sample

Even if you fell asleep halfway through the last chapter you could not have missed the point that bad polls have one major problem in common—that is, their samples are not representative. Obviously, the key to good polls is drawing and using a sample population that is representative of the total population that is being studied. I cannot stress this point enough. The first thing any poll critic will look at is the sample. Why? Because if the sample is not any good (i.e., if the sample is unrepresentative), the poll's findings can't be any good. Really, it is that simple!

To understand this, we must focus on the fundamentals of survey research. The basic assumption of polling is that valid inferences about the population universe can be made from the sample. To put it another way, pollsters assume that the opinions expressed by the respondents in their sample (e.g., 500–1000 polled New Yorkers eligible to vote) represent very accurately the opinions of the population universe (e.g., New York's total electorate). Ideally then, the sample, if properly drawn, is supposed to be a microcosm of the population universe, including in proper proportions all the various socioeconomic and political groupings (e.g., Protestants, Catholics, Jews, Republicans, Democrats, whites, African Americans, the haves and have-nots, and so on) actually found in the total population universe. Consequently, if the sample is not representative, the poll's basic assumption is false. If this assumption is false, findings from survey research would be worthless because no valid inferences could be made from the sample about the total population under study. In fact, pollsters rely heavily on inferential statistics to make sense of their raw data. These statistics permit pollsters to make inferences about certain traits and opinions in the population universe (N) based on the findings from a sample (n) taken from this population universe. However, employing "fancy" statistical tests means nothing if the sample is not representative, so conscientious pollsters are careful to make certain that their samples are representative.

Today, reputable pollsters in America almost exclusively rely on probability sampling since it has proven so reliable; it has replaced nonprobability sampling, which had proven so disastrous for pollsters who used this sampling method to make their erroneous 1948 presidential prediction that Dewey would defeat Truman. In nonprobability sampling there is no way of calculating the probability of a single sampling unit (e.g., an eligible voter) being included in the sample because the population universe is not specified. However, probability sampling allows survey researchers to calculate the statistical odds of a sampling unit being included in the sample because the population universe is known. Respected pollsters today use simple probability random sampling, which gives, at least theoretically, every person in the known population universe an equal chance of being selected. For example, if the population universe is 190,000,000 eligible voters in the United States and a sample of 1000 is drawn, although every eligible voter would have an equal chance of being selected, the statistical odds of an eligible voter being selected would be 1000 divided by 190,000,000, or 0.000005263.

Probability random sampling also gives pollsters the ability to calculate an error margin for their poll, given their sample size. For example, if the pollster uses a sample size of 500, the error margin would be approximately ±4.5% at 95% confidence. That means that if the pollster found that the president received a 60% job approval, the pollster would be 95% confident that the president's job approval could be as high as 64.5% or as low as 55.5%, but with the greatest probability that his job approval would be 60%, not at the error margin extremes. This point should be stressed because the media often note that a particular political race is in a "dead heat" when, say, candidate A leads candidate B by 46% to 42%, with an error margin of ±4%. Accounting for the error margin, this is technically true, but the odds are still greater that candidate A has a slight lead and not that candidate A is tied with or actually losing to candidate B. But since polling is not an exact science, we all feel more comfortable regarding these tight races as "too close to call."

Good polls can also be based on probability samples known as stratified sampling. This kind of sampling is used when the pollsters want to randomly sample various groups to make sure that they are represented proportionately in the poll. For example, I use stratified random sampling in the St. Louis region when I want to make certain that the different geographical areas of the St. Louis region are proportionately represented in my poll. For example, if St. Louis City constitutes 33% of the eligible voters and St. Louis County residents make up the remaining 67% of the eligible voters, I want to make sure that 67% of the respondents are from St. Louis County with only 33% from the city. As methodologists note, "Stratification does not violate the principle of random selection because a probability sample is subsequently drawn within each stratum."[4]

It should be pointed out that drawing and employing solid representative samples is not easy, even for the best pollsters. Problems are everywhere. To begin with, a sample is based on the population universe, yet it is difficult, if not impossible, to define precisely this population universe. For example, let's say the pollster wants to poll "voters" in Texas, but who are the voters? Should they be all the eligible voters? The registered voters? The likely voters? If the pollster decides to sample only registered voters, the pollster in reality could never get a definitive list of registered voters since these lists are never completely updated or accurate. In fact, no source lists (e.g., telephone, utility, welfare, driver license listings) are totally current, complete, and accurate. However, good pollsters work with the best source lists (known as sampling frames) available to try to make their samples as representative as possible. Usually they succeed, and that is why polls conducted by reputable polling firms are normally quite accurate.

Of course, once the not perfect but pretty accurate representative sample has been drawn, the problem of getting those in your sample to respond to the poll becomes another challenge for pollsters. As discussed previously, the "no response" problem, due to a variety of reasons (e.g., answering machines, Caller ID, respondents' growing unwillingness to cooperate), can contaminate the representative character of the carefully drawn random samples. However, I think the contaminating effect of this problem on sample representativeness has been exaggerated. Survey research purists hold that any time interviewers fail to reach and interview a specific randomly selected person, the representativeness of the sample is compromised. Yet, arguably, there are no real signs that simply going on to another randomly selected person on the random list of potential respondents has caused polls to be detectably less accurate. In fact, it appears that dedicated pollsters have done a laudable job overcoming any problems with sampling because, overall, polls by reputable firms today are more accurate than those of yesteryear despite the growing "no response" rate.

A Well-Designed Questionnaire

A poll is like a chain: if any link is weak, the whole chain becomes weak. Pollsters may do a good job in constructing a solid research design and drawing a representative sample, but if they drop the ball when developing the questionnaire, the poll will still turn out to be a poor one. Of course, good pollsters know this and they do everything they can to uphold standards during every step of the survey process, including the questionnaire design stage. As you can imagine, survey research scholars spend endless pages in methodology textbooks discussing the makings of good questionnaires, but my goal here is simply to cover the highlights, focusing in particular on the pitfalls in questionnaire construction that professional pollsters avoid.

One cannot forget that the questionnaire is the chief instrument of pollsters. The questionnaire is used to get the necessary information from respondents to satisfy the researcher's goals. In working closely with the client, the pollster must design a questionnaire that will answer all the survey research questions the client wants answered. This means that the pollster must listen very carefully to the client so that the client's needs are completely understood. To be honest, this is often a difficult chore since clients frequently don't know exactly what they want. However, experienced pollsters know how to listen, pose the right questions, and lead the way. Normally, pollsters must submit several rough drafts of the questionnaire to a client, each time responding to critical feedback, before the client agrees that this particular draft of the questionnaire will get the job done. Incidentally, professional ethics do not permit pollsters to administer a questionnaire unless their client gives final approval. Such approval also protects the business interests of the pollster as well. The last thing a pollster wants to hear from his or her client is: "This is not what we want! We are not paying you for this poll!"

Naturally, the questions constitute the fundamental building blocks of the questionnaire. Answers to enough properly designed questions should provide the information needed to satisfy the specific objectives and the general goals of the survey, as well as to adequately test the researcher's hypotheses. To do so, competent pollsters devote considerable attention to details pertaining to question content, structure, format, and order.

Question Content.   Questions are used to obtain both factual (e.g., sex, age, income) and subjective (e.g., opinions, attitudes) information from people. Factual questions need to be gathered so they can be linked to subjective information, allowing the subjective responses to be placed into a more meaningful perspective. For example, it may be important for city planners to know that generally 60% of the residents favor the city's proposed street improvements, yet the proposal receives only 34% support from residents living in the northwest quadrant of the city. In the spring of 2000, George W. Bush must have been delighted to find out that just over 90% of the Christian fundamentalists supported him for president, but disturbed to learn that about 95% of African Americans opposed him.

Asking factual questions is relatively easy (e.g., What is your marital status? __Married __Single __Separated __Divorced), but getting accurate answers can sometimes present problems. For instance, experienced pollsters know that personal questions regarding income, age, religious preference, and so on should be asked at the end of the questionnaire after the respondent is more comfortable, trusting, and more confident that the poll is a legitimate one. Nonetheless, some respondents are reluctant to answer truthfully, particularly very personal or sensitive questions or those that pertain to community standards that most respondents believe should be upheld even if they violated them. For example, pollsters know that consistently about 14–17% of those interviewed will say that they voted in the last presidential election even though they did not. The community standard is that good citizens should vote. However, inaccurate answers can also be given because the respondents may not understand the question; may not remember correctly; may not know the facts; or may purposely give false information for sundry reasons. Competent survey researchers have ways to minimize inaccurate answers to tolerable limits (e.g., repeating questions, using "comfortable" rhetoric, avoiding questions almost guaranteed to illicit unreliable responses, strategically placing questions, and even allowing respondents time to check the facts), yet false responses to certain problematic factual questions will continue to frustrate even the best pollsters.

Subjective questions are particularly popular in polls because normally pollsters want to understand public opinion on various matters. Duh, maybe this is why we commonly refer to such surveys as public opinion polls! But unlike factual questions, questions seeking to measure a person's opinion, attitude, intensity, and other subjective feelings about something can be very tricky. In fact, only experienced, professional pollsters do a good job constructing opinion questions and placing them in the proper sequence on questionnaires. It is not my purpose to cover the exhausting list of potential problems associated with drafting competent opinion questions, except to say that good pollsters know that they have to be careful with wording (no word is completely neutral), sentence development, emphasis, logic, transition from one question to the next, question placement, and the like. We all know about the sensitivity of words and how asking the "same" question using different words, emphases, and sentence structure can elicit very different responses. Despite the criticisms, however, professional pollsters do an admirable job handling question challenges and this is why these pollsters, surveying the same phenomenon, tend to obtain remarkably similar results.

Question Structure.   Professional pollsters know that questions must be structured differently to obtain the feedback from respondents that they need. There are three basic ways of structuring questions or questionnaires and they all serve different survey objectives. The most common structural type is the closed-end (also called "closed-ended") question in which respondents are asked a question, but they can only give a predetermined answer. An example of a closed-end question would be: "How would you rate President Clinton's job performance? __Excellent __Good __Fair __Poor __Don't know." Closed-end questions are very popular because they allow the pollster to easily quantify the responses (e.g., 283 or 37% answered "Excellent"), while also permitting poll results to be compared over time or even among different polling firms (e.g., "Today, 37% rated Clinton's job performance as excellent, while last month only 29% did.").

Obviously, the problem with closed-end questions is that they limit the kind of answer a respondent can give, often much to the frustration of the respondent. When pollsters need more elaborate responses, especially when the possible responses to a question cannot be easily anticipated, open-end questions are used. Open-end questions commonly follow closed-end questions when pollsters want respondents to elaborate or clarify. For example, to Clinton's job performance question, pollsters might want to ask: "What in particular do you like about Clinton's job performance?" Open-end questions may seem like better questions to the average person because they allow respondents the opportunity to give a "full" response, but the truth is that pollsters use them sparingly because answers tend to be "all over the place" and, therefore, hard to quantify (i.e., to place into meaningful numbers and percentages) and make understandable and useful. Also, interviewers cannot practically record the entire response, but only the "essence" of what is being said, calling into question the accuracy of the interpreted and recorded answer. Consequently, good pollsters occasionally employ open-end questions to shed some light on answers to closed-end questions, but are careful not to give them more weight than they deserve.[5]

Filter Questions. Filter questions are important to use when the pollster wants to screen respondents, to "filter out" those who should not answer certain questions. For example, a filter question may be: "Are you a registered voter living in the city of Boston?" If the respondent said "no," the interview would be terminated if the pollster only wanted to interview registered voters of Boston. Another filter question may be: "Have you been following the recent controversy over gun control?" If the respondent answered "no," the interviewer would not ask a series of questions on gun control because the pollster's objective is only to interview informed people who have been following the recent controversy over gun control. Filter questions are used to make sure that only the appropriate people are asked certain contingency questions (i.e., questions contingent on how respondents answered the filter questions). Experienced pollsters know how to use filter questions so that their questionnaires make logical sense.

Question Response Format. On occasion, pollsters want to find out how intensely people feel about simple "yes" or "no," "agree" or "disagree," and similarly oppositional answers, so they construct a response format that will measure intensity levels. For example, respondents might reply that they favor Al Gore for president, but are we to assume that all of these people who said that they favor Gore have the same level of enthusiasm for him? This would be an erroneous assumption. So to discover how "hard" or "soft" the support for Gore is, an insightful pollster might use the following follow-up intensity measure: "How would you rate your level of support for Gore? __Strongly support __Modestly support __Weakly Support." Obviously, knowing the level of support for someone or something is critically important to planners because they can normally count on "hard" support, but "soft" support can often abruptly evaporate in light of slight changes in circumstances, causing considerable problems for planners (e.g., campaign managers, governmental planners, marketing people). Also, given the high costs of some ventures, it may prove very cost-ineffective to implement some project that most people are very lukewarm toward. Consequently, when necessary, good pollsters choose from a variety of measures (rank ordering and rating scale techniques are also popular choices) to determine "support intensity."

Question Sequence. Question sequence is also crucial in questionnaire design because, clearly, good questions asked out of order or in an illogical sequence can ruin the worth of the questionnaire. Thus, professional pollsters make sure that they place questions in a logical sequence. For example, when the pollster's objective is to "narrow in" on a topic to get detailed information from respondents, the best approach is the *funnel sequence* in which broad questions are asked at first to place the following series of narrower and narrower questions into a proper, clearer perspective. However, sometimes it may be appropriate to use an *inverted funnel sequence* when respondents may find it difficult to respond to broader, more conceptual questions that essentially ask respondents to draw broad conclusions from a series of questions that focus on specifics. For instance, respondents may be asked: "Did you receive adequate treatment from your doctor during your last visit?" However, after a series of quite specific questions that may get broader in scope, the respondent is asked the broadest question: "Overall, how satisfied are you with your health care plan?"

Reputable pollsters must always pay careful attention to the general placement of all questions in their questionnaires, making sure, for instance, that the easy to answer (i.e., respond to) warm-up questions are placed at the beginning of the questionnaire to get respondents "into" the survey. This is critical because once respondents actually begin to respond, they tend to finish the survey. Just as important, as noted earlier in another context, sensitive, personal demographical questions (e.g., age, income) should be placed at the end of the questionnaire so that respondents are not "turned off" before the interview barely starts.[6]

Avoiding Other Questionnaire Pitfalls

Conscientious pollsters do their best to avoid pitfalls that tend to contaminate and bias answers to questions. Savvy pollsters make lead-in questions neutral to avoid biasing respondent answers. To achieve accurate answers, the wording of questions must be neutral and as clear as possible. Obviously, using sensational words (e.g., "killing babies" in a question dealing with the abortion issue) is going to bias the response. Also, using "big words" or words that are not generally understood, especially by less-educated respondents, such as "solvency," will generate unreliable answers. When I polled for Richard Gephardt, he wanted to obtain public opinion toward the solvency of the Social Security system. I told him that few people would understand the meaning of the word "solvency." Gephardt, being insightful, understood that we would have to use simpler terminology in the actual questions (e.g., future financial security of).

Veteran pollsters also learn to handle some words and questions with "kid gloves," particularly those that heighten anxieties in people. Unquestionably, questions pertaining to sexual preferences, sexual behavior, drug and alcohol use, extramarital activities, and so on will often yield very unreliable results because respondents will simply not answer the questions, grossly distort the truth, or flatly lie. Although carefully selected question rhetoric and lead-ins can minimize the problem, the truth is that there are simply some problematic questions that will not produce very reliable results, even when enormous resources are committed to doing the job right.

Finally, a "rookie" mistake that experienced pollsters would never make is asking two questions at once. A good example of such a double-barreled question would be: "The worst problems confronting Americans are declining family values and rising energy costs? __ Agree __ Disagree __ Unsure." Given the flawed wording, how could any sense be made out of the results to this question?

Well-Trained and Responsible Interviewers

It was made clear in the last chapter that George Gallup, when conducting polls during the 1930s and 1940s, had some problems with his interviewers. Despite their rigorous training, his interviewers had a very hard time adhering to the established interview procedures. They faced constant challenges in trying to interview enough people and the "right" people, in getting people to grant the interview, in obtaining the cooperation of the respondents during the interview so that they could get questions properly answered and questionnaires completed, and in simply dealing with the different, sometimes "impossible" personalities of respondents. Interviewing is not a science and, although some pollsters may not want to admit this to themselves or their clients, interviewers exercise broad, yet often quite unsupervised discretion in handling the various problems that emerge when conducting their interviews. Some people are "naturals" as interviewers, whereas others just can't seem to be successful in interviewing people. As a pollster for more than two decades now, I have always been amazed by the success rate of some interviewers and the dismal failure rate of others. And there does not seem to be any way I can predict whether those I hire and train will be successful or unsuccessful as interviewers. Some of my most successful interviewers have been women, housewives, retired people, and widows or widowers, while some of my worst have been younger people and students, yet just the opposite has also been true. As Gerald Adams and Jay Schvaneveldt conclude, "There is not a single predictable formula that can be used to assure that a person will be successful as an interviewer."[7]

To reiterate, interviewing is not a science! Pollsters can do their best to train and supervise their interviewers, but thorough training does not guarantee that interviewers will always "go by the book" or that in every instance they can or should. Also, supervision can only go so far. Obviously, interviewers in the field conducting personal interviews experience virtually no supervision, but even interviewers conducting interviews through phone banks still cannot realistically be supervised in such a way that all interviews will be conducted in the same manner.[8] The harsh reality for pollsters is that their interviewers cannot be turned into robots and all made to act in exactly the same way because they are real people with different backgrounds, personal traits, and personalities.

This is a harsh reality in the polling business, because the stark truth is that a plethora of studies over the years have made evident that the different characteristics of interviewers do affect at least somewhat the responses to survey questions.[9] Fortunately, this effect is minor, but the exact extent of contamination or bias cannot be measured precisely, especially since it would depend on the nature of the questions asked, to whom, and on the specific interviewers; it would not be valid to apply generalizations to individual interviewers.

Of course, this should not come as any surprise to anyone reading this book, because you know that you relate to various people differently. We all do. What is being said here, for example, is that common sense suggests that African American interviewers are going to elicit at least slightly different responses from white respondents than from black respondents when asking them questions about racial prejudice.[10] Likewise, younger interviewers will undoubtedly obtain different responses from much older respondents than from young respondents when asking them about Social Security or problems unique to the "new generation." Female interviewers will get somewhat different responses from women than from men when asking questions about feminist or sexual issues. For example, to an Eagleton Institute statement—"The decision to have an abortion is a private matter that should be left to the woman to decide without government intervention"—only

64% of the women interviewed by male interviewers agreed, while 84% of the female respondents agreed when interviewed by women.[11]

Let's focus on a practical interviewer problem that has no feasible solution, using the race of the interviewer as an example. Any experienced pollster knows that the race of the interviewer will affect the results of their polls because many questions on public opinion polls, especially when dealing with various socioeconomic and political issues (which are the primary focus of most polls), are race sensitive. Naturally, respondents can easily see the race of the respondent in a personal interview, but even in telephone interviews studies indicate that about three-quarters of the respondents could identify the race of the interviewer by his or her voice.[12] Consequently, whites tend to give black interviewers more "politically correct" responses to racially sensitive questions, whereas African American respondents are more likely to give more frank answers to racially charged questions to black interviewers, but more reserved or disingenuous responses to white interviewers.[13] So here we have a situation in which pollsters know that the race of interviewers can bias responses, yet what can even the most conscientious pollsters do about it? The answer is, about nothing. Practically and legally speaking, polling firms cannot hire interviewers based on their sex, age, race, nationality, social class, or personality. One time, when I was testifying in court, this message hit home. Under cross-examination, it was suggested that the fact that I had black and white interviewers biased my poll results, yet later it was implied that maybe I did not employ the "proper" percentage of black and white interviewers; even though I had proportionally more black interviewers than legally required.

In summary, professional pollsters do the best they can to recruit, train, and use competent interviewers. The accuracy of their polls depends on it. Pollsters need to make sure that their interviewers act as professionally as possible. This means that they must display some warmth and personality, yet conduct their interviews in a serious, neutral, and conscientious manner, following directions carefully, recording answers competently, and trying their best to uphold basic interviewing standards and ethics.

Interviewers cannot help that they are black or white, male or female, young or old, have different accents, and so on, so pollsters must live with the contamination to their poll data caused by these methodological deficiencies. However, given the impressive accuracy of polls conducted by professional polling firms over the past few decades, evidently these interviewer differences are not that significant overall, or, if they are, they somehow have a way of canceling each other out, or the training of interviewers has minimized the problem. However, it should be mentioned that poll accuracy is normally tested by comparing pollsters' predictions of election results with the actual results. Here interviewers are only asking respondents whether they plan to vote for certain candidates, something that is normally not very sensitive to the backgrounds and personal traits of the interviewers. So this does not mean that poll results for race, gender, and other sensitive questions are completely accurate, partially due to the personal differences in interviewers.

Careful Coding and Tabulation of Raw Poll Data

Once the interviewers have finished their interviews, the raw answers on all the questionnaires must be coded and electronically entered into a common data base for computer processing. Raw data are the answers to the closed- and open-end questions on the questionnaire. Coding is another important step in the polling process because improperly coded and entered data would generate inaccurate poll results. However, the coding and data entry processes are possibly the least challenging steps in the survey process because most public opinion polls today include mostly or exclusively closed-end questions that are very easy to code and enter.

Actually, closed-end questions are so easy to code that the coding scheme is almost self-explanatory to anyone with elementary logic (coding scheme example: 1 = Yes; 2 = No; 3 = Undecided). In fact, probably about all questionnaires today, including only closed-end response categories, are precoded, allowing interview-

tions to the same poll data because, in fact, most will reach quite similar conclusions as to what the survey results show. On the other hand, all poll data are open to some interpretation and pollsters naturally come from different backgrounds and possess different values and perspectives. Herbert Asher stresses that in analyzing poll data pollsters have "tremendous leeway in deciding which items to analyze, which sample subsets or breakdowns to present, and how to interpret the results." He points out that many things can influence an analyst, including time and budget constraints, a pollster's personal preferences, what he or she thinks is more or less important in the data, and the like. Appropriately, Asher concludes that it should not surprise anyone that two quite honest and dedicated pollsters "may interpret identical poll results in sharply different ways depending on the perspectives and values they bring to their data analysis; the glass may indeed be half full or half empty."[14]

Obviously, it is true that professional pollsters are human and are driven by different experiences, goals, values, and perspectives. But they are also professionals and have an obligation to analyze and interpret poll data in a fair and objective fashion. Frankly, that means that reputable pollsters should never cross the line into sleaze territory when interpreting poll data for their clients, the public, or anyone. So what does this really mean in practice? It means that clients can expect to buy a pollster's services, but not their integrity. Yes, pollsters can ethically put a "spin" on the poll data, emphasizing certain aspects of the poll's results that might please their clients. However, reputable pollsters still need to draw the line because they have an obligation to the polling profession and the public not to degrade the practice of polling. We know, for example, that we have Republican and Democratic pollsters and often they appear on political talk shows to discuss, among other things, how their Republican or Democratic clients are doing in the polls. We expect the Republican pollster to put a Republican spin on the poll data and the Democratic pollster to spin the results for the Democrats, but we shouldn't expect these professional pollsters to lie about the poll data or to act unprofessionally by intentionally distorting the data for the purpose of deceiving people. If pollsters purposely and maliciously misinterpret poll results to deceive, these pollsters will soon ruin their own credibility and do a great injustice to the polling industry.

I have listened carefully to established pollsters on television and radio giving news interviews and participating in the numerous talk shows. My overall impression has been that they certainly give their listeners the spin, but their interpretations of the poll data are basically quite honest, acknowledging, especially if pressed, certain negatives that their political clients might have. But as critics point out, the average American is normally confused by the disjointed and incomplete interpretation of poll data by partisan pollsters who are spinning their data, especially since the listeners or viewers are not survey research experts and do not have the advantage of having the questionnaire and completed poll results in their hands.

Most often, when it comes to the interpretations of political poll data, political analysts working for the media do the best job interpreting poll data because they are neutral and are honestly trying to present the poll results so they can be understood by their audience. At this writing, CNN's veteran political analyst, Bill Schneider, is probably the best in the business. Although his presentations go too fast because seconds are so precious in television, he does a laudable job giving a fairly comprehensive and objective view of the poll data.[15]

Interpreting poll data can be very tricky and even the best pollsters make mistakes, especially if they don't take time to think about what the results are really showing. For instance, in interpreting poll data, good pollsters know that they can grossly misread responses to questions if they place too much emphasis on a response to a single question or try to interpret responses out of context. For example, take the problem that plagued the Clinton administration when his advisors placed too much emphasis on certain answers to health care questions, while playing down or ignoring responses to other responses that would have placed public opinion on health care in a broader and more telling context. The Clinton administration pushed health care reform because they placed great weight on the answer to the following

June 1994 Gallup Poll question: "Which of these statements do you agree with more: The country has health care problems, but no health care crisis, or the country has a health care crisis?" Fifty-five percent answered "Crisis," 41% responded "Problems but no crisis," and 4% said "Don't know." With 55% saying "crisis," President Clinton felt he had a clear popular mandate and, therefore, swung for the fences on health care reform, only to strike out. Among other things, the Clinton administration failed to take other poll data into consideration, especially the poll results showing that the American people overwhelmingly opposed the "governmentalization" or the "public bureaucratization" of our health care system. In conducting a poll for Missouri Consumer Health Care WATCH, I found that the overwhelming majority of respondents said essentially that they were happy with their health care provider. However, a careful look at the poll data in context with other questions disclosed that actually only the vast majority of Missourians who had received only routine health care services were content, whereas the minority of respondents who had dealt with their health care providers for serious health problems were quite dissatisfied.

Herbert Asher urges that consumers of polls have an obligation as good citizens to become more sophisticated poll watchers and critics.[16] Although there are plenty of good pollsters giving reliable interpretations to poll data, citizens need to learn enough about the fundamentals of polling so they can consider the critical questions when poll results are being interpreted, such as: Who sponsored the poll? Was the poll conducted for the media and interpreted objectively or was the survey conducted for a special interest and probably interpreted in a biased way that would promote the special interests of the interest group? What data support the interpretations and conclusions? Have the analysts made logical inferences from the findings to substantiate their conclusions? Was the wording neutral or biased? Would different wording elicit very different results? Overall, was the questionnaire (e.g., wording, question placement, introduction, filter questions) constructed fairly and professionally to obtain unbiased public opinion or was the questionnaire designed to get "desired" results? Finally, have the entire questionnaire and results been made available for closer scrutiny?

Good Polls Can Be "Junked" by Bad Reporting

Definitely, one of the worst nightmares for pollsters, who have normally taken great care to make certain that their polls were done right, is to see their poll results poorly reported. After all, the public only learns about findings from the poll reports. Unfortunately, however, it is a common problem in the polling business to see good polls badly reported because most of the time poll results are not reported by the firm that conducted the poll, but by others (e.g., the media, interest groups, business organizations). For pollsters, the hapless truth is that they can exercise control over all of the steps in the survey research process, but they effectively lose control as soon as they turn over their poll findings to their clients or others. Yes, pollsters may have some say over how their poll results are reported, at least when results are initially reported, but they are mostly at the mercy of those doing the reporting. Well, so what? Big deal! But the problem is serious enough because too often comprehensive, accurate poll results are grossly distorted or evenly falsely reported by those doing the reporting because such reporters are rarely very sophisticated in survey research; in particular know very little about survey research methodology; frequently have different motives and objectives in reporting the data; often must use their inexpert discretion to edit, format, and simplify the poll results for the presentation or story; commonly operate under severe time and space constraints, as well as deadline pressures; have no real, long-term stake in the poll itself or the polling profession; and, compared to the pollsters, are not that aware or sensitive to the professional standards and ethics associated with poll reporting.

There is no doubt that one of the necessary ingredients in good polling is adept reporting of the results. Dedicated pollsters usually follow the American Association for Public Opinion Research's long list of standards for reporting poll findings (e.g., disclosing the sponsor of the survey, who conducted the poll, when the poll was conducted, specific population surveyed, sample size, error margin), but AAPOR's standards only apply directly to the professional pollsters and not, for example, to the journalists reporting poll results. Regarding the adherence to professional standards on poll reporting, scholar Herbert Asher aptly notes: "One reason the standards are not as effective as they appear is that they apply primarily to survey organizations and pollsters who release results rather than to the media that are covering the results; the impact of the standards is thus limited." Further, he stresses: "If the organization reporting the poll is different from the groups that sponsored it, the poll release and the actual news story may show major discrepancies in meeting the NCPP and AAPOR recommendations."[17]

The bottom line is that frequently the public gets irritated with how poll results are reported. Naturally, not giving much thought to it, people commonly blame the pollsters for simplistic reporting of findings that they believe twists the facts and distorts the truth. Yet such is usually not the fault of the pollsters, because they have very limited, if any, real control over the reporting of their poll data by secondary sources. Regarding the media, the typical reporting situations tend to promote the deficient reporting of poll findings. On television, the primary source for news for most Americans,[18] producers, reporters, and anchors, working together as professionals, normally do the best they can, under the circumstances, to present poll results to their viewers. But the opportunities for reporting poll results both thoroughly and insightfully are rare, although they may be adequate on special political reports appearing on cable stations such as C-SPAN, CNN, and CNBC. On the network and local TV, the producers, reporters, and anchors usually get poll data with little time to really examine the data, so they must scramble to put together a "poll report package," which is often used to supplement a one- to three-minute news story. The end result is a very superficial reporting of poll findings focusing only on the perceived "highlights" of the poll's results, and almost always excluding the exact wording of questions, complete response categories, anything on question placement, use of filter questions, response rates, weighting, a detailed explanation of methodology, and anything else that might be helpful in interpreting the results.

But television is a business too, and those responsible for programming have an obligation to the owners and shareholders to air programs that promote viewership and, thus, the ratings. The fact is that the typical viewer would quickly become bored by a comprehensive report on poll data, including even a cursory description of the methodology. Normally the station does the appropriate thing and invites those who are really interested in a complete reporting of the poll's results to visit their Web site (e.g., abcnews.go.com/sections/politics/PollVault). At these Web sites, the entire questionnaire with the answers reported in percentages may be found, but still the complete methodology is missing. Nonetheless, media polls are best viewed on the Web because people can then view the actual questionnaire and take time to study the responses. This is true even for polls reported in the newspapers, because newspaper space for polls is still quite limited, but normally one can find complete poll results reported at their Web sites (e.g., NYTimes.com), although poll data retrieval from their archives can be expensive since most newspapers charge fees for archival research.

To sum up, the best reporting of poll findings is done by the polling firms that conducted the polls. Overall, they do a commendable job and often their poll findings, along with commentary on their methodology, can be found by going to their Web sites (e.g., Galluppoll.com). Reporting by the media is usually presented in a neutral fashion, yet the reporting is nearly always superficial. Reporting by partisan political organizations, interest groups, and businesses should be viewed with a hefty dose of skepticism since such reporting is normally done to promote their interests, and so the reporting is almost always selective, incomplete, and slanted. Watch out!

EXAMPLES OF GOOD POLLS

In the last chapter I discussed several kinds of bad polls, pointing out why they were deficient. In this chapter I have focused on the ingredients of good polls. I want to conclude by discussing briefly two kinds of polls that can provide excellent poll data if conducted by competent pollsters—telephone polls and exit polls.

Telephone Polls Are Pretty Accurate

As noted in previous chapters, telephone polls are not perfect, but then what is? On the other hand, despite the apparent problems with telephone surveys, collecting survey data through telephone interviews has proved quite reliable, especially compared to other survey research methods. The fact is that pollsters must live with the reality that they cannot conduct a poll free of imperfections, and must strive to conduct the best possible polls they can. In the 1979 presidential address to the American Association for Public Opinion Research, Reuben Cohen made this point clear: "There are not perfect surveys. Every survey has it imperfections. The world is not ideally suited to our work. The best we can do is think through the ideal approach to a survey design, or implementation, or analysis problem—what we would do if we had our druthers— then get as close to the ideal as we can. . . . Practical work consists in good part of guessing what irregularities, where, and how much one can afford to tolerate. . . . The same is true for survey research. It should be done well. It can and should conform well, even if not perfectly, to an ideal approach."[19]

Dedicated pollsters have tried to find over the decades the best possible approach for collecting reliable survey research data. Personal interviews, mail surveys, telephone polls, and recently experimental Internet polls have all been tried. They all have their faults, yet telephone polls have proved to be the most cost-effective way to gather most kinds of survey data. Consequently, most reputable pollsters rely heavily on telephone polls.

In applying the ingredients of good polls, we can readily see why telephone polls have become so popular with professional pollsters. The plain truth is that at present telephone polling still encapsulates the best formula for sound polling standards, with the possible exception of exit polling used only on election days. As stressed earlier, the most crucial ingredient in good polling is a

Yes Mr. Wendel, but I'm afraid that our study on the polling industry is not good news for us

representative sample because an unrepresentative sample cannot be used to produce representative poll data. But unlike personal, mail, call-in, and Internet polls, which have serious problems with sampling, telephone polling can generate results that are not perfectly representative, yet still certainly representative enough to allow pollsters to have great confidence in their survey results. Decades ago, when a significant percentage of the population could not be reached by telephone, obviously survey researchers rejected telephone polls as a viable polling method. However, in the late 1950s only 72.5% of American households had telephones, whereas by the late 1980s almost 98% of Americans could be reached by phone, thus reducing sampling frame error to a tolerable level.[20] In addition, despite the concern over telephone poll response rates, the rate for telephone interviewing is very high compared to mail surveys and somewhat higher compared to door-to-door interviews, especially in certain dangerous metropolitan neighborhoods.[21] Also, while telephone interviews can reach the demographically "right" people during the evening, when most people are at home, door-to-door interviewers cannot feasibly interview at night for several reasons (e.g., difficulty in finding specified housing units in the dark, colder weather, heightened safety concerns, much greater interviewer intrusiveness). Personal interviews cannot always be conducted on weekends during the day because of time constraints, while door-to-door interviewing during the week is almost a waste of time since few of the "right" people are at home, especially because today a high percentage of both men and women are in the workforce. Of course, on a practical matter, telephone interviewing is still relatively inexpensive when compared to personal interviewing, since door-to-door interviewing is very time-consuming, causing labor costs to soar to really prohibitive levels for most pollsters, to say nothing of the significant cost-per-mile travel expenses. Another advantage of telephone polls is that interviewers frequently make their calls from a phone bank in a central location, allowing for better, but not perfect, monitoring of the interviewers, whereas personal interviewers are practically impossible to monitor.

Computer-assisted telephone polling has made telephone interviewing even more reliable. As noted previously, private companies have assembled terrific telephone number data bases that contain virtually all working residential and business telephone numbers, some consisting of even unlisted numbers. With a few clicks of the mouse, pollsters can target almost any specific population universe they want by, for example, region, state, county, city, or Zip code, including only business or residential phone numbers even within a specific area from a geo-coded starting point (e.g., 26 Main Street). After selecting the population universe they want, they can easily export the telephone numbers to a software program that can readily select the quantity of random numbers they need to conduct the survey.

New computer technology has also improved the use of a telephone sampling method called random digit dialing, which permits the pollster to call numbers randomly and proportionately in given exchanges (e.g., 30% of the numbers in exchange 619, 50% in 963, and 20% in 843). Because four-digit random numbers are generated to go with the three-digit prefixes, unlisted numbers are also included in the sample. However, many pollsters, but especially their interviewers, find the random-digit dialing method annoying and inefficient because so many unwanted telephone numbers exist (e.g., numbers not in service, fax machines, computer-allocated numbers, and pager numbers), preventing interviewers from reaching the "right" respondents. Consequently, many pollsters today prefer using the elaborate, updated telephone number data bases provided by private companies such as SelectPhone.

Many of the larger polling firms love to use CATI, Computer-Assisted Telephone Interviewing, because this system simplifies the interviewing process by allowing interviewers, assembled at a central site, to read the questions off of a computer screen and enter the questions directly. Survey researchers cite the following advantages to CATI: (1) it simplifies and speeds up the interviewing process by allowing direct entry of answers, thus reducing error; (2) it permits effective monitoring of interviewers not only by supervisors but through computer monitoring of interviewers (e.g., the time interviewers take to complete questionnaires, number of interviews completed, some error spotting); and (3) it allows pollsters to keep a running check on the overall status of the poll (e.g., total calls, refusals, and completions).[22]

Experts acknowledge that telephone polls have some problems. Specifically, they cite the nonresponse problem and the fact that telephone polls are not suited for certain kinds of interviewing in which more complex questions need to be asked, requiring many follow-up questions and extensive probing, especially involving sensitive subjects. Yet, on the whole, telephone polls have proved very useful and reliable for collecting a wide variety of survey data, permitting textbook authors on polling to conclude, in weighing the pros and cons of telephone polls, that "telephone surveys have gained general acceptance as a legitimate method of data collection in the social sciences."[23] In fact, compared to all other methods, considering their advantages and disadvantages for general survey data gathering, telephone polling is the only generally accepted survey research method.

Exit Polls Are Even More Accurate

As noted at length in Chapter 1, Americans love to attack pollsters. Some Americans, although out of ignorance, even berate exit pollsters, charging that their polls are wrong. But, as evinced in Chapter 2, how wrong can these critics be? Actually, exit polling has established a truly remarkable record for accuracy. Of course, if determined critics search long and hard, they might be able to find some exit poll predictions that missed their mark (e.g., the networks' call of the 2000 presidential race based on a misreading of their exit poll results in Florida), but statistically speaking, exit poll forecasts have been wrong only a tiny percentage of the time. Let's look at some expert endorsements.

Herbert Asher, who is an established survey research scholar, notes: "On rare occasions, exit polls are inaccurate."[24] Another renowned scholar in the field, Albert Cantril, contends that "as useful as pre-election polls may be for measuring the evolving disposition of the electorate, they are not nearly as powerful as exit polls in analyzing the message voters have sent by the ballots they cast."[25] Distinguished political scientists George Edwards III and Stephen Wayne place exit polls in context with other kinds of polls, concluding that "the most accurate poll is one taken after people vote and as they leave the voting booths." Ironically, they continue: "One of the problems with exit polls lies in their accuracy (rather than inaccuracy): They give the press access to sufficient data to predict the outcome before the elections have been concluded."[26] Political columnist David Broder, expressing appreciation for exit poll precision, comments: "They are the most useful analytic tool developed in my working life."[27] Fellow journalist Mark Jurkowitz helps to explain why. He claims that exit poll results are so reliable that the television networks, using exit poll data provided by the Voter News Service or VNS (a news fraternity including the Associated Press, ABC, CBS, CNN, Fox News, and NBC), confidently plan their election coverage in relative detail many hours before the polls close because the exit poll data have already told them who won, by about how much, and how (i.e., how the candidates fared with different voter groups). Consequently, packaged stories can be put together and anchors and political analysts can prepare their commentary on why candidates won and lost, while each network can air their teases that give rather obvious hints as to who won. For example, on Super Tuesday 2000, the big pileup of state presidential primaries, Fox News managing editor and anchor Brit Hume, knowing the election results from the exit poll data, began his 6:00 P.M. news broadcast, an hour before the polls closed on the East Coast, with the revealing tease that Bush and Gore "seemed poised to all but end the races in both parties."[28] Similarly, armed with my exit poll results of the 2001 mayoral race in St. Louis, *St. Louis Post-Dispatch* reporters and editors sat down with me to prepare their stories and editorials hours before any actual returns were reported, not having to alter them when the real count was completed.

Okay, so exit polls are incredibly accurate and reliable, but why are they? What distinguishes exit polls from others that are less impressive? Cantril claims that exit polls are more precise because they have obvious advantages over, for example, preelection polls. He explains: "By definition, exit polls sample only voters and interview them on election day, thus eliminating two difficulties inherent in pre-election polls: the need to identify likely voters and estimate turnout and the challenge of picking up last-minute shifts in opinion. In addition, exit polls can achieve larger samples more cost-effectively than most pre-election polls."[29]

As a pollster who conducts both preelection and exit polls, let me elaborate and stress a few points. The very fact that exit polls survey only those who have just voted necessarily makes these respondents very special to a pollster. In contrast to respondents in preelection polls, exit poll respondents are actual voters. Therefore, we do not have to speculate whether they will vote or not. We also don't have to figure out how the undecided vote will go. We know! Additionally, as Cantril notes, we don't have to worry about voters switching their vote preferences during the last few days of the campaign and thus screwing up our election predictions. And it cannot be emphasized enough that these respondents are people who voted just minutes before the exit interview was conducted. This means that these respondents are at least momentarily "into" the election and they are very likely to recall with great accuracy how they voted, though not necessarily how they voted on a long list of issue items (e.g., propositions) or on candidates for minor offices, which exit pollsters usually don't ask questions about anyway. But they certainly can remember which candidate they voted for in the presidential election and in the U.S. Senate, gubernatorial, and U.S. House races, making their responses very reliable, unless they were confused by the ballot and voted for the wrong candidate, which is exactly what was claimed by thousands of Florida voters in the 2000 presidential election.[30] In sharp contrast, in preelection polls, interviewers often interview people who are unlikely to vote (but may say they will vote); know little about the issues and candidates; may give opinions and preferences, yet eventually change their minds; and generally give more unreliable answers because they are not "into it" at the time of the interview and, therefore, are answering quite tentatively and without serious thought.

Exit polling techniques have improved over the past few decades to the point where today such polling is very sophisticated. For a presidential election, probability sampling is used to select representative sampling precincts within each state from a listing of all sample precincts. The number of precincts selected varies by size of the different states, but usually runs between twenty and sixty precincts. An interval formula is used to select the individual respondents to be interviewed at each precinct. In a national exit poll, well over 10,000 voters are interviewed (e.g., VNS interviewed 13,130 for the 2000 presidential election).

Exit poll questionnaires are relatively short, containing only fifteen to thirty questions. Thirty questions would be about the maximum number since completion rates tend to drop as the questionnaire length grows. Demographical questions such as age, sex, and race are also asked so analysts can interpret election results in the context of meaningful demographics (e.g., the black vote, the religious right vote). Once the questionnaire assignment is completed at the various precincts, the results are reported to central headquarters for immediate entry and quick data processing.

As a pollster who has conducted statewide and local exit polls in Missouri and Illinois, I need to point out that not all exit poll methods are identical. In fact, exit poll techniques must be adjusted to fit particular circumstances or exit pollsters will simply not get it right. For example, election contests in St. Louis are always characterized by racially polarized voting, with African Americans voting overwhelmingly for black candidates and white voters voting overwhelmingly for white candidates.[31] St. Louis is also typified by political units (wards and precincts) that are predominantly black or white, with only a minority of wards and precincts that are racially mixed. To an exit pollster, this means that normal random sampling methods cannot be used to select the precincts for placing interviewers because random selection, when selecting only twenty-two precincts, would risk getting a disproportionate number of black or white voters in the sample. Since commonly precincts in St. Louis can be 95% plus black or 95% plus white, with black and white voters voting in bloc fashion for the candidate of their race, especially black voters, over-representing or underrepresenting black or white voters would greatly affect the accuracy of the poll. Consequently, I must employ quota-random sampling because the black-white ratio must be presented perfectly in my sample or my results will be way off. Typically, when I send an interviewer to an African American precinct, at least 33 of the 35 respondents (voters) will have answered that they voted for the black candidate for, say, mayor, while in the predominantly white precincts roughly 31 of 35 will have indicated that they supported the white candidate. In interviewing a total of 770 voters (22 precincts × 35 voters in each = 770 voters), can you imagine how far off the exit poll results would be if just one extra black precinct was represented in the exit poll, especially at the expense of underrepresenting one white precinct? Instead of interviewing a proportionate number of black and white voters, thirty-five more voters from predominantly black precincts would be interviewed than proportionally justified and thirty-five fewer voters from predominantly white precincts than proportionately acceptable for a total of seventy voters or 9.1% of the sample. It should be noted that in national exit polls random sampling can more easily account for different demographical characteristics because interviewers are placed in hundreds of randomly selected precincts and interview over 10,000 voters. Consequently, the odds of proportionally representing, for example, the 12% black voting population[32] is much better, although sometimes weighting is still necessary to make certain the different demographics are represented proportionately.[33]

The lesson conveyed here is that exit polling has become very sophisticated and reliable, not only because pollsters have embraced sound survey research techniques, but because they have learned through experience to make valid critical adjustments to their polling methods when necessary.

Chapter Six

◙ ◙ ◙

Why the Media Love
(But Sometimes Hate) Polls

Without a doubt, sharp changes in polls make for spicy copy.
—James Bennett, *The New York Times*, October 4, 1996[1]

In Chapter 1 it was made abundantly clear that many Americans just don't like pollsters or their "silly" and "biased" polls. But it is also true that a hefty percentage of Americans don't like the media either, believing, among other things, that the media are biased too. Obviously, then, when we combine a discussion of polls with a discussion of the media and focus on media polls, we are dealing with a very unpopular combination. Pollsters can be disliked by a lot of citizens, yet still survive, as long as their clients still want their polls. However, the media are in a much more tenuous situation because they cannot afford to "turn off" too many of their readers, listeners, or viewers, after all these are the "clients" who pay their bills. Therefore, the media must be in the "pleasing business" to survive. Newspaper and magazine editors must please their readers to keep their circulations up, radio station managers must keep their listening audience happy to preserve their ratings, and television executives must keep their viewers content to hold on to them.

Yet media executives also have a responsibility to do the best job they can in reporting and analyzing the news, and they know that polls provide more honest, neutral, and representative information about, for instance, issues, institutions, public figures, and political candidates than probably any other source of information.[2] In fact, although the media may not be totally objective or unbiased in reporting the news or in their use of poll data because, as Larry Sabato acknowledges, "journalists are fallible human beings who inevitably have values, preferences, and attitudes galore—some conscious and others subconscious, all reflected at one time or another in the subjects or slants selected for coverage,"[3] a plethora of scholarly studies have found that the people charging the media and their polls as biased are in fact demonstrably much more biased than the media. For instance, in an article entitled "Biased Press or Biased Public," Albert Gunther concludes that the real bias seems to be with Americans who identify with various socio-economic and political groups. In his words, "The most prominent and certain conclusion to be drawn from these data is that group membership does indeed play a role in public perceptions of the fairness or credibility of mass media. The findings are consistent with the prediction that high involvement prompts not only more scrutiny but more biased scrutiny of media content and therefore increases the likelihood that a person will take a skeptical view of the source of that content."[4]

Gunther found that Republicans and Democrats could watch the same news coverage, yet "each perceive media coverage that favors the other side."[5] This finding should not surprise anyone in the media. As a media pollster and political analyst, I frequently am charged by sensitive partisans with favoring simultaneously the Republican and Democratic positions through my commentary or presentation of poll data. Shows such as *60 Minutes* love to air letters in response to a previous week's story demonstrating that different viewers thought the coverage was biased in opposite ways. Of course, those identifying with various groups (e.g., Democrats, Republicans, labor, management, pro-life, pro-choice) are particularly defensive when the media present any poll data related to their group, quickly charging bias if they don't like what they see.

Charles Jaco, award-winning journalist and popular radio talk show host of KMOX's *NewsMakers* in St. Louis, agrees, telling me in an interview that it has been his experience that people are quite hypocritical about polls, tending to agree with them when the polls support their views, but rejecting them when they don't.[6]

What does all of this mean? Although the media must try to please their readers, listeners, and viewers, they will never be able to keep everyone happy. In the context of using polls, media executives have to calculate the pros and cons of employing them. Ultimately, most executives decide to use polls because the advantages normally outweigh the disadvantages from the standpoint of upholding professional journalistic standards and serving their audiences. But despite some strong advantages of using public opinion polls, relying on such polls has some obvious liabilities for the media, and this is precisely why journalists have a love-hate relationship with their use of polls.

JOURNALISTS OF DIFFERENT "STRIPES" VIEW AND USE POLLS DIFFERENTLY

Columnist Byron Crawford of *The Louisville Courier-Journal* noted that he received an "old-fashioned, soapbox lecture" from one of his readers who complained about "the media's preoccupation with public-opinion surveys."[7] But what a sweeping generalization this is! The fact is that media people are very different and the industry is enormous, diverse, and complex. Some journalists in the industry may be obsessed with public opinion polls, while others clearly use them moderately, or sparingly, or not at all. For various reasons, some newspapers, magazines, radio stations, and television networks, network affiliates, and local independent stations rely heavily on poll data in their coverage of news events, whereas others do not. For example, *The New York Times* is famous for its commissioned polls and depends heavily on polls in presenting and analyzing the news; at the other end of the spectrum, *The Philadelphia Inquirer* has a policy of not commissioning polls or placing much stock in them. Robert Rosenthal, executive editor of the *Inquirer*, stressed in a telephone interview that his paper had taken an ethical position against the use of horse-race polls, although his paper occasionally uses issue-oriented polls. He believes that horse-race polls can influence political campaigns and that "they don't want to influence political races." He acknowledged candidly that "newspapers have enough problems, let alone having to deal with the problem of being accused of influencing the outcome of political races."[8]

Therefore, when we talk about the media's reliance on polls or the media's love-hate relationship with polls, the subject of this chapter, we need to be more discriminating when examining this enormous industry, placing it into a more meaningful perspective by looking at all the different players in it.

Valid generalizations about people in the media industry simply cannot be made. The players constitute an enormous array of "journalists" (even calling all of them in the industry journalists per se is a difficult generalization to make) who perform dramatically different roles with various responsibilities, objectives, clientele interests, and "bosses." They also do not necessarily share the same cultural backgrounds, educational credentials, life experiences, values, or personal and career goals. So making sweeping generalizations about the media is problematic. The charge, for example, that the media have a liberal bias is a gross generalization that presents problems. Yes, there are many liberals in the business, but we don't have to look very hard to find a lot of conservative Republican journalists jousting with their liberal Democratic colleagues over all sorts of public policy issues. These outspoken conservative journalists, such as William Safire, James Kilpatrick, George Will, Pat Buchanan, Robert Novack, David Limbaugh, and Rush Limbaugh, most of them harsh critics of polls or at least the polls that seem to favor the "other side," represent only a few of the conservatives who regularly get their message out through their columns and TV and radio talk shows.

Nonetheless, conservatives hold that the real liberal bias comes out in media stories written and produced by liberals posing as unbiased, professional journalists. However, not only do many studies disclose that overall media coverage is pretty fair,[9] but even the right-wing columnist James Kilpatrick acknowledges that, despite "a natural tilt" to the left, professionalism in the media tends to cause both left-wing and right-wing journalists to, by and large, bury their biases when presenting the news. And Kilpatrick recalls, "Walter Cronkite and I used to agree on eighteen of the twenty items that should be on the *CBS Evening News* on an average night, but our clashing vantage points could spark quite an argument over the other two!"[10]

But even if most journalists are to the left of center, the stark reality is that the owners and top managers in the media profession are typically "big business Republicans" and, overall, notoriously to the right of center. So what impact may this have on news coverage, political commentary, and the use of public opinion polls? Certainly, polls will not be used if the owners and top management do not want them. Putting the charge of media bias into a reasonable perspective, Larry Sabato concludes: "Aside from the far right and far left, no one believes the bias to be overwhelming."[11]

The Players

So when critics claim that media coverage is biased or that the media have a "preoccupation with public-opinion surveys," let's place these generalizations into proper perspective. In the first place, what constitutes the media? We have the print media, consisting mostly of newspapers and magazines, and the electronic media, represented mainly by network television and their affiliates, local TV stations, the expanding cable TV market, network and independently owned radio stations, and now the new frontier of Internet communications.

As noted, "journalists" of all descriptions serve these diverse media outlets in different capacities and they all view the value of polls for their purposes differently. Naturally, all of those in the media, if they use polls at all, want to use them to their advantage. Owners (rarely true journalists) are particularly interested in how polls can be used to promote their business interests, especially in boosting their profit margin. If polls are thought to be undermining profits, it simply would not be considered good business to continue to use them or to employ them to any significant extent. Top-level managers, such as general managers at radio or television stations or executive and managing editors in the print media business, answer directly or indirectly to the owners and also must be cognizant of the "bottom line," so they will shun polls if they do not prove cost-effective. However, "middle" managers, especially the closer they get to the actual production of stories and newsroom analysis (e.g., news directors in television and radio and newsroom and editorial editors in the print media), are often caught in what psychologists call cross-pressures or role conflict because they feel that they must respond simultaneously to demands from "above" and "below," which may be in conflict. The demand to not engage in any venture that won't prove profitable versus the demand to produce a quality news product is a common cross-pressure experienced by many middle managers in the news business. Top-level managers tend to focus more on the bottom line financial concerns, whereas middle managers seem most concerned with producing quality news coverage and analysis, although ratings or circulations that translate into advertising revenues are never completely ignored. Consequently, middle managers would more likely favor using polls if they felt that their use would help contribute to improving the coverage and analysis of the news, even though the tab for the polls may not look cost-effective to the organization's accountants. But Philip Meyer acknowledges that polls are so expensive that some editors use the high cost of the polls "as a rationale for moving that money to reporter travel and more one-on-one coverage of candidates."[12]

Local television anchors mostly read the news, but many of them are given some say over the news content. Since newscasts cannot but help to reflect on them, if they believe that informative poll data may make the news more substantive and attractive, they may use their power of persuasion with their respective producers and news directors to see to it that polls are used. Of course, circumstances may differ greatly from newsroom to newsroom, says former television anchor Don Marsh, noting that veteran anchors may command considerable respect because of their vast experience and be able to get less experienced and less confident and often younger producers to see it their way. He points out that although anchors often do not attend the morning meetings where the day's news coverage is planned, anchors nonetheless often attend certain key meetings where plans are made to cover major upcoming events such as elections, where they may adamantly present their case for the use of the polls. News directors would normally have the final say on whether polls should be used or not, but anchors often carry influence unless the anchor is regarded as "just another pretty face."[13]

At the network level the situation is very different. For example, ABC's Peter Jennings, CBS's Dan Rather, and NBC's Tom Brokaw are anchors who are also managing editors of their own newscasts because they are respected for their long, professional experience in the news business. If they insist on employing poll data to supplement news stories (e.g., political coverage), they get about all the poll numbers they want.[14] Obviously, these anchors see the value of public opinion polls because they often cite poll results to supplement their stories. How many times have we heard these anchors say, "According to the latest (ABC, CBS, or NBC) poll . . . ." Nonetheless, all of these anchors are individual journalists who see the value of polls differently. Using their professional discretion, they all use them or exclude them in their own unique way.

It is also difficult to generalize about how electronic and print media reporters regard and use polls in putting together stories. Over the past few decades I have worked closely with both electronic and print media reporters and I have concluded the obvious—that is, no two reporters are alike. Some of them love polls and see great value in them; some of them hate them and think they are destructive and useless; yet most are in between. But one thing is for certain—they all employ their professional discretion to use or not use them in the way they see fit, although they can't ignore their superiors' wishes completely. Columnists are no different. They are all professional journalists with their own opinions about the advantages and disadvantages of using poll data.

We cannot make valid generalizations about how columnists view and use polls in their work. They have different life experiences, perspectives, and goals. William Safire, for example, as noted, loves to take pot shots at pollsters and their polls, while David Broder seems to embrace reputable pollsters and polls, often citing in his columns, explicitly or implicitly, their meritorious worth in helping us to understand the dynamics of our democratic society.

With the help of cable television and the renewed popularity of syndicated radio programming, talk radio and TV "journalists" have emerged in the past decade or so to dominate the airwaves. These journalists all have their own styles and formats, but they basically raise and discuss the various issues of the day with their guests and callers. Of course, Rush Limbaugh, Larry King, Geraldo Rivera, Chris Mathews, and Brit Hume are quite notable, but there are many others, both liberal and conservative. Because poll data give persuasive weight to their positions, I have noticed that polls are cited frequently by the hosts, their guests, and the callers if it is thought that citing specific poll statistics can add something, especially credibility, to their arguments. Radio talk show host Charles Jaco told me that he doesn't use polls too much, yet he noted that they do "provide another source of information" and they are valuable "as a hook for a story" or "as a line leading into a story," giving guests and listeners something to respond to.[15]

Unfortunately but not unexpectedly, pollsters and their polls are frequently cited in a blatantly selective and hypocritical way. That is, if the poll statistic happens to bolster someone's argument, it is embraced as a valid poll finding by that provocateur, while poll numbers used to undermine that same person's argument are often rejected or explained off as irrelevant, out of context, or invalid. This brings to mind a CNN *Crossfire* show in which Pat Buchanan, after adamantly dismissing poll data for months as nonsense because the polls were consistently showing President Clinton to be enjoying high job approval ratings during the height of the investigation into the Clinton-Lewinsky scandal, decided to suddenly embrace the specific poll statistics that helped him make the argument that Special Prosecutor Ken Starr's testimony before Congress was well received by the American people. Needless to say, his

Crossfire colleagues got a chuckle out of his disingenuous use of polls, as did Buchanan himself, especially when Bill Press turned to Mark Broden and uttered "of course, you know, he [Buchanan] just discovered polls."[16]

Some talk show hosts even seem to have their favorite pollsters. Conservative talk show host Rush Limbaugh, for example, loved to cite John Zogby, who had a reputation as being a Republican pollster (actually, Zogby is an independent pollster). In fact, Zogby, although always a reputable pollster, has become a famous pollster in just a few years due in part to the enormous publicity Limbaugh gave to him on a regular basis. Of course, many talk show hosts have no choice but to cite constantly the polls of their networks since they are not in the business of promoting their competitors. But the point I am making is that polls normally play a significant role on these talk shows, yet sweeping generalizations certainly cannot be made on how these journalists regard and use polls. Again, some love them, others hate them, while some love or hate them depending on what the polls are showing, but it is clearly not the case that they all have a "preoccupation with public-opinion surveys."

TRADITIONAL JOURNALISM, PUBLIC JOURNALISM, AND THE DEBATE OVER THE USE OF POLLS

With declining newspaper and magazine circulations, television viewership, and radio listeners, media executives and journalists have searched for answers to try to get their readers, viewers, and listeners back. In fact, "soul searching" by the media empire has caused the industry to return to square one and ask the most basic question of all, "What are journalists for?" Actually, this is the title of a recent book by Jay Rosen, a journalism scholar who argues that traditional journalism has failed us and American democracy. In his introductory chapter, "What We're Doing Isn't Working," Rosen makes an emotional plea for abandoning traditional journalism, which incidentally includes the practice of using horse-race polls to track candidate progress, for a better kind of journalism—a less elitist journalism that more actively engages the public and promotes healthy debate that serves the best interests of our democratic society.[17] This new journalism, known as public or civic journalism, began about a decade or so ago and has attracted very harsh criticism from most in the journalism community—the traditional journalists, especially from the major news outlets in the big cities. In reality, the public journalism movement has had little success attracting many followers and its approach has only been partially implemented in a few newspapers, all of these relatively small ones such as the *Norfolk Virginia-Pilot*, *The Charlotte Observer*, the *Dayton Daily News*, the *Colorado Springs Gazette*, and *The Wichita Eagle*. Attempts were made to implement public journalism at one major newspaper, the *St. Louis Post-Dispatch*, but its editor, Cole Campbell, who succeeded in bringing public journalism to the *Virginia-Pilot*, failed in his efforts to make the *Post-Dispatch* a public journalism newspaper. There have been some efforts to bring civic journalism to television and radio in the past decade, probably best seen in "outreach programming" in which anchors actually do part of a newscast from a family's home, lead focus group discussions with a group of citizens, or host a New England-type town meeting to listen to citizens talk about what they think are the important issues.

It is worth going into this current battle between public journalist advocates and those defenders of traditional journalism because, unfortunately for the pollsters, they are stuck right in the middle of the debate. Why? Because to most public journalists, the use of polls, especially horse-race polls by traditional journalists, epitomize much of what is wrong with the traditional approach to reporting and analyzing the news, especially covering politics. Generally, public journalists find that poll data contribute little if anything of substance to "community discussions" and, possibly worse, detract from productive public discourse by dwelling on meaningless conflicts of who's winning or political divisions in our society, whereas traditional journalists contend that polls are very useful for telling journalists what Americans think about the issues and candidates. As Dick Polman, national political writer for

The Philadelphia Inquirer, told me, polls are very good "as tip sheets to give us ideas for stories. They tell us what the public is thinking and give us direction as to what kind of questions to ask." On the other hand, this veteran political reporter cautions that "polls should only be used as a guide because stories should not be 'poll driven.'"[18] What journalists love and hate about polls is certainly brought out in the debate between public and traditional journalists over the question "What are journalists for?" Let's look further at this philosophical yet passionate debate, because it places the media's use of polls into perspective and conveys why journalists are ambivalent about using poll data and, consequently, why they have a tormented love/hate relationship with polls.

Journalists Fall in Love with Polls

In a classic article for the fiftieth anniversary issue of the *Public Opinion Quarterly* in 1987, Albert Gollin, in "Polling and the News Media," traces the historical development of the use of polls by the news media. To make a very long story quite short, Gollin acknowledges that news journalists have always been attracted to polls because of the obvious "news value of polls,"[19] although in the early years the media struggled to justify the authoritative value of polls in light of the 1936 *Literary Digest* debacle and the failure of pollsters to accurately predict Harry Truman's 1948 presidential victory over Thomas Dewey. However, as the decades passed an increasing number of journalists were won over by the polls as methodological advances made the polls more reliable and extremely irresistible. Consequently, he notes, "The press, finding polls to be a highly useful means of supplementing their coverage of numerous topics, began to support polling as an *integral* feature of their news operations, instead of buying access to syndicated polling data or sponsoring special polls. Thus, the press—the vital 'organ' (shapes and mirror) of public opinion in standard treatments of the topic—became inevitably a leading actor in the evolving polling enterprise."[20]

Gollins contends that political polling became virtually impossible to ignore as more and more political candidates and interest groups turned to polls for their guidance. The various news media, he asserts, always competitive, simply could not stand on the sidelines while their competitors used polls to improve their election coverage. Besides, Gollin adds, by the 1970s polls had gained greater prestige among key political actors in the media's environment, especially among those movers and shakers in business and government. Thus, he concludes, "By the 1970s . . . a variety of influences flowed together to swell the demand for polling with the news media 'pulled' by the demonstrated value of polls for political coverage in particular."[21] Today, it seems like there is no turning back for the media. The apparent news value in the numerous preelection polls provides endless data for political journalists for their stories and columns, while exit poll data always "offer rich analytical possibilities for next-day in-depth coverage."[22]

Veteran Associated Press correspondent Jim Salter supports this contention, holding that the news value of polls, especially horse-race polls, is obvious. In a personal interview he told me that "Americans love a horse race, and polls give the only legitimate indication of where a race stands at a given time. If the polls show a close race, that's interesting. It makes a good story." Substantiating his point, he noted that "interest in the 2000 presidential primaries peaked when John McCain and Bill Bradley were seriously challenging the frontrunners." Salter also stressed that on a more substantial level, "Polls offer the only real insight about why people support or oppose a candidate." He noted that he and the AP particularly like the descriptive data provided by exit polls. Consequently, he explained, the AP takes exit polling "very seriously," spending months preparing by reading relevant materials and interviewing experts so election night and postelection stories can be filled with valuable analytical poll data to help explain the election results.[23]

The Public Journalists Cry Foul

Stop! Stop! Stop! the public journalists cry out! No wonder Americans hate the media, they exclaim. To the public journalists, the

American people are sick and tired of journalists relying on all sorts of experts, including political analysts and pollsters, when reporting and analyzing the news. Public journalists are convinced that to win back their readers, viewers, and listeners, journalists must change their tactics and rely much less on the experts and reach out to the citizenry and truly engage them; that is, ask them what issues really concern them. These public journalists vehemently urge their traditional journalist colleagues to largely forget the political analysts and pollsters and all their punditry that have been dominating media circles for decades now.

Public journalism advocates argue that traditional journalism has failed because the traditional approach is causing millions of Americans to turn off television and radio news and to stop reading their newspapers and news magazines. According to them, a major reason for this is that, in addition to being elitist, "reporting is too negative, too coldly objective, and too full of conflict."[24] Of course, to public journalists, the use of horse-race polls in particular only adds to the conflict, contributing little if any useful knowledge to a political campaign. These polls, they insist, tend to reduce the race to a contentious battle of who's winning and who's losing.

Public journalism guru Jay Rosen asserts that such emphasis on conflict, possibly best epitomized in horse-race polls and the detached objectivity of poll numbers, simply constitutes irresponsible journalism and helps to undermine our democratic society. In his book *What Are Journalists For?* he claims that journalists have the responsibility to not just report and give unbiased analysis of the news, but to get involved in their communities to promote healthy "community discussions" on the "real" issues that concern citizens.[25]

To Public Journalists, Pollsters Are Elitists

It must be stressed that at the core of the public journalists' argument is the belief that Americans have been alienated by the media because journalists have become too elitist. How can journalists "connect" to the average American, they posit, when journalists have become part of a new professional elite? To columnist Michael Kelly, this new professional class consists of "pollsters, news media consultants, campaign strategists, advertising producers, political scientists, reporters, columnists, [and] commentators," all committed to reporting and interpreting the news through an elitist value system far different from that of the average American.[26] Parenthetically, it is curious that Kelly listed pollsters first.

In "Those Darned Readers: The Gap Between Reporters and the General Public Is Huge," columnist John Leo cites, ironically, poll data displaying just how elitist and, therefore, socially disconnected journalists are from other Americans. Survey results showed that, compared to average Americans, journalists overall, not just those from the big-city media markets, "are more likely to live in upscale neighborhoods, have maids, own Mercedeses, and trade stocks, and they're less likely to go to church, do volunteer work, or put down roots in a community." They also were found to live in Zip codes where residents more typically than other Americans drank chablis and espresso, rented foreign movies, and read magazines like *Food and Wine* and *Architectural Digest*. The same survey found that their elitist perspective often develops early in life, since those majoring in journalism in college are more likely than their classmates to have come from richer families and have attended private schools. Not unexpectedly, journalists as a group were found to hold common cultural values and share similar social beliefs. For example, compared with Americans in general, journalists are much more likely to not identify with suburban or rural values, to identify with the "victims" of society, to support abortion rights,[27] and, yes, place great faith in experts, including pollsters.[28]

Public journalists argue that such elitism, especially if journalists pretend it doesn't exist, cannot but influence and bias their work, thus alienating the consumers of news. Leo asserts: "The astonishing distrust of the news media isn't rooted in inaccuracy or poor reportorial skills but in the daily clash of world views between reporters and their readers."[29] Public journalists acknowledge that traditional, elitist journalists are not bad reporters, they simply cannot seem to escape their class biases or their training in the Walter Lippmann school of elitist journalism.[30]

During his influential life, Walter Lippmann (1889–1974) pushed for a professionalized press in which journalists, working and socializing with various experts, gained an elevated status as they became experts themselves. As a result of their new expertise, Jay Rosen notes, "The journalist could claim elevated status as an expert commentator (a type Lippmann embodied), as a superior judge of what counted as news (the authority of *The New York Times* begins here), or as a professional 'adversary' keeping government in check (most notably *The Washington Post* during Watergate)."[31] But efforts to professionalize journalists, public journalists contend, "All placed the public at a comfortable distance; all were compatible with Lippmann's skepticism about the average person's competence."[32]

The use of polls fits in perfectly with the Lippmannian movement to professionalize the media. To many journalists of the 1930s and 1940s, polls represented the very "scientific objectivity" that they were seeking, that would help give them that elevated status. To these traditional journalists, scientific polling allowed journalists to measure public opinion "objectively" without even having to leave their desks to interview anyone. Besides, these polls seemed "better" than the unscientific, unrepresentative, and subjective interviews conducted by reporters. Now elitist reporters only needed to conduct supplemental interviews to provide examples of what the poll data were showing, making their jobs a lot easier and apparently more professional (i.e., objective). Rosen comments: "By learning to accept the polls as an approximation of public opinion, journalists 'solved' the problem of the public, at least to their own satisfaction."[33] As the decades passed, journalists became more dependent on poll data. Public journalists criticize the traditional journalists' heavy reliance on polls today in covering about every socioeconomic and political issue: "Publish a poll and 'public opinion' springs magically to life."[34] Or as political scholar Benjamin Ginsberg quips: "Poll results and public opinion are terms that are used almost synonymously."[35]

Public Journalists Urge "Community Discussions," Not Polls

The vast majority of traditional journalists today appear to embrace polls for a variety of reasons, but mostly because they believe sincerely that polls provide valuable public opinion data that can make their stories and commentary more informative and lively. In sharp contrast, most public journalists condemn the broad use of polls by traditional journalists, arguing basically that polls have very limited value because they don't provide citizens with what they need to engage them in deliberative, community conversations that are key to addressing and solving civic problems.

Certainly, one of the leading intellectual practitioners behind the public journalism movement in the United States is Cole Campbell. He rejects the elitism of Walter Lippmann, and positively endorses the more "sensitive" democratic works such as John Dewey's *The Public and Its Problems*, Robert Putnam's *Making Democracy Work*, Daniel Yankelovich's *Coming to Public Judgment*, and Michael Sandel's *Democracy's Discontent*. Campbell, as editor of the *Norfolk Virginia-Pilot*, sought to implement the core ideas of public journalism at the *Pilot* during the mid-1990s, meeting with relative success. He then moved to the *St. Louis Post-Dispatch* in early 1997, where his enthusiasm for public journalism was not well received. In April of 2000, he left the *Post-Dispatch* for a more friendly haven at the prestigious Poynter Institute for Media Studies in St. Petersburg, Florida. Because he has been and continues to be such an intellectual giant in the public journalism movement, I decided to give him a call and ask him just what role he thinks polls can play, if any, in journalism.[36]

Reflecting the wisdom of John Dewey, Campbell believes that any of the tools that journalists use, including polls, should help engage citizens in the political process. To Campbell, as for Dewey, it is not enough for journalists just to report the news, but it is the responsibility of the media to help stimulate "public discussions" about meaningful community issues, thereby turning journalists into "exemplary citizens" and citizens into actual participants in the democratic process looking for solutions to civic problems. In the wisdom of Dewey in 1927, which Campbell apparently endorses today: "The newspaper of the future will have to rethink its relationship to all the institutions that nourish public life, from libraries to universities to cafes. It will have to do more than 'cover' these institutions when they happen to make news. . . . The newspaper must see that its own health is dependent on the health of dozens of other agencies which pull people out of their private worlds. . . . Every town board session people attend, every public discussion they join . . . every gathering of citizens for whatever cause is important to the newspaper—not only as something to cover, but as the kind of event that makes news matter to citizens."[37]

For most public journalists, polls are too cold, impersonal, and superficial to engage citizens and make news really matter to them. As Campbell explained to me, polls tend to be too superficial, focusing on simplistic questions that can be easily answered in quick interviews. Consequently, he added, poll interviewers can't uncover what really matters to the citizens they interview. Campbell asserts that the important questions are: "What are the concerns of the community? What aspirations do they have? What do they want to do?" He emphasizes that possibly the chief weakness of polls is that they are "non-deliberative," that is, they "fail to get people to talk to one another." As an editor, he wanted "to find out what language people actually used, what they were actually thinking." For example, he says, pollsters may ask: "What do you think of President Clinton?" But when respondents answer, "All they give is off of the top of the mind opinion." To Campbell, again reflecting the thinking of Dewey, such does not constitute honest public opinion or at least meaningful public opinion. They both believe that true public opinion comes only from deliberative community conversations, not from polls or experts. To Dewey, expert opinion cannot be expected to ever replace the public opinion that is formed through community conversations about the issues: "Democracy must begin at home and its home is the neighborly community."[38] He believed that real public opinion is formed through community deliberations in which a collective "we" opinion is reached.[39] Or as Campbell explained to me, community conversations allow citizens to work through issues through open deliberations, permitting them to reach well-thought-out "public judgments."

It is important to understand what Campbell means by *public judgment* since this is key to understanding why public journalists tend to reject public opinion polling as a helpful or reliable journalistic tool. He made it clear to me that editors have an obligation to "depict reality" in their news coverage. Polls cannot deliver this reality because they, to reiterate, only tend to measure "off of the top of the mind opinion." Public opinion realities, to Campbell, are much more likely to be generated in community conversations in which people learn about the issues, discuss them in relative depth, weigh different circumstances and alternatives, and, as a result, reach informed "best public judgments" about the issues and what to do.[40]

Campbell told me that editors should be more concerned about their news product and whether they have "de-valued political discourse, not whether you have alienated your readers." For him, polls represent one form of knowing, and public discussions represent another form of knowing. Obviously, Campbell favors the latter. But he does not reject the use of polls completely, even horse-race polls, which have been a favorite target of many public journalists. In fact, the first thing he said when I asked him what he thought of horse-race polls was: "I have changed my mind on horse-race polls." Campbell noted that "horse-race polls make good side bars, but weak main bars." Elaborating, he said that he had changed his mind, assuming they are good polls, because they actually can add something to community conversations. Specifically, "horse-race polls create interest in the outcome of elections and can help get citizens more involved in the electoral process." As a practical matter, he confessed to me, he has come to realize that "Americans like that kind of conversation" and naturally like to talk about "who is ahead and behind." Campbell thinks that horse-race polls can be good as long as they get citizens involved and thinking about why candidates are ahead or behind. However, the use of such polls, he stressed, "can hurt if they become the whole process," thus distorting what is going on in the electoral process. "Polls," he reiterated, "must be side bars!"[41]

When he said this, I interjected, noting that when I did exit polls for the *St. Louis Post-Dispatch*, he had placed my polls on the front page above the fold. He quickly responded that, in the first place, "other issues" prevented him from significantly implementing public journalism at the *Post-Dispatch*, but secondly, exit polls are not horse-race polls, but the most "valuable form of polls" because they provide valuable data for postelection analysis, essentially explaining to citizens what happened and why.[42]

In sum, public journalists seem to have their hearts in the right place. They have looked around and seen that consumers of news have become increasingly more alienated from the media. Public journalists have concluded that journalists are largely to blame. Consequently, they have been looking for better ways to reconnect with their readers, viewers, and listeners. To reconnect, they are convinced that the traditional journalist's role of "elitist detachment" must be replaced with one that engages citizens and promotes democracy. Frankly, public journalists are shocked at the dramatic increase in political apathy and the sharp decline in voter turnout in the past few decades.[43] To save democracy, they believe journalists must *serve* their communities by taking an active role in sponsoring public discussions about civic problems and helping citizens seek solutions to these problems. To most public journalists, serving democracy also means placing polls on the "back burner" because they maintain that polls promote unnecessary, divisive conflict and contribute nothing of real substance to public policy discussions.

Traditional Journalists Gang Up on Public Journalists

Cole Campbell and other public journalists seem to have good intentions and many of their arguments appear reasonable, especially considering the fact that journalists are losing their followers and our republic is losing its voters. So why have traditional journalists vehemently blasted the public journalism movement? The reason, I suppose, may be because the public journalists' attack strikes at the very foundation of what traditional journalists have been doing for their whole careers. So when public journalist proponent Jay Rosen asks "What are journalists for?" and answers that traditional journalists have been doing it all wrong, naturally a strong rebuttal from these traditional journalists should be expected. When told that they should essentially "throw away the polls," which they have forever relied on, stiff resistance and bitter resentment are predictable reactions.

In a critique of public journalism in the *Columbia Journalism Review*, a critique that seems to capture the feelings of most traditional journalists, David Shaw refers to public journalism as "a kind of New Age gobbledygook."[44] He admits that journalists, especially those in the big cities where some have become "even more famous and highly paid than the people they cover," have become overly cynical, too focused on campaign strategies, too inclined to resort to name calling, and too much in love with polls, especially horse-race polls, failing to focus as much as they should on those policy issues that are of vital concern to citizens. However, to Shaw, the fact that these problems exist does not at all justify the remedies proposed by the public journalists. In fact, he states frankly, "as a cure for what ails the body politic (and the body journalistic), civic journalism is likely to prove worse than the disease." He claims that it is one thing for editors to be concerned with what readers want in newspapers, but "editing a newspaper based largely on focus group research is—shudder!— quite another." More specifically, Shaw warns that, given the uninformed nature of average citizens, journalists who take their cues primarily from civic forums "will inevitably ignore or glide lightly over issues essential to the well-being of the family, the community, and a democratic society."[45]

Actually, the traditional journalists cannot understand the logic behind the public journalists' criticism of polls, particularly horse-race polls. The former support polls basically because they feel that George Gallup was right when he argued that polls can represent the democratic mainstream.[46] In sharp contrast to the public journalists, traditional journalists defend the use of issue polls, as well as horse-race polls, not just because they add "color" to their coverage, but because polls allow journalists to include democratically sanctioned public sentiment in their stories and analyses.

Ironically, critics of public journalism charge that horse-race polls actually help to engage citizens in the political process and even help them understand and comprehend political and election coverage better. In pointing out where public journalists have gone wrong in an *American Journalism Review* article, Philip Meyer argues that "ignoring the horse race is a mistake. When voters are deprived of information on which candidate is ahead, their interest in the election declines. So does their knowledge about issues."[47] Meyer asserts that public journalists rationalize that "Dumping the polls, so this arguments goes, will free up readers' brain cells to hold issue information." But he notes that "Recent research tells us otherwise." In one experiment, for example, people were divided equally into two groups and given two fictitious news stories about a political campaign, one including issue information only and the other including both issue and poll information. Both groups were tested on their knowledge of the issues, and the group that received the information within the horse-race context did significantly better. Like spectators at a basketball game, their knowledge of the score helped them understand and appreciate the action. A more comprehensive study sponsored by the Poynter Institute produced similar results: "The poll followers learned more about the issues even after we adjusted for their greater interest and education."[48] This makes me wonder whether Cole Campbell possibly changed his mind about polls after he joined the Poynter Institute and became familiar with this study.

The traditional journalists are also quick to attack the public journalists' assumption that conflict is a destructive force in democratic government and that polls, not just horse-race polls, add to the conflict. It is not that public journalists avoid conflict, it is just that they seem to fail to recognize its importance to the vitality of democracy. Political scientists have long recognized, for example, that vigorous intra- and interparty competition is healthy for democracy. In fact, in a series of studies decades ago, V. O. Key Jr.,

Duane Lockard, and John Fenton showed that the greater the intra- and interparty competition in states, the more the citizens benefited from public policy outputs. Why? Because if elected officials in competitive situations didn't produce, they tended to be voted out of office.[49] Besides, notes Philip Meyer and Deborah Potter, "Conflict resolution is what representative democracy is all about. . . . Reporting of conflict has to be the first step in resolving it. The second step is getting different factions to understand one another."[50] So, it seems reasonable that polls should be used to gain information about what various groups like or dislike, what they support or oppose, or what they regard as acceptable or unacceptable. In this sense, polls can be employed to help various groups understand one another, particularly their differences, ultimately allowing poll data to be used to promote healthy discussions among the diverse groups that reside in any legitimate democratic society.

Even horse-race polls do not need to be viewed as a divisive force. Knowing where political candidates stand in the polls begs many questions. Why is candidate X behind? Why is candidate Y ahead? What is it about candidate Y that so many people like? What groups support candidate X and Y? Is candidate X or Y closer to my public policy viewpoints? Are candidate Y's issue stands more sound than candidate X's?

Finally, traditional journalists have always recognized the value of polls to spice up the stories and attract the audience. As James Bennett wrote in *The New York Times*, "Without a doubt, sharp changes in polls make for spicy copy."[51] Tom Warhover, an editor at the *Norfolk Virginia-Pilot*, charged that when Campbell, as editor of the *Pilot*, decided to stop using horse-race polls, stories proved to be "pretty dull copy. . . . We moved too far to the citizen agenda and cut out the candidates."[52] Let's face it, the traditional journalists make a good point, because if the "copy" is dull, people won't read or listen or watch it, and then where will we be? Educators such as myself understand that it would be irresponsible if we didn't employ the pedagogical techniques necessary to attract the attention of students—to arouse their curiosity. Within limits, you use what works! Most journalists today recognize the lure of poll data. They would be foolish to abandon such a lure that not only shines, but glitters with information.

A CONCLUDING COMMENT

Steve Kraske, a political correspondent and columnist for *The Kansas City Star*, told me that he views polls "pretty skeptically" because he has noticed over the years that simple, technical problems in polls can "sway the results." For example, he noted: "Just a subtle difference in wording can make a significant difference in the poll results."[53] Of course, thousands of journalists share Kraske's skepticism about polls. Abraham McLaughlin, staff writer for *The Christian Science Monitor*, is one. He says that polls may be useful for the moment, providing "a little bit of help," but "everything can change so fast" so "I don't put much stock in them."[54] John Judis, senior editor of *The New Republic*, is another. Judis uses polls in his articles, but he stressed to me that he prefers to "use poll data to show long-range trends because the overall trend is more important. Consequently, he employs polls very sparingly, not only because he questions their day-to-day accuracy and worth, but because he does not want to mislead the public with questionable poll statistics involving close elections."[55]

But despite the reservations that journalists have toward using polls, very few decide ultimately not to use them. Why? Because the plain fact is that, although cursed for their flaws, polls provide valuable, unique, authoritative, and generally acceptable public opinion information on various topics that simply cannot be ignored. Even the skeptical Kraske admitted to me that this is the case: "Whether we admit to it or not, we can't ignore poll data."[56]

The hard truth, whether journalists want to admit to it or not, is that they depend on polls for their very survival. Can one imagine a political journalist during the 2000 presidential campaign writing a story or a column essentially saying that Alan Keyes will likely be the winner of the presidential race, ignoring all poll data to the contrary? Would not such journalists lose credibility? Could not a journalist actually get fired for being "so out of touch" with reality? When I asked Kraske these questions, his immediate response was, "You're right!"[57] In the end, did not Cole Campbell change his mind about polls, despite his perceived problems with them, because he could not ignore their clear net value? In the next chapter we shall see that politicians are even more addicted to polls than journalists.

Chapter Seven

◙ ◙ ◙

Today's Politicians
Live and Die by Polls

*Polls have become for modern politicians and pundits what the Oracle
at Delphi was to the ancient Greeks and Merlin was to King Arthur:
A mysterious and almost divine source of wisdom.*
—Stephen Budiansky, *U.S. News and World Report,*
December 4, 1995[1]

Politicians curse the polls and question their accuracy, yet these
same politicians hire pollsters and pay them big bucks to get
elected and, if elected, to help hold office. Such is the hypocritical
nature of the world of political polling. The objective of this chapter is to point out how politicians "live" and "die" by polls. It is
stressed that while politicians get angry and frustrated when polls
disclose what they don't like, they nonetheless rely heavily on
polls to guide their political careers. Since the early days of
polling, politicians could not but notice their potential use as
strategic tools. After all, no astute politicians could ignore the
power of public opinion. Savvy politicians realized that democracy meant *government by the people*. Polls offered politicians the
opportunity to test the waters of public opinion to their strategic
advantage in running for office, for marketing controversial policy

programs, or for anything else that they wanted to consult the public on before stepping into those always potentially "troubled waters."[1]

Franklin D. Roosevelt was the first president to use pollsters. For example, FDR used pollsters George Gallup and Hadley Cantril in 1940 to try to understand how he could mobilize support from isolationist Americans to help Britain resist the Nazi war movement.[2] Since that time, presidents and other politicians have employed polls at an increasing rate. Today, it seems that political candidates and elected officials just cannot survive without them. Polls, noted one former White House insider, "become addictive. They work once, and then they become a crutch; you don't do anything without them."[3] Fortunately or unfortunately, the modern political reality is that, as the title of this chapter suggests, today's politicians live and die by polls. This chapter focuses on: (1) the apparent addiction of politicians to polls; (2) how they use them; and (3) how they abuse them.

POLITICIANS HAVE BECOME ADDICTED TO POLLS

Before going into the specifics of how politicians use polls, let's look for a moment at the claim of so many political observers that politicians have developed a hard-core addiction for polls. Carl Cannon in "Hooked on Polls" argues that today's politicians conduct polls so often and on so many different issues that essentially representative government has been turned into an "electronic town meeting . . . elevating the public opinion polls to the status of a kind of super-Congress."[4] In 1992 when Ross Perot was running for president, he pushed this "electronic town meeting" concept as a good democratic idea. Vice-President Dan Quayle at the time condemned Perot's plan as absurd, exclaiming that it essentially amounted to "nullifying representative democracy with a bizarre scheme of government by polls."[5] When Perot suggested that President Bush could have built public support for liberating

Kuwait through the electronic town meeting approach, Bush quipped that Perot "was out of touch with reality."[6] But given the enormous use of polls by Bush himself when he was president, his rebuttal seems somewhat hypocritical. His son, George W. Bush, seemed to have adopted the same hypocrisy when running for the presidency in 2000. He constantly told voters, "I don't need polls to tell me what to think," even though Bush had a reputation for heavily relying on polls and focus groups to help him determine his issue stands during the campaign. This blatant hypocrisy prompted James Carney and John Dickerson, two *Time* magazine journalists, to ask sarcastically: "Did a pollster tell him to say that?" My answer is, very, very likely![7]

Sidney Blumenthal, a journalist who joined the Clinton administration, holds that political polling has gotten so out of hand that it seems that the Madisonian system of checks and balances has been "replaced by the Geraldo system; checks and balances by applause meter."[8] Cannon notes that many years after the fall of Ross Perot, "polls are being used more aggressively than ever before by the President and his loyalists."[9] Given the money the Democratic National Committee has paid to Clinton's White House pollsters, it is projected that the Clinton administration has been cranking out polls at a brisk rate of about one every three days for Clinton's entire administration.[10]

But it is not just our recent presidents who have become poll junkies. Virtually all politicians have become addicted. For example, political scientist Lawrence Jacobs claims that presidents and legislators alike, for a few decades now, have relied heavily on polls to help them understand issues and mold their responses, even using polls to discover what buzz words work best with different constituents. "They use polls to learn how to manipulate the language and to employ buzz words and symbols,"[11] he asserts.

The bottom line, says Republican pollster Frank Luntz, is that politicians use "polls to decide what to do" and "what to say."[12] Political journalist Stephen Budiansky agrees, contending in disgust that today's "queasy politicians" consult polls for virtually everything from what to say to what to wear. He says, "There are polls to help politicians decide which euphemisms to use for orphanages, if they're in favor of them, and what epithets to use for government employees, if they're against them (call them 'foster homes' and 'bureaucrats'). There are polls to tell them what kind of shirt to wear (the checkered, lumberjack variety)."[13] Political writer Chris Adams points out that countless political polls are conducted for politicians because "Americans are the most fickle people around. What they say one week, they condemn the next. What they like today, they hate tomorrow."[14] Obviously, then, if this is true (and probably most insecure politicians think so), they cannot afford the political risks of supporting what was popular "yesterday." Republican pollster Brian Tringali recognizes that the rapidly changing political climate can undermine politicians if they don't keep up, so their strategists must constantly consult the newest poll data. He adds that politicians and their strategists are so spoiled with such new poll data almost always on tap that "they have a tough time making a decision without it."[15]

So, when politicians claim emphatically that they don't like polls or give them much attention, don't believe them. The odds are that they rely on them a lot more than it is politically wise for them to admit. On the other hand, it is easy for pundits to blast politicians for being so dependent on polls because, after all, these critics have nothing to lose. However, to be honest about it, the politicians have a lot to lose, namely, their political careers.

HOW DO POLL-DRIVEN CANDIDATES USE POLLS?

The first fundamental thing to remember is that candidates use polls to try to win election to office. As political scientist Sandy Maisel notes, candidates in "most modern campaigns do not rely on hunches to determine what the public is thinking nor to evaluate how different approaches to campaigning are working. Public opinion polling has acquired a prominent role in modern campaigns."[16] Polls provide valuable information to candidates and their staffs that helps the campaign organization decide practically anything from whether a potential candidate should actually get into the race to what attack ads to run against an opponent to whether the candidate should drop out of the election contest. In a nutshell, notes Charles Roll Jr. and Albert Cantril, "Polls are political intelligence."[17]

In making their campaign decisions, candidates use media polls, their own private polls, and "shared" polls conducted for friendly candidates within their party and polls done within their party's organization (e.g., National Democratic or Republican Committee polls; state Democratic or Republican Committee polls). Although candidates for minor offices (e.g., city council, country assessor, state representative) usually don't have the funds to pay for relatively expensive polls, virtually all candidates for major offices spend a lot of money on polls. The present going rate charged by many pollsters is about 5% of the total campaign budget. This can be quite lucrative for pollsters since some campaign budgets run into hundreds of thousands or even many millions of dollars. Probably in most campaigns (e.g., for a typical U.S. House, U.S. Senate, gubernatorial, or mayoral race), only a handful of polls are done, but for hotly contested statewide races in large states, such as California and New York, an enormous number of polls may be conducted. Of course, in presidential contests polls are taken practically nonstop.

WHAT TYPES OF POLLS
DO CANDIDATES USE?

Basically, most respectable pollsters use very similar methods, but different kinds of polls are used by political candidates to serve their particular needs. Some candidates running in major races with big budgets may make use of all the poll types, whereas others with limited budgets campaigning for lesser offices may employ only a few kinds or even none. Some candidates, even those running for relatively high offices like the U.S. House of Representatives, don't use any polls at all because they believe that they don't need them to win. Incumbents in "safe seats" who face only token opposition and win by large margins in election after election often feel that they would only be wasting campaign contributions if they commissioned polls. For example, Congressman Bill Clay (Democrat–St. Louis, Missouri), who won sixteen consecutive congressional elections by comfortable margins, once told me that he has not needed to hire pollsters to win. Remember, polls provide valuable information to candidates to help them map out a winning campaign strategy. Obviously, any candidate seeking election in a noncompetitive race does not need to spend money needlessly on polls.

Benchmark Polls

The first poll that is commissioned by a candidate for political office is called a benchmark poll. These polls are usually conducted very early in a campaign or even before any active campaigning begins. When I have conducted such polls for candidates, I have referred to them descriptively as "get-to-know-your-district" polls. A benchmark poll is usually a quite comprehensive poll that is used to find out a lot of basic information about the political district (e.g., city, legislative district, state, nation). The term "benchmark" comes from the surveyor's trade, where a *benchmark* serves as a basic, stationary reference point from which, for example, elevations or tidal observations can be measured. In political campaigns, benchmark polls also serve as a basic reference or starting point for the campaign.

Candidates can use the information collected in a benchmark poll to chart a basic strategy for the campaign because it will:

- tell the candidate about the demographical characteristics of the district;
- reveal attitudes of the citizenry toward various socioeconomic and political issues;
- disclose how various voters within the district prioritize different issues; and

- provide key information on how people perceive the candidate versus their opponent(s) regarding name recognition, favorability, greatest strengths and weaknesses, the horse race, and, for incumbents, job performance.

Naturally, benchmark polls may encounter some problems. The greatest problem is that the poll is conducted so early that much of the information obtained may not be worth very much. What do I mean by this? For openers, a benchmark poll may be run so early that people are not at all focused on the upcoming election. At this time they often do not know who the candidates are and have given little, if any, thought to the issues. Of course, there are always issues that voters have contemplated, but will the issues in, say, February or March of the campaign year turn out to be critical campaign issues in the fall campaign? Consequently, too often benchmark polls tap issues that may vanish by the active campaign season since issues naturally evolve and change, while certain events (e.g., a sudden stock market plunge) may dramatically alter the nature and priority of some issues. Can you imagine, for example, how worthless the early benchmark polling was for Hillary Clinton after an unfortunate event, the discovery of prostate cancer in Rudolf Giuliani, her likely opponent, caused him to drop out of the race before he was even officially in it? Although some of the poll information would still be useful, all of the "match-up" information between Clinton and Giuliani would be useless. This would not prove to be a big deal for a well-funded campaign like Clinton's, but it would drain valuable resources from any candidate with limited resources. Because of such problems, I have frequently advised my political clients, who I know are "hurting for money," to skip the benchmark poll or to combine some of the ingredients of a benchmark poll with a later tracking poll.

Tracking Polls

Basically, there is only one other kind of poll commissioned by political candidates during the campaign. These are called, generally speaking, tracking polls. My experience has been that people are confused about just what constitutes a tracking poll, because the term is used to refer to two different kinds of polls. However, before I make the distinction, any privately commissioned poll that is used to measure or track a candidate's progress or how a candidate is doing versus an opponent during the campaign may be called a tracking poll. Such polls are viewed as critically important to campaign strategists because they provide valuable information that will be used to steer the campaign in the "right" direction. Tracking poll information is used to maximize the candidate's vote potential. For example, tracking poll data may be used to answer questions such as:

- Should our candidate modify his or her position on any issues?
- Is this television ad effective?
- Should our candidate go on the attack?
- Has he been too aggressive in the debates?
- Should she do more to capture the rural vote?
- Should he "soften" his pro-death penalty position?
- Do we need to conduct a media blitz to catch up?

In short, tracking polls are used to monitor the campaign so that appropriate, tactical adjustments can be made to the campaign plan.

The truth is that tracking polls are so expensive that only the most well-funded campaign organizations can afford what purists would call "true" tracking polls. In these elaborate tracking polls, pollsters use "polling" sample clusters and the polling continues (rolls) for many consecutive days in an attempt to measure any significant changes in public opinion over time. It works this way. On the first day, 150 "likely voters" may be interviewed, on the second day another 150, on the third day another 150, and on the fourth day another 150. But on the fifth day, when another 150 are interviewed, the first day's 150 sample is dropped, while on the sixth day when another 150 are interviewed, the second day's cluster of 150 "likely voters" are dropped, and so forth for as many days as the rolling tracking poll may last. Obviously, these tracking polls are particularly useful for measuring electoral shifts due to changing events in the campaign. In presidential campaigns and other high-stakes campaigns in which enormous sums of money are spent (e.g., U.S. Senate or gubernatorial campaigns in our biggest states), such tracking polls may be run almost continuously for the last two months of the campaign.

However, in most campaigns funds are quite limited, and such tracking polls are conducted only a few times during the campaign to provide campaign managers the vital feedback they need to make the necessary adjustments. In many campaigns "regular" tracking polls are run that do not follow the rolling sampling technique, but they are still referred to as tracking polls because they are used to track a candidate's progress. In addition to an early benchmark poll in a typical limited-budget campaign, one or two nonpurist tracking polls may be run, usually in the last six weeks of the campaign.

Of course, a favorite question in a tracking poll is the horse-race question because these polls can show clearly whether a candidate is gaining or losing ground and possibly why. The information obtained from tracking polls is particularly useful for *targeting* specific areas or groups that a candidate may have to pay more attention to in order to win.

SPECIFIC POLITICAL POLLING TECHNIQUES

Political pollsters know that when it comes to measuring voter opinion, there are many ways to "skin a cat." Consequently, pollsters may rely on cross-sectional, random sampling, "targeted" random sampling, various forms of focus groups, or a combination of them. If a campaign organization can afford only one kind, it is highly likely that it will use cross-sectional, random sampling. In such a poll anywhere from 400 to 1200 or so citizens (e.g., eligible voters, registered voters, "likely voters") will be randomly selected and interviewed. In big-budget campaigns, many of these polls may be conducted, and each time a different random sample of citizens may be selected and interviewed, whereas in low-budget campaigns only a few will be done, including the benchmark poll.

Since random sampling techniques are employed to draw the sample, poll results should proportionately reflect valuable, representative opinions of the various subgroups in the population. From these polls, candidates can learn, among other things: (1) how far ahead or behind they are; (2) what voters like or do not like about them and their opponents; (3) what campaign policy positions and tactics are working or not working; and (4) what levels of support they have from particular groups.

If candidates commission several of these polls, they can monitor their relative standing before the general electorate and among specific groups every, say, three weeks. For instance, candidate X might find out that, although he trailed candidate Y 45% to 36% in the early September horse-race question, in the late September poll he now trails by only three percentage points, 47% to 44%. Since many demographical questions are asked in these polls, by cross-tabulating the horse-race question with the demographical data a candidate can find out, for example, how he or she stands with various groups such as African Americans, women, Catholics, Independents, labor organizations, and so on. By cross-tabulating the horse-race question with answers to issue questions, a candidate can also find out the extent to which voters, who hold different issue positions, support him or her.

However, one serious problem with these polls is that the number of people represented in subgroups (e.g., black voters) is often so small, with the exception of gender because any decent sample would have to include a large number of men and women, that the true opinion of a subgroup may be inaccurately represented. Only foolish candidates would put too much stock in opinions based on a very small subsample.

Nonetheless, such a poll, even if the sample size is small for the subgroup, may reveal accurate subgroup opinions. If it is important to a campaign to probe the opinion of a particular subgroup, another poll may be run that targets this subgroup. Let's say that the initial cross-sectional poll indicated that black voters were not very supportive of the candidate. Since the campaign manager might feel that his candidate cannot win without a majority of black voter support, it would probably be appropriate to conduct a follow-up random sample poll targeting black voters, perhaps interviewing many hundreds of African American voters. Such a poll would disclose quite accurate, representative opinion that could be used by the candidate's staff to try to develop a campaign strategy to win more African American support.

Some candidates, particularly those in major races, may use various forms of focus groups to make up for the inherent deficiencies of polls. Although I am a strong supporter of polls, I must admit that polls are not very good for measuring in-depth public opinion. For example, polls don't measure the reasons that stand behind public opinion very well, nor the intensity of opinion. Polls measure what people think superficially, but do they measure what voters really think, especially if they were given more information and allowed to discuss the issues? In polls, respondents are asked to respond to mostly preset response categories such as "Favor," "Oppose," or "Undecided." But candidates might be very interested in finding out how solidly voters favor them or what it would take to convince the "Undecideds" to support them. Follow-up questions may be used to measure intensity (e.g., simply asking voters how *strongly* they favor the candidate in closed-end questions or asking an open-end question to allow respondents to say something about their intensity level in a few words), but such measures are still plagued by problems and normally can measure only "superficial," instant opinion. Also, parenthetically, the coding of open-end questions in such polls is not very systematic or rigorous, often turning out to be a methodological farce.

In any event, candidates who favor the use of focus groups believe that such groups can be used to provide more insights into the classic "Yes, but . . ." response. In focus groups, usually consisting of about a dozen participants, campaign organizations can spend hours probing the opinions of voters. Ideally, these lengthy, in-depth discussions can provide useful information to a campaign. Campaign managers who use them claim that they are good for getting behind the "shallow" poll numbers, providing real human input. They are particularly good for measuring voter reactions, and these reactions can then be probed for better understanding. For example, focus groups are used to see how voters may react to different political ads, allowing campaign staffs to air only those commercials that seem to work best. Focus groups are also used to test-market all sorts of ideas (e.g., which candidate to nominate, issues to push, rhetoric to use, clothes to wear) in a setting where campaign staffers can observe reactions behind a one-way glass screen so that discussions are more spontaneous and candid.

A particular version of a focus group that is popular for measuring immediate reactions to political speeches allows voters to react to the speech using computer keyboards. Robert Dole's campaign manager, Scott Reed, used this focus group technique when Dole gave his acceptance speech at the 1996 Republican National Convention. "Electronic dials measured the reactions of these groups word by word as they listened to the speeches in San Diego. If a phrase excited them, the 'spike' would show up on the computer screens below the podium." Of course, the irony here is that this kind of focus group measures only the instant visceral, "thoughtless" reactions of voters to the speech as it is being delivered, virtually redefining the original purpose of a focus group, which is to measure in-depth opinions as a result of long discussions.

Most political polls do tend to measure only the superficial, but does that mean that focus groups can serve candidates better? I think not! The focus group approach suffers from a very serious problem, namely, that twelve or so participants in a focus group cannot be representative of anything. As Herbert Asher points out, drawing from the wisdom of Richard Morin, "Certainly one caveat is that focus groups are not mini-public opinion surveys. Focus groups may suffer from problems of external validity—that is, the results of the focus group may not be generalizable to any broader population because the participants in a focus group may not be representative." Focus groups also suffer from the "group think" phenomenon. In my experience in running focus groups, the facilitator has a hard time stopping people from falling prey to "group think," in which many in the group just blindly adopt the thinking of some authoritative voice in the group. One time I ran back-to-back focus groups on the same topic. In the first group a few early comments led to an overall very positive view, while in the second group early comments led people down a negative path, turning the group into one big gripe session. Asher has observed the same thing, noting that "One focus group participant relates a particular horror story, leading other participants to join in with their own awful anecdotes. Soon the focus group becomes a gripe session."

Focus groups seem to have become more popular with political candidates, possibly because they are not totally happy with those "impersonal, superficial" polls. One political scientist, James Fishkin, even developed a "deliberative poll" to try to solve the problems caused by a poll's superficiality and a focus group's unrepresentative character. The "deliberative poll" supposedly combines the best of both worlds by drawing a random, representative sample of hundreds of citizens and then assembling them in a "focus group" to provide them with additional information before the "more informed" discussions take place. Actually, his idea was tried in Austin, Texas, in January of 1996, where 459 people participated at a cost of about $8 million. (Obviously, few candidates, even presidential candidates, will opt for these outrageously expensive "polls.") After days of informal discussions, several original issue stands changed, suggesting to proponents that more informed voters would hold different and "better" positions. The flaw in this thinking for political candidates, of course, is that superficial opinion will be much more represented at the ballot box than "informed opinion," since typical voters make their choices on the basis of their superficial knowledge. The normal political polls that have been traditionally used by candidates may measure only superficial opinion, yet the truth is that such polls have proved to be quite accurate because voters indeed act on superficial knowledge that forms the basis of their opinions and voting behavior.

A POTPOURRI OF EXAMPLES OF HOW CANDIDATES USE POLLS

As I have made clear by now, it is obvious that candidates use polls in a large variety of ways to advance their candidacy. In fact, it is accurate to say that most modern candidates are poll-driven. In this section, focus is on the specific, legitimate, real-life examples of how political aspirants use polls in their campaigns, although we all may argue over what constitutes legitimate use. However, common sense and an understanding of polling ethics and laws certainly help to separate the legitimate from illegitimate uses of polls by candidates. Illegitimate uses are discussed later in the chapter.

Getting In and Out of Races

Many candidates dream of winning political office, but in reality there are many more dreamers than winners. Polls are often used to determine whether these dreamers have any realistic chance of winning the election contest. Since political campaigns, especially major ones, require a lot of time and money from supporters, those thinking of committing to a candidate may require some proof that the candidate has a reasonable chance of winning. Evidence of at least a threshold level of public support in a poll can provide the "reality check" necessary to attract supporters, money, media attention, and other things necessary to help build a viable campaign. For example, in June of 2000, Representative Rick Lazio (R-New York) decided to run against Hillary Clinton for the U.S. Senate in New York. Naturally, other Republican hopefuls wanted to challenge Clinton after New York City's mayor, Rudolf Giuliani, decided ultimately not to run, but Lazio was the only candidate given the green light by New York's Republican establishment because he looked like the best candidate in the "match-up" polls against Clinton.

Polls are also used to tell candidates that they should probably fold their tents and drop out of the race. Often candidates simply cannot build the support they need to win during their campaign. Polls might show that their opponents are gaining increasing electoral strength at their expense as each day passes and that they now have no realistic chance of winning. Although some candidates refuse to acknowledge these poll signals, others read "the writing on the wall" and withdraw. For example, in 1994 former Virginia governor Douglas Wilder decided to end his race as an independent candidate for the U.S. Senate against incumbent Democrat Charles Robb and Republican Oliver North when polls showed he had only 12–13% support among voters, while Robb and North were running considerably stronger in the polls. As a veteran politician, Wilder knew the score. He knew that if he stayed in the race, things would only get worse for his candidacy as the money would dry up, staff desertion would occur, the media would turn out the lights on him, and on election day he would only be embarrassed.

Help Making the Campaign Organization Viable

Polls provide vital information on how the campaign is doing. Good poll results for a candidate can help energize a campaign in many ways. In politics people love to jump on the bandwagon of a winner. For instance, in the 2000 presidential campaign, George W. Bush showed so much early support in the polls that his opponents' campaign organizations were wiped out. Candidates grimace at feeble showings in the polls because, even though they may publicly curse them as inaccurate, they know in their hearts that they are not and they fear how their supporters and outside observers will react. While candidates in good standing in the polls can attract large donations, in-kind contributions, positive media attention, interest group and party support, and valuable endorsements from party leaders and even celebrities, and recruit the best staffers and keep their volunteers happy and motivated, those candidates ranking poorly in the polls will not experience these benefits. Predictably, contributors will be hard to find, supporters will start to flee like spooked geese after gun shots, endorsements will be almost impossible to secure, essential staffers and volunteers will desert and even defect to "enemy" camps, the media will ignore you, and the political analysts will add you to their candidate obituary list.

Michael Traugott and Paul Lavrakas assert that when the polls present a bleak picture for a candidate, "the campaign staff will try to produce an explanation or spin that minimizes the damage that such polls can produce." But the truth is that normally very little can be done to stop the mounting tidal wave. Dan Quayle found this out during his quest for his party's presidential nomination in 2000 as he desperately, but unsuccessfully, tried to hold his campaign organization together in the face of his pathetic poll numbers.

Help with the Planning and Running of the Campaign

Polls help with the development of a campaign plan. Every candidacy is different because each candidate faces different obstacles in a unique political climate. Some incumbents face no real opposition, tough competition, or complex opposition involving third-party candidates; opponents of incumbents almost always face uphill battles where the odds of them winning are usually very low; while those running in open-seat races face many unknowns. The types of races (e.g., mayoral, prosecutor, state senate, U.S. representative, U.S. Senate, U.S. presidency) also make a big difference when developing a campaign strategy because the districts may be so different in size, partisanship, attitudes, subculture, affluence, race, ethnicity, and the like. Consequently, polls would be needed to provide vital information about relevant political aspects of a particular district (e.g., city, county, state, the entire country) to help campaign managers devise an intelligent, strategic plan.

As an example, let's consider Missouri's 2000 gubernatorial race, which pitted Republican U.S. Representative Jim Talent against

Democratic State Treasurer Bob Holden. This contest posed some very interesting and unique challenges to both candidates. Talent, a very popular conservative Republican in his quite conservative Second Congressional District just west of St. Louis, was expected to do well in the relatively affluent Republican suburbs in and around his own district and in the Republican suburbs of Kansas City. However, Talent, reigning from a suburban-urban area, faced the unique problem of being a "city slicker" trying to win in a state where rural Missourians have historically voted against city slickers, making it virtually impossible for them to win. The last time a gubernatorial candidate won from the "city" (i.e., the Kansas City or St. Louis areas) was in 1940. Holden, in sharp contrast, grew up in the boondocks of Missouri, where most successful candidates seeking statewide office come from.

Pollsters for Talent had the critical task of gathering the essential poll data that could allow his camp to develop a game plan that would somehow attract the support of rural voters. Holden's pollsters, on the other hand, had the responsibility of strengthening his hold on rural voters, while giving him the savoir faire necessary to allow him to erode some of Talent's suburban electoral base.

Experienced pollsters know that in high-visibility races the greatest determinant of vote choice is image, followed by the voters' partisanship and position on campaign issues. Obviously, then, the pollsters for Talent had to find out what impression rural people had of him, specifically, what they liked and didn't like about him. To develop a more salable image of Talent, they first had to know what Missourians, especially rural voters, really thought of his overall appearance, dress, mannerisms, speech pattern, education, the fact that he is a lawyer, and anything else that is pertinent to his persona.

Once this poll information was gathered, it was used in virtually all aspects of the Talent campaign. Specifically, some of his political commercials were designed to target rural voters. For example, poll data were employed to help him dress "more appropriately" when campaigning in rural areas, say things that ring "true" for rural voters, produce the right kind of Web site, and generate rurally sensitive political commercials, all while simultaneously maintaining his suburban electoral strength. Of course, as the campaign progressed, tracking polls were used to see if the campaign plan was working, specifically focusing on whether Talent was "playing well enough" in rural areas. Naturally, the Holden PR specialists were using their poll data to keep Talent looking as much like an out-of-touch city slicker as they could, hoping to hold their rural base. Holden's camp succeeded and Talent lost.

Missouri is large and diverse enough to have caused the Talent and Holden campaign managers, drawing from poll data, to target different groups of voters in various areas of the state to maximize their candidate's vote potential. In presidential campaigns, targeting is much more complicated since there are so many different groups and radically different subcultures spread over a huge country composed of fifty separate states. As diverse as the different voters in Missouri may seem to Talent and Holden, the diversity pales in comparison to the dissimilarity of voters nationwide. Also, candidates running for statewide office in any state only need to be successful in their own state to win, but presidential candidates must focus on enough individual states to first win enough state delegates to secure their party's nomination, then go on to capture enough states in our winner-take-all electoral college system to obtain the necessary 270 electoral votes to win the presidency.

Sophisticated targeting schemes cannot be designed without poll data, and lots of it. As the campaign matures during the fall campaign, for example, presidential candidates consult poll data regularly to get "must" questions answered, such as: What states are hopeless for me and so should "write off"? What states am I so far ahead in that I can afford to ignore? What states am I trailing in, but I can possibly win if I devote more attention to them? What states am I ahead in, but could lose if I don't concentrate on them? What campaign tactics and messages need to be employed to maximize my vote in them?

In 1996, Republican presidential nominee Bob Dole was trailing President Clinton badly in the polls, so Dole's pollsters and strategists employed a desperate targeting strategy to "bail him out."

Poll data suggested that Dole had to target the southern states, a traditional Republican base that Dole was losing, although the situation was not perceived as hopeless if the Dole camp developed the right tactics to win the South back. Data suggested that Dole must stress his war record to the more "hawkish" southerners, while countering the Clinton charges that Republicans want to weaken Medicare, Medicaid, and Social Security, especially focusing on electoral vote-rich Florida, where the growing number of Independents, if they vote, tend to vote Republican.

In the 2000 presidential race, polls suggested that the contest would be close and the Hispanic and African American voters could decide the winner. Consequently, George W. Bush and Al Gore originally decided to target key states with large Hispanic and/or black voters, such as New York, California, and the bloc of southern states, especially Florida. With affirmative action ending in states like Florida and Texas, problems with Hispanic voters for Bush in California, the Cubans in Miami angry with Gore over Elian Gonzales being sent back to Cuba, the controversy over the Confederate flag flying over the state capitol in South Carolina, and the release of a sensitive report on police-race relations in New York City, the poll-driven campaigns of Bush and Gore decided to push civil rights. Early polls showed that Bush in particular had to do more to appeal to minorities because he trailed Gore 55% to 28% when voters were asked which candidate "would do the best job of improving conditions for minority groups."

In political campaigns, as in physics, for every action there is a reaction. This means that the poll data must be interpreted and applied to maximize benefits and minimize the losses. Consequently, polls are used constantly in major campaigns to "fine-tune" strategy and minimize any damage caused, especially by unexpected events during the campaign. Often the damage is self-inflicted when candidates blunder during their campaigns, causing their pollsters to conduct immediate polls to assess the damage so the candidates can start their "damage control" efforts. For example, Bush, desperate after losing the New Hampshire primary to John McCain, decided to give a speech at Bob Jones University to help him win the South Carolina primary. Guided by his pollsters, Bush took a calculated risk by delivering the speech to this controversial, ultra-right-wing school. Although the speech probably helped him win in conservative South Carolina, reaction to the speech soon turned into a major problem for Bush when it was learned that Bob Jones embraced anti-Catholic and anti-interracial policies—policies that Bush seemed to tacitly accept by saying nothing about them in his speech. The media soon made a major issue out of this and Bush suddenly had the problem of being labeled insensitive to interracial relationships and vulnerable to the charge that he was an "anti-Catholic bigot."

His pollsters sprang immediately into action and surveyed the public's reactions. They found the obvious, that Bush could not afford to alienate two major voting blocs, Catholics and African Americans, and expect to win the presidency. Bush's remedies were not quick enough and he lost the Michigan primary a week later, losing too many of the plentiful Catholic and black voters in that state. To win the Catholic vote back, he sent a letter of apology to Cardinal John O'Connor, archbishop of New York, and immediately scheduled and delivered a speech at St. Louis University, a major Catholic university. To appease African American voters, he started focusing on black issues and concerns, even pointing to an "interracial" marriage in the Bush family.

Help with the Final Stretch Run

Although polls are used throughout the campaigns, especially to fine-tune the campaign tactics as new developments occur and different "spins" need to be added (e.g., for the candidate's speeches, political commercials, targeting different voter blocs), polls are usually used the most during the final few weeks of the campaign when staffs search desperately to resolve any tactical problems in order to turn their campaigns into winning ones.

During this stretch drive, polls, often in combination with focus groups, are employed especially to help design the political ads that air during the media blitz over the final weeks. It is during this critical period of the campaign that candidates, especially those who are trailing, resort to "endless" negative commercials. As dirty and unethical as they may appear, numerous studies over the years have shown that negative commercials are normally the most effective. Consequently, poll information is used to design political ads, mostly negative ones, to exploit the vulnerabilities of opponents while playing up their own positive traits and records. Because "truth in advertising" is not required in political commercials, in contrast to regular consumer commercials regulated by the Federal Trade Commission, very often these ads greatly distort and even contain blatant lies about opponents. In federal elections, for example, the Federal Election Commission has taken the position that it would be practically impossible for the FEC to monitor the content of candidate commercials, leaving it up to the media, the candidates, and others to point out the distortions and inaccuracies. Unfortunately for the victims of such commercials, "correcting" a negative ad may only promote the message even more, while in many cases the most nasty negative ads are aired during the final days before the election when the victimized candidates do not have enough time to respond. Nonetheless, pollsters work overtime during these final weeks and days to tap voter opinion with an eye toward using this opinion research to help design those positive or negative commercials that will work best for their candidates, frequently helping to design those ads that counter the negative commercials run against their clients.

Polls are also used by campaign organizations during their candidate's stretch run to target voters whom they can recruit to help them with their campaigns. Toward the end of campaigns, campaign staffs are desperate for volunteers to help with final mailings, door-to-door literature drops, phone banks to call those most likely to vote for their candidate, and the get-out-the-vote drive on election day. Pollsters have identified from previous polls those most likely to enthusiastically support their candidate. Staffs often contact these people in an effort to solicit contributions, but mainly to ask them whether they can serve as volunteers to help with the aforementioned end-of-campaign activities. Poll information is also essential for making certain that the voters most likely to vote for their candidate are reminded to vote and even asked whether they need transportation to their polling place.

WHAT CONSTITUTES THE MISUSE OF POLLS BY CANDIDATES?

The question posed in this section's title is virtually impossible to answer. Most of us would agree that the most flagrant abuses of polls constitute misuse, while most of us would also agree on certain uses that are completely acceptable. However, candidates, pundits, journalists, and ordinary citizens disagree about the many poll uses that fall in between. Roll and Cantril noted decades ago that polls can be misused by political candidates in two basic ways, that is, polling procedures can be exploited as well as their product—the poll itself. Roll and Cantril acknowledged that unscrupulous candidates could get unethical pollsters to contaminate their procedures enough so that the poll could not but favor their candidate. Regardless of whether legitimate procedures were followed to produce accurate results, candidates still had the opportunity to manipulate the poll itself by, for example, distorting the true picture by strategically leaking to the media only the most favorable parts of the poll.

It is very interesting to discover that many of the uses of polls that Roll and Cantril considered abuses in 1972, when they wrote *Polls: Their Use and Misuse in Politics*, are considered common, tolerable, and even expected practices in political polling circles today. For example, wallowing in what most today would regard as political idealism, they argued that using polls to tailor candidate views on the issues to conform with what's popular and to employ polls to package and sell political candidates at least borders on the unethical, tending to undermine democratic elections. Ideally, one can sympathize with this viewpoint because packaging and selling candidates like toothpaste does seem ignoble, but the political reality is that this is exactly why candidates hire pollsters, media, and public relations experts. Candidates want to win and, therefore, they want to be packaged "properly" and sold to the voters.

There are several other uses of polls that Roll and Cantril condemn as misuses or at least "unfortunate" or "regrettable" uses of polls because, in their eyes, they "can be injurious to the democratic process." For example, they criticize the use of early "trial heat" polls as unfair because they are used to eliminate candidates from races before the campaign season even begins, thus depriving voters of the opportunity to scrutinize and possibly elect those candidates who might turn out to be good leaders. This is particularly true for lesser-known candidates who want to challenge incumbents. It cannot be denied that incumbents win reelection at very high rates (e.g., well over 90% for U.S. Representatives) in part because normally preelection "trial heat" polls show relatively unknown challengers so weak that they can't attract the money, staffers, and media attention to mount a viable campaign. Roll and Cantril hold that results from such polls undermine democracy because they "do not provide a realistic assessment of the potential strength of the candidates. The non-incumbent usually is less well known, and it is not until the campaign's in full swing that the public becomes really aware of him."

Unquestionably, preelection trial heat polls do present such obstacles to some candidates, especially those little-known candidates who want to challenge incumbents. But the implication is that such polls constitute misuse and possibly should be banned because they are bad for democracy. However, such a ban would be worse for our democracy, being a blatant violation of a candidate's First Amendment right to free expression. The root of the problem is not in the trial heat polls that uncover the obvious strength of the incumbents, but in the inherent advantages of incumbency in our electoral system. Placing term limits on incumbents, although I oppose them, still makes more sense than suggesting that trial heat polls constitute an abusive practice that should be prohibited. Yes, the publicity of the results of trial heat polls is unfair to little-known candidates, but the reality is that life itself is inherently unfair.

Roll and Cantril also condemn the practice of candidates leaking their poll data, especially to the media, to help advance their candidacies. They assert that such leaks of selected poll data can show a candidate looking stronger than he or she really is, placing the candidate in a better position to raise money more easily and obtain publicity through heightened press coverage. But assuming the poll results are honest, the leaking of some poll data to the media that can benefit a candidate's campaign only makes good PR sense from the standpoint of the candidate. Campaign staffs have a right to give out any legal information they want to promote their candidates, so such selective leaks do not constitute a misuse of polls. On the other hand, journalists and others should not blindly accept any leaked poll statistics. In particular, journalists have an obligation not to use leaked poll data in their stories unless they have examined the poll statistics in the context of the entire poll, including all the questions in the actual order asked, all possible responses, and a thorough description of the methodology.

On a related matter, Roll and Cantril think that it is wrong for candidates to try to trick the media and voters by flatly lying to them about what their internal polls show, especially by creating a "phantom" or false impression of their own standing in the polls. They note that John Kennedy in 1960 did this in the critical West Virginia primary. He told reporters on election eve that he would be "lucky to get 40 percent of the vote" against rival Hubert Humphrey even though he knew that his own polls showed that he would likely "blow out" Humphrey. When he did win easily with over 60% of the vote, the press interpreted it as a big upset and an unexpected display of his great strength among voters, helping Kennedy to mount the momentum he needed to capture his party's nomination. Of course, lying is not an admirable trait, but for the media to expect candidates not to lie and distort the actual picture in political campaigns is downright naive. Many may consider it unethical for candidates to misrepresent and lie about poll numbers to the press, but it is not illegal and only the most gullible reporters would trust virtually anything candidates say during political campaigns. I am not condoning the practice by candidates because blatantly lying about your polls to deceive the media, potential contributors, and the voters is simply dishonest, does constitute a misuse of poll data, and tends to turn people off toward the electoral process. But anyone receiving poll information should ask to see the entire computer printout of the poll. If the candidates won't release it, and the odds are high that he or she won't, then dismiss it.

Lying about poll numbers is unethical, but the greatest misuse of political polls occurs when candidates persuade their pollsters to manipulate polling procedures for the purpose of generating totally deceptive poll statistics that favor their clients. Only sleazy, irreputable pollsters would comply with such requests, but biasing procedures to produce client-favorable results is, unfortunately, methodologically easy to accomplish. For example, a pollster could design the sample so only obvious candidate supporters are interviewed. Questions or response sets could be slanted to guarantee positive responses for the candidate. Candidates have even been desperate and iniquitous enough to offer to pay a pollster more money for a poll showing them above a certain percentage. This happened to me one time when a candidate planning on running in a U.S. Senate primary race offered me a pile of dollars extra for a poll showing at least 5% voter support, thus allowing the candidate to approach the media and possible contributors with the "good news." I turned the "creative" aspirant down and so did the voters.

As noted, many years ago Roll and Cantril condemned certain uses of polls as at least "unfortunate," yet some of these uses have become "acceptable" or tolerated in today's modern campaigns because, if for no other reason, they are now expected or commonplace. However, some groups monitoring the use of polls in campaigns have become concerned about the flagrant misuses, such as the use of "push polls," which were discussed at length in Chapter 4. One such group, the National Council on Public Polls, announced at the beginning of the 2000 campaign season that the NCPP was going to "scrutinize the conduct and reporting of polls, particularly those about the 2000 elections, and to comment on cases of misuse of surveys or distortions of findings." Andrew Kohut, president of NCPP, held that it was the intention of NCPP's quality control panel to make sure that poll misuses were short-lived and would not seriously jeopardize the electoral process.

THE INCREASING USE OF POLLS BY ELECTED OFFICIALS: FOCUS ON THE PRESIDENT

Carl Cannon wrote the following about President Clinton: "As President, Clinton has commissioned polls on issues ranging in gravity from whether he ought to stop genocide in Bosnia . . . to whether it was better public relations to vacation in Wyoming or Martha's Vineyard." However, Clinton is not the first president to use polls in a major way, nor the first elected official to do so. Overwhelming evidence exists that virtually all of our elected leaders from local officials to the president of the United States consult and employ polls regularly, and have done so for many years. But the focus in this section is mainly on how our recent presidents have come to rely more heavily on polls and how they have specifically used them. As one would expect, although lower-level elected officials use polls much more today than a few decades ago, modern presidents have learned to use them on a grand scale, devoting considerable money and personnel to polling and related public relations operations.

Instinctively, our elected leaders have always been interested in tracking public opinion because, to a large extent, their very survival depends on what their constituents think of them and their actions. For example, even in the 1800s, long before modern polling, presidential staffs tried to keep a thumb on the public pulse by using straw polls, sending workers out to canvass voters, and analyzing public sentiment as expressed in newspapers, magazines, and at public gatherings. President Franklin D. Roosevelt did show an interest in polls when scientific public opinion polling first began during his administration, but he didn't really use polls very much. President Harry Truman rejected them as quite useless and annoying. Of course, Truman probably had little respect for them because the "great scientific pollsters" of his day all wrongly predicted that he would lose to Thomas Dewey in the 1948 presidential election. His successor, Dwight Eisenhower, saw the potential value in polls, but like FDR, he didn't set up any apparatus to use them.

However, beginning with President John Kennedy, extensive use of public opinion polls began. As noted in Chapter 3, Kennedy was the first presidential candidate to hire a professional pollster, Lou Harris, to help develop a campaign strategy. Impressed with Harris and the insights provided by polls, Kennedy also used Harris as a pollster while president, although Kennedy used him informally and did not establish any formal White House polling operations. President Lyndon Johnson and especially President Richard Nixon were the first presidents to really become "hooked" on the value of polls, not just for electioneering purposes, but for helping them run their administrations.

In a most enlightening article, "The Rise of Presidential Polling," Lawrence Jacobs and Robert Shapiro traced the development of presidential polling from JFK through Nixon, arguing that Kennedy and Johnson did much to bring polling to the White House, but Nixon was the first president to institutionalize public opinion polling in the presidency by establishing an elaborate White House administrative apparatus aimed at centralizing all aspects of polling and related media and PR activities under presidential control. According to Nixon's chief of staff, H. R. Haldeman, who headed White House polling operations, only days after Nixon took office in 1969 he ordered a polling operation to be established in his administration that could monitor "what moves and concerns the average guy," because he was convinced that it is easy to fall "out of touch" since the White House is "almost in total isolation from the real world." According to Jacobs and Shapiro, Nixon's desire to develop an elaborate White House polling capacity was driven in large part by his frustration at having to depend exclusively on Harris and Gallup for public opinion information. Nixon wanted poll exclusivity, control, and political loyalty, something that media-oriented pollsters like Harris and Gallup could not give him. Consequently, Nixon insisted on building a private and quite secretive polling operation that went way beyond that of Kennedy and Johnson in both quantity and quality. Nixon felt that "processing secret information that was denied other politicians (in an era of limited polling) provided . . . a critical advantage in anticipating future public reactions. . . . Nixon believed that keeping the poll results confidential maximized the 'power in having the statistics yourself.'" He also understood that by setting up private polling machinery under his direction, he could order polls conducted when he wanted them, make them more comprehensive than "superficial" media surveys, and tailor all poll questions to suit his political needs.

Nixon became the first president to conduct and consult polls regularly to help with the almost daily activities of his administration. Compared to Kennedy and Johnson, Nixon commissioned many more polls, especially for "governing" purposes. According to Jacobs and Shapiro, JFK commissioned 93 polls, but 77 were campaign polls, and only 16 were conducted while he was president. Johnson had 130 polls conducted, with 48 being campaign polls and 82 used during his administration for governing matters. While most (153) of Nixon's polls between 1969 and 1972 (a count was not taken after 1972) were used for his 1972 campaign, he commissioned 80 during his 1969–1971 "governing period," at an unprecedented rate of about one poll every two weeks. This does not count the media polls that he influenced, collected, and analyzed. According to Haldeman, he met with Nixon at least once a week to discuss matters related to public opinion polling.

Because Nixon used these polls to make important administration decisions, he insisted on having only quality polls conducted. What he did to increase poll quality and the status of polling operations in the White House cannot be stressed enough, because Nixon's push for poll excellence set a new standard that was followed and improved upon by his successors. Specifically, Nixon centralized polling operations; secured ample, almost totally private funding for his polls; recruited skilled survey research methodologists and analysts to design, implement, and interpret poll results; advanced statistical applications from simple univariate and bivariate data summaries to more complex multivariate analysis; conducted numerous polls to permit adequate, comparative "trend analysis"; and shortened the time period for completing polls by using what his staff called "telephone quickie polls" rather than the slow door-to-door polls used by Kennedy and Johnson. In sum, Nixon's polling apparatus brought to the presidency "innovative and technically sophisticated methods for analyzing public opinion and political behavior; methods used to advise Nixon and his senior aides were genuinely state-of-the-art—a level of expertise that was never approached under Kennedy or Johnson."

Clearly, President Nixon paved the way for poll use by modern presidents. His use of polls three decades ago was not that dissimilar to how, for example, President Clinton has employed polls. Nixon, like Clinton, used polls regularly to monitor public opinion so his presidential actions would not be greeted by unexpected public reactions. They both used opinion polls to find out what most and least concerned the public; whether the public was aware of certain presidential actions and whether they approved or disapproved of them; where they stood regarding presidential favorability and job performance; what to say and not to say at press conferences and in speeches; how to attack political opponents and various critics; how to target specific groups and citizens in various areas of the country; how to develop, defend, and sell public policy positions; and, finally, how to survive in office, especially during those crises that inevitably inflict presidential administrations.

Nixon was particularly keen on using polls to test the popularity of different issue stands. Before acting, Nixon would want to know, for example, what the public thought about a certain issue relating to the environment, jobs, inflation, taxes, the Strategic Arms Limitation Talks, admitting China to the United Nations, Vietnam, and eventually the Watergate affair. Of course, the poll-driven Clinton also felt it was imperative to consult the polls on the issues. For Clinton, the issues were health care reform, welfare reform, campaign finance reform, gay rights, care for the elderly, teen violence, drugs, education, Bosnia, Middle East peace talks, what to do with the mounting budget surplus, and free trade. Regarding the Clinton-Lewinsky scandal and impeachment, polls became, according to one Clinton insider, "our religion. We cite them, we flog them, we beat people over the head with them." Judging from Nixon's prolific use of polls before Watergate, I can't believe that polls were used much differently in the White House during the Watergate affair.

CONCLUDING COMMENTS

Obviously, whether they like it or not, most of our political candidates and elected leaders live and die by polls. Politicians simply cannot escape their use or their impact on their political careers. Consequently, our politicians have developed a love/hate attitude toward polls. Of course, the crucial question is whether the increased use of political polls has damaged our electoral processes and harmed the way our elected leaders govern. Although I devoted considerable space to the possible damage that political polling has done to election politics and democratic government in Chapters 1 and 2 especially, I feel it is appropriate to argue against the apparent assumption that the increased use of polls by candidates and our elected officeholders has necessarily been a bad thing.

Senator John McCain, for example, a candidate for the Republican presidential nomination in 2000, blamed the use of polls by politicians in part for "the pervasive public cynicism that is debilitating our democracy." Specifically, he noted that politicians have earned "the public's contempt with our poll-driven policies, our phony posturing, the lies we call spin, and the damage control we substitute for progress." This makes for good speech rhetoric, but what proof does he offer to support his contention that poll-driven politicians are somehow partially to blame for our political leaders squandering the "public trust"? The fact is that there isn't any hard or pervasive evidence to substantiate the claim that, overall, the increasing use of polls alone by candidates and officeholders has been damaging the electioneering or governance in America or has contributed to the undermining of the public trust. This is not to say that critics can't legitimately cite specific misuses of polls,

I don't need polls to make decisions

even abuses that have certainly not promoted the best interests of democracy (e.g., push polls, early candidate and media polls used to prematurely eliminate candidates from campaigns, using poll data to play to popular public opinion at the expense of principled judgment, blatant manipulation of poll data, or using poll results to unfairly and undemocratically eliminate potentially good candidates from the presidential debates). However, is there really any convincing evidence to suggest that our democracy is performing worse now than before the use of political polls by our candidates and elected officials? I have not seen any. In fact, the American polity and its economy seem to be doing better than ever.

Nonetheless, a mythical perception has been advanced and accepted by many without any real proof that our candidates and elected leaders are less noble, principled, and competent than those of yesteryear because they use polls to help them make campaign and governmental decisions. This mythical perception is so prevalent that even politicians, who rely on polls so heavily, often try to hide from the media and the public their dependence on the polls out of fear that they will be chastised, particularly for not being strong, principled leaders. For instance, Jacobs and Shapiro noted that Kennedy, Johnson, and Nixon, like most politicians today, tried to hide their use of polls because they didn't want the public to find out that they used polls as a "crutch." Harry Dent, a Nixon aide, explained that Nixon was adamant about hiding his reliance on polls because he wanted the American people to "believe that he was a political genius and . . . prime strategist . . . [who] didn't need to go by public opinion polls." And obviously things have not changed, as evidenced by George W. Bush's repeated declaration in his 2000 presidential campaign that "we take stands without having to run polls and focus groups to tell us where we stand," despite his obvious addiction to polls and focus groups.

But candidates and political officeholders are probably much better off today because they do use polls to help them in their decisionmaking. Naturally, polls can be misused and overused, like any tool. However, polls can also be underused too. That is, only a foolish politician would ignore the obvious advantages of polling on the issues. Given Abraham Lincoln's curiosity for public opinion in his day, it would be hard to believe that he would not have used polls if scientific polling had been around during his presidency. Good polls provide valuable information to help make decisions. Naturally, politicians should not be "poll-driven," ignoring all other considerations, but it seems incongruous that sensible Americans would condemn any politician for using any additional information that can help in the making of wise decisions, especially since approximately 95% of the money spent on polls in America, as noted in Chapter 3, are for surveys to help guide private business decisions.

Chapter Eight

◨ ◨ ◨

Polls, the Clinton-Lewinsky Scandal, and Democracy

And, despite Starr's protestations that he was only doing the job he was appointed to do, he leaves the office as one of the most negatively evaluated public figures measured in Gallup Poll annals.
—Frank Newport, Gallup News Service, October 19, 1999[1]

Polls were relentlessly attacked during the Clinton-Lewinsky scandal for all sorts of reasons. Not only were pollsters attacked for being wrong, but also for playing an illegitimate role in the nation's democratic processes. The Clinton-Lewinsky affair seemed to bring the criticisms against pollsters to a head. Ironically, however, the polls held up very well. All major polling firms essentially showed the same results month after month as they tracked the public reaction to the almost daily developments in the scandal. During this period, pollsters performed at their best, asking citizens relentless questions about the scandal from many different perspectives and providing valuable insights into how Americans interpreted the complex dynamics of one of the greatest scandals ever to plague the American presidency. As the decades pass, political historians, no doubt, will become increasingly appreciative of the mounds of public opinion information collected by these pollsters.

Nonetheless, during the whole episode, many in the general public, in the media, and in pundit and political circles questioned the motives and integrity of the pollsters, even attacking them for undermining and disrupting constitutional government, especially pertaining to the impeachment processes. "Should we follow the pollsters or the Constitution?" was a constant sarcastic outcry. Reflecting on the pressures placed upon U.S. House members by polls showing that the American people were solidly against impeachment, reporter Jill Lawrence of *USA Today* wrote: "Will they serve their constituents, their consciences, their parties, the Constitution, or the national polls that show the country does not want impeachment?"[2]

The chief purpose of this chapter is to show how a variety of poll data can help us to understand the Clinton-Lewinsky scandal and, especially, how Clinton, remarkably, managed to "survive" it. Special emphasis is given to poll statistics relating to what Americans thought of the charges brought against Clinton, the impact of these charges on public perceptions of Clinton, as a man and as our president, and the impact on his accusers, especially Ken Starr and the congressional Republicans. In the chapter's summary, the sordid affair is put into perspective.

THE MAIN EVENT: CLINTON V. STARR

When the first stories appeared on the Clinton-Lewinsky scandal on January 21, 1998, the Clinton White House denied the charges. President Clinton's now infamous animated, finger-waving statement, "I did not have sexual relations with that woman, Miss Lewinsky!"[3] was given within a few days of the breaking story, followed a couple days later by Hillary Clinton's more credible assertion that her husband was the victim of the "politically motivated" special prosecutor, Ken Starr, who was part of "a vast right-wing conspiracy."[4] Whether or not such a conspiracy was behind the relentless attacks on President Clinton, his upcoming year was about to turn into the worst nightmare of his life. Still fighting off sexual harassment charges filed by Paula Jones, as

1998 unfolded, his denials of his vile affair with Monica Lewinsky became less and less compelling and were definitively undercut by the humiliating DNA "proof positive" discovery that the stains on Lewinsky's dress were from Clinton's semen, convincingly substantiating the once-believed to be preposterous claim that White House intern Monica Lewinsky had performed oral sex on our president in the exalted White House. By year's end, Independent Counsel Ken Starr had disclosed more details about Clinton's illicit, adulterous affair with Lewinsky than the public wanted to hear,[5] including Clinton's ability to perform remarkable sex tricks with a cigar and also being able to enjoy sex with Lewinsky while simultaneously talking on the phone to high-ranking political officials.[6] As 1999 began, Starr had convinced most of us that Clinton was guilty of this adulterous affair, of lying under oath and to the American people, and of obstructing justice.[7] Consequently, Clinton became only the second American president ever to be impeached, and he faced an impeachment trial in the Senate.

However, the remarkable truth is that Clinton survived, and Starr and his fellow Republicans did not. House Speaker Newt Gingrich, who largely orchestrated the House Republican efforts to get Clinton, felt obliged to resign after the November 1998 congressional election when House Republicans actually ended up losing six seats to the Democrats in a year in which they were expected to make big seat gains. Starr, especially, was devastated. Never "getting it," he left office as one of the most unpopular political figures ever, while Clinton's job approval only continued to soar. According to the Gallup News Service, "And, despite Starr's protestations that he was only doing the job he was appointed to do, he leaves the office as one of the most negatively evaluated public figures measured in Gallup Poll annals. About two-thirds of Americans said they had a negative opinion of Starr earlier this year, after the impeachment crisis was over, and the same number said they disapproved of the job he did as Independent Counsel."[8] Let's look carefully at the voluminous poll numbers to help explain Clinton's ability to survive, not forgetting that Clinton and his staffers consulted the polls often to help them understand the public's thinking on developments concerning the scandal so the

White House could develop the best "damage control" strategies. A curious question arises: Would Clinton have resigned had he served during an era when presidents did not have access to poll data, not knowing that he, incredibly, had broad public support?

Polls Show High Job Approval for Clinton, Despite Scandal

With the release of the weighty Starr Report detailing the sexual escapades of President Clinton with Monica Lewinsky, journalists in the United States and abroad were having a field day writing Clinton's obituary. "Hasta la vista, amigo?" read the headline of a prominent newspaper in Mexico City. "Comeback Kid Plots Moves in Last Chance Saloon" was the headline in *The Times* (London). *The Sydney Morning News* in Australia reported in a prophetic tone: "Two dark vans that drove [the report] to the Capitol were akin to hearses arriving to take away the corpse of the Clinton presidency."[9] But according to the American people, to borrow from the wit of Mark Twain, reports of the death of the Clinton presidency had been "greatly exaggerated." In fact, according to the numerous polls on the Clinton-Lewinsky scandal, the vast majority of Americans gave their ceaseless support to Clinton throughout the entire ordeal, even though they came to realize that Clinton had sexual relations with Lewinsky, lied about it, and engaged in an obstruction of justice when trying to cover it up. In poll after poll, Clinton's favorability scores (i.e., ratings regarding his personal and moral character) did decline, yet his critical "job approval" ratings remained strong, even surging to new highs during the height of the scandal. The American public sent the clear message in these and related polls that they still wanted Clinton as their president because they regarded him as quite competent, yet flawed.

Toward the end of 1998, Richard Brody, after reviewing countless polls, concluded in *Polling Report.com* that the scandal "has had a very selective effect on public opinion. Over the past nine months the American public has substantially changed its view of Clinton as an individual but barely readjusted its perception of President Clinton as a political leader." He continued to stress that Clinton's job approval, as measured in 194 separate samples by eleven major polling firms, showed that during the course of the scandal consistently better than 60% of the American public assessed his job performance positively.[10] Before examining Clinton's actual job performance evaluations by the American public, it is necessary to emphasize that job approval ratings are the most critical to a president's survival because, unlike other rankings (e.g., favorability), job approval scores constitute "bottom line" public opinion relating directly to a president's ability to survive. That is, they answer the question, all things considered, including his weaknesses, "Is his job performance, nonetheless, acceptable?" For example, no U.S. president has ever been reelected with job approval percentages below 50% because, not surprisingly, job approval scores and percent voting for the reelection of a president are very closely related. In fact, pollsters knew that George H. W. Bush was in deep trouble in 1992 when his job approval plummeted to around 37%—about the same percentage who voted for him in the 1992 presidential election.

Table 8.1 uses the poll data from the four most popular news media polls, plus the most famous and respected private polling firm, the Gallup Poll, to track Clinton's job approval ratings from just before the news of the scandal broke on January 21, 1998, to just after the Senate voted not to pursue a full impeachment trial and to end the scandalous ordeal on February 12, 1999. These data show that Clinton's job approval percentages remained comfortably high throughout 1998 and into February of 1999, despite relentless efforts by Ken Starr, the Republican Congress, and the conservative media to uncover and present evidence of his affair with Monica Lewinsky that they hoped would discredit him enough before the American people to force him to resign or to allow the House to impeach him and the Senate to remove him with a conviction in an impeachment trial. As the fall congressional elections approached, Republicans, led by House Speaker Newt Gingrich, also hoped to pick up seats in Congress by dishonoring

Clinton. As Alison Mitchell commented in *The New York Times*, "Although Mr. Clinton's job approval ratings in polls remain confoundingly high, Republicans believe that a constant drumbeat of revelations about the President's behavior with Ms. Lewinsky in the Oval Office and efforts to cover it up will bring his ratings down as the mid-term election approaches."[11]

But no matter what Starr or the Republican Congress did, Clinton's job approval ratings remained high, even soaring to a record high for his presidency. This frustrated Starr and those sympathetic to Starr's cause, especially since Clinton's job approval scores appeared strongest when Clinton faced his worst moments of the scandal—immediately following the breaking news of the Lewinsky affair and learning that Starr was going to investigate; just after he was compelled to give a nationally televised explanation and apology in mid-August; soon after Starr released in September the grand jury tapes and 2800 pages of documents describing the details of his sexual conduct with Lewinsky; and immediately after the House voted to impeach Clinton. Not all of these slight jumps in his ratings can be seen in Table 8.1 because some of the polls disclosed were not taken immediately following these events, but some were. Note Clinton's uniformly high approval ratings in February, 1998, just a few weeks after Americans were informed about the affair. Here we see that his job approval scores jumped about ten points above his ratings just prior to the breaking news about the scandal.[12] In middle to late August, around the time Clinton gave his public apology, his job approval scores jumped slightly to 68% and 70%, as measured by the CBS and NBC News polls, respectively. Though Clinton's job approval tapered off a little by early and mid-September, his ratings increased again to 66% just after Starr released the documents and grand jury tapes, as tracked by NBC, and increased according to all polling organizations shown in Table 8.1 by mid-October. Again, as Starr and congressional Republicans seemed to close in for the kill after Starr's testimony before Congress and after the House Republicans led the successful impeachment vote, Clinton's job approval percentages surged to a record high of 73% in December as captured by the polling of CBS and Gallup.[13] After the

TABLE 8.1 Clinton's Monthly Job Approval Ratings from Just Before Scandal to Just After Scandal

Polling Organization	Just Before Scandal	Feb. 1998	Mar. 1998	Apr. 1998	May 1998	Jun. 1998	Jul. 1998	Aug. 1998	Sept. 1998	Oct. 1998	Nov. 1998	Dec. 1998	Just After Scandal
ABC News	55	67	66	65	64	59	63	62	61	63	61	66	60
CBS News	55	67	67	64	62	60	64	68	61	63	68	73	65
CNN/Gallup/USA Today	56	66	66	63	64	60	64	65	63	65	66	63	68
Gallup	59	66	67	63	64	60	65	62	63	65	66	73	69
NBC News	57	66	NA	66	NA	63	64	70	66	68	NA	65	67

SOURCE: The source for the polling was nationaljournal.com (poll track). Although poll track lists over forty polling organizations, I used only poll data from the four most prominent media polls (ABC News/Washington Post; CBS News/New York Times; CNN/Gallup/USA Today; and NBC News/Wall Street Journal), plus the best-known private polling firm, the Gallup Poll. Poll data are sometimes reported by the networks alone or with their print media partners, so the particular percentage might have come from, for example, a CBS poll or a CBS/New York Times poll. Numbers represent the percentage approving of "the way Bill Clinton is handling his job as President." Some polling organizations conducted more than one poll in a month. When they did, I consistently picked the job approval percentage that was nearest to the middle of the month to try to provide better comparative data, but this was not always possible. NBC's 70% in August 1998 and CBS's and Gallup's 73% in December 1998 were taken late in their respective months when Clinton's job approval was higher than during the middle of the month when other polls were taken. "Just Before Scandal" means within two months before the news of the scandal broke on January 21, 1998, and "Just After Scandal" is within two months of when the Senate voted on February 12, 1999, not to pursue a full impeachment trial.

whole "year-of-the-scandal" ended, Clinton's job approval ratings leveled off to comfortable, yet lower levels than he had before his crisis year. By mid-1999, his job approval stood at 60%, and by mid-2000 it registered an identical 60% (Gallup polls, 6/13/99; 6/7/00).

Many political observers, even some experienced pollsters, seemed quite perplexed by Clinton's strong and consistent job approval scores, especially in light of many poor ratings in other areas, as will be discussed in subsequent sections. What's particularly puzzling to some is that Clinton's job approval percentages did not dip, but they actually went up for the entire duration of the Starr probe. Ethel Klein, president of EDK Associates, a non-profit firm in New York City that conducts social and public policy polls, explained in September of 1998 that these jumps in job approval for Clinton meant that many Americans were "coming to the defense of their guy because he's under major attack," but she suggested that once the people "digest" all of this information, Clinton's popularity would likely be placed in greater jeopardy and he would probably be forced to resign.[14] Political scientist Donald Ferree also speculated at the same time that despite "little or no slippage in his job rating, there are certain indications that the rating of the President as a person or a leader may be at some risk" and the American people might decide that "not only has he done bad things, but they don't want this kind of person as President."[15] However, not only were these plausible speculations wrong, but Clinton's job approval ratings, as noted, peaked after all of the "dirt" of the scandal was well known by the public. Explaining why requires a careful and thorough analysis of all relevant poll data.

Richard Brody, professor emeritus of political science at Stanford University and expert on the presidency and the media, admits that he is baffled by Clinton's ability to win the approval of the public and to survive so well in office. Brody's insights are fascinating and worth exploring for a moment. He claims that "given saturation coverage of the affair and a rising tide of criticism of President Clinton by the media and political opinion leaders, we are hard-put to account for this pattern of support." Acknowledg-

Monica, I can't tell you how much you have meant to me

ing that poll data indicate that public opinion on Clinton's character has plummeted, he stresses that "most explanations of the dynamics of public opinion would lead us to expect a negative public judgment of the President's 'handling of his job.'" He continues to explain that "presidents often get boosts in approval from major international crises but there has been, in this period, no such crises. Without a rally to offset the Lewinsky affair, we have to rethink our standard explanations of what the public is responding to when it forms opinions on presidential performance."[16]

Professor Brody concludes that "the Lewinsky affair has produced a large volume of negative news which should have reduced Clinton's support." But despite all the news on the affair that he describes as "bad news" for Clinton, the vast majority of Americans were pleased with his job performance. Reflecting on the past revelations of poll data, Brody asked: "Why did conventional wisdom and past research fail in this case? What does this tell us about how the American public forms its opinions?"[17]

We could conclude that the American people continued to give Clinton high job approval ratings because they were not following the news on the scandal and, therefore, ignorantly continued to support Clinton. But, as we shall see from an analysis of the poll data, this is certainly not the case. Americans followed this scandal very closely, showed impressive knowledge about the details of the scandal, and, in fact, responded quite rationally to the scandal.

Polls Show Clinton with Strong Ratings in Related Job Areas

Clinton's nightmare must have seemed quite surreal to those closely following the poll numbers during the course of the scandal. As 1998 ended a few weeks after the House voted to impeach Clinton, the Gallup Poll released its January 1999 poll statistics on Clinton, numbers that undoubtedly caused experts such as Professor Brody to scratch their heads with even greater disbelief. Beyond his 73% job approval rating, a record high for his administration and, according to Frank Newport of the Gallup News Service, "one of the highest job approval ratings given any President since the mid-1960s,"[18] President Clinton's rankings in other job-related areas were also quite impressive. Of course, Clinton benefited immensely from the booming economy that seemed to put Americans in a euphoric mood, generously giving Clinton an 81% approval score for his handling of the economy.

Historically, overall job approval ratings are closely linked to how well the nation's economy is doing, and thus to how most Americans are doing. Even though most Americans consistently acknowledge in polls that the president is not very responsible for upturns or downturns in the economy, polls have nonetheless constantly shown over the decades that public perceptions of the president's handling of the economy are directly associated with the nation's economic performance. That is, as the economy goes, so goes a president's approval ratings regarding his handling of the economy. The simple political reality is that the health of the economy is key to the president's ability to survive his presidency. When the economy is robust, a president is going to get not only solid ratings for his management of the economy, but good ratings will tend to spill over into other job performance areas as well. When the economy turns sour, the job approval ratings of presidents have dropped quickly, as did George Bush's in the early 1990s, causing him to lose the presidency to Clinton in 1992. Of course, the Great Depression ended Herbert Hoover's reelection chances in 1932, and serious "stagflation" caused Jimmy Carter to be defeated by Ronald Reagan in 1980.

David Moore, interpreting the poll data for the Gallup News Service, claimed that the strong economy had put Americans in a record-shattering, "historically good mood, with 60 percent feeling the economy is the best it has been in their lifetime, and 70 percent expressing overall satisfaction with the way things are going in the country—the highest percentage to say this since the question was first asked two decades ago." Clinton's 81% rating for his handling of the economy, Moore notes, was also the highest score obtained by any president since the Gallup Poll first asked the question in the 1960s. But he stresses that the euphoria over the economy affected other policy areas, most likely causing Clinton to score high in the public opinion polls in these areas, too.[19]

According to Moore, in January of 1999, President Clinton received the highest ratings of his presidency in the Gallup Poll for "his handling of foreign affairs (64%), race relations (76%), education (69%), the environment (69%), the federal budget deficit (68%), crime (66%), taxes (58%), Medicare (53%), health care (52%), and poverty and homelessness (47%)."[20] No wonder the vast majority of Americans (64%) on February 12, 1999, said in a CBS News poll that they approved of the Senate voting not to convict Clinton. Regardless of his personal misdeeds, in the same CBS poll, 58% still felt that "Clinton can be trusted to keep his word as President," while in a February 1, 1999, CBS/New York Times poll, 72% believed that "Clinton can still be an effective President." Moore concludes that everywhere you look in the poll data, Clinton receives rave reviews from the people for his leadership "with 82 percent describing him as a president who can get things done, 76 percent saying he is an effective manager, and 73 percent as an effective leader—all record high ratings for his presidency."[21]

Defensive Posture of Americans Toward Their President Benefits Hillary

To the American people, Ken Starr and company went after not only President Clinton, but Hillary Clinton as well. When Starr struck out in trying to pin anything concrete on the Clintons during his Whitewater investigation, he decided to enter the "bedroom politics" of the Clintons' private sexual lives. In a sense, Starr successfully proved that the president lied when Clinton said, "I did not have sexual relations with that woman, Miss Lewinsky"; he demonstrated that Clinton was an adulterer and a liar, and that he even engaged in an obstruction of justice while trying to cover up his involvement with Monica Lewinsky during the investigation. However, as Margery Eagan quipped in "Starr-Crossed President Always Comes Out on Top," "Ken Starr, in the end, is not the sort of man America wants toppling its President, is he?" To Eagan, Starr is a pathetic figure who never figured out that overall the American people detested and resented his investigation into the Clintons' private sexual lives.[22] According to the polls, even a significant percentage of Republicans felt Starr was wrong in turning the Whitewater real estate investigation into an investigation "all about just sex," violating what most Americans consider personal privacy rights. For example, on August 18, 1998, 34% of Republicans thought of this whole situation as "more of a private matter having to do with Bill Clinton's personal life" than as "a public matter having to do with Bill Clinton as President," while 51% said, "the investigation of Bill Clinton's relationship with Monica Lewinsky should be dropped."[23] Consequently, Starr's investigation caused more people to side with the Clintons than ever before, inspiring Eagan to write: "Poor Ken Starr. It must drive him nuts."[24]

As Hillary Clinton defended her husband and attacked Starr as part of a right-wing conspiracy out to get her husband, her poll numbers went up and, as we shall see, Starr's numbers went way down. In fact, only during Starr's endless probe did Hillary enjoy such high favorability ratings in the polls. In other words, polls convey clearly that not only did the American people rally to defend President Clinton in light of Starr's investigation, but they turned to support the First Lady as well. According to CNN/Gallup/*USA Today* polls, Hillary's favorability in 1994 stood at 48%. But just two weeks after news of the scandal broke in January of 1998 and after she first blasted Starr as part of the right-wing conspiracy targeting her husband, her favorability percentage jumped to 64%, and remained in the sixties until the end of the scandal. In December of 1998, a CNN/Gallup/*USA Today* poll showed her with a 63% favorability, while a February 1999, *Washington Post* poll tracked her at 63% favorability.[25] However, since the Starr investigation ended and the Senate voted not to convict President Clinton in February of 1999, Hillary's favorability ratings have tapered off to prescandal levels. A CNN/Gallup/*USA Today* poll ranked her at 56% favorability in June of 1999, and an ABC/*Washington Post* poll recorded only a 49% favorability score in September of 1999.

Polls Disclose Lack of Public Support for Congress's Handling of the Clinton-Lewinsky Affair, Especially by Partisan Republicans

History has shown that "attack politics" sometimes works, but sometimes it doesn't. Whether attack tactics work depends largely on whether or not the public perceives the attacks as justified and fair. Poll data seem to support the contention that the attack politics of congressional Republicans backfired on them, actually turning many Americans off to Congress, especially the Republicans, and compelling many Americans, including even a hefty percentage of Republicans, to support Clinton. A plethora of polls reveal that the country opposed Congress's assault on Clinton, often expressing clear anger toward the Republican-controlled Congress for how they were handling the Clinton-Lewinsky affair. Polls showed from many different opinion perspectives that Americans never thought the affair involved a serious public matter worthy of diverting Congress's time and resources away from important public policy issues. Consequently, polls conveyed consistently the clear message that President Clinton was guilty as charged, but sexual misconduct and lying about it simply did not justify the Republican Congress trying to remove him from office. According to repeated polling, Americans said, "Just drop it!" When the Congressional Republicans kept on the attack, the polls turned against the Republicans, and the voters in the 1998 House elections sent the House Republicans a clear message by giving the Democrats six new House seats. Of course, House Speaker Newt Gingrich, as well as more neutral political observers, expected House Republicans to pick up as many as forty-plus seats. Let's look at the poll data.

By the end of 1998, most Americans were expressing their frustration, anger, and disapproval of Congress, especially in its handling of the Clinton-Lewinsky matter. While Clinton's job approval ratings continued to soar to record highs, as noted, Congress's job approval continued to decline, reaching a 42% job approval rating in a CBS/*New York Times* poll by December 20, 1998. A majority of citizens (53%) disapproved of Congress's job performance, with even a notable percentage of Republicans (30%) expressing disapproval. Public opinion was running against the handling of the Clinton-Lewinsky situation, in particular, with only 34% asserting approval and barely a majority of Republicans (54%) saying they approved.

ABC News found in an earlier poll completed on October 25, 1998, that only a tiny percentage of Americans were happy with the way the Republicans in Congress were handling the Clinton-Lewinsky matter. Only 9% said they were "happy," 27% noted that they were "satisfied/not happy," while the vast majority (59%) expressed "dissatisfaction/not anger" (37%) or "anger" (22%). Public displeasure with Congressional Republicans seemed to stem from their insistence on refusing to drop the Clinton-Lewinsky issue and relentlessly moving toward impeachment. Throughout 1998, public opinion was strongly in favor of dropping the matter and overwhelmingly against the House effort to impeach Clinton. For example, a CBS News poll on October 4, 1998, revealed that only 37% of the American people felt the House Judiciary committee should even conduct impeachment hearings, with over one-third of GOP respondents believing the hearings to be unnecessary. Once the Committee completed the hearings, according to an ABC News poll on December 6, 1998, 59% of the citizenry disapproved of the way the Committee was "handling the investigation." In a follow-up ABC News poll on December 11, 60% of the public said that they did not want to see the full House "impeach Clinton and remove him from office." Once the House did vote to impeach, 61% of the public disapproved, including 27% of the Republicans, 87% of the Democrats, and 59% of the Independents.

Such disapproval was to be expected since all year long Americans were telling Congress, especially the House Republican leadership, to drop the investigation or simply scold the president with an official censure and move on to more important policy matters. Shortly before the impeachment hearings were to begin, ABC News asked on November 20–22, 1998, "Do you think Congress should proceed with the impeachment hearings, or drop the matter?" Consistent with what the polls had been showing all year long, a high percentage of Americans (59%) replied, "Drop it." This response can be largely attributed to the public's unwavering position that the charges against Clinton were not "serious enough" and that the Republican-led vote to impeach Clinton was aimed mostly at damaging Clinton and the Democrats (63%). According to a CBS/*New York Times* poll (12/20/98), even a significant percentage of Republicans (29%) and a very solid percentage of Independents (65%) felt this way.[26] Most Americans did eventually favor censuring or officially reprimanding Clinton (61%) in a December 11, 1998, ABC News poll, but not impeachment (60%).

During 1998, Americans came to the rather quick conclusion that the Republican effort "to impeach the President has more to do with partisan politics than with doing what is best for the country." Almost three out of four Americans (71%) agreed somewhat (16%) to strongly (55%) with the above statement, while 74% agreed somewhat (12%) to strongly (62%) that "instead of spending time on a lengthy impeachment trial, Congress and the President should focus on issues and legislation important to average families" (AFL-CIO poll, 12/17/98).

Poll numbers make clear that congressional Republicans did not win many public relations battles with President Clinton, although, as we shall see, the Republican lawmakers were successful in seriously tarnishing Clinton's image as a person. Although Clinton's favorability ratings dipped significantly as a result of the investigation, the behavior of Congress evidently did not impress very many Americans, causing favorability scores for Democrats in Congress, but especially Republicans, to decline considerably to embarrassing levels. According to ABC/*Washington Post* polls, in June of 1996 Republicans in Congress had a favorability rating of 41%; just after news of the scandal broke on January 31, 1998, their approval score was still at 41%, but by year's end their score had fallen precipitously to a dismal 23%. Partisan bickering over the scandal didn't help the Democrats either. The same polls showed Democrats in Congress with a favorability score of 43% in June of 1996, increasing to 49% by January 1998, but then plunging to 29% by December 20, 1998, a percentage Democrats could hardly boast about.

At the end of 1998, Americans told Congress, especially the Republicans in Congress, that they didn't like what they had done. When ABC News/*Washington Post* asked in a December 19–20, 1998, poll, "Overall, how much do you think Congress has accomplished in the past year?" only 8% said a "great deal," while 52% answered "not too much" (43%) to "nothing at all" (9%).[27] Also, this poll disclosed that by year's end Americans were much more likely to trust Clinton than the Republicans in Congress with doing "a better job coping with the main problems the nation faces over the next few years." Fifty-two percent of the public trusted President Clinton, and only 34% trusted the Congressional Republicans.

Starr Scores with a Few "Punches": Clinton's Favorability Ratings Dip, But His Character Rankings Plunge

Political science professor Jeffrey Cohen, in "The Polls: The Components of Presidential Favorability," points out that throughout 1998 "some pundits and observers predicted the end of the Clinton presidency, that he would be convicted of the impeachment charges levied against him, citing the fact that his favorability poll results had taken a nosedive."[28] However, he notes that others predicted Clinton would survive because he was receiving such lofty job approval scores. But Cohen also points out that there were still many others who "were perplexed by the disconnect between his approval and favorability ratings."[29] To Professor Cohen, this confusion is understandable because, although job approval ratings have been studied for many decades and are fairly understandable, favorability as a public perception appears much more complex and has been examined far less.[30]

Cohen, like many pollsters, acknowledges that the components of favorability are quite mysterious because it is impossible to understand what people really mean when they say they have a favorable or unfavorable impression of the president, or any person being rated. Common sense would suggest that job approval perceptions must influence favorability and vice versa because, obviously, favorability ratings would have to be affected by good or bad job performance by a president, while positive or negative favorability scores would have to have some impact on a president's job approval rankings. But in what way and to what extent? My opinion is that we will never be able to answer these questions to our complete satisfaction because the determinants of favorability perceptions are too complex and we lack the methodological sophistication to measure the dynamics behind the human thought processes that cause people to rate presidents favorably or unfavorably. Commonsensical explanations will have to suffice.

Pollsters have used favorability to measure public perceptions related to a president's "likability," which in turn appears to be related to character traits and general image, although a linkage to perceptions of job performance cannot be ignored. Therefore, to understand a president's general favorability rating, we need to look at more specific ratings pertaining to character, although questions relating to a president's persona could be endless. Nonetheless, the more public opinion information obtained on a president's character, the more insights we will gain on the president's favorability rating, allowing us to give plausible explanations for various favorability ratings.

In 1998 Ken Starr and the Republicans made Clinton's character the issue in trying to bring his presidency to an end, while in the 2000 presidential campaign the Bush-Cheney Republican ticket once again tried to make character the chief issue ("It's all about integrity"), trying to link Gore to Clinton's low character standings in the polls. So what is character? Can a president have weak favorability/likability/character ratings, yet survive with positive job approval ratings?

Obviously, the answer is "yes"! Clinton did. Polls showed that Starr and the Republican leadership were quite successful during 1998 in damaging Clinton's favorability ratings, as well as specific rankings relating to character. But, as previously documented, Clinton's job approval ratings soared as his ratings on character dropped. A thorough look at the various poll data on favorability/likability/character seems to show why.

Pollsters have used a large variety of questions to measure public perceptions of a president's character. General questions have asked mainly whether respondents have a favorable or unfavorable impression or positive or negative impression of the president, and specific questions have focused on traits such as morals, integrity, honesty, respect, personal values, honor, trust, appearance, charisma, mannerisms, friendliness, whether you would want to "hang out" with him, and all sorts of other questions pertaining to character. Of course, pollsters asked a lot of questions pertaining to character in the context of the Lewinsky affair to try to understand how the scandal affected public opinion of Clinton. Unquestionably, the scandal damaged public perceptions of Clinton's character, but probably not as badly as one would think.

Starting with general favorability rankings, data from various polling organizations all disclosed the same downward trend, as long as the question asked respondents to answer whether they have a favorable or unfavorable impression of Clinton *as a person* (Clinton's favorability scores tended to be somewhat higher if "as a person" or something very similar was not in the question).[31] For example, on January 19, 1998, just before news of the scandal, an ABC News poll showed Clinton with a respectable 59% favorability rating, but by January 25, just four days after the news broke, his favorability percentage fell five points to 54%. By August 23, only five days after Clinton tried to explain the Lewinsky affair on national television, his favorability dipped to 45%, and then to 42% by November 1, and to 41% by December 15.[32]

There is no doubt that Clinton's decline in favorability ratings in these polls from 59% at the beginning of 1998 to 41% at the end of 1998 was significant, representing a drop of eighteen percentage points. Considering that President Clinton enjoyed favorability ratings in the sixties in some polls before the scandal (e.g., 62% in an October 1997 Gallup poll), but has never regained his comfortable favorability scores, we can conclude that the damage to his image was also permanent. Polls conducted after the scandal reveal that Clinton's favorability percentages have stabilized at this lower level, normally being found in the high thirties to high forties (e.g., 48% in a June 27, 1999, Gallup poll; 37% in a January 16, 2000, ABC News/*Washington Post* poll; 47% in a January 10, 2000, Associated Press poll; and 41% in a July 13, 2000, Fox News/Opinion Dynamics poll).

However, a "silver lining" can be seen. Despite the negative impact of the scandal on Clinton's favorability ratings, his scores nonetheless stabilized at a level higher, sometimes much higher, than for others associated with the scandal. Table 8.2 compares Clinton's favorability with others linked to the scandal, along with a few notable personalities to help place favorability ratings of political figures in perspective. Although the Gallup polls were not always taken on the same dates for all persons in the table, they still convey quite clearly that the American people have a much more favorable attitude toward Clinton than toward the others involved in the Clinton-Lewinsky affair. For whatever reason, the women did the worst in the favorability ratings, with Tripp, Lewinsky, and Jones generating absolutely dismal favorability percentages. The men, Ken Starr, House Speaker Newt Gingrich, and Senate Majority Leader Trent Lott, received better favorability ratings than the women, yet their scores still are noticeably worse than Clinton's.

Evidently, even given the immoral and boorish behavior of our president, most Americans concluded that the actions taken by these other people were demonstrably worse. However, politicians fail to impress Americans favorably compared to those in the world of entertainment and sports. As I scanned Gallup's favorability rankings of "people in the news," I could not help but notice the lofty favorability ratings given to entertainer Jerry Seinfeld (63%), but especially to baseball stars Sammy Sosa (83%) and Mark McGwire (87%). Also very telling is the fact that McGwire and Sosa received only negligible unfavorability percentages of 3% and 2%, respectively, while those linked in some way to the scandal had unfavorability scores many times that of McGwire and Sosa (e.g., Lewinsky's 82% is forty-one times higher than Sosa's 2%, Tripp's 76% is thirty-eight times greater, and Starr's 66% is thirty-three times more).

Although news coverage of the scandal did not lower Clinton's general favorability ratings as much as many would have expected, coverage did have quite a negative effect on public perceptions of Clinton's character and his likely reputation in U.S. history. Professor Brody, after acknowledging Clinton's high job approval scores, nonetheless emphasized that public "judgments of the president's character and other personal qualities suffered substantially."[33] By late January 1999, David Moore, after analyzing poll data for the Gallup News Service, reached the same conclusion, recognizing Clinton's record-breaking job approval status in general and in specific policy areas, but noting that Clinton was also setting negative records regarding his character. "At the same time, never have Americans been so critical of the President on a personal level. Just 20 percent of those interviewed think he provides good moral leadership, and only 24 percent characterize

Table 8.2   Clinton Favorability Scores After the Scandal Compared to Others Associated with the Scandal, Along with a Few Notable Personalities to Put Favorability Ratings in Perspective

Name	Poll Dates	Favorable	Unfavorable	Never Heard Of	No Opinion
Bill Clinton	6/27/99	48	50	0	2
	8/4/99	52	46	0	2
	4/99	51	47	0	2
Newt Gingrich	12/29/98	38	51	2	9
	11/22/98	32	53	4	11
	2/15/98	37	48	4	11
Monica Lewinsky	3/7/99	15	79	0	6
	12/29/98	11	82	0	7
	2/15/98	13	63	4	20
Ken Starr	3/7/99	24	66	4	6
	12/29/98	32	58	4	6
	2/1/98	25	42	19	14
Linda Tripp	2/21/99	11	76	6	7
	11/22/98	9	74	6	11
Kathleen Willey	12/29/98	20	30	27	23
	3/16/98	23	29	25	23
Paula Jones	12/29/98	16	72	2	10
	3/16/98	18	62	6	14
Trent Lott	2/21/99	30	26	27	17
	12/29/98	29	25	24	22
Mark McGwire	12/29/98	87	3	5	5
Sammy Sosa	12/29/98	83	2	8	7
Jerry Seinfeld	12/29/98	63	23	4	10

SOURCE: All poll data are taken from Gallup polls. To compare favorability ratings, it is important to observe the ratio between favorability–unfavorability–never heard of–no opinion, especially since a lower favorability may be due to the fact that a significant percentage of respondents never heard of the person and/or had no opinion (e.g., Lott and Willey in this table).

him as honest and trustworthy—a new low for Clinton's presidency."[34]

If we look further into public opinion pertaining to Clinton's character, we find, as Brody claims, "that the public changed its opinion of the President's honesty, trustworthiness and personal moral and ethical standards after being informed of the Lewinsky affair."[35] Basically, Clinton's character ratings plummeted because the vast majority of Americans (86%), according to a Fox News/Opinion Dynamics poll (2/13/99), felt that he had done something wrong. Specifically, 73% believed that he perjured himself when testifying before the grand jury about the Lewinsky affair, but in a later Fox poll, 72% felt he had probably not learned his lesson and "would lie again" (7/29/99). And, according to a CNN/Gallup/*USA Today* poll, hardly anyone (3%) thinks that Clinton's moral standards are "higher than the average married man," while 61% believe his moral standards are lower (3/4/99).

The bottom line is that, as a result of the scandal that led to his impeachment, many more Americans "think less of him" (42%) than "more of him" (7%), although 49% "think about the same of him"(Gannett poll, 1/11/99). Also, a majority of Americans (57%) hold that Clinton's presidency has "damaged the country's moral values" and 73% contend that he broke his 1992 promise to have "the most ethical administration in the history of the republic" (Fox poll, 2/13/99). As a result, few Americans (20%) think historians will remember Clinton as "a highly respected leader," but a high percentage (68%) believe he will be remembered as "a President under the cloud of constant scandals" (Fox poll, 10/21/99).

But despite such negative public opinion relating to Clinton's personal character, other poll data cast doubt on how much weight should be given to these grim character ratings. It has already been shown that, despite what Americans think of his flawed character, they nonetheless refused to give him anything but high job approval ratings. Polls have also revealed that, despite everything, they have not lost that must respect for him. According to a January 21, 1999, CNN/*Time* poll, almost half of the citizenry (48%) say they still respect Clinton, while 50% said in a Fox News/Opinion Dynamics poll (2/12/99) that he "has the honesty and integrity to serve as President."[36] More enlightening, however, is the public sentiment, expressed months after the scandalous ordeal ended, that 61% of the American people believe "the country is better off today than it was before Bill Clinton was elected President" (Fox poll, 12/7/99). This is not surprising, since earlier in a CNN/Gallup/*USA Today* poll (8/23/98), 56% said "yes" to the question, "All things considered, are you glad Bill Clinton is President, or not?"

But in trying to make sense out of the public's general tolerance of the Clinton-Lewinsky affair, a few key public opinion findings must be stressed. In the first place, as noted, most Americans never believed the Lewinsky affair to be a serious public matter, but regarded it as a private one. In fact, in a series of 1998–1999 CNN/Gallup/*USA Today* polls, the majority of Americans consistently held that "Bill Clinton's personal life does not matter . . . as long as he does a good job running the country" (57%, 56%, 54%, 56%, on 9/1, 7/29, 3/22, and 1/28, respectively). But most importantly, apparently few Americans were shocked by Clinton's personal behavior, possibly reflecting a decline in the moral standards in modern American society. In an ABC News poll, 59% said they believed that "most Presidents [had] extramarital affairs while President," and a very high percentage (75%) asserted that "Clinton's faults" were "no worse than other Presidents'" (2/1/98).

In summary, Americans acknowledged Clinton's personal defects, yet they (64%) still regarded him as a strong leader. They also evidently considered these personal flaws as dishonorable, yet at the same time quite human and not surprising. In fact, most Americans thought that Clinton's personal behavior was similar to that of past presidents. But very importantly, most Americans felt that Clinton's private sexual life was not related to how he performed as president. In Brody's words: "It appears, however, that the judgment of Clinton as a person is largely irrelevant to the judgment of his performance as President. Indeed, a large fraction of the public has resisted efforts to convert the Lewinsky affair into a politically consequential matter."[37]

Ken Starr: He Never Did "Get It"

"My job is my duty!" Starr exclaimed. It is about "the integrity of the oath" and "the sanctity of the political process," he bellowed.[38] But the American people never believed him. To them, it was once again about sordid partisan politics and it was clear to them, even to many scrupulous Republicans, that Starr was pursuing President Clinton for blatantly partisan reasons. The polls showed, in no uncertain terms, that from the beginning to the end of Starr's investigation, a clear consensus of Americans wanted Starr to halt his probe into the Lewinsky affair, even if his charges were true.

Once Starr proved that Clinton indeed did have a sexual relationship with that woman—Ms. Lewinsky—and lied about it, the American people still did not support Starr's probe. To most Americans, it was still all about sex—the sexual acts, cigars and all, and the lies to try to cover up the affair. Starr tried to elevate it to the equivalent of Watergate, or the Iran-Contra affair, but he failed to convince the American people, not only because his goals were so transparently partisan, but mainly because the constitutional questions he had raised about obstruction of justice and perjury were not related to the public's business. In covering Starr's investigation for *The New York Times*, Alison Mitchell reported: "A difficulty is that Mr. Starr has raised such serious constitutional questions about perjury and obstruction of justice, [yet] this cover-up is all about sex, not about a burglary against a political party or using the Central Intelligence Agency to hinder an investigation by the Federal Bureau of Investigation."[39]

But despite his inability to persuade the American people to see it his way and his growing unpopularity in the polls, Starr pressed on, even though the American public opinion seemed to oppose virtually every step he took. Why? Public opinion poll data, as already noted and to be explored still further, suggest that Americans resented Starr because his inquisition, unlike the much more popularly supported probes into Watergate and Iran-Contra, constituted a blatant disregard for the personal privacy rights of the president. To Americans, not only was Starr's investigation not worth the enormous time and millions of dollars spent, but to the majority of Americans Starr exhibited incredible mean-spiritedness in his attempt to trash Clinton and the institution of the presidency for some partisan advantage (e.g., to possibly enable the Republicans to pick up a few more House and Senate seats in the 1998 congressional elections). To countless Americans, Starr's relentless probe into Clinton's personal life not only lacked dignity, but also showed a flagrant and tasteless disrespect for the office of the president of the United States. Because of this, Ken Starr earned the pathetic distinction of being one of the most unpopular public personalities in the history of public opinion polling. According to Frank Newport, "despite Starr's protestations that he was only doing the job he was appointed to do, he leaves the office as one of the most negatively evaluated public figures measured in Gallup Poll annals. About two-thirds of Americans said they had a negative opinion of Starr earlier this year, . . . and the same number said they disapproved of the job he did as Independent Counsel."[40]

Specific poll numbers reveal that most Americans disliked Starr and the job he was doing from the very beginning to the end of his investigation. Newport points out that as soon as the public became aware that Starr was going to investigate the Clinton-Lewinsky affair, "Starr's image quickly turned more negative."[41] In January of 1998, Starr had only a 24% unfavorability rating in the Gallup poll, but by mid-February his unfavorability rating had doubled to 46% and was rising at a record pace. By mid-October, not long after Starr released his controversial report to Congress, his unfavorability score reached a new high of 60%, increasing to 62% on February 8, 1999, shortly after the Senate voted to acquit Clinton, and then continued to climb to an almost unbelievable 66% unfavorable by March 7, 1999. In this same March Gallup poll, only 28% said they approved of the job Starr had done as independent counsel, with only a bare majority of Republicans (52%) approving of his job performance. In fact, the vast majority of Americans (73%) regarded Starr as "a loser" in the whole impeachment process.[42]

Newport asserts that there are plenty of poll data that help to explain why most Americans held such a negative impression of Starr. In the first place, it appears that most Americans never perceived Starr's probe into the Lewinsky matter as anything but partisan, with 53% claiming that Starr was "acting more like a 'persecutor' than prosecutor" (39%). Americans (71%) also were not happy with Starr's decision to release his report to Congress with the sexual details of Clinton's affair with Lewinsky. According to the polls, Starr's behavior was not regarded as professional, but motivated with a goal of simply trying to damage Clinton politically. Only 38% felt Starr was concerned with "finding out the facts," while 57% felt his objective was to destroy Clinton.[43] In fact, to the Fox News/Opinion Dynamics question, "Who do you think is more of a stalker: Monica Lewinsky or Kenneth Starr?" 47% said Starr and only 22% answered Lewinsky, with 31% saying, "not sure."

In the final analysis, only a relatively small percentage of Americans appreciated Starr's efforts to take down President Clinton. In fact, only an unimpressive percentage (35%) felt, all things considered, that "Starr did a good job dealing with the Monica Lewinsky matter, while 54 percent held that he had done a 'bad job'" (*Newsweek* poll, 4/16/99). Also, according to this same poll, Americans had become disenchanted with the way independent counsels like Starr had been using the law to investigate wrongdoing by top government officials. Consequently, 58% answered "should not be extended" to the following question: "Do you think the law should be extended because independent counsels are important in preventing abuses of power, or the law should not be extended because independent counsels waste taxpayers' money and leave people under suspicion too long?" Starr's perceived misuse of the Office of Independent Counsel, causing a majority of Americans to want to abolish it, may be Starr's greatest legacy. The independent counsel law did die in mid-1999, but ironically the investigation into the Clinton-Lewinsky scandal did not. Hours before Democratic presidential nominee Al Gore delivered his acceptance speech at the 2000 Democratic Convention, news spread that Starr's successor, Robert Ray, had impaneled a new grand jury to determine whether Clinton should face criminal charges in connection with the Lewinsky affair. Predictably, an overwhelming percentage of the American people (67%) quickly said that, regarding the Lewinsky matter, "no further action against Clinton is needed" (CNN/*USA Today*/Gallup Poll, 8/19/2000). On January 19, 2001, Ray decided to close the book on the ugly Lewinsky matter after Clinton agreed to: accept a five-year suspension of his law li-

cense in Arkansas; acknowledge that he knowingly gave misleading and evasive answers during discovery under Judge Susan
Webber Wright; and forfeit the collection of any legal fees in connection with the case.

CONCLUDING COMMENTS

Since this book is about public opinion polling, the real purpose of
this chapter was to demonstrate how polls can be used to help us
understand a complex social event; in our specific example, public
reaction to the Clinton-Lewinsky scandal and the impact public
opinion likely had on the political processes regarding the handling of the affair. For example, public opinion itself played a role
in how the various political actors (e.g., Clinton, Starr,[44] Congress)
responded to the scandal, the most obvious being Clinton's decision not to resign because public opinion was strongly behind him
and the Senate's decision not to convict Clinton in an impeachment
trial because public opinion was strongly against a conviction.

I hope I have succeeded in showing how examining a legion of
poll data can help us gain valuable insights into a complex situation, helping us to understand it better. On the surface, the Clinton-Lewinsky affair seemed simple enough, but beneath the surface a complex and high-stakes political power struggle was being
played out. As a married man, Clinton committed an immoral act
by having an ignoble adulterous affair, but as our president, he
frankly took a really stupid risk. If found out (and he must have
known that the chances would be fairly high in this new age of
"anything goes" in politics and the press), he risked not only his
presidency and his reputation in history, but his party's present
standing and future.

Overall, pollsters did an excellent job tracking public reaction to
breaking news on the Clinton-Lewinsky scandal from the start to
the finish. Public opinion scholars have long noted that the American people don't display that much specific knowledge about the
American political system, but as one of the most distinguished
political scientists of the twentieth century, V. O. Key Jr., often

stressed, they are not fools either. To Key, voters have an incredible instinct to understand the basics and respond with appropriate collective wisdom.[45] I think Key was right. An abundance of poll data, much of it presented in this chapter, conveys that most Americans not only followed the various developments in the Clinton-Lewinsky affair quite closely, but demonstrated remarkable sophistication by placing the scandal in "proper" perspective—in fact, in a perspective that matched the thinking of most objective legal and political scholars commenting on the dynamics of the scandal.

To summarize, the polls showed that the vast majority of Americans saw Starr's probe into the Clinton-Lewinsky affair for what it really was—dirty partisan politics. They were convinced that Clinton was guilty of the charges Starr brought against him, yet they vehemently disagreed with Starr over the seriousness of the matter. To most Americans, the affair involved a very private sexual matter unrelated to Clinton's performance as president. Consequently, most Americans consistently told pollsters that Starr and the Republican Congress should stop wasting the taxpayers' money and devote their attention to more important public policy concerns. When Starr and the Republicans refused to drop the matter, public opinion turned increasingly negative toward Starr and the Republicans, and, somewhat predictably, defensively supportive of President Clinton. Throughout the whole nasty ordeal, public opinion remained quite stable against the inquisition and impeachment. Starr may have won several petty court battles against Clinton, but in the end he lost the war to Clinton and, most clearly, the public opinion crusade.

Chapter Nine

□ □ □

Polling in Other Countries

In Albania, for example, we were offered the choice of riding a mule
or going miles by foot to conduct interviews in many rural areas.
—Mary McIntosh and Ronald Hinckley,
The Public Perspective, July/August, 1992[1]

George Gallup Jr. exclaimed in an interview a few years ago that "Polling is in its infancy—it's just getting started!"[2] But this remark seems quite strange in light of his father's legendary pioneering efforts in survey research nearly sixty years ago. The comment is also odd because he is certainly well aware of the heralded accomplishments in the polling profession over the past few decades, making pollsters highly paid and respected professionals eagerly sought by those who feel that they simply must have an accurate reading of the public's pulse to survive and prosper. The truth is that most observers have applauded polling as a field that "has arrived."

But Gallup Jr. is not talking about the status of polling in the United States, he is referring to the position of polling worldwide, where its overall status is less than lofty. He and his brother, Alex Gallup, want to see public opinion research expand into many other countries and eventually reach the level of sophistication that it enjoys in the United States, and they want to be part of this movement. Why? Because they want to help promote their father's dream through the George H. Gallup Institute, a nonprofit polling organization dedicated to using public opinion research to help societies solve their problems. As Gallup Jr. reflected: "My father's continuing dream was to identify constructive ideas that would help humanity and then help leaders refine them in light of public opinion. He always felt that the public was ahead of most politicians anyway, and that public opinion research could be used to help enlighten our leaders."[3] Of course, George Gallup felt passionately that public opinion polling was a true friend of democracy and an enemy of totalitarianism. Consequently, to Gallup and his sons, the expansion of polling in the world would necessarily help promote democracy at the expense of totalitarian dictators.

The purpose of this chapter is to explore the spread of public opinion polling in other parts of the world. Specifically, the goal is to shed some light on the following questions:

What has been the influence of the American polling industry on the development of public opinion polling in other nations?

Why has public opinion research expanded so rapidly and successfully in some countries, yet has failed to do so in others?

What specific obstacles have pollsters faced in trying to conduct and publicize poll results in various countries of the world?

More specifically, what differences in "polling climates" can be seen in modern democratic nations versus emerging democratic nations versus authoritarian and totalitarian societies?

Have public opinion research efforts helped to promote democracy in other countries?

THE INFLUENCE OF AMERICAN POLLSTERS ON POLLING IN OTHER COUNTRIES

Public opinion polling is an American creation and, by now, an American institution. Led by the pioneers in scientific polling—George Gallup, Archibald Crossley, and Elmo Roper in the 1930s and 1940s—these pollsters and their successors were responsible for building a giant and successful polling industry in America that attracted worldwide attention and admiration. Given the obvious benefits of public opinion polling for those involved in business, entertainment, politics and government, and academic research, opinion polling was destined to spread to many other countries throughout the world. Of course, the desire to bring public opinion polling to other nations naturally created a demand for American pollsters since they were, as a whole, the best-trained and most experienced pollsters in the world.

American pollsters were first recruited to help develop a polling industry in the other mature and relatively affluent democracies in the world, such as Britain, Canada, Germany, and Australia, to name only a few. Britain was the first country to recruit and use American pollsters to help with the development of their polling profession. At first, during the early years of polling in Britain, the British tried to employ probability sampling, the popular sampling techniques used by American pollsters, but for sundry reasons random sampling simply did not work well in Britain, so it gave way to quota sampling. Ironically, this was the method that proved so unreliable in the early years of scientific polling in the United States. Humphrey Taylor notes that "the relative failure of random sampling in Britain is still a mystery for which I have seen no satisfactory explanation."[4]

Polling spread rapidly in developed democracies because these nations could easily see how beneficial polling had been to various consumers of polls in America. Businesses felt that these new scientific polls could be used to help business leaders get to know their markets better, specifically by finding out about consumer preferences so they could increase their sales and, thus, their profits. Educational institutions realized how much scientific polling could help in their research, especially among scholars wanting to shift their emphasis from qualitative to quantitative studies. Modern survey research methods afforded them the opportunity to collect reliable public opinion in their countries on all sorts of subjects, ranging from attitudes toward various social institutions and processes to human sexual behavior. Of course, politicians elsewhere, aware of the effective use of polls in American politics, wanted to employ American pollsters to work that "old poll magic" for them in their political careers. According to John Maggs, the demand for American pollsters has become so acute that possibly "America's latest and greatest export may be Washington political consultants, who are polling, focus-grouping, and triangulating all over the world."[5] Naturally, to keep pace with the use of polling by others, the media in these countries have also had to develop a taste for polling, resulting in more sophisticated analysis of polls by the media, as well as a growing number of media polls.

Although American polling firms such as Gallup International have been polling in many countries for decades now and American pollsters have assisted those in other countries in the development of their own polling firms, the presence of American pollsters elsewhere in the world today is more prevalent than ever because of all the newly developing democratic nations that have emerged in the last few decades. The fact is that the number of democracies in the world has doubled in the last twenty-five years.[6] As we shall see later in this chapter, legitimate public opinion polling is practically impossible to conduct under authoritarian or totalitarian governments, yet can flourish in democratic states. As more countries have become democratic, the demand for American pollsters has surged, although the demand for pollsters from Britain and other mature democracies with veteran pollsters has also increased. Maggs asserts that American pollsters are now commonly "on display in governments and election campaigns throughout Europe, Latin America, and even Africa." Sarcastically, he contends that this army of American pollsters and political consultants, "many of whom worked for Clinton, may well be the President's most lasting contribution to world politics."[7]

In addition to seeing more American polling firms expanding their international polling business (e.g., Zogby International expanded into Nigeria in 2000),[8] Maggs is right in saying that many American pollsters, some so famous that they are virtually household names, can be seen serving as campaign consultants and pollsters for governments and candidates in many different countries. In the 2000 presidential election in Mexico, for example, former Clinton pollsters and political consultants James Carville and Dick Morris served the two frontrunners for the Mexican presidency. Carville coached Francisco Labastida, the candidate of the once dominant Partido Revolucionario Institucional (PRI), to defeat, while Morris advised challenger Vincente Fox to a dramatic upset victory. Previously, Carville and Morris had gone head-to-head in Honduras and Argentina. In fact, they now claim that they only want to poll and consult for candidates in foreign countries. They are not alone, given that the money is often very good and in cash. Stan Greenberg, another former Clinton confidant and pollster, also claims that he only likes to poll abroad for politicians, boasting a string of election successes in foreign countries for left-of-center candidates in the 1990s. He successfully polled for and advised to victory Nelson Mandela and Thabo Mbeki in South Africa in 1994 and 1999, respectively; Tony Blair in Britain in 1997; Gerhard Schroeder in Germany in 1998; and Ehud Barak in Israel in 1999; but did fail with Eduardo Duhalde in Argentina in 1999.[9]

Although the influence of American pollsters intensified during the Clinton era, they had been polling for governments and political candidates before Clinton. For example, Dick Wirthlin and other Republican pollsters and consultants worked for right-of-center candidates in the 1980s,[10] while the "godfather" in the business of political consulting/polling, Joe Napolitan, who worked for John Kennedy, Lyndon Johnson, and Hubert Humphrey, has been exporting his expertise for decades, not always serving the most righteous political leaders. Napolitan has worked for Ferdinand Marcos of the Philippines, dictator Hugo Banter in Bolivia and Omar Torrijos in Panama, a Communist politician in Italy, and a Gaullist aspirant in France. However, he drew the line with President Alberto Fujimori of Peru, refusing to work in his corrupt "reelection" campaign in 2000.[11]

American political consultants and pollsters have been desperately sought after in former Communist regimes that have been emerging topsy-turvy into tenuous, shaky democracies. As Ronald Hinckley and Andrew Kohut note, "Public opinion polling is a product of modern democracies, but today it is being practiced quite successfully in former Soviet bloc countries where democratic traditions are just developing. In a region turned upside down, where one formerly interpreted affairs in terms of who stood next to whom on the review atop Lenin's mausoleum, the thought of being able to conduct scientific surveys does seem a little strange."[12] Despite the problems of conducting polls in these countries, Western pollsters, including many Americans, have nonetheless been conducting modestly successful polls in many of these countries, although success has been uneven in former Communist nations owing to their unique socioeconomic and political climates.

Veteran American pollster Warren Mitofsky, former media pollster and now president of Mitofsky International, describes exit polling in Russia as "exhilarating, but frustrating." Nevertheless, he believes that his polling in Russia has been quite successful, especially considering the reality that legitimate public opinion polling is a new phenomenon in Russia.[13] Although polling has met with moderate success there, American pollsters report that polling has generally not been as successful in Eastern European countries. Mary McIntosh and Ronald Hinckley, commenting on their frustrations of overseeing the conducting of valid polls for the United States Information Agency in Eastern Europe, lament: "Our experience indicates that the quest for reliable East European survey data has often taken a path as Byzantine as their region's pursuit of democratic politics and free markets."[14]

The influence of American pollsters can also be seen in many countries in the Middle East and Asia, either directly or indirectly. Gallup International and the Roper Center for Public Opinion Research not only conduct polls in several Asian countries, for example, but the Roper Center has done a laudable job cooperating with the Japanese to develop archives of polling data on Japanese society so that it can be better understood.[15] Gallup pollsters have also done a commendable job conducting comprehensive polls in China in an attempt to disclose little-known public opinion facts about the Chinese. Brian Palmer remarks that Gallup interviewers have randomly interviewed thousands of Chinese citizens in the past few years from the "far-flung corners of the country," using their findings to reveal "a snapshot of a country in the vortex of change." But, according to Palmer, such polling may be more difficult or impossible in the foreseeable future because the Chinese government in August of 1999 issued new regulations that will "sharply restrict foreign market research firms—both in what they can ask and what they can release."[16] From all indications, China is still a rather closed totalitarian society and is particularly leery about the motives of foreign pollsters.[17] However, Du Yan, director of China Survey Research, acknowledges that, although the Chinese government has been skeptical about permitting foreigners to poll in China, under most circumstances insiders have been allowed to conduct "approved" surveys.[18]

Overall then, the apparent obsession with polls in the United States has, not surprisingly, spread to countries all over the world, even to countries that supposedly detest Western culture and practices, such as Iran. Even there the influence of American consultants and pollsters is blatant. As Howard Schneider observes, Iranians "read American political journals to glean campaign tactics, use modern polling techniques to hone their message and offer alluring close-up photos of their leading candidates."[19] Iranians, especially the younger Iranians, just can't seem to resist the benefits that modern polling offers to those seeking political change or political office. These Iranians, especially those educated in survey research at Western universities, can be seen using polls to, for example, persuade "the reformist President, Mohammad Khotemi, to don a snappier shirt under his cleric's robes" or to launch "negative attacks that helped galvanize youths against former President and parliamentary contender Ali Akbar Hashemi Rafsanjani, considered a possible barrier to change."[20]

POLLING IN MATURE
DEMOCRATIC COUNTRIES

Since the 1960s and 1970s, public opinion polling has spread rapidly outside the United States, but especially in the more mature and modern democracies such as Canada, Israel, Australia, Japan, and in Western Europe. Successful polling cannot be conducted very easily in just any country because certain prerequisites are required. Polling has normally flourished in modern, stable democratic societies because generally these societies have satisfied the basic prerequisites of acceptable opinion research. Developed democratic countries, for example, are open and free, allowing their citizens to feel comfortable in giving honest answers to interviewers without fearing that their responses may be found out by the government and retaliatory steps taken against them for answers that governmental officials do not like. For polling to prosper, there has to be at least minimal respect for the practices of public opinion research. Despite the predictable and sometimes harsh criticisms of pollsters in democratic countries, pollsters nonetheless do receive enough respect and cooperation in modern democracies to permit them to conduct decent polls. Polling in mature democracies is also generally accepted by the media as a valid method for gathering public opinion, and reporters, columnists, and editors normally do a pretty good job in reporting and analyzing poll data free of government and interest group influence that in nondemocracies or struggling democracies has had a way of corrupting the honest, free, and independent reporting of poll results. In short, as international expert Tim Lomperis stresses, polling cannot flourish in countries that do not provide an acceptable climate for opinion research, but fortunately democratic countries do provide that necessary climate.[21]

Modern democracies also tend to be relatively affluent and technologically advanced, making it far easier for pollsters to conduct costly yet methodologically sophisticated polls. An affluent and technologically developed society is not theoretically an absolute prerequisite for public opinion polling, but practically speaking, advanced polling techniques are quite expensive and clients in poorer countries simply cannot afford them. Also, valid polling can be virtually impossible to conduct in countries that have poor communication and transportation systems, making it practically impossible to reach and interview people, to say nothing about the almost prohibitive costs associated with trying to reach respondents. J. David Kennamer, professor of mass communications at Virginia Commonwealth University, asserts that those in affluent democracies often take for granted the developed communications infrastructure that makes polling much easier and relatively inexpensive. In most countries, however, quality polling is very challenging because few people have phones and, overall, people are extremely difficult to reach for interviews, causing pollsters to develop survey "solutions that are certainly creative but perhaps indefensible from a methodological perspective."[22]

Polling in Britain

Britain provides a good example of what it's like to poll in a mature democracy other than the United States. British society satisfies all of the basic prerequisites just mentioned to facilitate modern public opinion research. Britain is affluent, technologically advanced, has a free and sophisticated press, and its citizens are relatively well educated and informed and quite respectful of its democratic institutions and practices, including the place of opinion polling in its open, democratic society. Yet every democratic country is still somewhat different because of their unique histories, customs, and traditions, which pollsters must acknowledge and accommodate to poll successfully. The British are no different. They are unique, just ask the French. Consequently, polling in Britain presents similar challenges to pollsters who also poll in other developed democratic countries, yet still pollsters must confront unique challenges in Britain because, for example, often words, expressions, gestures, symbols, and images convey different meanings to people of different countries. James Carville, for example, found this out the hard way when advising and polling for Francisco Labastida in the 2000 presidential election in Mexico (not that Mexico is a mature democracy). Carville's "It's the economy, stupid" slogan worked well for Bill Clinton during the 1992 presidential campaign, but his slogan for Labastida, "It's the right kind of change, stupid," backfired terribly when Mexicans were offended because they thought that Labastida was calling them stupid. Labastida, once ahead by 20 points, lost and Carville's reputation for his political acumen plummeted.[23]

Britain has a long, unique, and rather impressive history in public opinion polling, although, as in the United States, British pollsters have certainly blown calls and faced public humiliation from time to time. Although opinion research, especially political opinion research, didn't really take off until the 1960s in Britain, the British have engaged in modest market research and some political polling since the mid-1940s. In fact, Winston Fletcher, in reviewing the development of survey research in Britain, notes that records on political polling in Britain date back to 1945. He emphasizes that political polling, as in the United States and in most developed democracies, is overwhelmed by the ubiquity of market surveys, constituting only a small percentage of the total pounds spent on opinion surveys. Fletcher points out that market research in Britain is very well developed, with the United Kingdom's Market Research Society having celebrated its fiftieth birthday in 1997. He stresses that "market research is now pretty big business. With £7 bn [billion] in turnover and steady, compound growth of 8–10 per cent a year, the UK research business has done extremely well of late. Moreover, the Association of Market Survey Organizations (AMSO) forecasts growth of 15–20 per cent this year."[24] Additionally, he boasts that Britain is a "world leader" in market research exportation, reporting that "about 20 percent of UK market research turnover comes from international surveys, and international work is growing faster than domestic." He concludes that market surveys in Britain are so pervasive that "today there are few manufacturing companies, media houses, government departments, public bodies, academic institutions or even retailers in Britain which do not integrate research into their decision-making processes."[25]

Despite the reality that about 95% of opinion research money in Britain is spent on market surveys, as is the case in the United States, it still seems that political polling receives practically all of the attention. Of course, this is because political polls are thrust into the limelight during elections by the media. As in the United States and other modern democracies, the use of political polls in Britain by politicians, interest groups, and the media has always generated controversy, frequently centering on the charges that political campaigns and media stories are too "poll-driven" and poll predictions tend to unduly influence election results or at least, according to the outspoken Welsh Deputy Labour Party leader Aneurin Bevan, "take the poetry out of politics."[26] The Brits, possibly just for "the bloody fun of it," love to criticize the political polls, as Americans do. Despite the fact that most poll predictions have been fairly accurate since 1945 when the first poll predictions of elections were recorded, the British press and people love to dwell on the occasions when the pollsters misfired, most notably in the 1970 and 1992 British elections.

But British critics, especially the media critics, seem to be harsher than their American counterparts, attacking pollsters mercilessly unless the pollsters are almost exactly on target. Nick Sparrow, for example, writing for *The Guardian* (London), refuses to give pollsters a break, noting that "the 1992 election was an undoubted disaster for the pollsters—they failed to predict Major's victory—but 1997 was seen as a success." However, he contends that their predictions in 1997 when they successfully predicted Tony Blair's Labour Party victory was not good enough, stressing that "the pollsters' average error of 2% that year was the third worst result for the industry since 1945. It was as bad as the 1970 election . . . that provoked a Market Research Society investigation into our methods."[27] Fletcher, another journalist, employs the same rigorous standards, pointing out initially that for pollsters "1992 was not their only cock-up. They also bombed in 1970. And in the 13 elections between 1945 and 1987, some 40 percent of pollsters' forecasts were inaccurate by more than plus or minus 2 percent."[28] Wow! I'm glad I am polling in America, where most critics feel that calling elections within a 3% error range is reasonably acceptable.

To make their polls more precise, British pollsters, sometimes working with American pollsters and methodologists, have experimented with various survey research techniques. Veteran polling guru Humphrey Taylor applauds the British for trying to improve their polling techniques by experimenting with different survey methods because, in a study of polling in many different countries, he found that few polling firms in these countries have seriously tried to improve their survey methods. He maintains that this is so because most polling is used for market research and the results of such polls "are never validated and cannot be."[29] Business clients, who use marketing surveys, are not willing to pay for expensive new polling techniques that may improve accuracy, while the media normally judge polls "on their newsworthiness, not on their quality," Taylor claims. He stresses that it is unfortunate that his research found only a few polling companies that were interested in changing their survey methods to upgrade their polls. "Indeed," he concluded, "with the exception of the Brits, only the Japanese polling firms seem to be thinking of making changes."[30]

Henry Durant, who headed the Gallup Poll in Britain for many years, once exclaimed that political polling is "the stupidest of professions" because, he reasoned, who else would be so stupid as to risk career suicide by making election calls that can prove to be so humiliating when the actual election results are posted? Yet, as George Gallup rightfully held long ago, the real acid test of polling is having poll predictions of political contest outcomes virtually square with the actual election returns. Apparently, British political pollsters, like American political pollsters, have tried hard to improve their polling techniques, especially in light of blown election predictions. After British pollsters miscalled the 1970 British election, they sought to improve their polling techniques by experimenting with various survey methods, as well as looking more carefully at the impact turnout rates and late electoral shifts can have on their poll predictions.[31]

A unique feature of British polling is that their pollsters, even most of the American pollsters polling in Britain, have relied primarily on quota sampling, even though adequate sampling frames exist that could be used for probability (random) sampling. Quota sampling has been rejected by survey researchers as unacceptable in America since the early 1950s, yet in Britain and in most European countries it is the dominant approach. Taylor regards the use of quota sampling in Britain as the most striking difference between American and British polling practices, but he admits that for sundry reasons random sampling has proved overall less successful in accurately forecasting British election results than has quota sampling. Taylor asserts, "Given that Britain, unlike the United States, publishes electoral registers that include all possible voters—a perfect sampling frame—the relative failure of random sampling in Britain is still a mystery for which I have seen no satisfactory explanation."[32] Some British pollsters considered abandoning quota sampling for random sampling, and did experiment with random sampling in the 1997 British election, for which most pollsters accurately predicted Blair's Labour Party victory.[33]

In Britain, as in the United States and in many other modern democracies, polls play a dominant role in the political process, like it or not. As Taylor observes, "Polls do influence political agendas, financial support for candidates, media coverage of issues and candidates, and congressional voting. A president or prime minister with high poll ratings can influence the legislature much more . . . and parliamentary and congressional . . . members are avid poll readers."[34] But not only are British politicians poll-driven, as are probably most politicians in modern democracies today, but British journalists tend to be poll-driven too. Just a cursory review of political coverage by the British media would soon convince observers.

However, despite the love affair that British politicians, journalists, and citizens seem to have with polls, John Parker, Washington bureau chief of The Economist and longtime observer of the use of polls in Britain, told me in a personal interview that the "British obsession of polling is nothing like the obsession Americans have with polling." To him, most British really perceive polling as a sort of "pseudo-science," making the typical Brit place less faith in the poll numbers than do Americans. The British, he claims, are generally less quantitative and more qualitative oriented than Americans. Unlike so many Americans, Brits tend to see "more shades of gray," believing that polls just "capture the tip of the iceberg." Parker believes that the British are much more likely than Americans to distrust polls because they are more likely to lie to pollsters. He admits that the British people also love to focus on the horse-race aspects of political campaigns, but not as much as Americans, because Brits seem more concerned with more substantive social welfare issues than are Americans. Additionally, he notes, polling is somewhat more difficult in Britain because parliamentary elections are more complex (e.g., prime ministers are elected indirectly) and third parties play a greater role, presenting unique problems for pollsters. Parker also points out that polls get much more publicity in the United Sates than in Britain because of the enormous number of news organizations competing against each other, whereas in Britain there are basically only two broadcast networks (BBC and ITN) and only a handful of national newspapers.[35]

POLLING IN EMERGING DEMOCRACIES: RUSSIA, EASTERN EUROPE, AFRICAN, AND LATIN AMERICAN COUNTRIES

The experiences of most pollsters in developing democracies are quite similar, although clearly specific polling challenges are somewhat unique to each particular country because no two emerging democracies are exactly alike. In reviewing the literature regarding polling in developing democracies, as well as interviewing some who have polled in these countries, I found that pollsters tend to zero in on the same sort of challenges for conducting opinion surveys.

Probably the most obvious problem that pollsters face when polling in emerging democracies is that polling itself is a new, foreign phenomenon, and the role of polls has not been well established. In fact, polling is such a recent phenomenon in most of these emerging democracies that their whole culture and infra-structure can't as yet comfortably embrace and support public opinion polling. Kennamer points out that "Opinion polling has come to be one of the most important and visible manifestations of democratic and free-market societies. It is therefore only natural to expect that countries developing in these political and economic directions will want to adopt and adapt polling to their own situations."[36] However, he stresses that sophisticated public opinion polling cannot flourish in these countries in quick fashion because "opinion researchers in emerging democracies face challenges that are in many ways far more severe than those faced by the pioneers of American polling back in the 1930s."[37] For example, in America, democracy was already well established and respected by the time George Gallup and other survey researchers started to develop polling, providing a very friendly atmosphere for the development of a successful polling industry in the United States. Of course, the same was true for Britain and other mature democracies when polling developed in those countries. Even then, it took many decades for public opinion polling to reach a sophisticated level in these countries.

In sharp contrast, Kennamer contends that opinion research has simply come to these new, emerging democracies too fast, posing some obvious problems. He asserts, "Opinion polling, a product of mature democracies and market economies, has parachuted into an emerging economy and democracy, which certainly does not have the communications infrastructure to support it, may not have the institutional independence necessary to manage it, and with few exceptions does not have the critical facility within the media and universities to place the results in perspective."[38] Virtually no pollsters with experience conducting polls in emerging democracies disagree with this assessment. Let's look at some of the most problematic challenges in these developing democracies.

For many pollsters, especially those polling in former Communist countries or other countries formerly dominated by authoritarian or totalitarian rule, remnants from past histories and cultural tradition pose some problems in being able to conduct polls in a free manner, independent of the corrupting influence of political elites. Such elites are often suspicious of the intention of poll-sters, especially foreign pollsters and journalists, and may still have a knee-jerk tendency of biasing stories to protect and pro-mote the interests of politicians in power. For instance, Emmanuel Uwalaka, who has polled in Nigeria, a country that has struggled to develop a stable and enduring democracy, warns pollsters that "given the fragile nature of government in Third World Countries in general, and Africa in particular, the leaders look with suspi-cion at any research projects with foreign backing."[39] Conse-quently, he notes, pollsters will normally have to "go through offi-cial red-tape" in applying for a permit to gain clearance for conducting a poll.

Humphrey Taylor maintains that the greatest challenge in polling in emerging democracies is, in fact, being able to conduct freely "honest and independent polls" that, when completed, will be reported fairly and accurately. He claims that too often in these emerging democracies, which lack a lengthy democratic tradition, published polls "are, in varying degrees, corrupted by govern-ments, political parties, the media, and business interests."[40] For example, Taylor notes that politicians who have been elected in these developing democracies now have to live with a "painful truth" that they may learn to not like. "What democracy giveth, it can also take away."[41] That is, some of these politicians who ap-plauded public opinion polls and free elections as democratic ne-cessities suddenly try to undermine and corrupt the polls and the democratic elections as their popularity slips away and they are faced with losing their political office, as did Alberto Fujimori in Peru and Slobodan Milosevic in Yugoslavia in the 2000 elections.[42] To unscrupulous leaders hanging precariously on to their power, polls become a clear target since, as Taylor rightfully points out, "it is harder to steal elections when honest and accurate pre-elec-tion opinion polls and exit polls show someone else ahead"[43] (e.g., Alejandro Toledo tied or ahead of Fujimori in Peru and Vojislav Kostunica far in front of Milosevic in Yugoslavia in the 2000 races).

In "The Challenges of Surveying Public Opinion in an Emerging Democracy," Ansu-Kyeremeh Kwasi focuses on the emerging de-mocracy in Ghana. He argues that Ghana's "long historical experience of authoritarianism and dictatorships, including a period of a 'culture of silence,' to freedom of expression," poses a serious problem for honest, independent polling.[44] He holds that, despite the fact that Ghana has had eleven years of democracy, "the political conditions that enable polling have hardly prevailed long enough in Ghana for a tradition of public opinion surveys to develop."[45] Specifically, he contends that legitimate public opinion polling today cannot help but suffer from a recent history in which "successive one-party and military dictatorships" suppressed free expression, sometimes brutally, in Ghana, discouraging "the open statement of citizens' views and consequently measured public opinion."[46]

Kwasi emphasizes that Ghana's mostly nondemocratic tradition has caused journalists, who are basically ignorant of polling methodology and rather insensitive to the legitimizing role that polls should play in a democracy, to routinely misinterpret poll data, jump to erroneous conclusions, and have a tendency to bias the reporting of polls in favor of the leaders in power. These journalists are still fearful of possibly angering those in control who might want to flex their political muscle against any "disrespectful" journalist.[47] Furthermore, the citizenry is fearful of responding truthfully to pollsters. But how broadly can Kwasi's allegations about polling problems in Ghana be applied to the experiences of pollsters in other emerging democracies? The answer seems to be that it depends a lot on the particular country.

Generally, however, pollsters are more troubled with journalists doing a poor job in the reporting of poll results than with public reluctance to answer survey questions truthfully. The reality is that even journalists in mature democracies still have problems with reporting polls in an accurate and conceptually sophisticated manner, mostly because it takes considerable training and experience with the nuances of polling practices to do so. So naturally, pollsters are especially bothered by how their polls are interpreted and reported by the media in many developing democracies because journalists tend to be particularly inexperienced in the interpretation and reporting of poll data, as well as more prone to intentionally shade poll results to avoid any possible retaliation

against them by the politically powerful. Humphrey Taylor acknowledged the following about media reporting of polls in
emerging democracies:

> Many polls quoted in the media were wildly inaccurate, either
> because the numbers were changed or because they were
> never actually conducted. Some clients will pay handsomely
> for these phony polls.
> Honest, independent poll findings have been suppressed by the
> media because they displeased those with power.
> Polling firms not providing their clients with numbers they like
> (and are unwilling to alter the data) sometimes do not get
> paid.
> Contracts for multiple polls—for both the media and
> politicians—with reputable polling firms have been
> canceled because those with power did not like the early
> poll numbers and the polling firms would not change them.
> Some courageous media executives have suffered because they
> published accurate findings.[48]

However, despite the problems with accurate and honest reporting of poll results by the media, pollsters have generally found
that respondents in emerging democratic countries normally try to
answer poll questions very truthfully. For instance, Professor
James Gibson, who has polled extensively in Russia, told me in a
personal interview that he had experienced no unusual problem
obtaining truthful answers from the Russian people. In fact, he
stressed that he has "been impressed with their desire to have
their true, honest opinions expressed to the interviewers, including the 'don't knows.'"[49] Professor Ellen Carnaghan, who has
studied Russian responses to interviews in depth, agrees, telling
me that "under Communism, Soviet respondents may have feared
repercussions for truthfully answering survey questions, but there
is no evidence that Russians fear repercussions today. Indeed, they
are rather quick to provide negative information."[50] And in a specific study of "don't know" responses by Russian respondents, she
concluded that "while it is not possible to conclude definitively

that fear played no role in making Russians reluctant to answer survey questions, its role does not seem to have been a particularly large one. Instead, for most Russians, most of the time, if they did not answer questions it was because they had little interest and minimal information: they did not have an opinion."[51]

Professor Uwalaka also told me that in his experience polling in Nigeria, "The average Nigerian feels free to speak his or her mind to interviewers, despite a long, past tradition of authoritarian military rule in Nigeria." He noted that not only would Nigerian respondents not fear repercussions for truthfully responding to interviewers, but they are eager to answer truthfully, even if their answers are critical of the government, because they believe that their answers may be used to bring about positive change.[52] Regarding the giving of truthful responses to survey questions in Russia, Eastern Europe, Mexico, and Argentina, other pollsters have also concluded that, for the most part, respondents in these emerging democracies, despite their past experiences living under authoritarian regimes, seem to provide quite honest opinions to interviewers, apparently undercutting the myth that people living in these countries fear answering poll questions in a truthful manner.

But of all the problems reported by pollsters in trying to conduct reliable polls in emerging democracies, practical problems apparently present the greatest frustrations. Experienced pollsters acknowledge that possibly their worst problem is recruiting and training personnel, especially interviewers and supervisors who will learn, accept, and seriously uphold rigorous Western polling standards. For example, McIntosh and Hinckley have stressed how difficult it has been to find and train people to conduct polls in Eastern European nations: "We wanted people who were open to conducting polls by Western standards, and who did not have a political agenda."[53] When I asked the renowned pollster John Zogby point blank what he expected to be his biggest challenge in expanding his polling operations in Nigeria, he immediately responded, "Training interviewers and field supervisors!" He noted more specifically that it would be a challenge to get interviewers and supervisors (and supervisors for supervisors) to respect the importance of actually interviewing representative people who would satisfy his quota sampling demands. He told me that in the United States, by sharp comparison, a CATI system is typically used by pollsters, by which all of the well-trained interviewers conduct telephone interviews and enter responses on their computers in the same room monitored closely by supervisors.[54]

Of course, Zogby is also touching on another basic survey research problem encountered by pollsters in emerging democracies. That is, few people have phones, so face-to-face interviewing is a must. Survey researcher Gibson, for example, estimates that probably around 40–45% of Russian citizens have phones.[55] Uwalaka speculates that the home phone penetration rate in Nigeria is about 10%,[56] while Kennamer says that only one in seven have a phone in Argentina.[57] Of course, the very fact that face-to-face field interviews have to be conducted to collect survey data causes a lot of problems for pollsters that are not present in America. Obviously, just reaching respondents poses a serious problem. In fact, Gibson describes face-to-face sampling in South Africa as "a bit of a nightmare" because the costs of interviewing are driven up "sky high" since many whites live in very inaccessible gated communities, whereas some blacks live in "hostiles," which tend to be potentially violent areas controlled by "unfriendly" political parties, making them too dangerous for field interviewers. These obstacles make it practically impossible to represent all people in a national poll.[58]

Virtually all pollsters who conduct face-to-face polls in developing democracies report similar problems, although the specific obstacles vary from country to country. Since emerging democracies are normally much less affluent than most developed democracies, pollsters are forced to work with woefully inadequate transportation and communication systems as well as unreliable energy supplies. When polling in Eastern Europe, McIntosh and Hinckley noted that unexpected "power outages have resulted in a day's data processing being lost. Inadequate transportation systems in many countries often made it impossible to get to rural areas. In Albania, for example, we were offered the choice of riding a mule or going miles by foot to conduct interviews in many rural areas."[59] In Russia, Gibson says the vast size of the country makes face-to-face interviewing very tough, especially since the transportation is quite unreliable—trains frequently do not run on time and plane flights are often canceled. As in so many struggling democracies, he adds that the communications network is antiquated, affecting the reliability of phone, fax, and Internet use. All of this, he emphasizes, makes polling more inconvenient, time-consuming, and expensive.[60] Beyond these difficulties, in some countries even obtaining basic and essential supplies such as paper, typewriter ribbons, and ink for copying machines can be a problem. According to McIntosh and Hinckley, "Some pollsters in the region have adopted the practice of making just one copy of the questionnaire for each interviewer and then instructing the interviewer to record the responses on a separate sheet of paper. While this is a creative solution, we find it too error prone."[61]

Unlike in such countries as the United States, Britain, France, Germany, and Japan, where only one language is spoken prevalently, in many of these developing democracies no single official language is recognized, making questionnaire construction and interviewing very difficult and costly. Gibson explains how questionnaire design and implementation is exceptionally tedious in South Africa because eleven official languages are recognized, although he said you could get 100% penetration by using eight.[62] Uwalaka says that drafting and implementing workable questionnaires in Nigeria is even more challenging because "there are over 200 other languages being spoken in Nigeria," besides Igbo, the language he used to interview people in just two local areas. Because of the absence of a universal language in so many of the developing democracies, he claims that survey research is made particularly difficult, especially since words and concepts such as democracy, freedom, and human rights, when translated into different languages, take on such different meanings. Consequently, he concludes, because of the enormous number of languages and subcultures, the administration of valid national polls becomes, for all practical purposes, impossible.[63]

The rather low literacy rates in so many of these emerging democracies also present a problem for pollsters, although some of these countries, such as Russia and the Czech Republic, have quite high literacy rates. However, in countries like South Africa, Nigeria, Ghana, and Mexico, to cite only a few, literacy rates are low, sometimes around 25–35%, making effective interviewing very hard. To overcome this problem, interviewers have had to use special translators and picture or illustrative show cards to convey a question, yet too often something gets lost in the translation.[64]

Finally, another source of frustration for pollsters in most developing democracies is the lack of adequate sampling frames, especially ones that reliably account for all adults within the country. No sampling frame in any country, even in the United States, is perfect, yet in most mature, affluent democracies adequate sampling frames are available that can be used to draw respectable representative samples. However, reliable sampling frames, even for partial populations within most emerging democracies, are not normally available, mostly because such countries do not have the technologies or the money to maintain costly and technologically challenging current sampling frames.[65] Consequently, pollsters, without reliable representative sampling frames for the entire adult population, cannot even think about conducting polls nationwide using random sampling techniques. As a result, pollsters almost exclusively use versions of quota sampling or even "representative" panels to survey public opinion, sometimes devising quite creative ideas for developing makeshift sample frames that can adequately serve their quota sampling needs.[66]

POLLING IN AUTHORITARIAN OR TOTALITARIAN COUNTRIES

Reliable public opinion polling cannot be conducted in authoritarian or totalitarian countries for one obvious reason—such societies are closed or controlled by their governments. A basic prerequisite of public opinion polling is openness and freedom, because meaningful polling cannot be carried out in a country where its political leaders dominate their people, as well as the pollsters, and where freedom of expression does not exist. Naturally, if opinion researchers cannot measure what the people in a country really think, what sense does it make to conduct a public opinion poll? More specifically, if the people do not feel free to criticize their political leaders for their actions or if pollsters cannot ask the questions they want to the people they want, what purpose does a public opinion poll serve? If political leaders rule as dictators, ignoring the will of the people, is it not a waste of time and money to conduct a public opinion poll?

China as an Example

Even in struggling, emerging democracies such as Peru under Fujimori or Yugoslavia under Milosevic, where democratic traditions like free elections and public opinion polling have been inconsistently accepted and rejected, the use of polling has at least begun, which is not the case in a totalitarian country such as China, where free elections and legitimate public opinion polling have no history at all. This does not mean, however, that no polling is conducted whatsoever.

Du Yan, who founded and became director of the China Survey Research (CSR) and who has been referred to as "China's Gallup," acknowledges that polling in China is very different than in Western democracies because the Chinese political culture has no genuine tolerance for free or open polling, instead placing restrictions on what pollsters can ask and how poll results can be reported. For example, he points out that political polls especially are not commonly conducted in China because the results may be too politically sensitive and disturbing to the Chinese leadership. Chinese politicians particularly restrict polling on international issues because "the government is concerned that survey findings may be regarded as China's official stand because the newspapers in which survey results are published are official. The government wants to be the only spokesman for China in international politics." Du Yan mentions that once his CSR firm polled on the Persian Gulf War, but the government would not permit the release of the poll's results.[67]

In fact, he asserts that in their closed society, the government controls the reporting of polls and, as a result, "on the whole not many polls are published in China." He does claim that those polls "conducted for the media still stand a better chance to be made public." But the problem is that the content of the polls and the release of the polls are still censored and monitored by the government. Also, most polls are conducted for private consumption and very few for public consumption, and consequently few poll results are released to the media. The ones that are released normally are reviewed by governmental officials first. "If some journalist tries to learn from us about a survey conducted for a government agency, we'll direct him to the agency."[68]

Du Yan states that face-to-face, telephone, and mail surveys are all used in China, but because few Chinese have phones with direct lines in urban areas (e.g., only one direct phone line may run to an apartment complex), and rural people have almost no phones, while mail surveys are methodologically problematic and normally used only to target special populations, the most common polls in China are done through face-to-face interviews at respondents' homes. Such interviews, however, are not always convenient for pollsters to conduct, especially if they involve interviewing people on the streets. Du Yan cautions that "When conducting in-person interviews on streets, we have to inform either the local police bureau or the traffic police bureau first for their approval," because some police "will regard polling as a problem and make some trouble."[69]

Obviously, polling in China does not constitute legitimate public opinion polling. Although polling is not forbidden, it is carefully monitored and controlled. Consequently, the polling industry in China is very small, extremely unsophisticated, under the corrupting influence of the Chinese government, and struggling for its very survival. In the United States polling is a thriving and expanding $5 billion industry; polling firms in China are very few in number and generate only millions of dollars. In fact, Du Yan reports that, besides his own CSR, as of 1993 "there are three other substantial polling groups, all located in Guangzhou."[70] He adds that only his firm polls nationally, but what he means by this is that CSR polls in seven major cities in China, not in the entire country. True national surveys cannot be conducted in China, not only because of the lack of an adequate sampling frame that can account for all adult residents, but because rural Chinese are too difficult to reach and too isolated to know enough to answer questions in an informed manner (e.g., Gallup pollsters report that "while almost everyone in the ten big cities surveyed has seen a foreigner, more than half of the rural Chinese have not").[71]

Of the polls that are conducted in China, most (about 95%) are market surveys. Only about 5% could be classified as polls on social and political issues. Du Yan contends that this is because the government is rather "cool" toward such polls, but also because very little funding exists for sociopolitical polls. He exclaims, "What organizations are willing to fund social or political surveys? China's media have not attached enough attention to funding and publishing polls." He notes that there is no evidence that even government-sponsored polls are used to influence government policymaking. "As I said, never has a leader expressed any opinion on any survey in China."[72] Ironically, this is unfortunate because "the Chinese people think positively of polling as a means of expressing themselves." They are also willing to trust the pollsters, believing that their answers will not be manipulated. Incredibly, the refusal rate by the Chinese is lower than 5% (much lower than in the United States). The response rate is high, Du Yan speculates, because the Chinese are very curious about polling since very few have ever been interviewed and, thus, they are very eager to respond. Nonetheless, the Chinese people don't think their opinions carry much influence with the Chinese leaders.

In conclusion, it is worth noting that not only is polling not expanding very much in China, but there is evidence to suggest that the little polling that is done is on the decline. In 1997, the government-run China Poll and Survey released the following bizarre statement: "As most of the controversial issues concerning China have been polled, the Board of China Poll and Survey (CPS) has recently reached an agreement that CPS will DISSOLVE HERSELF as an organization. . . . There will be no more poll [sic] here."[73] Could any informed citizen from a Western democracy relate to a statement that conveys the absurd message that polling is no longer needed because "most of the controversial issues concerning the country have been polled," implying strongly that no future controversial issues will emerge that need to be surveyed? Gallup International, which conducted polls in China in 1994, 1997, and 1999, has run into serious problems there due to new governmental regulations published in August 1999 that "sharply restrict foreign market firms—both in what they can ask and what they can release."[74] Although the polling situation just described is unique to China, there is no reason to believe that legitimate public opinion polling could prosper in any similar closed society.

POLLING HELPS TO PROMOTE DEMOCRACY IN THE WORLD

There are those who argue that public opinion polls do not serve democracy very well, whether here in the United States or elsewhere in the world. Their main contention is that leaders should act on principle and not be slaves to public opinion polls, especially considering that the public is so often ill-informed, misinformed, fickle, and easily manipulated by the media and misunderstood events. But such arguments have historically too often served the interests of tyrants, who have enthusiastically embraced such convenient arguments to justify a course of action blatantly contrary to the will of the people. As Celinda Lake and Jennifer Sosin assert, public opinion polling promotes democracy quite well, especially democratic decisionmaking, because polling information can "play a valuable role in setting direction and in checking political excess." Additionally, they note, "public opinion polling keeps elected representatives, who are increasingly isolated, more in touch with their constituencies than they would be without it."[75] It is also false to think that opinion polls measure public ignorance on public policy matters just because people in general do not know many of the details regarding policy choices. The reality, according to Lake and Sosin, is that most people understand the basics quite well and "are clear in their minds about their priorities and values to make choices about the elected officials they support and the issues they emphasize."[76]

The demonstrable fact is that public opinion polling helps to promote democracy because it promotes popular government, a basic and necessary ingredient in any true democracy. In this light, Humphrey Taylor rightfully points out that "Most people's definition of bad government would apply to countries in which public opinion is not heard and has little influence, and where unpopular governments 'win' grossly unfair elections or steal them with fraudulent vote counts."[77] Taylor, as well as other pollsters, admit that polls are not perfect, but they do provide "the only reasonably reliable way to measure public opinion." Honest, independent public opinion polls published in various countries help to tell leaders what the people think and, as Taylor maintains, "it is reasonable to suppose that their having a good knowledge and understanding of public opinion is better for democracy than not having it."[78]

More specifically, opinion polls serve to set the record straight, preventing dictators or minority interests from advancing self-serving policies that obviously carry little public support. As Taylor espouses, "Without polls, it is much easier for rich, powerful, and influential minorities to claim they speak for the majority when they do not." Consequently, he adds, "Dictators, communist governments, and other authoritarian regimes have never allowed free independent political polls in their countries because the truth would be damaging. Most real democracies allow opinion polls complete freedom."[79] Ansu-Kyeremeh Kwasi, who has witnessed Ghana's struggle to secure democratic government, agrees with Taylor, holding that public opinion polling can help promote a democratic culture in Ghana by compelling its leaders to finally pay attention to public opinion.[80] Once leaders start paying attention to what the people really think, because public opinion polls are accepted as a legitimate aspect of political participation in the "public, deliberative process,"[81] then sensitive, publicly sanctioned democratic policy making and planning can take place.[82] However, it is crucial to stress that it is especially important for journalists in these countries to recognize the importance of public opinion polling too, so they can use the "power of the pen" to check political leaders who choose to ignore the dictates of public opinion. After all, in well-established democratic systems the media play a critical watchdog role.

In the short run, however, honest pollsters can best serve the development of democracy worldwide by alerting journalists and the public to not-so-democratic politicians who try to steal elections. Warren Mitofsky believes that independent, credible pollsters can, in a sense, function like election result auditors, confirming or not confirming such results. For example, he explains that his exit poll in Russia served to verify the actual results of the 1993 Russian election because his results were very close to the actual election results, thus easing the widespread suspicion that "the Yeltsin-dominated election commission would not produce an honest count." To Mitofsky, "Exit polls, when produced by neutral pollsters, are an independent verification of the result produced by the election commission."[83]

Humphrey Taylor agrees emphatically. He says that a "major contribution of polls in new and emerging democracies is that they make it much harder for governments to steal elections."[84] He acknowledges that an unscrupulous leader can easily claim that he won the election if no polls are conducted to verify the results. For instance, in the 1988 Mexican presidential election, most observers believed that Carlos Salinas stole the election from Cuauhtémoc Cárdenas, but "with no reliable pre-election polls and no exit polls, there was little evidence to support a challenge to the official results."[85] Of course, when Vincente Fox won the 2000 Mexican presidential election in dramatic fashion, no one questioned the results since numerous preelection polls and exit polls made it clear that Fox had actually won. And when Slobodan Milosevic tried to tell the world that he had not lost to Vojislav Kostunica in the 2000 presidential election in Yugoslavia in the midst of public opinion polls that suggested otherwise, pressure from foreign governments and riots by his own people forced him to concede that he had lost. In this case, no doubt the pollsters served democracy and the Yugoslavian people very well.[86]

Chapter Ten

◻ ◻ ◻

Testing the Pollsters

How Accurate Were the Pollsters' Predictions in the 2000 Presidential, U.S. Senate, and Gubernatorial Races?

In Chapter 2 we looked at the track record of several polling organizations and found that, after a very shaky start in the 1930s and 1940s, polling accuracy has gotten considerably better as survey research techniques have been scrutinized and improved by pollsters. Many skeptics still love to cite the dreadful 1948 election predictions to bolster their argument that polling is crude witchcraft that seldom hits its target. But such charges are patently unfair and are certainly not rooted in fact. The allegations are unjust because, frankly, 1948 was a long time ago when scientific polling was in its infancy and survey research methodology was unrefined. But as the decades have passed, as with other developing fields, polling has become more sophisticated and respected as dedicated pollsters have experimented with various polling techniques, eventually adopting those procedures that have consistently produced quite reliable results. Consequently, today pollsters usually hit the bull's-eye or come very close.

So let's look at how well the pollsters did in forecasting the 2000 election results. First, we are going to compare the tracking polls of major polling organizations in the 2000 presidential election from June through their last prediction before election day on November 7. Focus will then turn toward scrutinizing how well the major pollsters did in predicting the presidential election results, calculating how far off each forecast was from the actual results. Then we will look at how well major and local pollsters did in predicting the election outcomes in the U.S. Senate and gubernatorial races, and in forecasting the presidential results in the individual states.

HOW WELL DID THE POLLSTERS TRACK THE 2000 PRESIDENTIAL RACE?

Obviously, the objective of tracking polls is to accurately track the degree of electoral support for candidates throughout a campaign. However, only the very last tracking polls that pollsters conduct just days before the election, constituting their final predictions, can be tested by comparing their forecasts with the actual election results. Consequently, there is no real way that we can absolutely test for the accuracy of all those tracking polls that supposedly measure voter fluctuations leading up to election day, especially for those conducted several weeks or even months before the election. Nonetheless, it seems reasonable to give more credibility to the precision of the tracking polls if the level of support for the candidates shows similar results on about the same dates leading up to the election and if their final election predictions were accurately within a reasonable error margin (e.g., ±3%) of the actual election results. Let's apply the testing criteria to the tracking polls conducted by the major polling organizations for the 2000 presidential campaign.

Table 10.1 shows the tracking poll statistics for the major polling organizations from June 2000 through their last predictions shortly before election day on November 7, 2000. The table is very

TABLE 10.1 2000 Presidential Election Tracking Polls from June Through Last Poll Before November 7, 2000, Election

Polling Org.	Candidate	June	July	Aug.	Sept.	Oct.	Last Poll	Actual Result
Date		12	25	20	8	23	11/6	11/7
ABC/	Bush	49	51	50	49	47	49	48.0
Washington	Gore	45	45	45	47	47	45	48.3
Post	Others	3	3	2	1	4	4	3.7
	Undecided	3	1	3	2	2	2	—
Date		—	24	—	12	22	11/6	11/7
CBS/	Bush	—	46	—	43	46	44	48.0
New York	Gore	—	40	—	46	45	45	48.3
Times	Others	—	1	—	2	2	5	3.7
	Undecided	—	11	—	9	7	6	—
Date		8	25	20	12	23	11/6	11/7
CNN/	Bush	48	49	46	40	50	48	48.0
Gallup Poll/	Gore	44	41	47	49	41	46	48.3
USA Today	Others	1	4	5	4	5	5	3.7
	Undecided	7	6	2	7	4	0	—
Date		9	21	26	8	23	11/6	11/7
Fox/	Bush	39	43	40	43	45	43	48.0
Opinion	Gore	32	37	44	46	42	43	48.3
Dynamics	Others	7	8	6	4	5	4	3.7
	Undecided	22	12	10	7	8	10	—
Date		21	25	16	18	30	11/5	11/7
Harris	Bush	47	45	42	41	48	47	48.0
	Gore	40	40	43	49	43	47	48.3
	Others	10	11	11	4	6	5	3.7
	Undecided	4	8	2	5	3	0	—
Date		22	31	14	12	19	11/6	11/7
Hart (D)	Bush	49	47	44	42	45	47	48.0
Teeter (R)	Gore	41	42	41	45	43	44	48.3
NBC/	Others	5	5	8	5	5	6	3.7
Wall Street	Undecided	5	6	7	8	7	3	—
Journal								
Date		—	—	29	25	31	11/5	11/7
International	Bush	—	—	39	40	43	46	48.0
Communi-	Gore	—	—	46	46	41	44	48.3
cations	Others	—	—	5	6	10	9	3.7
Research	Undecided	—	—	10	8	6	0	—

TABLE 10.1　(Cont'd.)

Polling Org.	Candidate	June	July	Aug.	Sept.	Oct.	Last Poll	Actual Result
Date		24	29	21	14	23	11/1	11/7
Princeton	Bush	42	47	42	40	48	46	48.0
Survey	Gore	40	40	48	46	41	43	48.3
Research/	Others	5	6	4	6	6	7	3.7
Newsweek/	Undecided	13	7	6	8	5	4	—
Bloomberg								
Date		—	—	12	13	26	10/26	11/7
Greenberg	Bush	—	—	48	41	42	42	48.0
Quinlan	Gore	—	—	39	45	44	44	48.3
Research (D)	Others	—	—	9	7	7	7	3.7
	Undecided	—	—	4	7	7	7	—
Date		—	—	21	—	25	11/6	11/7
MSNBC/	Bush	—	—	46	—	45	46	48.0
Reuters/	Gore	—	—	43	—	43	48	48.3
Zogby/NBC	Others	—	—	4	—	5	6	3.7
	Undecided	—	—	7	—	7	0	—
Date		21	27	—	—	25	11/5	11/7
Pew	Bush	41	42	—	—	45	49	48.0
Research	Gore	42	41	—	—	45	47	48.3
Center	Others	7	8	—	—	5	4	3.7
	Undecided	10	9	—	—	5	0	—
Date		—	—	—	10	31	11/6	11/7
Tipp/	Bush	—	—	—	42	49	47.9	48.0
Christian	Gore	—	—	—	42	40	46.0	48.3
Science	Others	—	—	—	5	5	3.7	3.7
Monitor	Undecided	—	—	—	11	7	0	—
Date		22	31	17	21	20	11/6	11/7
Voter.com	Bush	52	46	45	42	44	50	48.0
Battleground/	Gore	40	38	40	39	40	45	48.3
Lake (D)	Others	—	4	4	4	5	3.5	3.7
Goeas (R)	Undecided	8	11	10	15	11	0	—

NOTE: In this table tracking polls refer to any polls used to track candidates even though they may not technically be rolling, tracking polls. Comparing poll results for different polling organizations is difficult because polls were not necessarily conducted on the same dates, questions were not exactly the same, and reporting of results was not uniform (e.g., results for registered voters, likely voters, including or excluding learners, combining or not combining Don't Know/Undecided/Other). Nonetheless, the table is useful for showing general tracking trends.

useful for comparing general trends revealed by the different polling organizations, but precise comparisons cannot be made because polls were not necessarily conducted during the same days or even weeks, the questions asked were not necessarily identical, and poll results were not always reported in the same way (e.g., some separated "undecided" from "other" and "don't know," while others did not; results may have been reported for registered voters or likely voters). An effort was made, however, to use polls conducted about the same time, if possible, and to use likely voters, if reported. Contrary to those who bashed the pollsters, especially in the media, contending that tracking polls on the presidential candidates were "all over the place," Table 10.1 discloses that most polling organizations detected similar shifts in popular support for Bush and Gore from June through election day. Of the eight polling firms that conducted polls in June, all but one (Pew Research Center) showed Bush leading Gore, and Pew only showed Gore up by 1%, well within the statistical margin of error. Five of the polling organizations showed Bush ahead by 5, 4, 7, 7, and 8 percentage points, respectively, while Princeton Survey Research/*Newsweek* placed Bush ahead by only 2% and the Voter.com Battleground poll had Bush leading by 12%.

July polls disclosed that Bush continued to maintain his lead over Gore. Of the nine polling organizations that conducted polls in July, each showed Bush in the lead. In fact, all but one (Pew) indicated that Bush was ahead by about the same margin. These polling firms showed that Bush led Gore by 6, 6, 8, 6, 5, 7, and 8 percentage points, respectively, but Pew had Bush ahead by only 1%. The August polls, however, noted a dramatic turnabout, with Bush leading in most early to mid-August polls, but Gore closing the gap and even going ahead in some post-Democratic Convention late August polls, indicating that Gore received a hefty bounce from his Democratic Convention, held August 14–17. The Greenberg Quinlan Research (a Democratic firm) poll released just prior to the Democratic Convention on August 12 disclosed that Bush led Gore by 9%, while an NBC/*Wall Street Journal* poll released on the day the Democratic Convention began, August 14, showed Bush up by just 3%. A Voter.com poll made public on August 17 showed Bush up by 5%, indicating a decline from its July poll in which Bush led by 8% and its June poll where he led by 12%. Only the Harris poll, released on August 16, showed that Gore had actually moved ahead by 1%, 43% to 42%. Harris had previously showed Bush ahead by 7% in June and 5% in July. But the trend, noted by all of these pollsters, indicated that Bush was starting to slip in the polls.

Although polls released during or immediately after the Democratic Convention disclosed gains by Gore in the polls, the late August polls shown in Table 10.1 reveal that Bush's lead had evaporated. A Fox poll released on August 26 now showed Gore ahead by 4%, while an International Communications Research poll made public on August 29 had Gore leading by 7%. Frank Newport of Gallup News Service acknowledged this turnabout in the polls in Gore's favor, noting: "Prior to the start of the conventions this summer, Bush led Gore in almost every poll conducted for the past year and was ahead by a 7.5 percent point margin in an average of four June and July polls. Now, in an average of the two polls conducted after the Democratic Convention, the two candidates are dead even."[1]

Overall, Table 10.1 shows that September was a good month for Gore, especially early to mid-September.[2] In the ten polls posted between September 8 and 25, Gore led in eight of them by a relatively consistent margin of 3, 9, 3, 8, 3, 6, 6, and 4 percentage points. Gore trailed by 2% in an ABC/*Washington Post* poll released on September 8 and the Voter.com poll by 3% disclosed on September 21, but these two polls are the exception in Table 10.1.

In sharp contrast to September, October was overall not a good month for Gore. Most polls measured Bush's comeback in the polls, which really started in late September. All thirteen polling organizations displayed in Table 10.1 conducted polls in October, with ten showing that Bush had regained the lead, two indicating the race was tied, and only one, Greenberg Quinlan Research, showing Gore ahead, but by only 2%. But the resurgence of Bush was short-lived. Most pollsters, who had accurately tracked the ups and downs in the polls of Bush and Gore throughout the campaign, detected that Gore had bounced back to move into a statistical dead heat with Bush. Eleven of the thirteen polling organizations reported polls indicating that the two candidates were within the standard ±3% margin of error of each other. Nine of the eleven showed the race within ±2%, with three being within 1% and two, Fox and Harris, showing Bush and Gore absolutely tied.

In summary, Table 10.1 demonstrates that the pollsters did a laudable job tracking the fluctuations of Bush and Gore support in the 2000 presidential campaign. Most polling organizations in this table tracked the same general trends. That is, that Bush was ahead, sometimes comfortably, in June and July, but then fell behind after Gore benefited from a solid Democratic Convention bounce that lasted until late September. Then, Table 10.1 conveys that Bush surged back and moved ahead in most of the October polls, only to have Gore fight back and move into a virtual tie with Bush by election day. To reiterate, the fact that most of these pollsters revealed the same general trends attests to their apparent accuracy during the presidential campaign. But adding to the credibility of their tracking accuracy is the reality that all but two showed Bush and Gore by election day to be within a statistical dead heat—a forecast that proved very true!

HOW WELL DID THE POLLSTERS DO IN PREDICTING THE OUTCOME OF THE 2000 PRESIDENTIAL RACE?

Table 10.2 displays the last poll predictions in the 2000 presidential race by thirteen major polling organizations.[3] Analysis of this table reveals that these thirteen organizations were pretty accurate with their presidential predictions. Ten out of thirteen were within the ±3% error margin of picking the exact popular vote winning percentage, 48.3%, Gore would receive. And of the three that missed, their average error was 3.7%, not exactly that far outside the respectable ±3% error margin. Almost half of the pollsters (six) were within the ±2% error margin range, while four

TABLE 10.2   2000 Presidential Election Predictions Showing Calculated Error by Comparing Last Poll Prediction Before Election with Actual Election Results

Polling Org.	Candidate	%	A/U	Actual Result 11/7	Error	Polling Org.	Candidate	%	A/U	Actual Result 11/7	Error
ABC/	Bush	49	50	48.0	2	NBC/	Bush	47	48.5	48.0	0.5
Washington	Gore	45	45.9	48.3	2.4	Wall Street	Gore	44	45.4	48.3	2.9
Post	Other	4	4.1	3.7	0.4	Journal	Other	6	6.2	3.7	2.5
11/6	Undec.	2	—	—	—	11/6	Undec.	3	—	—	—
CBS/	Bush	44	46.9	48.0	1.2	Internatl.	Bush	46	46	48.0	2
NYTimes	Gore	45	47.9	48.3	0.4	Communic.	Gore	44	44	48.3	4.3
11/6	Other	5	5.4	3.7	1.7	Research	Other	9	9	3.7	5.3
	Undec.	6	—	—		11/5	Undec.	0	—	—	—
CNN/	Bush	48	48	48	0	Princeton	Bush	46	47.9	48.0	0.1
Gallup/	Gore	46	46	48.3	2.3	Survey	Gore	43	44.8	48.3	3.5
USA Today	Other	5	5	3.7	1.3	Research/	Other	7	7.3	3.7	3.6
11/6	Undec.	0	—	—	—	Newsweek/	Undec.	4	—	—	—
						Bloomberg					
						11/1					
Fox/	Bush	43	47.8	48.0	0.2	Greenberg	Bush	42	45.2	48.0	2.8
Opinion	Gore	43	47.8	48.3	0.5	Quinlan	Gore	44	47.3	48.3	1.0
Dynamics	Other	4	4.5	3.7	0.8	Research (D)	Other	7	7.5	3.7	3.8
11/6	Undec.	10	—	—		10/26	Undec.	7	—	—	—
Harris	Bush	47	47	48.0	1	MSNBC/	Bush	46	46	48.0	2.0
11/5	Gore	47	47	48.3	1.3	Reuters/	Gore	48	48	48.3	0.3
	Other	5	5	3.7	1.3	Zogby/NBC	Other	6	6	3.7	2.3
	Undec.	0	—	—	—	11/6	Undec.	0	—	—	—
Pew	Bush	49	49	48.0	1.0	Voter.com	Bush	50	50	48	2
Research	Gore	47	47	48.3	1.3	Battleground	Gore	45	45	48.3	3.3
Center	Other	4	4	3.7	0.3	11/6	Other	5	5	3.7	1.3
11/5	Undec.	0	—	—	—		Undec.	0	—	—	—
Tipp/	Bush	47.9	47.9	48.0	.1						
Christian	Gore	46.0	46.0	48.3	2.3						
Science	Other	6.1	6.1	3.7	2.4						
Monitor	Undec.	0	—	—	—						
11/6											

Average prediction error for Gore: 1.98%
Average prediction error for Bush: 1.15%
Combined prediction error: 1.56%

NOTE: Most polling organizations rounded their poll percentages, consequently error estimates are calculated by comparing rounded poll predictions with actual election results rounded to the nearest 1/10th of a percent. This could contaminate the estimated error by 0.5%. If pollsters did not allocate their undecideds, the proportionate method was used to allocate the undecided (A/U) so fair error estimates could be made.

missed predicting Gore's exact winning percentage by only 1% or less. Remarkably, three polling companies, CBS/*New York Times*, Fox/Opinion Dynamics, and MSNBC/Reuters/Zogby/NBC nearly hit the bull's-eye, being off by 0.5% or less.

Despite the pollsters' admirable record in predicting Gore's winning percentage, they did even better in predicting the popular vote percentage that Bush would get. Not only did all thirteen polling organizations make calls within the ±3% error margin, but twelve of them were within ±2% error range, and seven made predictions within 1% of the popular vote Bush would obtain. Laudably, five came within a 0.5% error margin, with Fox/Opinion Dynamics missing by only 0.2%, Princeton Survey Research/*Newsweek*/Bloomberg by 0.1%, while CNN/Gallup/*USA Today* hit it right on the button with 0% error.

There is little reason to scrutinize the calls for "Other" because the percentages for the other candidates are normally low and one would expect the error, therefore, to be not far off, although three of the thirteen polling firms had high estimates for Nader, causing their predictions for "Other" to fall outside the ±3% error range. Predictably, far fewer Americans ended up voting for Ralph Nader than they indicated to pollsters, presumably not wanting to "waste" their vote by voting for Nader over Gore, who was the most prevalent second choice by far for would-be Nader voters according to the preelection polls. The pollsters who were outside the ±3% error margin on "Other" probably failed to weight this rather predictable "wasted vote factor" in their predictions and so lower their predicted percentage for "Other."

Overall, Table 10.2 conveys that the pollsters did very well in predicting the vote percentages that the presidential candidates would likely receive in the 2000 presidential election. In calling the popular vote percentage for Gore, the pollsters were off by an average error margin of only 1.98%, while for Bush their average error margin was a very impressive 1.15%. The pollsters' average error for both the winner (Gore) and loser (Bush) of the popular vote was a very respectable error of 1.56%.[4] These low error averages are particularly impressive given the fact that two significant third-party candidates, Ralph Nader and Pat Buchanan, were in the race, making predictions for the two frontrunners even more challenging. The apparent volatility of the electorate, given the ups and downs in the polls of the presidential candidates during the campaign, also would make the election more difficult for the pollsters to predict accurately, yet they closely followed the electoral swings of the voters during the campaign and predicted the popular vote percentages of the candidates with praiseworthy precision. Instead of bashing these pollsters, these pollsters deserve resounding applause.

HOW WELL DID THE POLLSTERS DO IN PREDICTING THE RESULTS OF THE 2000 U.S. SENATE RACES?

One hundred and two election predictions by major and local polling organizations for thirty U.S. Senate races were compared to the actual 2000 election results to determine the accuracy of these projections.[5] Major polling organizations, the most prevalent in 2000 being Mason-Dixon and Zogby International, are those firms that conduct polls nationally on a regular basis, whereas local polling companies are those that do not, instead concentrating their polling in a single state or region. Predictions were examined for all of the polling organizations together, as well as for major and local polling organizations separately.

These data are given in Table A.1 in the Appendix; this lengthy table displays all 102 predictions taken from each polling firm's last poll results before the November 7, 2000, U.S. Senate elections.[6] Also shown in this table is whether the polling firm is major or local, the allocation of the undecided voters (A/U), the actual election result, and the calculated error. However, Table A.1 is summarized in Table 10.3.

Analysis of Table A.1 shows that, of the 102 U.S. Senate election calls by the pollsters for the winning candidate's vote percentage, 16 fell within the ±1% error margin and another 28 were within the ±3% error margin, for a total of 44 or 43.1% of the predictions not exceeding ±3% error. Another 30 calls (29.4%) were found to be in the 3% plus to 6% error range, 23 (22.5%) fell between 6% plus to 10%, while only 5 calls (4.9%) exceeded 10% error. That is, out of 102 Senate predictions for the vote percentage of the winning candidate, almost three-quarters (72.5%) fell within ±6% error. Only an insignificant percentage, 4.9%, were way off or exceeding 10% error. The average error for all 102 predictions of winning percentages was 4.35%, over twice as high as the error (1.98%) by the thirteen major polling organizations that predicted the popular winning vote percentage or percentage that Gore would receive in the 2000 presidential election.

In projecting the winning percentage in the U.S. Senate contests, the major and local polling organizations performed about the same statistically, except that many more predictions falling within <±1% error were made by the major polling firms. Of the 16 winning percentage predictions that were within the <±1% error margin, 12 were conducted by the major polling companies with an exemplary average error of only 0.6%. The four local polling firm projections in the <1% error range had an average error of 0.7%. For the error range from 1% plus to ±3%, the average error for the 12 calls by major firms was 2.1%, while it was 2.15% for the 16 calls by the local firms. In the 3% plus to ±6% error range, the 15 predictions by major firms had an average error of 4.2%, while the 15 calls by local companies had an average error of 4.4%. In the 6% plus to ±10% error range, the 14 projections by major organizations posted an average error of 7.4%, while the 9 predictions by local firms had an average error of 8%. Only in the >10% error range did the major polling firms have an average error greater than that for the local firms, but there were only 5 calls in this range (4 by major firms and 1 by a local company), with the major organizations having a 14.45% average error and the local firm having a 13% error. Because of this one range, major polling firms actually had an average error of 4.5%, slightly above the average error of 4.2% for the local organizations. However, excluding this one range, which distorts a more accurate portrayal because so few predictions are included, the average error for the 53 predictions made by major polling organizations was 3.7%, while it was 4.0% for the 44 calls made by the local ones.

Turning to the 102 predictions by the pollsters in the Senate races for the losing candidate's popular vote percentage, an examination of Table A.1 reveals that 19 of the election forecasts fell within the <±1% range and 29 were found to be in the 1% plus to ±3% error range, for a total of 48 or almost half of the projections (47.1%) having an error of only ±3% or less. Another 32 or 31.4% fell within the 3% plus to ±6% error range, while 15 predictions or 14.7% had a less than respectable error of between 6% plus to ±10%. Only 7 or 6.9% of the election calls were way off the mark with an embarrassing error exceeding ±10%. The average error for all 102 projections of the losing percentages in these U.S. Senate contests was 4.13%, slightly lower than the 4.35% found for the winning percentage forecasts.

Once again, the major and local polling firms performed about the same in their prediction accuracy, except, as before, more predictions by major firms (13) fell within <±1% error compared to the calls (6) made by the local companies, with the major firms also having a slightly lower average error than the local firms in this error range, 0.42% to 0.43%. For 1% plus to ±3%, 13 predictions came from the major companies for an average error of 1.7%, while 16 were from the local firms with an average error of 2%. In the 3% plus to ±6% error range, 17 predictions came from major polling organizations with an average error of 4.9%, and 15 were made by local firms with an average error of 4.5%. In the less respectable 6% plus to ±10% error range, 10 calls were made by major companies with an average error of 7.65%, while 5 by the local firms had an average error of 4.5%. In the >±10% error range, 4 calls came from major organizations with a pathetic average error of 13.5%, and 3 were made by local firms with an almost equally discomforting average error of 12.4%. The total average error for the major polling organizations in their 57 predictions of the popular vote percentage for the losing Senate candidate was 4.2%, while it was slightly lower, 4.0%, for the local firms. Table 10.3 summarizes the major findings from Table A.1.

TABLE 10.3 Summary of Prediction Error for the Winning and Losing 2000 U.S. Senate Candidates

	Error Prediction for Winning Senate Candidates					
Error Range (± %)	No. of Predictions	% in Range	Major Polling Org.	% in Range	Local Polling Org.	% in Range
> ± 10	5	4.9	14	7	1	2.2
6 ± ± 10	23	22.5	14	24.5	9	20.0
3 ± ± 6	30	29.4	15	26.3	15	33.3
1 ± ± 3	28	27.5	12	21.1	16	35.6
< ± 1	16	15.7	12	21.1	4	8.9
Total	102	100	57	100	45	100

Total average prediction: 4.35%
Average prediction error for major polling firms: 4.5%
Average prediction error for local polling firms: 4.2%

	Error Prediction for Losing Senate Candidates					
Error Range (± %)	No. of Predictions	% in Range	Major Polling Org.	% in Range	Local Polling Org.	% in Range
>±10	7	6.9	4	7	3	6.7
6± ±10	15	14.7	10	17.6	5	11.1
3± ± 6	32	31.4	17	29.8	15	33.3
1± ± 3	29	28.4	13	22.8	16	35.6
< ±1	19	18.6	13	22.8	6	13.3
Total	102	100	57	100	45	100

Total average prediction: 4.1%
Average prediction error for major polling firms: 4.2%
Average prediction error for local polling firms: 4.0%

In assessing how well the pollsters did in forecasting the outcomes in the 2000 U.S. Senate races, a few cautionary notes on how to interpret their predictions need to be emphasized, and many of these cautions apply to interpreting any predictions by pollsters. In the first place, pollsters often take offense when others interpret their poll results as predictions. As pollster John Zogby stressed to me one time, people keep on insisting that poll results constitute predictions of election outcomes, but they really don't because poll results are just "snapshots of the race at that moment in time."[7] Technically speaking, Zogby is absolutely right, because many things can change during a campaign to alter the standing of the candidates in the polls. Therefore, the predictive accuracy of polls becomes less valid as the gap widens between the last poll taken by the pollster and election day. This reality must be taken into consideration when drawing conclusions from Table A.1 or the other tables in this chapter that compare poll results to actual election results. Most of the poll results in Table A.1 were taken within a week or so or even a few days before the election, making their predictive value quite solid. Unfortunately, some "last polls" were used that were much older, lowering their predictive utility. These older polls tended to be conducted in races that were not very competitive and/or in states where there was less interest and even possibly less money available to sponsor the polls. For example, though an enormous number of polls were taken in states such as Michigan, Missouri, New York, New Jersey, and Florida, few polls, many not very close to election day, were conducted in states such as Maine, North Dakota, Vermont, and Wyoming. Consequently, the pollster's average error in these "low-profile" states tended to be considerably greater than for the "high-profile" states. For example, the average error for the last polls conducted by 10 polling organizations for the winner in the Michigan Senate race was 3.6%, whereas the average error for the last two polls conducted for the winner in the Senate contest in Maine was 11.2%.

In sum, extreme caution must be taken when drawing conclusions about average error statistics. To be fair to the pollsters, all factors that may affect average error should be considered. For instance, note that one of the reasons the average error was so low for the 13 polling organizations that made calls in the presidential election, as contrasted to several that conducted polls for the Senate races (Table 10.2.), was because well-funded, professional, experienced polling firms polled almost up to election day. Having said all this, still too many pollsters were not very accurate in their Senate predictions.

HOW WELL DID THE POLLSTERS DO IN PREDICTING THE RESULTS OF THE 2000 GUBERNATORIAL RACES?

A total of 34 election predictions by major and local polling companies for all 11 gubernatorial races in 2000 were compared to the actual election results to determine the accuracy of their projections. Clearly, the poll forecasts for the gubernatorial elections proved to be considerably better than the projections were for the 2000 Senate contests. Also, the election calls by the major polling firms were much better than those made by the local polling organizations.

A review of Table A.2 (see Appendix) discloses that 8 of the 34 total "last poll" projections (23.5%) for the winning gubernatorial candidates were within the ±1% error range, 11 (32.4%) were in the 1% plus to ±3% error range, 11 more (32.4%) were in the 3% plus to ±6% error, only 4 fell within the 6% plus to ±10% error range, and no projections exceeded ±10% error. The calls by the major polling firms were particularly impressive. Almost 4 of 5 of their projections (77.7%) fell within ±3% error, with one-third (33.3%) being within <1% error for an average error of 0.6% within the <1% range and 1.9% in the 1% plus to ±3% error range. The average error for the major polling organizations was 4% in the 3% plus to ±6% error range, while it was 7.8% for the 6% plus to ±10% range. In sharp contrast, only 2 or 12.5% of the 16 calls for the winning gubernatorial candidates made by the local polling firms fell in the <±1% error category, while only another 3 (18.75%) were within 1% plus to ±3% error, for a total of only 31.25% with ±3% error—less than half the percentage of calls by the major firms in this range. Another 8 (50%) were in the 3% plus to ±6% range, while 3 (18.75%) were in the 6% plus to ±10% range. The average errors for the local firms were, respectively, 0.6%, 1.8%, 4.3%, and 7.7% for the lowest to highest error ranges.

Overall, in forecasting the winning percentage of the popular vote in the 2000 gubernatorial contests, the predictions were quite accurate, significantly better than the predictions for the U.S. Senate contests. Whereas the average error for the winning percentage in the Senate races was 4.35%, the average winning percentage error in the gubernatorial contests was 3.1%. As noted, the major polling organizations performed much better than local polling firms in predicting the percentage that the winning gubernatorial candidate would get, with the average being an impressive 2.2% error for the major companies, almost half that (4%) for the local polling firms.

Table A.2 reveals that the election forecasts were fairly accurate in predicting the losing percentage in these gubernatorial races, although not as accurate as the forecasts for the winning percentage. Exactly half (50%) of the 34 total projections fell within ±3%, with 7 (20.6%) within <±1% error. Just over one-third (35.3%) of the predictions were in the 3% plus to ±6% range, while only 14.7% were in the 6% plus to ±10% range, with no errors found to exceed 10%.

Two-thirds of the calls made by the major polling organizations were within ±3% error, and 88.8% were within ±6%, with no projections exceeding ±10% error. The average errors for the major firms in each error range from lowest to highest were 0.6%, 1.9%, 3.6%, and 6.3%, respectively. For the local polling companies, less than one-third of their calls (31.25%) fell within ±3% error, with only 1 call (6.25%) being within <±1% error. Another 8 (50%) were found in the 3% plus to ±6% error range, while 3 (18.75%) were in the 6% plus to ±10% range, with no predictions above 10% error. The average errors for the local polling firms in each error range from lowest to highest were 0.5%, 2.1%, 4.2%, and 8.6%, respectively. Both major and local polling organizations performed pretty well, with an average error of 3.3% for their 34 forecasts, but the major firms had an average error of only 2.4%, whereas the error for the local firms was nearly twice that, 4.3%. Table 10.4 summarizes the findings of Table A.2.

TABLE 10.4   Summary of Prediction Error for the Winning and Losing 2000
Gubernatorial Candidates

Error Prediction for Winning Gubernatorial Candidates						
Error Range (± %)	No. of Predictions	% in Range	Major Polling Org.	% in Range	Local Polling Org.	% in Range
>10%	0	0	0	0	0	0
6+ – 10	4	11.8	1	5.6	3	18.75
3+ – 6	11	32.4	3	16.7	8	50.0
1+ – 3	11	32.4	8	44.4	3	18.75
<1	8	23.5	6	33.3	2	12.5
Total	34	100.1	18	100.0	16	100.0

Total average prediction error: 3.1%
Average prediction error for major polling firms: 2.2%
Average prediction error for local polling firms: 4.0%

Error Prediction for Losing Gubernatorial Candidates						
Error Range (± %)	No. of Predictions	% in Range	Major Polling Org.	% in Range	Local Polling Org.	% in Range
>10%	0	0	0	0	0	0
6+ -10	5	14.7	2	11.1	3	18.75
3+ - 6	12	35.3	4	22.2	8	50.0
1+ - 3	10	29.4	6	33.3	4	25.0
<1	7	20.6	6	33.3	1	6.25
Total	34	100	18	99.9	16	100

Total average prediction error: 3.3%
Average prediction error for major polling firms: 2.4%
Average prediction error for local polling firms: 4.3%

HOW WELL DID THE POLLSTERS DO IN FORECASTING THE RESULTS OF THE 2000 PRESIDENTIAL ELECTION IN EACH STATE?

Finally, the pollsters were subjected to one more test, which involved taking the last poll prediction for the presidential race in each state, plus the District of Columbia, made by a major or local polling organization and comparing it to the actual result in each state and the District (Table A.3 in the Appendix). An analysis of the data in Table A.3 shows that the pollsters once again did a fairly decent job in forecasting the vote percentage that the winning and losing candidates would likely obtain. Remarkably, of the 51 winning percentage forecasts, 31 or 60.8% were found to be within ±3% error with almost a quarter (23.5%) within ±1% error. Close to 80% (78.4%) were within ±6% error. Although 51.6% of the calls did fall within the undistinguished 6% plus to ±10% range, no predictions topped a ±10% error. The average errors were 0.525% for <±1% error, 2% for 1% plus to ±3% error, 4.3% for 3% plus to ±6% error, and 7.3% for the 6% plus to ±10% error range, for a total average error of 3.2%.

Contrary to what was found for the gubernatorial predictions, where the major polling firms outperformed the local ones, in calling the presidential results in the states the local polling companies easily "outpredicted" the major organizations. Of the 15 predictions made by the local firms, surprisingly over half (8 or 53.3%) actually were within ±1% error, while only 11.1% fell within ±1% error for the major polling firms. In fact, 73.3% of the winning presidential candidate forecasts fell within ±3% error for the local firms and 90.3% were within ±6% error, as compared to 55.5% and 72.2%, respectively, for the major organizations. For the "hot" local polling firms in this test, their average error was 0.6% for <±1% error, 1.9% for 1% plus to ±3% error, 4.9% for 3% plus to ±6% error, and 8.1% for the 6% plus to ±10% error range for a total average error of 2.2%, as contrasted to 0.45%, 2%, 4.1%, and 7.2%, respectively, for a total average error of 3.6% for the major companies. Note that the total average error is considerably lower for the local firms because most of their predictions (8 of 15%) fell within <±1% error.

Of the 51 forecasts in the states for the losing presidential candidates by the major or local polling firms, their overall predictions were even better. Thirty-six or 70.6% were within ±3% error, and 46 calls or 90.2% fell within the ±6% error range. Only 5 calls or 9.8% exceeded ±6% error, while no calls surpassed ±10% error. The average error in the <±1% range was 0.6%, 1.9% for 1% plus to ±3%, 4.2% for 3% plus to ±6%, and 7.3% in the 6% plus to ±10% range, for a respectable total average error of 2.6%.

Again, as would be expected given the performance of the local polling organizations in predicting the vote percentage for the winning presidential candidates in the states, their projections for the losing percentage proved even more impressive. Laudably, 12 out of their 15 calls (or 80%) were within ±3% error, while only 1 (6.7%) exceeded ±6% error. In contrast, 24 of the 36 predictions by the major polling companies (or 66.7%) fell within the ±3% error range and 4 (or 11.1%) fell beyond ±6% error, but no predictions exceeded ±10% error. The average errors for the local firms were 0.6% for <±1% error, 1.8% for 1% plus to ±3% error, 3.95% for 3% plus to ±6% error, and 6.8% for 6% plus to ±10% error, for a total average error of only 2.1%. For the major polling organizations, their average errors were 0.6%, 2.1%, 4.3%, and 7.5% for these respective error ranges for a total error of 2.8%. Table 10.5 summarizes the major findings of Table A.3.

While the performance was impressive for both the major and local polling firms in their 51 forecasts of the vote percentages for the winning and losing presidential candidates in the 50 states plus the District of Columbia, the performance by the local organizations was even more impressive. Given the normally greater resources and experience of the major polling companies, it is somewhat surprising that they were outperformed by the local firms.

THE ARROGANCE AND "UNTESTABILITY" OF THE VOTER NEWS SERVICE'S EXIT POLLING

If you search the Web for coverage of the Voter News Service (VNS), you will immediately find a plethora of articles vehemently attacking them. So what is VNS and why is this service so attacked? VNS was assembled by the major television networks, newspapers, and news services about three decades ago and has served in relative secrecy since its creation. For several elections now, VNS has functioned as a monopoly conducting exit polls for all of the major networks, including CNN and Fox, *The New York Times*, *The Washington Post*, other papers, and the wire services,

TABLE 10.5   Summary of Prediction Error for the Winning and Losing 2000 Presidential Candidates in Each State by the Last Poll Conducted

			Error Prediction for Winning Presidential Candidates			
Error Range (± %)	No. of Predictions	% in Range	Major Polling Org.	% in Range	Local Polling Org.	% in Range
>10%	0	0	0	0	0	0
6+ – 10	11	21.6	10	27.8	1	6.7
3+ – 6	9	17.6	6	16.7	3	20.0
1+ – 3	19	37.3	16	44.4	3	20.0
<1	12	23.5	4	11.1	8	53.3
Total	51	100	36	100	15	100

Total average prediction error: 3.2%

Average prediction error for major polling firms: 3.6%

Average prediction error for local polling firms: 2.2%

			Error Prediction for Losing Presidential Candidates			
Error Range (± %)	No. of Predictions	% in Range	Major Polling Org.	% in Range	Local Polling Org.	% in Range
>10%	0	0	0	0	0	0
6+ – 10	5	9.8	4	11.1	1	6.7
3+ – 6	10	19.6	8	22.2	2	13.3
1+ – 3	25	49.0	16	44.5	9	60.0
<1	11	21.6	8	22.2	3	20.0
Total	51	100	36	100	15	100

Total average prediction error: 2.6%

Average prediction error for major polling firms: 2.8%

Average prediction error for local polling firms: 2.1%

especially the Associated Press. But VNS has more than exclusivity in conducting exit polls for the media, it "participates" in the counting of the actual votes.[8] In fact, VNS projections on election night are based on both exit polling and actual returns. That is, VNS is "plugged in" to the computers nationwide that actually tally the votes. Of course, the reason why the networks originally called Florida for Gore, then recanted and put Florida in the undecided column, then called Florida for Bush, but then decided to pull that call and once again place Florida in the undecided column (which naturally threw the whole 2000 presidential election into chaotic limbo because of Florida's decisive 25 electoral votes) is because all of these media outlets were relying on VNS for their election information.[9]

It is precisely because VNS, as a monopoly, plays such an instrumental public role in our democratic society that its polling procedures and projections should be carefully scrutinized by independent researchers, especially by "independent" journalists and by electoral behavior and survey research methodologists at various universities and think tanks. In fact, professional polling associations such as the American Association of Public Opinion Research, under their Best Practices section, state that "Excellence in survey practice requires that survey methods be fully disclosed/ reported in sufficient detail to permit replication by another researcher and that all data . . . be fully documented and made available for independent examination."[10]

However, when I called VNS and requested their exit poll results (i.e., their actual exit poll data based on the 13,130 respondents who were interviewed by VNS, excluding any "contamination" of this pure exit poll data with actual election results) so I could compare VNS's results to the actual election results in the U.S. presidential, Senate, and gubernatorial races, they would not give the data to me.[11] Murray Edelman, editorial director of VNS, insisted that such data were confidential, constituting private, proprietary corporate information. Noting that he has superiors that he must answer to, he told me that "You are not going to get what you need to do your analysis."[12] Consequently, I could not test the accuracy of VNS exit poll results with actual election results even though I could for other polling companies because they "stuck their necks out" and allowed their poll predictions to be scrutinized.

This position taken by VNS is very unfortunate, especially given the monopolistic status of VNS and the enormous role their exit polls play in U.S. elections. Unlike the competitive polls conducted by numerous preelection pollsters, VNS, to reiterate, conducts the only polls that are used by the media to project election results on election night. Such projections, critics charge, are routinely made before the polls are closed in our nation's more western time zones and, occasionally, even before all of the polling places are closed in the same state. For example, in the 2000 election VNS was criticized for calling Florida for Gore before the polling places had closed in the western counties of Florida (i.e., the area from Panama City to Pensacola), which are in the Central Time Zone. Of course, critics claim that such calls may influence voter turnout and possibly alter election results in close contests, such as the incredibly close 2000 presidential race in Florida that was decided by a tiny fraction of 1% of the total vote. The question is, why are the Voter News Service and the TV networks so arrogant, taking the position that their exit polls and their behavior are above the usual public scrutiny? As one prominent national journalist told me, "This arrogance is ironic given the media's normal position that things that affect the public should be made public."[13]

SUMMARY REMARKS

Obviously, it depends on one's standards, but I feel that overall pollsters did a laudable job in their 2000 election year polling. Poll data in Table 10.1 show that the pollsters performed quite well in tracking the apparent shifts in voter preference for the presidential candidates from the preconvention period until right before election day. Contrary to the charges by so many not-so-observant critics, most polling organizations were not showing radically different levels of voter support for the presidential candidates, but in fact detected the same pattern of electoral shifts in voter preferences throughout the 2000 campaign, ending their tracking by showing that the election would be very close. Of course, Table 10.2 displays clearly that almost all of the polling companies were very accurate with their 2000 presidential predictions, with an average prediction error for both the winner and loser of the popular vote percentage of only 1.56%.

For sundry reasons, pollsters had the most problems in predicting with reasonable accuracy the outcomes of the 2000 U.S. Senate races. It is not that the major and local polling firms were, generally speaking, that far off, although a few were, but that they could do somewhat better. Their average prediction error for 102 preelection calls for the percentages of the popular vote for both the winning and losing senatorial candidates was 4.2%. This is not an average prediction error that the pollsters can celebrate, yet a careful examination of Table 10.3 does show that the average error would be much more respectable if the error was calculated for the 90 calls that did not exceed ±10% error, and/or if only the polls conducted within two weeks of election day were included—something that many of my critics would contend that I should have done to be fairer to the pollsters.[14]

The pollsters did do considerably better in forecasting the outcomes of the gubernatorial contests. Their average prediction error for the popular vote percentage for both the winners and losers in all eleven gubernatorial elections was ±3.2%, or just outside the generally acceptable error margin of ±3%. However, it must be pointed out that the average error for the major polling firms in these gubernatorial races was a very respectable ±2.3%.

Finally, the pollsters also did reasonably well in predicting the popular vote percentages that the presidential candidates would obtain in the fifty states, plus the District of Columbia. In comparing the very last recorded poll projections, by either a major or local polling company, with the actual presidential results, it was found that the pollsters' average error in predicting the popular vote percentages that Gore and Bush would receive was ±2.9%, with the local pollsters being slightly more accurate than the major pollsters.

Chapter Eleven

◨ ◨ ◨

Epilogue

Public Opinion Polling Can and Should Be Defended

*In this class I learned that properly conducted
scientific polls are not only amazingly accurate,
but are valuable tools in understanding society.*
—Meghan Gavura, St. Louis University student,
responding to a final exam question in my
"Polls, Politics, and Society" class,
December 11, 2000

I wrote this book, *In Defense of Public Opinion Polling*, because I believed that a book devoted to a general defense of public opinion pollsters was warranted. I felt that such a sympathetic defense of the polling profession was needed because it had become very apparent to me, as a pollster and political scientist who closely follows polls, that pollsters and their polls were commonly misunderstood and, quite frankly, unfairly maligned. Consequently, I wanted to help set the record straight on the polling profession. One major goal was to present an easy to understand overview of the polling industry, explaining its development and present role in society and its growing importance worldwide. More specifically, I wanted to present and discuss the pros and cons of public opinion polling, conceding that opinion polling definitely poses some problems, yet stressing that overall the pros of public opinion polling far outstrip the cons and that the frequent attacks on pollsters and their polls are too often rooted more in bias and disingenuous hype than rational thought.

In concluding this book, I simply want to revisit each chapter, highlighting the most important points in a way that furthers my central thematic contention that public opinion polling can and should be defended.

The chief point of Chapter 1 is that many Americans, often for sundry reasons, hate pollsters and polls and take great joy in constantly ridiculing them. For these people, poll bashing has become an American "sport" that has aroused their fury. They simply refuse to allow any credible arguments or facts to change their closed minds about pollsters and polls. They don't like them and that's it!

Certainly, it is not that some gripes about pollsters and polls are not legitimate. Some definitely are, as has been noted in this book, but the reality is that most of them are not. For example, how legitimate is it to constantly complain about how the polls are way off in their predictions when most are very accurate, as was demonstrated in Chapter 10? What sense does it make to argue that polls are undemocratic when common sense dictates that nothing could be more in the democratic mainstream in a democratic country than conducting polls to find out what the people think? Is it not absurd to declare polls illegal or unconstitutional and try to ban them when clearly poll taking is unquestionably lawful, obviously protected under our First Amendment? Is it fair or even in good taste to call pollsters all sorts of names (e.g., sleazy, slimy, nasty) when most pollsters comply with professional and ethical standards in trying to do the best job they can?

The basic problem is that this prejudice against pollsters and their polls is like any other prejudice. That is, the prejudicial attacks are seldom fair or reasonable, being mostly rooted in distortions of facts, faulty logic, arguments that defy common sense, denials, biases, and selfish agendas.

The main contention in Chapter 2 is that polls can easily be defended from their detractors, as long as one is willing to listen, because pollsters are indeed mostly professionals with integrity and their polls have obviously proved quite valuable to so many. The second chapter, "In Defense of Pollsters," constitutes the cornerstone of this book because my central theme is that pollsters can and should be defended—a theme that pervades the entire book. Although I contend that polls provide us with accurate and very useful data; have helped us record and interpret history; continue to help us in understanding the present; and have proved invaluable for planning purposes; my favorite argument is that polls have helped to promote democracy itself. This remains my favorite argument because, as a political scientist and citizen, I simply cannot understand the contention of those who hold that public opinion polling somehow undermines American democracy. Of course, there are some unfortunate consequences of polling that present problems for democratic politics (e.g., some politicians may be too "poll-driven," or polls may have the consequence of eliminating "prematurely" candidates from election contests or excluding them "unfairly" from campaign debates), but these negatives are minor compared to the many advantages of public opinion polling for any democratic society. The reality is that public opinion polling helps promote democracy by making almost certain that our political leaders do not get too out of touch by ignoring public opinion. Polls provide our leaders with constant and essential feedback from the citizenry, which helps guide our officials when they make *public* policy decisions.

The basic defense given for public opinion polling by George Gallup and Saul Rae in their 1940 book, *The Pulse of Democracy*, still remains the best argument. They asked, "Shall the common people be free to express their basic needs and purposes, or shall they be dominated by a small ruling clique?"[1] For a true democracy, the answer is obvious.

The overriding theme in Chapter 3 is that the polling profession has grown into a giant, $5 billion industry, not because public opinion polling is irritating and useless, but because it is viewed by serious professionals as an industry that yields a valuable product. The key point in this chapter is that, despite the poll critics, most have figured out that public opinion polling provides absolutely essential information that can be used for a variety of purposes. The very fact that polls are in such demand attests to their value and perceived worth. Businesses have found them invaluable for assessing the acceptability of their products and services. Politicians rely heavily on polls to help them with their political campaigns and to gauge the level of public support for various public policies. Journalists have long used polls to help place news stories into perspective and to attract readers, listeners, and viewers, while various interest groups have employed polls to help assess and gain public support for their causes.

Unquestionably, public opinion polling in the United States has come a long way since the days of the unscientific, unreliable, and laughable straw polls of the 1800s and early 1900s. But since the early years of scientific polling in the mid-1930s, polling has become increasingly more sophisticated and reliable. Today, public opinion polling may still have its enemies, but most, especially among the informed, seem to respect the polling profession and many pay considerable sums of money for polls. Actually, public opinion polling is not only flourishing in America, but it is starting to really blossom worldwide. Consequently, one credible way to defend the polling profession today is to simply point to the industry's booming status here and abroad.

The chief point of Chapter 4 is that, admittedly, there are some bad pollsters and bad polls. The problem is that these "pollsters" and their polls tend to give the truly legitimate, professional pollsters a bad name. That is, too many unthinking people throw all pollsters and polls into the same basket, making the reputable pollsters, unfortunately, guilty by association.

Naturally, this failure to distinguish the good from the bad pollsters is most unfortunate because the professional pollsters would have nothing to do with sleazy push polls, which are not really legitimate polls at all, or flagrantly unrepresentative and otherwise methodologically flawed polls such as media call-in polls or blatantly biased interest-group polls. Good pollsters have also abandoned or not adopted those survey research techniques that have proved unsound, such as methodologically inferior mail surveys, mall surveys, and other survey approaches that have failed to generate sound, representative poll data. Internet polls may be the wave of the future if many more people can be reached on-line and proper weighting procedures are developed, but thus far responsible pollsters have refused to shift to Internet polling because of the unrepresentative nature of such polls.

Nonetheless, in any profession, there are those who insist on adopting flawed approaches and methods, which lead to dismal displays of a profession's product. These unprofessionals do not have the integrity of the profession at heart and may abandon professional codes of conduct and ethics for short-term gains, monetary or other. The polling industry, like any industry, cannot escape such unfortunate realities.

Fortunately, however, most pollsters are professionals and try in earnest to uphold the professional and ethical standards of the polling profession. One would have to be in blatant denial not to notice all the good, representative polling that is going on. In fact, my main contention in Chapter 5 is that, despite those terrible polls that irritate the good pollsters, the truth is that plenty of commendable polls are being cranked out by professional pollsters. Most of this laudable polling is done rather quietly for private clients (e.g., market surveys, private political polls, rigorous academic survey research), so the general public does not become aware of all of the solid survey research that takes place each year. But remember, as George Gallup noted, that the real acid test of public opinion polling, which is very visible to the public, is accurately predicting election results. Well, as was shown in Table 10.2, the average prediction error of the thirteen polling organizations forecasting President Bush's popular vote percentage was only 1.15%, and only 1.98% for Gore. This is very visible evidence that excellent polling is taking place in the United States, despite what those poll bashers would want people to believe.

An important, related point made in Chapter 5 is that professional polls have become increasingly accurate because pollsters have done a much better job over the years in drawing representative samples. Remember, there are many elements that go into good polling, such as quality questionnaire design, but the key to solid survey research is representativeness, because any sample that cannot reasonably represent the total population universe under study (e.g., the American voters) cannot possibly produce any worthwhile poll results.

The simple point that I was trying to make in Chapter 6 is that many journalists have a very uncomfortable love-hate relationship with public opinion polls. In working closely with print and electronic journalists for over two decades now, I must say that most journalists love to use polls in their stories because poll data can help to boost credibility among the informed, as well as interest. However, despite their heavy reliance on polls, I have always found it both hypocritical and a bit amusing that only a minority of journalists will admit openly in chats about polls or in formal interviews that they believe in the accuracy or authoritative value of polls. Really, my honest impression is that journalists love to use polls, but at the same time they like to stress that they really don't place much stock in them. Why is this so?

One reason why so many journalists feel genuinely uneasy accepting or defending polls may be because they know that many of their readers, viewers, or listeners just hate those "sleazy, manipulative" polls. Consequently, in somewhat demagogical fashion, many journalists like to deny their reliance on polls before their audiences, even though if you check their stories you will often find them citing polls, especially to strengthen certain points they are trying to make, particularly points that they may personally embrace.

Of course, another apparent reason why journalists show ambivalence toward public opinion polling is that they really do not have the necessary survey research methodological background to really appreciate and understand polls. This is obvious in the way journalists sometimes fail to explain properly poll results or polling methodology in their stories. For instance, Professor Terry Jones, who is a pollster and author of a textbook on polling, argues in "Newspapers Often Misunderstand Their Own Polls" that journalists are often "self-described statistically challenged souls" who are attracted to journalism by "words and images, not numbers and formulas." Jones was inspired to write this article because he was very critical of the *St. Louis Post-Dispatch*'s misreporting of a Zogby poll on the 2000 presidential race, particularly because of its demonstrable misapplication of the poll's error margin.[2]

The glaring message in Chapter 7 is that politicians have become obviously very addicted to polls, yet they like to pretend before the public that they are too strong and principled to have to rely on polls to help them make decisions. It is clear that politicians have knee jerk or stock answers to any questions they may have to field about polls. Virtually all politicians disingenuously minimize their reliance on polls by saying such things as "I don't really put much stock in polls" or "I don't need polls to tell me what to do," or utter the old classic, "The only poll that counts is the one on election day."

But nearly all of the politicians who say such things about polls are blatant hypocrites and it is hard to believe they are fooling very many people because their heavy reliance on polls is so obvious to even the casual political observer. The simple truth is that candidates running for any major public office at the local, state, or national level must rely on polls to campaign competitively. There are few exceptions (e.g., incumbent legislators in very safe districts). Once in office, only rarely does one find a politician who would not consult polls to find out what the public is thinking about various political issues, public policy proposals, and his or her popularity. The question is, when will politicians feel comfortable in admitting publicly that polls should not be regarded as something taboo, but as a source of valuable information that can be used for positive purposes?

In Chapter 8 I set out to explain how a plethora of public opinion poll data could be used to help resolve an apparent mystery to a lot of people, many of them on Capitol Hill. How could President Clinton not only "survive" the sordid Lewinsky scandal, but also actually soar to new highs in those job approval polls?

Certainly, during the year of the scandal, there was no shortage of polls on the Lewinsky affair. Various polling organizations asked the American people every conceivable question related to the scandal. To the surprise of no one who trusted the pollsters, but to practically everyone who did not, virtually all of the polls revealed the same thing. In a nutshell, the pollsters found that the American people overall resented Ken Starr's probe into the Lewinsky matter, even though they believed that Clinton was guilty of having sexual relations with "that woman," Monica Lewinsky. The polls disclosed that, in fact, the more feverish Starr and the Republican Congress became in pursuing Clinton, the higher he climbed in his job approval ratings (although his character scores dipped), in part because the economy was booming along, but mainly because the scandal was perceived to be about sex and not government business. Also, apparently many Americans believed that Starr's investigation committed an invasion of privacy, that the probe was mostly about gaining a partisan advantage over the Democrats, and that Clinton's affair was not unlike the behavior of other politicians and past presidents. Overall, the pollsters did an admirable job placing the Clinton-Lewinsky affair into perspective, helping us understand how Clinton managed to survive it while explaining why Starr and House Speaker Newt Gingrich did not.

The prevailing theme in Chapter 9 is that public opinion polling is becoming increasingly popular in other countries of the world. At first, many veteran American pollsters worked to promote the acceptance of polling in other developed democracies, and in recent decades polling has been spreading rapidly in many emerging democracies as well. Public opinion polling has even been experimented with in some authoritarian and totalitarian countries, but legitimate polling cannot emerge in such closed societies where people are dominated and intimidated by their government.

Public opinion polling has quickly expanded into other countries because those citizens have undoubtedly recognized the obvious benefits of opinion polling. For example, businesses have realized the advantages of opinion polling in their market research, and academic institutions have successfully used polling to advance various research interests. However, the emphasis in Chapter 9 was on how public opinion polling has helped to develop democracy in various parts of the world by providing a check against corrupt, undemocratic elections, while serving to sensitize political leaders to the genuine will of the people.

In concluding this summary chapter, as well as the book, it is essential that I stress why I decided to write Chapter 10. To reiterate one final time George Gallup's acid test for good polling, he believed that public opinion polling must pass and continuously pass the acid test of accurately predicting election results or else the polling profession would simply not earn the respect it needs to flourish.

Consequently, in Chapter 10 I once again subjected pollsters to Gallup's test. Can we say that they passed with flying colors? Probably not, but certainly, taken together, they did a fairly commendable job. Clearly, the pollsters were at their best in tracking and making predictions in the 2000 presidential election, for which the thirteen polling organizations examined missed predicting Bush's popular vote percentage by an average error of just 1.15% and Gore's by only 1.98%. The pollsters' predictions for the U.S. Senate and gubernatorial races were less impressive, yet altogether their predictions were reasonably precise with many polling organizations making very accurate calls. Would George Gallup be happy with the pollsters' 2000 election predictions? Probably not, because he would maintain that they can and must do even better. And this remains the challenge for pollsters—to keep refining their methods with the goal of performing even better.

Appendix

TABLE A.1   2000 U.S. Senatorial Election Predictions Showing Calculated Error by Comparing Last Poll Prediction Before Election with Actual Election Results (in percent)

State Poll Org Date	Candidate	Last Poll Pred.	A/U	Actual Result 11/7	Error
CA Zogby[M] 11/2	Feinstein, D, I	51	55.1	56.0	.9
	Campbell, R	34	36.7	36.4	.3
	Other		8.2	7.6	.6
	Undecided	15*			
CA Field[L] 11/4	Feinstein, D, I	52	56.8	56.0	.8
	Campbell, R	32	34.9	36.4	1.5
	Other		8.3	7.6	.7
	Undecided	16*			
CA LATimes[M] 10/27	Feinstein, D, I	60	60	56.0	4.0
	Campbell, R	35	35	36.4	1.4
	Other	5	5E	7.6	2.6
	Undecided	0			
CT UConn[L] 10/3	Lieberman, D, I	60	66.7	63.5	3.2
	Giordano, R	27	30.0	34.2	4.2
	Other	3	3.3	2.3	1.0
	Undecided	10			
DE Mason-Dixon[M] 11/3	Carper, D	44	48.9	55.5	6.6
	Roth, R	44	48.9	43.7	5.2
	Other	2	2.2	.8	1.4
	Undecided				
FL CBS/NYTimes[M] 10/25	Nelson, D	45	50.6	51.0	.4
	McCollum, R	36	40.5	46.2	5.7
	Other	7	7.9	2.8	5.1
	Undecided	11			
FL McLaughlin[M] 10/20	Nelson, D	38	47.5	51.0	3.5
	McCollum, R	38	47.5	46.2	1.3
	Other	4	5.0	2.8	2.2
	Undecided	20			
FL Mason-Dixon[M] 11/3	Nelson, D	45	50	51.0	1.0
	McCollum, R	40	44.4	46.2	1.8
	Other	5	5.6	2.8	2.8
	Undecided	10			
FL Schroth[L] 10/8	Nelson, D	45	54.2	51.0	3.2
	McCollum, R	34	41.0	46.2	5.2
	Other			2.8	2.0
	Undecided	17			
FL Tarrance (R)[M] 10/9	Nelson, D	42	50.7	51.0	.3
	McCollum, R	38	45.9	46.2	.3
	Other		3.4	2.8	.6
	Undecided	10*			
FL Zogby[M] 11/5	Nelson, D	44	47.8	51.0	3.2
	McCollum, R	43	46.7	46.2	.5
	Other	5	5.5	2.8	2.7
	Undecided	8			
GA Atlanta Const[L] WSB-TV 11/4	Miller, D, I	55	63.2	57.4	5.8
	Mattingly, R	32	36.8	38.7	1.9
	Other		0.0	3.9	4
	Undecided	13			
GA Shapiro (D)[L] 10/12	Miller, D, I	50	58.1	57.4	.7
	Mattingly, R	32	37.2	38.7	1.5
	Other	4	4.7	3.9	.8
	Undecided	14			
GA Mason-Dixon[M] 10/19	Miller, D, I	49	60.5	57.4	3.1
	Mattingly, R	30	37.0	38.7	1.7
	Other	2	2.5	3.9	1.4
	Undecided	19			
IN McLaughlin (R)[M] 10/2	Johnson, D	15	17.2	31.9	14.7
	Lugar, R, I	70	80.3	66.5	13.8
	Other	3	3.4	1.6	1.8
	Undecided	13			
IN Market Shares[M] 11/1	Johnson, D	10	12.2	31.9	19.7
	Lugar, R, I	69	84.1	66.5	17.6
	Other	3	3.7	1.6	2.1
	Undecided	18			
IN Research 2000[M] 11/3	Johnson, D	20	22.2	31.9	9.7
	Lugar, R, I	68	75.6	66.5	9.1
	Other	2	2.2	1.6	.6
	Undecided	10			
ME Critical Insights[L] 10/18	Lawrence, D	16	17.8	31.4	13.6
	Snowe, R, I	73	81.2	68.6	13.0
	Other	0	0	0	0
	Undecided	10			
ME Market Decisions[M] 10/29	Lawrence, D	15	20	31.4	11.4
	Snowe, R, I	60	80	68.6	11.4
	Other	0	0	0	0
	Undecided	25			
ME RKM Research[L] 9/15	Lawrence, D	19	21.1	31.4	10.3
	Snowe, R, I	70	77.7	68.6	9.1
	Other	2	2.2	0	2.2
	Undecided	10			
MD Mason-Dixon[M] 11/1	Sarbanes, D, I	59	66.3	63.3	3.0
	Rappaport, R	30	33.7	36.7	3.0
	Other	0	0	0	0
	Undecided	11			
MA Boston Herald[L] 9/1	Kennedy, D	68	81	72.6	8.4
	Robinson, R	16	19	13.0	6.0
	Other	0	0	14.4	14.4
	Undecided	16			
MA U. of Mass.[L] 10/8	Kennedy, D	60	72.3	72.6	.3
	Robinson, R	23	27.7	13.0	13.3
	Other	0	0	14.4	14.4
	Undecided	17			
MI Anderson (R)[L] 10/7	Stabenow, D	37	42.5	49.3	6.8
	Abraham, R, I	50	57.5	48.0	9.5
	Other	0	0	2.7	2.7
	Undecided	13			
MI Detroit News[L] 11/5	Stabenow, D	38	46.9	49.3	2.4
	Abraham, R, I	41	50.6	48.0	2.6
	Other	2	2.5	2.7	.2
	Undecided	19			
MI Detroit Free Press[L] 10/27	Stabenow, D	41	48.3	49.3	1.0
	Abraham, R, I	41	48.3	48.0	.3
	Other	2	2.4	2.7	.3
	Undecided	15			

State Poll Org Date	Candidate	Last Poll Pred.	A/U	Actual Result 11/7	Error
MI EPIC-MRA[M] 11/4	Stabenow, D	42	46.3	49.3	3.0
	Abraham, R, I	47	51.3	48.0	3.3
	Other	0	2.9	2.7	.2
	Undecided	11*			
MI Hickman-Brown (D)[L] 10/4	Stabenow, D	42	46.3	49.3	3.0
	Abraham, R, I	46	50.7	48.0	2.7
	Other	0	3.0	2.7	.3
	Undecided	12*			
MI Hill Research (R)[L] 10/26	Stabenow, D	41	44.3	49.3	5.0
	Abraham, R, I	49	52.9	48.0	4.9
	Other	0	2.9	2.7	.2
	Undecided	10*			
MI Marketing Resource (R)[L] 10/4	Stabenow, D	36	40.4	49.3	8.9
	Abraham, R, I	50	56.1	48.0	8.1
	Other	4	4.5	2.7	1.8
	Undecided	11			
MI MI Democratic Party (D)[L] 10/12	Stabenow, D	40	46.5	49.3	2.8
	Abraham, R, I	46	53.5	48.0	5.5
	Other	0	0	2.7	2.7
	Undecided	14			
MI Research 2000[M] 11/4	Stabenow, D	44	51.8	49.3	2.5
	Abraham, R, I	39	45.9	48.0	2.1
	Other	2	2.4	2.7	.3
	Undecided	15			
MI Zogby[M] 11/5	Stabenow, D	47	49.6	49.3	.3
	Abraham, R, I	45	47.5	48.0	.5
	Other	0	2.9	2.7	.2
	Undecided	8*			
MN Mason-Dixon[M] 10/31	Dayton, D	47	50.0	48.7	1.3
	Graham, R, I	42	44.7	43.3	1.4
	Other	5	5.3	8.0	2.7
	Undecided	6			
MN MN Star Tribune[L] 11/5	Dayton, D	46	52.3	48.7	3.6
	Graham, R, I	37	42.0	43.3	1.3
	Other	5	5.7	8.0	2.3
	Undecided	12			
MN St. Cloud U.[L] 10/27	Dayton, D	48	55.2	48.7	6.5
	Graham, R, I	33	37.9	43.3	5.4
	Other	6	6.9	8.0	1.1
	Undecided	13			
MN Tarrance (R)[M] 11/3	Dayton, D	44	47.8	48.7	.9
	Graham, R, I	43	46.7	43.3	3.4
	Other	6	6.5	8.0	1.5
	Undecided	8			
MO Ayres-McHenry (R)[L] 9/15	Carnahan, D	38	45.8	50.5	4.7
	Ashcroft, R, I	43	51.8	48.4	3.4
	Other	2	2.4	1.1	1.3
	Undecided	17			
MO Mason-Dixon[M] 10/27	Carnahan, D	46	49.5	50.5	1.0
	Ashcroft, R, I	46	49.5	48.4	1.1
	Other	1	1.1	1.1	0.0
	Undecided	7			
MO Mason-Dixon[M] 10/27[b]	Carnahan, D	47	50.5	50.5	0
	Ashcroft, R, I	45	48.4	48.4	0
	Other	1	1.1	1.1	0
	Undecided	7			
MO Research 2000[M] 11/3	Carnahan, D	47	52.8	50.5	2.3
	Ashcroft, R, I	42	47.2	48.4	1.2
	Other	0	0	1.1	0
	Undecided	11			
MO Zogby[M] 11/5	Carnahan, D	47	51.1	50.5	.6
	Ashcroft, R, I	45	48.9	48.4	.5
	Other	0	0	1.1	0
	Undecided	8			
MT A & A Research[L] 10/19	Burns, R, I	48	53.9	51.0	2.9
	Schweitzer, D	40	44.9	46.8	1.9
	Other	1	1.1	2.2	1.1
	Undecided	11			
MT Mason-Dixon[M] 10/26	Burns, R, I	45	50	51.0	1.0
	Schweitzer, D	44	48.9	46.8	2.1
	Other	1	1.1	2.2	1.1
	Undecided	10			
MT Mellman (D)[L] 10/18	Burns, R, I	48	53.3	51.0	2.3
	Schweitzer, D	40	44.4	46.8	2.4
	Other	2	2.2	2.2	0
	Undecided	10			
MT MT State U.[L] 10/25	Burns, R, I	41	45.6	51.0	5.4
	Schweitzer, D	43	47.8	46.8	1.0
	Other	6	6.7	2.2	4.5
	Undecided	10			
MT Talmey-Drake (D)[L] 9/11	Burns, R, I	49	55.1	51.0	4.1
	Schweitzer, D	40	44.9	46.8	1.9
	Other	0	0	2.2	2.2
	Undecided	11			
NE Hackman-Braun[M] 9/8	Nelson, D	54	58.1	51.0	7.1
	Stenberg, R	39	41.9	49.0	7.1
	Other	0	0	0	0
	Undecided	7			
NE Moore Info (R)[L] 9/23	Nelson, D	44	49.4	51.0	1.6
	Stenberg, R	45	50.6	49.0	1.6
	Other	0	0	0	0
	Undecided	11			
NE RKM Res.[M] 10/29	Nelson, D	49	57.0	51.0	6.0
	Stenberg, R	37	43.0	49.0	6.0
	Other	0	0	0	0
	Undecided	14			
NV Mason-Dixon[M] 11/1	Bernstein, D	37	40.2	39.7	.5
	Ensin, R	54	58.7	55.1	3.6
	Other	1	1.1	5.2	4.1
	Undecided	8			
NV Public Opinion Strategies (R)[M] 9/22	Bernstein, D	36	40.9	39.7	1.2
	Ensin, R	47	53.4	55.1	1.7
	Other	5	5.7	5.2	.5
	Undecided	12			
NV Mellman (D)[M] 9/20	Bernstein, D	37	45.7	39.7	6.0
	Ensin, R	41	50.6	55.1	4.5
	Other	3	3.7	5.2	1.5
	Undecided	19			
NJ Gannett NJ[M] 11/5	Corzine, D	41	53.2	50.6	2.6
	Franks, R	36	46.8	46.6	.2
	Other	0	0	2.8	2.8
	Undecided	23			
NJ Mahoney, Strimple, Gano (R)[M] 10/5	Corzine, D	41	53.2	50.6	2.6
	Franks, R	36	46.8	46.6	.2
	Other	0	0	2.8	2.8
	Undecided	23			
NJ New Star-Ledger[L] 10/29	Corzine, D	46	55.4	50.6	4.8
	Franks, R	37	44.6	46.6	2.0
	Other	0	0	2.8	2.8
	Undecided	17			
NJ NYTimes[M] 10/18	Corzine, D	53	57.1	50.6	6.5
	Franks, R	37	40.0	46.6	6.6
	Other	0	3.0	2.8	.2
	Undecided	10[a]			
NJ Penn, Schoen, Berland (D)[L] 11/5	Corzine, D	51	53.1	50.6	47.5
	Franks, R	45	46.9	46.6	.3
	Other	0	0	2.8	2.8
	Undecided	4			

State Poll Org Date	Candidate	Last Poll Pred.	A/U	Actual Result 11/7	Error
NJ Quinnipiac College^L 11/6	Corzine, D	43	48.9	50.6	1.7
	Franks, R	45	51.1	46.6	4.5
	Other	0	0	2.8	2.8
	Undecided	12			
NJ Research 2000^M 10/1	Corzine, D	48	58.5	50.6	7.9
	Franks, R	34	41.5	46.6	5.1
	Other	0	0	2.8	2.8
	Undecided	48			
NJ Tarrance (R)^M 9/29	Corzine, D	43	49.5	50.6	1.1
	Franks, R	41	47.2	46.6	.6
	Other	0	3.2	2.8	.8
	Undecided	16*			
NM Mason-Dixon^M 11/5	Binaman, D, I	60	66.7	62.5	4.2
	Redmand, R	30	33.3	37.5	4.2
	Other	0	0	0	0
	Undecided	10			
NM Research & Polling^L 11/5	Binaman, D, I	61	65.6	62.5	3.1
	Redmand, R	32	34.4	37.5	3.1
	Other	0	0	0	0
	Undecided	7			
NY Blum & Weprin^L 11/5	Clinton, D	47	50.0	55.1	5.1
	Lazio, R	40	46.0	43.1	2.9
	Other	0	0	1.8	1.8
	Undecided	13			
NY CBS/NY Times^M 10/29	Clinton, D	49	54.4	55.1	.7
	Lazio, R	41	45.6	43.1	2.5
	Other	0		1.8	
	Undecided	10			
NY I I Newsday/ WB11 (R)^L 10/17	Clinton, D	51	53.1	55.1	2.0
	Lazio, R	45	46.9	43.1	3.8
	Other	0	0	1.8	1.8
	Undecided	4			
NY Marist Inst.^L 11/6	Clinton, D	49	51.0	55.1	4.1
	Lazio, R	46	47.9	43.1	4.8
	Other	2	2.1	1.8	.3
	Undecided	4			
NY Princeton Survey^M 11/2	Clinton, D	48	50.5	55.1	4.6
	Lazio, R	47	49.5	43.1	6.4
	Other	0	0	1.8	1.8
	Undecided	5			
NY Quinnipiac College^L 11/6	Clinton, D	51	56.7	55.1	55.1
	Lazio, R	39	43.3	43.1	43.1
	Other	0	0	1.8	1.8
	Undecided	0			
NY Zogby^M 11/5	Clinton, D	48	51.1	55.1	4.0
	Lazio, R	46	48.9	43.1	5.8
	Other	0	0	1.8	1.8
	Undecided	6			
ND Garin-Hart (D)^M 9/19	Conrad, D	61	69.3	61.7	7.6
	Sand, R	27	30.7	38.3	7.6
	Other	0	0	0	0
	Undecided				
ND MN State U.^L 10/30	Conrad, D	66	71.0	61.7	9.3
	Sand, R	27	29.0	38.3	9.3
	Other	0	0	0	0
	Undecided	12			
OH EPIC-MRA^M 9/19	Celeste, D	27	36.4	35.7	.7
	Dewine, R	48	64.6	60.0	4.6
	Other	0	0	4.3	4.3
	Undecided	26			
OH Mason-Dixon^M 11/4	Celeste, D	32	36.4	35.7	.7
	Dewine, R	56	63.6	60.0	3.6
	Other	0	0	4.3	4.3
	Undecided	12			
OH Ohio State U.^L 10/25	Celeste, D	36	39.9	35.7	4.2
	Dewine, R	50	55.4	60.0	4.6
	Other	0	4.8	4.3	.5
	Undecided	14*			
OH U. of Cincinnati^L 11/6	Celeste, D	34	35.1	35.7	.6
	Dewine, R	63	64.9	60.0	4.9
	Other	0	0	4.3	4.3
	Undecided	3			
OH Zogby^M 11/5	Celeste, D	29	32.6	35.7	3.1
	Dewine, R	60	67.4	60.0	7.4
	Other	0	4.3	4.3	4.3
	Undecided	11			
PA Commonwealth Lincoln Inst.^L 0/25	Klink, D	38	42.7	45.4	3.0
	Santorum, R, I	49	55.1	52.4	2.7
	Other	2	2.2	2.2	0
	Undecided	11			
PA Decision Forecasting^L 11/6	Klink, D	34	38.2	45.4	7.2
	Santorum, R, I	55	61.8	52.4	9.4
	Other	0	0	2.2	7.2
	Undecided	11			
PA Mason-Dixon^M 11/5	Klink, D	36	39.6	45.4	5.8
	Santorum, R, I	55	60.4	52.4	8.0
	Other	0	0	2.2	2.2
	Undecided	0			
PA Millorsville U.^L 10/31	Klink, D	27	35.0	45.4	10.4
	Santorum, R, I	48	62.2	52.4	9.8
	Other	0	2.8	2.2	.6
	Undecided	25*			
PA Public Opinion Strategies (R)^M 10/31	Klink, D	31	36.0	45.4	9.4
	Santorum, R, I	53	61.5	52.4	9.1
	Other	0	2.6	2.2	.4
	Undecided	16*			
PA Westchester U.^L 10/25	Klink, D	35	43.6	45.4	1.8
	Santorum, R, I	43	53.6	52.4	1.2
	Other	22*	2.7	2.2	.5
	Undecided				
PA Zogby^M 11/5	Klink, D	33	38.7	45.4	6.7
	Santorum, R, I	50	58.7	52.4	6.3
	Other	0	2.6	2.2	.4
	Undecided	17*			
RI Brown U.^L 10/29	Weygand, D	28	34.1	41.3	7.2
	Chafee, R, I	52	63.4	56.7	6.7
	Other	2	2.4	2.0	.4
	Undecided	18			
RI Fleming Assn.^L 11/2	Weygand, D	34	38.2	41.3	3.1
	Chafee, R, I	53	59.6	56.7	2.9
	Other	2	2.2	2.0	.2
	Undecided	11			
TN Mason-Dixon^M 10/2	Clark, D	23	26.2	32.2	6.0
	Frist, R, I	62	70.7	65.1	5.6
	Other	0	3.1	2.7	.4
	Undecided	15*			
TN Zogby^M 11/5	Clark, D	28	30.9	32.2	1.3
	Frist, R, I	60	66.2	65.1	1.1
	Other	0	3.0	2.7	.3
	Undecided	12*			
TX Scrips Data Ct.^M 11/5	Kelly, D	21	25.4	32.3	6.9
	Hutchison, R, I	59	71.4	65.1	6.3
	Other	0	3.1	2.6	.5
	Undecided	20*			
UT Jones & Assoc. (R)^L 10/15	Howell	24	26.7	31.5	4.8
	Hatch, R, I	64	71.1	65.6	5.5
	Other	2	2.2	2.9	.7
	Undecided	10			

State Poll Org Date	Candidate	Last Poll Pred.	A/U	Actual Result 11/7	Error
UT Salt Lake Tribune[L] 9/3	Howell	27	31.0	31.5	.5
	Hatch, R, I	59	67.8	65.6	2.2
	Other	1	1.1	2.9	1.8
	Undecided	13			
VT Mason-Dixon[M] 9/1	Flanagan, D	28	31.5	25.8	5.7
	Jeffords, R, I	61	68.5	66.7	1.8
	Other	0	0	7.5	7.5
	Undecided	11			
VT Research 2000[M] 10/27	Flanagan, D	33	35.1	25.8	9.3
	Jeffords, R, I	61	64.9	66.7	1.8
	Other	0	0	7.5	7.5
	Undecided	6			
VA Mason-Dixon[M] 11/3	Allen, R	49	52.7	52.3	.4
	Robb, D, I	44	47.3	47.7	.4
	Other	0	0	0	0
	Undecided	7			
VA Media General[L] 11/4	Allen, R	45	51.1	52.3	1.2
	Robb, D, I	43	48.9	47.7	1.2
	Other	0	0	0	0
	Undecided	12			
VA Old Dominion U.[L] 9/18	Allen, R	42	56.8	52.3	9.1
	Robb, D, I	32	43.2	47.7	4.5
	Other	0	0	0	0
	Undecided	26			

State Poll Org Date	Candidate	Last Poll Pred.	A/U	Actual Result 11/7	Error
WA Elway Res.[L] 10/26	Cantwell, D	43	47.3	48.7	1.4
	Gorton, R, I	46	48.6	49.3	1.4
	Other	0	2.2	2.0	.2
	Undecided	11*			
WA Moore Inf (R)[M] 9/12	Cantwell, D	28	33.7	48.7	1.5
	Gorton, R, I	45	54.2	48.6	5.6
	Other	10	12.0	2.6	9.4
	Undecided	17			
WA Zogby[M] 11/5	Cantwell, D	50	52.7	48.7	4.0
	Gorton, R, I	43	45.3	48.6	3.3
	Other	0	2.1	2.7	.6
	Undecided	7*			
WI Market Shares[M] 11/?	Kohl, D, I	60	67.9	61.6	6.3
	Gillespie, R	2	30.6	37.1	6.5
	Other	0	1.5	1.3	.2
	Undecided	13*			
WI Zogby[M] 11/5	Kohl, D, I	62	65.7	61.6	4.1
	Gillespie, R	31	32.9	37.1	4.2
	Other	0	1.4	1.3	.3
	Undecided	7*			
WY Mason-Dixon[M] 9/21	Logan, D	14	16.3	22.1	5.8
	Thomas, R, I	68	80.0	73.7	6.3
	Other	3	3.5	4.2	.7
	Undecided	15			

NOTE: Major poll organizations (M) include those that poll nationally on a regular basis; local poll organizations (L) are those that normally do not, but poll mostly in one state or a region. It is not always easy to make the distinction between major and local polling organizations, but I feel generally comfortable with the classification. Arizona, Hawaii, Mississippi, and West Virginia U.S. Senate races are excluded because no polls or no recent polls were conducted in these noncompetitive Senate contests. I, D, R, and A/U indicate Incumbent, Democrat, Republican, and allocation of undecided voters.

[a] Unfortunately these poll results, when reported, grouped "other," "undecided," and "don't know" categories together. This forced me to use a "necessity formula" to separate the "undecided/dk" from "other" so the undecided percentage could be determined so a "prediction error" could be calculated. To estimate the "undecided," the actual "other" percentage was subtracted from the "undecided/other/dk" grouping. Once this was done, the proportionate allocation method, as used in Table 10.2, was used to allocate the undecided so poll predictions could be compared to the actual results so "prediction error" could be figured. Granted, subtracting the actual percent for "other" biases the calculation of error, but no good choice remained. It is irresponsible for poll results to be reported without separating "other" from the "undecided/dk" category.

[b] Question acknowledged that Jean Carnahan would be appointed if her deceased husband, Mel Carnahan, won.

TABLE A.2 2000 Gubernatorial Election Predictions Showing Calculated Error by Comparing Last Poll Prediction Before Election with Actual Election Results (in percent)

State / Poll Org / Date	Candidate	Last Poll Pred.	A/U	Actual Result 11/7	Error
DE Mason-Dixon[M] 11/3	Minner, D	48	57.1	59.2	2.1
	Burris, R	36	42.9	39.7	3.2
	Other	0	0	1.0	1.0
	Undecided	16			
DE U. of Delaware[L] 10/2	Minner, D	52	61.8	59.2	2.6
	Burris, R	33	39.2	39.7	.5
	Other	0	0	1.0	1.0
	Undecided				
IN Gavin-Hart Yanal (D)[M] 10/12	O'Bannon, D, I	57	64.8	56.6	8.2
	McIntosh, R	31	35.2	41.6	6.4
	Other	0	0	1.8	1.8
	Undecided	12			
IN Indiana U.[L] 9/12	O'Bannon, D, I	44	62.0	56.6	5.4
	McIntosh, R	26	36.6	41.6	5.0
	Other	1	1.4	1.8	.4
	Undecided	29			
IN Indianapolis Star[L] 9/13	O'Bannon, D, I	50	62.5	56.6	5.9
	McIntosh, R	29	36.6	41.6	5.3
	Other	1	1.2	1.8	.6
	Undecided	20			
IN McLaughlin (R)[M] 10/2	O'Bannon, D, I	48	58.0	56.6	1.4
	McIntosh, R	34	41.0	41.6	.6
	Other	0	0	1.8	1.8
	Undecided	17			
IN Market Shares[M] 11/1	O'Bannon, D, I	49	58.2	56.6	1.6
	McIntosh, R	33	39.2	41.6	2.4
	Other	3	3.6	1.8	1.8
	Undecided	16			
IN Research 2000[M] 11/1	O'Bannon, D, I	52	57.1	56.6	.5
	McIntosh, R	37	40.7	41.6	.9
	Other	2	2.2	1.8	.4
	Undecided	9			
MO Ayes McHenry (R)[M] 9/15	Holden, D	35	47.5	49.1	1.6
	Talent, R	34	46.1	48.2	2.1
	Other	4	5.4	2.7	2.7
	Undecided	26			
MO Mason-Dixon[M] 10/28	Holden, D	45	49.6	49.1	.5
	Talent, R	43	47.4	48.2	.8
	Other		3.0	2.7	.3
	Undecided	12*			
MO Zogby[M] 11/5	Holden, D	42	48.8	49.1	.3
	Talent, R	42	48.8	48.2	.6
	Other	2	2.3	2.7	.4
	Undecided	14			
MT A&A Research[M] 10/21	O'Keefe, D	44	51.2	47.1	4.1
	Martz, R	41	46.7	51.0	4.3
	Other	1	1.2	1.9	.7
	Undecided	14			
MT Mason-Dixon[M] 10/27	O'Keefe, D	46	50.5	47.1	3.4
	Martz, R	44	48.4	51.0	2.6
	Other	1	1.1	1.9	.2
	Undecided	9			
NH American Res.[L] 11/5	Shaheen, D, I	41	44.0	50.1	6.1
	Humphrey, R	45	48.4	44.1	4.3
	Other	8	8.6	5.8	2.8
	Undecided	7			
IN Franklin Pierce College[L] 10/31	Shaheen, D, I	51	58.1	50.1	8.0
	Humphrey, R	30	34.2	44.1	9.9
	Other	5	5.7	5.8	.1
	Undecided	12			

State / Poll Org / Date	Candidate	Last Poll Pred.	A/U	Actual Result 11/7	Error
NH Research 2000[M] 11/3	Shaheen, D, I	51	53.1	50.1	3.0
	Humphrey, R	42	43.7	44.1	.4
	Other	3	3.1	5.8	2.7
	Undecided	4			
NH RKM Research[M] 11/2	Shaheen, D, I	43	45.7	50.1	4.4
	Humphrey, R	44	46.8	44.1	2.7
	Other	7	7.4	5.8	1.6
	Undecided	6			
NH U. of Conn[L] 10/3	Shaheen, D, I	44	51.7	50.1	1.6
	Humphrey, R	35	41.1	44.1	3.0
	Other	7	7.2	5.8	1.4
	Undecided	15			
NH U. of New Hampshire[L] 9/8	Shaheen, D, I	49	53.3	50.1	3.2
	Humphrey, R	36	39.2	44.1	4.9
	Other	7	7.6	5.8	1.8
	Undecided	8			
NC KPC Research[L] 10/21	Easley, D	43	51.5	51.9	.4
	Vinroot, R	37	44.3	46.4	2.1
	Other	1	1.2	1.7	.5
	Undecided	16			
NC Mason-Dixon[M] 11/2	Easley, D	48	52.7	51.9	.8
	Vinroot, R	41	45.1	46.4	1.3
	Other	2	2.0	1.7	.5
	Undecided	9			
NC Research 2000[M] 11/2	Easley, D	48	53.9	51.9	2.0
	Vinroot, R	40	44.9	46.4	1.5
	Other	1	1.1	1.7	.6
	Undecided	11			
ND Minn. State U.[L] 10/29	Heitkamp, D	46	48.2	45.0	3.2
	Hoeven, R	49	51.6	55.0	3.4
	Other	0	0	0	0
	Undecided	5			
ND Public Opinion Strategies (R)[M] 9/1	Heitkamp, D	41	46.6	45.0	1.6
	Hoeven, R	47	53.4	55.0	1.6
	Other	0	0	0	0
	Undecided	12			
UT Jones & Assoc. (R)[L] 9/26	Ortem, D	36	39.2	42.3	3.1
	Leavitt, R, I	52	56.6	55.8	.8
	Other	3	3.3	1.9	1.4
	Undecided	8			
UT Deseret News/ KSL-TV[L] 10/15	Ortem, D	37	40.7	42.3	1.6
	Leavitt, R, I	52	57.1	55.8	1.3
	Other	2	2.2	1.9	.3
	Undecided	9			
UT Salt Lake Tribune[L] 9/3	Ortem, D	29	34.1	42.3	8.2
	Leavitt, R, I	55	64.7	55.8	8.9
	Other	1	1.2	1.9	.7
	Undecided	15			
VT Mason-Dixon[M] 10/24	Dean, D, I	48	51.6	50.6	1.0
	Dwyer, R	39	41.9	38.1	3.8
	Other	6	6.5	11.3	4.8
	Undecided.	7			
VT Public Opinion Strategies (R)[M] 9/27	Dean, D, I	44	50.0	50.6	.6
	Dwyer, R	39	44.3	38.1	6.2
	Other	5	5.7	11.3	5.6
	Undecided.	12			
VT Research 2000[M] 10/27	Dean, D, I	49	53.8	50.6	3.2
	Dwyer, R	35	38.5	38.1	.4
	Other	7	7.7	11.3	3.6
	Undecided.	9			

State Poll Org Date	Candidate	Last Poll Pred.	A/U	Actual Result 11/7	Error
WA	Locke, D, I	56	63.2	58.2	5.0
Elway Res.[L]	Carlson, R	31	32.4	40.2	7.8
10/26	Other	0	1.8	1.6	.2
	Undecided.	13*		1.6	
WV	Wise, D	42	46.7	50.2	3.5
Ohio State U.[L]	Underwood, R, I	44	48.9	47.2	1.7
10/30	Other	4	4.4	2.6	1.8
	Undecided	10			

State Poll Org Date	Candidate	Last Poll Pred.	A/U	Actual Result 11/7	Error
WV	Wise, D	38	45.5	50.2	4.7
Ryan-McGinn-	Underwood, R, I	43	51.4	47.2	4.2
Samples (R)[L]	Other		3.1	2.6	.5
10/25	Undecided	19*			
WV	Wise, D	36	46.8	50.2	3.4
W. Va. Res. Ct.[L]	Underwood, R, I	39	50.6	47.2	3.4
9/29	Other	2	3.4	2.6	.8
	Undecided	23			

NOTE: Major poll organizations (M) include those that poll nationally on a regular basis; local poll organizations (L) are those that normally do not, but poll mostly in one state or a region. I, D, R, and A/U indicate Incumbent, Democrat, Republican, and allocation of undecided voters.

[a] Unfortunately these poll results, when reported, grouped "other," "undecided," and "don't know" categories together. This forced me to use a "necessity formula" to separate the "undecided/dk" from "other" so the undecided percentage could be determined so a "prediction error" could be calculated. To estimate the "undecided," the actual "other" percentage was subtracted from the "undecided/other/dk" grouping. Once this was done, the proportionate allocation method, as used in Table 10.2, was used to allocate the undecided so poll predictions could be compared to the actual results so "prediction error" could be figured. Granted, subtracting the actual percent for "other" biases the calculation of error, but no good choice remained. It is irresponsible for poll results to be reported without separating "other" from the "undecided/dk" category.

TABLE A.3 2000 Presidential Election Predictions in Each State by the Last Poll Conducted Showing Calculated Error (in percent)

State Poll Org Date	Candidate	Last Poll Pred.	A/U	Actual Result 11/7	Error	State Poll Org Date	Candidate	Last Poll Pred.	A/U	Actual Result 11/7	Error
AL Mason-Dixon^M 11/4	Bush	55	57.9	56.4	1.5	KS American Research Group^M 9/21	Bush	55	61.1	58.2	2.9
	Gore	38	40.0	41.7	1.7		Gore	32	35.6	37.1	1.5
	Other	2	2.1	1.9	1.1		Other	3	3.3	4.7	1.4
	Undecided	5					Undecided	10			
AK Amer. Research Group^L 9/21	Bush	47	52.2	59.0	6.8	KY Mason-Dixon^M 11/4	Bush	51	54.3	56.5	2.2
	Gore	26	28.9	27.9	1.0		Gore	41	43.6	41.4	2.2
	Other	.8	20.0	13.1	6.9		Other	2	2.1	2.2	.1
	Undecided	10					Undecided	6			
AZ Arizona Republic^L 11/3	Bush	49	53.3	50.9	2.4	LA Mason-Dixon^M 10/29	Bush	52	55.4	52.5	2.9
	Gore	39	42.4	45.2	2.8		Gore	39	41.9	44.9	3.0
	Other	3	3.3	3.9	.6		Other	2	2.1	2.6	.5
	Undecided	8*					Undecided	6			
AR Memphis Commercial Appl^L 11/5	Bush	47	49.6	50.9	1.3	ME RKM Research^M 10/31	Bush	42	46.2	44.0	2.2
	Gore	44	46.5	45.4	1.1		Gore	42	46.2	48.9	2.7
	Other		3.9	3.7	.2		Other	5	5.5	7.1	1.6
	Undecided	9					Undecided	9			
CA Zogby^M 11/5	Bush	44	44	41.8	2.2	MD Mason-Dixon^M 10/21	Bush	40	42.5	40.0	2.5
	Gore	47	47	53.3	6.3		Gore	48	51.0	56.8	5.8
	Other	8	8	4.9	3.1		Other	7	7.4	3.2	3.2
	Undecided	0					Undecided	6			
CO Ciruli^L 11/2	Bush	47	52.2	50.8	1.4	MA American Research Group^M 9/21	Bush	26	28.9	32.6	3.7
	Gore	38	42.2	42.4	.2		Gore	57	63.4	59.9	3.5
	Other	5	5.6	6.8	1.2		Other	6	6.7	7.6	.9
	Undecided	10					Undecided	10			
CT Hartford Courant U. of Conn.^L 10/4	Bush	32	36.9	38.5	1.6	MI Zogby^M 11/5	Bush	43	43	46.4	3.4
	Gore	48	55.3	56.1	.8		Gore	50	50	51.1	1.1
	Other	5	5.8	5.4	.4		Other	6	6	2.5	3.5
	Undecided	13					Undecided	0			
DE Mason-Dixon^M 11/3	Bush	46	49.5	41.8	7.7	MN Minneapolis Star Tribune^L 11/5	Bush	47	50.5	45.5	5.0
	Gore	42	45.2	55.1	9.9		Gore	37	39.8	47.9	8.1
	Other	5	5.4	3.9	1.5		Other	9	9.7	6.6	3.1
	Undecided	7					Undecided	7			
FL Zogby^M 11/5	Bush	49	49	48.8	.2	MS Mason-Dixon^M 11/4	Bush	52	55.3	56.9	1.6
	Gore	46	46	48.8	2.8		Gore	41	43.6	41.4	2.2
	Other	5	5	2.4	2.6		Other	1	1.1	1.6	.5
	Undecided	0					Undecided	6			
GA Atlanta Journal Const.^L 11/4	Bush	53	55.8	55.0	.8	MO Zogby^M 11/5	Bush	49	49	50.4	1.4
	Gore	37	38.9	43.1	4.2		Gore	45	45	47.1	2.1
	Other	5	5.3	1.9	3.4		Other	5	5	2.5	2.5
	Undecided	5					Undecided	0			
I II American Research Group^M 9/21	Bush	29	32.6	37.5	4.9	MT Mason-Dixon^M 10/28	Bush	49	52.7	58.4	5.7
	Gore	57	64.0	55.8	8.2		Gore	37	39.8	33.4	6.4
	Other	3	3.4	6.7	3.3		Other	7	7.5	8.2	.7
	Undecided	11					Undecided	7			
ID Mason-Dixon^M 10/28	Bush	56	60.2	68.8	8.6	NE RKM Research^M 10/28	Bush	56	62.2	62.6	.4
	Gore	30	32.3	28.3	4.0		Gore	31	34.4	33.0	1.4
	Other	7	7.5	2.8	4.7		Other	3	3.3	4.4	1.1
	Undecided	7					Undecided	10			
IL Zogby^M 11/5	Bush	40	40	42.7	2.7	NV Mason-Dixon^M 10/31	Bush	47	50.5	49.5	1.0
	Gore	53	53	54.5	1.5		Gore	43	46.2	46.0	.2
	Other	6	6	2.8	3.2		Other	3	3.2	4.5	1.3
	Undecided	0					Undecided	7			
IN Market Shares^M 11/1	Bush	53	61.2	57.1	4.1	NH American Research Group^M 11/5	Bush	48	49.5	48.2	1.3
	Gore	30	35.2	41.3	6.2		Gore	38	39.2	47.0	7.8
	Other	1	3.6	1.6	2.0		Other	11	11.3	4.9	6.4
	Undecided	15					Undecided	3			
IA Des Moines Register^L 11/5	Bush	42	46.7	48.3	1.6	NJ Quinnipiac College^L 11/6	Bush	41	43.2	40.4	2.8
	Gore	44	48.9	48.6	.3		Gore	49	51.6	56.0	4.4
	Other	4	4.4	3.2	1.2		Other	5	5.3	3.6	1.7
	Undecided	10					Undecided	5			

State Poll Org Date	Candidate	Last Poll Pred.	A/U	Actual Result 11/7	Error
NM Mason-Dixon[M] 11/5	Bush	45	47.4	47.9	.5
	Gore	45	47.4	47.9	.5
	Other	5	5.3	4.3	1.0
	Undecided	5			
NY Zogby[M] 11/5	Bush	39	39	35.5	3.5
	Gore	53	53	59.8	6.8
	Other	7	7	4.7	2.3
	Undecided	0			
NC Research 2000[M] 11/2	Bush	52	55.3	56.1	.8
	Gore	42	44.7	43.2	1.5
	Other	0	0	.7	.7
	Undecided	6			
ND American Research Group[M] 10/7	Bush	47	55.3	60.6	5.3
	Gore	35	41.2	33.2	8.0
	Other	3	3.5	6.3	2.8
	Undecided	15			
OH Zogby[M] 11/5	Bush	52	52	50.2	1.8
	Gore	43	43	46.3	3.3
	Other	4	4	3.5	.5
	Undecided	0			
OK Mason-Dixon[M] 11/4	Bush	54	56.8	60.3	3.5
	Gore	39	41.1	38.4	2.7
	Other	2	2.1	1.3	.8
	Undecided	5			
OR Davis Hibbitts[L] ll/1	Bush	44	45.4	46.7	1.3
	Gore	45	46.4	47.0	.6
	Other	8	8.2	6.3	1.9
	Undecided	3			
PA Zogby[M] 11/5	Bush	45	45	46.4	1.4
	Gore	47	47	50.6	3.6
	Other	7	7	3.0	4.0
	Undecided	0			
RI Brown U.[L] 10/29	Bush	29	34.1	32.0	2.1
	Gore	47	55.3	61.4	6.0
	Other	9	10.6	6.1	4.5
	Undecided	15			
SC Mason-Dixon[M] 11/4	Bush	53	56.4	56.9	.5
	Gore	38	40.4	40.8	.4
	Other	3	3.2	2.3	.9
	Undecided	6			
SD KELO-TV[L] 11/3	Bush	51	58.0	60.3	2.3
	Gore	33	37.5	37.6	.1
	Other	4	4.5	2.1	2.4
	Undecided	12			

State Poll Org Date	Candidate	Last Poll Pred.	A/U	Actual Result 11/7	Error
TN Zogby[M] 11/5	Bush	50	50	51.2	1.2
	Gore	46	46	47.4	1.4
	Other	3	3	1.4	1.6
	Undecided	0			
TX Mason-Dixon[M] 11/4	Bush	64	66.7	59.3	7.4
	Gore	30	31.3	38.0	6.7
	Other	2	2.8	2.7	.7
	Undecided	4			
UT Salt Lake Tribune[L] 11/5	Bush	60	67.4	66.9	.5
	Gore	24	27.0	26.3	.7
	Other	5	5.6	6.8	1.2
	Undecided	11			
VT Research 2000[M] 10/27	Bush	36	38.3	41.0	2.7
	Gore	52	55.3	51.0	4.3
	Other	6	6.4	8.0	1.6
	Undecided	6			
VA Media General[L] 11/4	Bush	46	52.3	52.4	.1
	Gore	40	45.5	44.7	.8
	Other	2	2.3	3.0	.7
	Undecided	12			
WA Zogby[M] 11/5	Bush	44	44	44.8	.8
	Gore	48	48	50.2	2.2
	Other	8	8	5.0	3.0
	Undecided	0			
WV W. Va. Research Ct.[L] 11/3	Bush	41	50.0	51.8	1.8
	Gore	39	47.6	45.7	1.9
	Other	2	2.4	2.5	.1
	Undecided	18			
WI Zogby[M] 11/2	Bush	47	47	47.7	.7
	Gore	45	45	47.9	2.9
	Other	8	8	4.4	3.6
	Undecided	0			
WY American Research Group[M] 9/21	Bush	60	66.8	69.2	2.4
	Gore	26	29.0	28.3	.7
	Other	2	2.2	2.5	.3
	Undecided	10			
DC American Research Group[M] 9/21	Bush	14	15.2	9.0	6.2
	Gore	73	79.3	85.4	6.1
	Other	5	5.4	5.6	.2
	Undecided	8			

NOTE: Major poll organizations (M) include those that poll nationally on a regular basis; local poll organizations (L) are those that normally do not, but poll mostly in one state or a region. A/U indicates Incumbent, Democrat, Republican, and allocation of undecided voters.

[a] Unfortunately these poll results, when reported, grouped "other," "undecided," and "don't know" categories together. This forced me to use a "necessity formula" to separate the "undecided/dk" from "other" so the undecided percentage could be determined so a "prediction error" could be calculated. To estimate the "undecided," the actual "other" percentage was subtracted from the "undecided/other/dk" grouping. Once this was done, the proportionate allocation method, as used in Table 10.2, was used to allocate the undecided so poll predictions could be compared to the actual results so "prediction error" could be figured. Granted, subtracting the actual percent for "other" biases the calculation of error, but no good choice remained. It is irresponsible for poll results to be reported without separating "other" from the "undecided/dk" category.

Notes

CHAPTER 1

1. Archibald M. Crossley addressing The Iowa Conference on Attitude and Opinion Research. Conference proceedings published in Norman C. Meier and Harold W. Saunders, eds., *The Polls and Public Opinion* (New York: Henry Holt and Co., 1949), p. 160.

2. William Safire, "Sampling Is Not Enumerating," *New York Times* (December 7, 1997), sec. 4, p. 17.

3. Daniel S. Greenberg, Editorial, "Thwarting Pollsters," *Journal of Commerce* (June 26, 1996), p. A9.

4. Steve Neal, Editorial, "Williamson's Bandwagon Steers Toward Low Road," *Chicago Sun-Times* (September 21, 1992), p. 23.

5. Herbert Asher, *Polling and the Public: What Every Citizen Should Know,* 4th ed. (Washington, D.C.: Congressional Quarterly Press, 1998), p. 19.

6. Ibid. The study is by Tom W. Smith, "How Comics and Cartoons View Public Opinion Surveys," *Journalism Quarterly* 64 (1987): 208–211.

7. Ron Fournier, "Quayle Chides GOP for Rush to Back Bush," *Buffalo News* (May 27, 1999), p. A16.

8. B. Drummond Ayres Jr., "Political Briefing: 99% Margin of Error on Polls' Relevance," *New York Times* (June 11, 1999), p. A24.

9. Casey Meyers, Letter to the Editor, *Wall Street Journal* (March 11, 1999), p. A23.

10. Case No. 991-879, Div. 2 (August 11, 1999).

11. William Morris, ed., *The American Heritage Dictionary of the English Language* (Boston: Houghton Mifflin Co., 1981), p. 402.

12. Humphrey Taylor, "Myth and Reality in Reporting Sampling Error: How the Media Confuse and Mislead Readers and Viewers," *The Polling Report* (May 4, 1998).

13. Genie Dickerson, "Why Do I Hate Opinion Polls? Let Me Count the Ways," *Houston Chronicle* (July 14, 1999), p. A24.

14. Allan Rivlin, "Do You Trust Polls or Not? (Or Are You Undecided?)," *National Journal* (July 3, 1999), vol. 31, p. 1970.

15. Editorial, *Wall Street Journal* (April 7, 1999), p. A22.

16. Ibid.

17. Walter Lippmann, *Public Opinion* (New York: Macmillan Co., 1960).

18. Harry DeWese, "Time for Some Self-Analysis," in *Printing Impressions* (Philadelphia: North American Publishing Co., 1999), vol. 41, p. 94.

19. Michael Moseby, "Voters Show Big Ten Bias," *Omaha World Herald* (October 19, 1997), p. C1.

20. Bryan Burwell, "Subjective Polls Taint Glory of National Title," *USA Today* (January 3, 1996), p. C1.

21. Arnold J. Oliver, "End the Pollsters' Tyranny—Don't Play Along," *Houston Chronicle* (October 16, 1996), p. A29.

22. Ibid.

23. Jacqueline Calmes, "Exit Polls Targeted: Method Sought to Restrict Broadcast Vote Predictions," *Weekly Report* (March 10, 1984), p. 565.

24. Ibid.

25. In Hardin County, Kentucky, election officials and Kentucky election law prevented WHAS-TV's exit interviewer from interviewing within 500 feet of any voting site. WHAS sued the Hardin County election officials and won the suit. Federal District Judge Charles Allen ruled that the state law restricting exit polling is unconstitutional because it violates the constitution's First Amendment, which "protects the right of the media to gather news." Deborah Yetters, "Exit-Poll Limit Is Ruled Unconstitutional," *Louisville Courier Journal* (October 25, 1988), p. 28.

26. 888 F2d 380, 387 (9th Cir. 1988).

27. Associated Press, "Appeals Court Voids Ban on Surveys at the Polls," *New York Times* (February 3, 1988), p. A23.

28. 888 F2d 380, 387 (9th Cir. 1988).

29. Steven Walters, "Elections Board Seeks to Curb Fake Poll Calls, Caller Must Disclose Who Is Paying for Call or Face $500 Forfeitures," *Milwaukee Journal Sentinel* (February 2, 1996), News section, p. 5.

30. Dan Miller, *USA Today* (February 3, 1999), p. A12.

31. Editorial, "Courts Should Allow Use of Sampling," *Minneapolis Star Tribune* (August 31, 1998), p. A14.

32. Jennie H. Dunkley, "Modern Judicial Process: It's a Sad Day in America," *Boston Globe* (September 22, 1998), p. A22.

33. Martin Dyckman, "Polls Shatter Creativity, Fun in Politics," *St. Petersburg Times* (August 31, 1999), p. A11.

34. David W. Moore, *The Superpollsters: How They Measure and Manipulate Public Opinion in America* (New York: Four Walls Eight Windows, 1992).

35. Asher, *Polling and the Public*, p. 22.

36. Chris Adams, "Polls' Words Can Sway Answers," *Sarasota Times-Picayune* (January 23, 1994), p. A4.

37. Ibid.

38. Norman Solomon, "Polls Provide the Numbers, But the Truth Is Hard to Figure," *Cleveland Plain Dealer* (May 11, 1996), p. B11.

39. Rivlin, "Do You Trust Polls Or Not?" p. 1971.

40. Ibid.

41. Asher, *Polling and the Public*, p. 23.

42. William H. Flanigan and Nancy H. Zingale, *Political Behavior of the American Electorate,* 9th ed. (Washington, D.C.: Congressional Quarterly Press, 1998), pp. 12–15.

43. Ibid., pp. 13–14.

44. Ronald D. Elving, "CQ Roundtable: Early Polls Best Served with a Grain of Salt," *Weekly Report* (December 18, 1993), p. 3498.

45. I use *major* public office because those campaigning for "minor" public offices (e.g., city council, state representative) do not normally have the money to hire pollsters, nor do their opponents, so their campaigns are infrequently directly affected by poll numbers.

46. Editorial, "The Only Poll That Counts," *Nation's Business* (November 1996), p. 87.

47. I have lived in St. Louis since 1974. I first met Richard Gephardt in 1981 when I started serving as his pollster and co-campaign manager with Joyce Aboussie for his 1982 congressional campaign. Because of other work commitments I stopped working for Gephardt in 1983, but I still maintain contact with him. Aboussie is still directing his operations and has quietly emerged as one of the leading Democratic organizers and fund-raisers in the United States.

48. Ross Perot's unique candidacy in 1992 offered an alternative to the usual Republican and Democratic candidates for president, thus attracting more than the usual number of voters to the polls, increasing the turnout to an abnormal high of 55%.

49. Jeremy Rabkin, "The Case for Censorship," *The Weekly Standard* (August 23, 1999), p. 28.

50. Holly Idelson, "From Every Poll, Several Opinions," *Weekly Report* (January 5, 1991), p. 15.

51. Dyckman, "Polls Shatter Creativity," p. A11.

52. Alexis de Tocqueville, *Democracy in America*, 2nd ed., Henry Reeve, trans., 2 vols. (Cambridge, Mass.: Sever and Francis, 1863).

53. Editorial, "A Matter of Privacy," *St. Petersburg Times* (November 3, 1999), p. A18.

54. Charles J. Sykes, *The End of Privacy* (New York: St. Martin's Press, 1999).

55. Dickerson, "Why Do I Hate Opinion Polls?" p. A17.

56. Corey Kilgannon, "New Yorkers and Co.; When New York Is on the End of the Line," *New York Times* (November 7, 1999), sec. 14, p. 4.

57. Oliver, "End the Pollsters' Tyranny," p. A29.

58. Dickerson, "Why Do I Hate Opinion Polls?" p. A17.

59. Max Frankel, "Word and Image; Cyberights," *New York Times* (February 12, 1995), p. C26.

60. Ibid.

61. Ibid.

62. Ibid.

63. Quoted in Dana James, "Techie Techniques Find Target; Precision Decision; Speedy New Standard in Web Research Feeds Accuracy, Privacy Concerns," *Marketing News TM* (September 27, 1999), p. 23.

64. Ibid.

65. Roberta Furger, "On the Web You Have No Secrets," *PC World* (July 1999), pp. 29–32.

66. Ibid.

67. In computer jargon, spam is unsolicited e-mail, mostly "junk mail."

68. James, "Techie Techniques Find Target," p. 23.

69. Brendan I. Koerner, Doug Pasternak, and David E. Kaplan, "Can Hackers Be Stopped," *U.S. News and World Report* (June 14, 1999), p. 46.

70. Ibid.

71. Ibid., p. 23.

72. Furger, "On the Web You Have No Secrets."

73. Quoted in Corey Kilgannon, "New Yorkers and Co.," sec. 14, p. 4.

74. Ibid.

75. Nick Sparrow, "The Spiral of Silence, Predictions Made by Pollsters Are Famously Inaccurate, But How Much Do Surveys Actually Drive Election Results?" *The Guardian* (London) (October 27, 1999), p. 19.

76. Oliver, "End the Pollsters' Tyranny," p. A29.

77. Andy Rooney, "A Few Observations on Life," *Buffalo News* (January 10, 1999), p. H3.

78. Quoted in John Futty, "Poll Exaggerates Lashutka Lead in Mayoral Race, Moss Charges," *Columbus Dispatch* (October 10, 1995), p. C3.

79. Clifford J. Levy, "The 1998 Elections: New York State—The Polling; The Experts Examine Their Miscalculations," *New York Times* (November 5, 1998), p. B14.

80. Dickerson, "Why Do I Hate Opinion Polls?" p. A17.

81. Levy, "The 1998 Elections," p. B14.

82. Ibid.

83. John J. Watson, "Key to Validity of Polls," *USA Today* (January 7, 1999), p. A14.

84. Kathleen Frankovic, "Pollsters Must Be Above Suspicion," *The Public Perspective* 9 (August 1998): 34.

85. Godfrey Sperling, "The Genuflection to Campaign Polling Begins," *Christian Science Monitor* (July 13, 1999), Opinion section, p. 11.

86. Don Van Natta, Jr., "Polling's 'Dirty Little Secret': No Response," *New York Times* (November 21, 1999), sec. 4, p. 1.

87. Ibid. (Ladd died on December 8, 1999.)

88. Flanigan and Zingale, *Political Behavior*, p. 110.

89. Watson, "Key to Validity of Polls," p. A14.

90. "Satisfice," by now a very popular term in the social sciences, was coined by Nobel Prize-winning author Herbert Simon. To Simon, decisionmakers cannot possibly know all of the facts that may be relevant to a decision, so decisionmakers, limited by "bounded rationality," must rely on the facts that are "good enough" or will satisfice. Likewise, pollsters can only try to "satisfice" or conduct polls that are "sound enough" since pollsters cannot possibly eliminate or even know all of the possible sources of contamination. See Herbert A. Simon, *Administrative Behavior: A Study of Decision-Making Processes in Administrative Organization*, 3rd ed. (New York: Free Press, 1976).

91. Jim Salter, AP reporter, interviewing me on election night, November 3, 1998.

92. Herbert Asher, in *Polling and the Public*, does a commendable job informing citizens what they should know about polling and what they can do, as citizens, to make polling in our society better.

93. Rooney, "A Few Observations on Life," p. H3.

94. Michael R. Kagay with Janet Elder, "Numbers Are No Problem for Pollsters. Words Are," *New York Times* (August 9, 1992), sec. 4, p. 5.

95. William Safire, "The Gorebush Era," *New York Times* (June 24, 1999), p. A27. But the election did turn out to be between Gore and Bush.

96. Ibid.

97. Frankovic, "Pollsters Must Be Above Suspicion," p. 34.

98. James Bennet, "The Polls; Use of Daily Election Polls Generates Debate in Press," *New York Times* (October 4, 1996), p. A24.

99. Associated Press, "Eligibility Age for Social Security Will Soon Rise," *St. Louis Post-Dispatch* (November 30, 1999), p. A1.

100. Bennet, "The Polls," p. A24.

CHAPTER 2

1. Humphrey Taylor, "Myth and Reality in Reporting Sampling Errors: How the Media Confuse and Mislead Readers and Viewers," *The Polling Report* (May 4, 1998).

2. Ibid.

3. John P. Robinson and Robert Meadow, *Polls Apart* (Washington, D.C.: Seven Locks Press, 1982), p. 14.

4. Francis Kissling, "Polls Apart," *Washington Post* (November 20, 1990), p. A22.

5. American Association for Public Opinion Research, "Best Practices for Surveys and Public Opinion Research," www.aapor.org/ethics/best.html.

6. American Statistical Association, *What Is a Survey?* (Washington, D.C.: ASA, 1995), p. 11.

7. American Association for Public Opinion Research, "Best Practices."

8. Ibid.

9. Charles F. Turner and Elizabeth Martin, eds., *Surveying Subjective Phenomena*, vol. 1 (New York: Russell Sage Foundation, 1984), p. 90.

10. American Association for Public Opinion Research, "Best Practices."

11. American Association for Public Opinion Research, "Statement Condemning Push Polls," http://www.aapor.org/ethics/best.html.

12. Ibid.

13. George Gallup and Saul F. Rae, *The Pulse of Democracy* (New York: Simon and Schuster, 1940), p. 6.

14. Walter Lippmann, *Public Opinion* (New York: Macmillan Co., 1960).

15. Gallup and Rae, *The Pulse of Democracy*, p. 13.

16. Ibid., pp. 1–26.

17. Ibid.

18. J. Michael Sproule, *Propaganda and Democracy: The American Experience of Media and Mass Media* (Cambridge: Cambridge University Press, 1997), pp. 60–61.

19. Ibid.

20. Gallup and Rae, *The Pulse of Democracy*, pp. 218–270.

21. Plato, *The Republic*, edited and translated by Francis MacDonald Cornford (New York: Oxford University Press, 1956), p. 283.

22. Aristotle, *The Politics*, edited and translated by T. A. Sinclair (Baltimore: Penguin Books, 1962), p. 132.

23. Ken Dautrich, "The Ethics of Polls and the Press" (Arlington, Va.: Media Studies Center Forum, October 29, 1996).

24. Gallup and Rae, *The Pulse of Democracy*, p. 12.

25. Ibid., pp. 1–26.

26. Daniel S. Greenberg refers to polls as "pernicious voodoo" in "Getting Back at the Pollsters," *Journal of Commerce* (March 31, 1999), p. A5.

27. Stephen J. Wayne, *The Road to the White House: The Politics of Presidential Elections* (New York: Bedford/St. Martin's, 2000), pp. 330–331.

28. James P. Pfiffner, *The Modern Presidency*, 3rd ed. (New York: Bedford/St. Martin's, 2000), p. 39.

29. George C. Edwards III and Stephen J. Wayne, *Presidential Leadership: Politics and Policy Making* (New York: St. Martin's/Worth, 1999), p. 83.

30. Warren J. Mitofsky, "Was 1996 a Worse Year for Polls Than 1948?" *Public Opinion Quarterly* 62 (summer 1998): 230.

31. Jennifer G. Hickey, "Were the Polls Right or Wrong?" *Insight on the News* (December 7, 1998), p. 12.

32. Ibid.

33. See Mitofsky, "Was 1996," where he discusses the pros and cons of methods for measuring the accuracy of polls, concluding that some methods are better than others, but each poses some problems.

34. Ibid., pp. 240–249.

35. Ibid., pp. 244–249.

36. Pfiffner, *The Modern Presidency*, p. 39.

37. William H. Flanigan and Nancy H. Zingale, *Political Behavior of the American Electorate*, 9th ed. (Washington, D.C.: Congressional Quarterly Press, 1998), pp. 111–115.

38. Shelley E. Taylor, Letitia Anne Peplau, and David O. Sears, *Social Psychology* (Upper Saddle River, N.J.: Prentice Hall, 2000), chaps. 1–10, 15.

39. Ibid.

40. Jo-Ann Barnas, "Marge's World," *Houston Chronicle* (May 12, 1996), Sports section, p. 7.

41. Kenneth F. Warren, "We Have Debated Ad Nauseam the Legitimacy of the Administrative State, But Why?" *Public Administration Review* (May/June 1993), pp. 249–254.

42. Kristeane M. Ridgway, "Our Times/Orange County Communities," *Los Angeles Times* (December 16, 1999), p. B5.

CHAPTER 3

1. George H. Gallup addressing The Iowa Conference on Attitude and Opinion Research. Conference proceedings published in Norman C. Meier and Harold W. Saunders, *The Polls and Public Opinion* (New York: Henry Holt and Co., 1949), p. 218.

2. Ronald D. Elving, "Polling: From Infancy to Ubiquity," *Weekly Report* (August 19, 1989), p. 2189; Dana James, "Techie Techniques Find Target," *Marketing News TM* (September 27, 1999), p. 23.

3. Elving, ibid.; James, ibid.; Anon., "Pollster Shift," *AdWeek* (April 15, 1996), vol. 36, p. 10.

4. Cited by *AdWeek*, ibid.

5. Ibid.

6. Quoted in Albert H. Cantril, *The Opinion Connection: Polling, Politics, and the Press* (Washington, D.C.: Congressional Quarterly Press, 1991), p. 13.

7. David W. Moore, *The Superpollsters: How They Measure and Manipulate Public Opinion in America* (New York: Four Walls Eight Windows, 1992), p. 33.

8. Ibid., p. 33. *The Raleigh Star* also published in 1824 a presidential preference poll, yet most sources for sundry reasons seem to ignore the *Star* poll.

9. Jean M. Converse, *Survey Research in the United States: Roots and Emergence 1890–1960* (Berkeley: University of California Press, 1987), pp. 121–122.

10. Carroll J. Glynn, Susan Herbst, Garrett J. O'Keefe, and Robert Y. Shapiro, *Public Opinion* (Boulder: Westview Press, 1999), p. 33.

11. Moore, *The Superpollsters*, pp. 37–38.

12. Quoted in Moore, *The Superpollsters*, p. 47.

13. Ibid., pp. 47–48.

14. Ibid., p. 48.

15. Ibid., chap. 2; Cantril, *The Opinion Connection*, chap. 1; Glynn et al., *Public Opinion*, chap. 2.

16. Moore, *The Superpollsters*, p. 44.

17. Cantril, *The Opinion Connection*, pp. 93–106; Moore, *The Superpollsters*, pp. 66–68.

18. Moore, *The Superpollsters*, pp. 61–68.

19. Quoted in Moore, *The Superpollsters*, p. 70.

20. Ibid., pp. 71–72.

21. Ibid., p. 72.

22. Cantril, *The Opinion Connection*, p. 12.

23. Moore, *The Superpollsters*, pp. 73–74.

24. Ibid., p. 74.

25. Ibid., p. 121.

26. Ibid., p. 89.

27. George C. Edwards III and Stephen J. Wayne, *Presidential Leadership: Politics and Policy Making*, 3rd ed. (New York: St. Martin's Press, 1994), p. 78; George C. Edwards III and Stephen J. Wayne, *Presidential Leadership: Politics and Policy Making*, 5th ed. (New York: St. Martin's/Worth, 1999), p. 83.

28. Compounding the matter was the unfortunate reality that survey research textbooks, especially those written by math professors, used examples in their problems that were "foreign" and counterproductive for social science students. Consequently, it was difficult to relate to various statistical tests being taught when the authors insisted on using widgets (What the hell is a widget, and who cares anyway?) instead of variable examples that social scientists could relate to (e.g., percent of blacks and whites voting for Republican and Democratic candidates).

29. I am constantly told by my clients that there are few polling companies willing to compete for jobs, especially ones who can do a good job at a reasonable price. In fact, at this writing I just told a desperate lawyer in Illinois that I may not be able to do a pretrial publicity poll for his murder case because I am pretty booked. He begged me to do the poll, telling me that he just can't seem to find any pollsters who conduct such polls. He claimed that pollsters who conduct pretrial publicity polls seem to be a "rare breed" (his rhetoric).

30. William H. Flanigan and Nancy H. Zingale, *Political Behavior of the American Electorate*, 9th ed. (Washington, D.C.: Congressional Quarterly Press, 1998), chap. 2.

31. John M. Barry, "The Polling Business; From 'CATI' to 'CATS,'" *The Public Perspective* 6 (June 1995/July 1995): p. 60.

32. Don Van Natta, Jr., "Polling's 'Dirty Little Secret': No Response," *New York Times* (November 21, 1999), sec. 4, p. 1. Note the Pew Research Center found that poll results were "strikingly similar" between polls where the "no response" rate differed significantly.

33. Gordon S. Block and George Terhanian, "Using the Internet for Election Forecasting," *The Polling Report* (October 26, 1998), www.pollingreport.com/internet.htm (2/15/01).

34. Ibid.

35. Ibid.

36. Tom Abott, "This Election Night, the Internet Could Turn Out To Be a Big Winner, Accuracy of Online Surveys May Make Phone Polls Obsolete," *San Francisco Chronicle* (November 3, 1998), Business section, p. D1.

37. Brian C. Tringali, "Three Trends to Watch in Political Polling," *Campaigns and Elections* (August 1995), p. 20.

38. Herbert Asher, in his book *Polling and the Public: What Every Citizen Should Know*, 4th ed. (Washington, D.C.: Congressional Quarterly Press, 1998), does an excellent job, as the title clearly suggests, in telling citizens what they should know about polls and the polling business so they can become responsible consumers of polls.

CHAPTER 4

1. Quoted in Chuck Henning, *Wit and Wisdom of Politics* (Golden, Colo.: Fulcrum Publishing, 1996), p. 172.

2. William Safire, "Sampling Is Not Enumerating," *New York Times* (December 7, 1997), sec. 4, p. 17.

3. Herbert Asher, *Polling and the Public: What Every Citizen Should Know*, 4th ed. (Washington, D.C.: Congressional Quarterly Press, 1998), p. 14.

4. Allan Rivlin, "Do You Trust Polls or Not? (Or Are You Undecided?)," *National Journal* (July 3, 1999), p. 1970.

5. Asher, *Polling and the Public*, p. 12.

6. David W. Moore, *The Superpollsters: How They Measure and Manipulate Public Opinion in America* (New York: Four Walls Eight Windows, 1992), p. 66.

7. Michael R. Solomon and Elnora W. Stuart, *Marketing: Real People, Real Choices*, 2nd ed. (Upper Saddle River, N.J.: Prentice Hall, 2000), p. 131.

8. Asher, *Polling and the Public*, p. 12.

9. Tim Cuprisin, "Miss America Pageant," *Milwaukee Journal Sentinel* (September 19, 1995), Cue and Family section, p. 3.

10. Andrew Kohut, "The Vocal Minority in American Politics" (Washington, D.C.: Times Mirror Center for the People and the Press, July 16, 1993).

11. Planned Parenthood, "National Survey on Reproductive Health," May 1999 (cover letter signed by Gloria Feldt, president). I want to stress that I am not singling out Planned Parenthood. As noted, the Planned Parenthood survey is simply typical.

12. Asher, *Polling and the Public*, pp. 8–11.

13. David Broder, "When Push Comes to Shove, Fake Polls Become Dirty Trick," *St. Louis Post-Dispatch* (October 10, 1994), p. B7.

14. Ibid.

15. The example I used is almost identical in content to a "push poll" question used in the Jefferson Parish Council race in Florida in 1999. See Pam Louwagie, "Jeff Council Runner-Up Drops Suit Against Pollster," *New Orleans Times-Picayune* (December 15, 1999), p. B3.

16. I am quoting the "push" question from Jerry Berger's column that appeared in the *St. Louis Post-Dispatch* on August 27, 1999, p. A2. However, after I denounced this "push poll" in the *St. Louis Post-Dispatch* on September 5, 1999, p. B2, Frederick S. Yang, of Garin-Hart-Yang Research Group and Slay's pollster, denied that he had asked this question in a response to my "Letter to the Editor" (*St. Louis Post-Dispatch*, September 10, 1999, p. C18). In November 1999, he again denied that he had asked this "push poll" question in a phone conversation with me, although he did say to me that the quoted question is "not necessarily" a "push" question. In a phone conversation with Berger, which I had before I condemned the "push" question, Berger insisted that the question he had quoted in his column constituted the exact wording of the question. I am left baffled. However, the lesson here is that, for obvious reasons, no one wants to be associated with a "push poll."

17. Editorial, "Political Sleaze Grows," *Boston Herald* (February 15, 1996), p. 34.

18. See Don Van Natta Jr., "The 2000 Campaign: The Polling," *New York Times* (February 15, 2000), p. A22. The article focuses on allegations that the Bush camp used "push polling" against McCain in the South Carolina primary campaign.

19. Quoted in Sarah Schafer, "To Politically Connect, and Profitably Collect," *Washington Post* (December 13, 1999), p. F10.

20. Ibid.

21. Gail Collins, "Public Interests: Forget Iowa," *New York Times* (January 25, 2000), p. A23.

22. Quoted in Anne E. Kornblut, "Putting the Public in Policy Internet Polling Rekindles Debate over Voter Role in Politics," *Boston Globe* (December 12, 1999), p. A13.

23. Ibid.

24. Ibid.

25. Schafer, "To Politically Connect," p. F10.

26. Ibid.

27. Deborah Frazier, "Skiers Schuss to Web to Support Ajax Snowboard Ban," *Denver Rocky Mountain News* (January 6, 2000), p. A7.

28. Harris_Poll@hpol.gsbc.com, "Thank You for Your Continued Participation in the Harris Poll Online" (February 18, 2000).

29. Harris_Poll@hpol.gsbc.com, "Harris Poll Online Survey Reminder" (February 18, 2000).

30. Moore, *The Superpollsters*, p. 65.

31. Ibid., p. 63.

32. Ibid., pp. 60–66.

33. Chava Frankfort-Nachmias and David Nachmias, *Research Methods in the Social Sciences*, 4th ed. (New York: St. Martin's Press, 1992), p. 228.

34. Ibid.

35. Brian C. Tringali, "Three Trends to Watch in Political Polling," *Campaigns and Elections* (August 1995), p. 20.

36. Telephone interview, February 8, 2000. Yes, we are related. He is my older brother and, of course, we all have to listen to our big brothers.

37. Group think is a psychological concept that refers to the tendency for people to conform to what they think the group wants to hear, out of respect or fear for the group or the group's leader(s).

38. For an overview on focus groups, see Elizabeth O'Sullivan and Gary R. Rassel, *Research Methods for Public Administrators*, 3rd ed. (New York: Addison Wesley Longman, Inc., 1999), pp. 40–43, 47, 193–196.

39. J. Ronald Milavsky, "How Good Is the A. C. Nielsen People-Meter System: A Review of the Report by the Committee on Nationwide Television Audience Measurement," *Public Opinion Quarterly* 56 (1992): 114.

40. Don Aucoin, "Local TV Stations Giving Nielsen Low Ratings," *Boston Globe* (November 18, 1999), p. A1.

41. Telephone interview with Jeff Allen, news director at KDNL-TV, St. Louis, on February 29, 2000.

42. Milavsky, "Nielsen People-Meter System," pp. 102–115.

43. Clarence Jones, "TV Ratings—How They Know Who's Watching," excerpts from *Winning with the News Media* (1999), www.winning-newsmedia.com/ratings.htm (2/15/01).

44. Ibid.

45. Matthew Greenberg, "FAQ: The Nielsen Ratings," *Washington Post* (December 9, 1997), www.washingtonpost.com/wp-srv/style/tv/permanent/faqnielsen.htm (2/15/01).

46. Aucoin, "Local TV Stations."

47. Quoted in Aucoin, "Local TV Stations."

48. Aucoin, "Local TV Stations."

CHAPTER 5

1. David S. Broder, *Behind the Front Page: A Candid Look at How the News Is Made* (New York: Simon and Schuster, 1987), p. 253.

2. This summary is based on the professional standards and ethics set forth by the Research Industry Coalition, the National Council on Public Polls, the American Association for Public Opinion Research, and the American Association of Political Consultants as reported by Herbert Asher, *Polling and the Public: What Every Citizen Should Know*, 4th ed. (Washington, D.C.: Congressional Quarterly Press, 1999), pp. 19–20, 89–92, 122–123; Albert H. Cantril, *The Opinion Connection: Polling, Politics, and the Press* (Washington, D.C.: Congressional Quarterly Press, 1991); and a statement on professional ethics and standards published by the Research Industry Coalition, www.researchindustry.org/Pages/indeth1.html February 13, 2000.

3. Chava Frankfort-Nachmias and David Nachmias, *Research Methods in the Social Sciences*, 4th ed. (New York: St. Martin's Press, 1992), p. 98.

4. Ibid., p. 180.

5. Open-end questions may be more appropriate and useful for specialized surveys of doctors, judges, etc., where in-depth responses are sought, but they are not as useful in the typical public opinion poll.

6. I relied on my experiences as a pollster for much of what was presented in this discussion on questionnaire design, but I also drew from the insights of Asher, *Polling and the Public*, pp. 44–60; Frankfort-Nachmias and Nachmias, *Research Methods*, pp. 239–267; and Gerald R. Adams and Jay D. Schvaneveldt, *Understanding Research Methods*, 2nd ed. (New York: Longman, 1991), pp. 197–251.

7. Adams and Schvaneveldt, *Understanding Research Methods*, p. 219.

8. It is common practice today to use phone banks where interviewers gather at one location to conduct their interviews on the many phones supplied. A supervisor is usually present.

9. Asher, *Polling and the Public*, pp. 83–87.

10. Ibid., pp. 85–86.

11. Richard Morin, "Women Asking Women About Men Asking Women About Men," *Washington Post* (January 15–21, 1990), National Weekly edition, p. 37.

12. Asher, *Polling and the Public*, pp. 85–86.

13. Ibid. Asher cites several studies substantiating this point.

14. Ibid., p. 141.

15. One time Schneider was presenting my own poll data on the 1997 mayoral race in St. Louis, but I could not even adequately follow the presentation because the data were presented so fast. To understand poll data, one has to really

look at it and give it time to sink in. Consequently, I often record the presentation of poll results so I can play it until I really understand it.

16. Ibid., pp. 141–182.

17. Ibid., p. 90.

18. Studies disclose consistently that 65–80% of Americans report that they rely primarily or exclusively on TV for their news, especially their political news.

19. Reuben Cohen, "Close Enough for All Practical Purposes," *Public Opinion Quarterly* 43 (fall 1979): 421–422, 424.

20. Chava Frankfort-Nachmias and David Nachmias, *Research Methods in the Social Sciences*, 5th ed. (New York: St. Martin's Press, 1996), p. 242.

21. Ibid., pp. 242–245.

22. Elizabethann O'Sullivan and Gary R. Rossel, *Research Methods for Public Administrators*, 3rd ed. (New York: Addison Wesley Longman, Inc., 1999), pp. 179–187.

23. Frankfort-Nachmias and Nachmias, *Research Methods* (1996), p. 242.

24. Asher, *Polling and the Public*, p. 118.

25. Cantril, *The Opinion Connection*, p. 142.

26. George C. Edwards III and Stephen J. Wayne, *Presidential Leadership: Politics and Policy Making*, 5th ed. (New York: St. Martin's Press, 1999), p. 84.

27. Broder, *Behind the Front Page*, p. 253.

28. Mark Jurkowitz, "The Media: Fox-Trotting Around Taboo of Exit Polls," *Boston Globe* (March 9, 2000), p. F1.

29. Cantril, *The Opinion Connection*, p. 142.

30. Whether true or not, thousands of Florida voters said that they were confused by a "butterfly" ballot, which caused them to mistakenly cast a vote for Pat Buchanan instead of Al Gore. Of course, if some of these voters were interviewed, they probably told exit poll interviewers that they had voted for Gore, which would have thrown off the exit poll results in Florida by a fraction of 1%, if they had actually voted for Buchanan by mistake. Supposedly, only later did these voters realize that they had cast their presidential vote in error.

31. Racially polarized voting is not unique to St. Louis and almost always exists when black and white candidates run against each other in communities with significant white and black populations. Such polarized voting is not evident when white and black candidates are not running against each other.

32. Roughly 12% of the voting population is black, although the black vote percentage is less since African Americans tend to vote less proportionately than do white voters.

33. This is particularly true at the state level when the Voter News Service may underrepresent, say, the black vote percentage. Since the Voter News Service polls simultaneously for state races, it may have to use weighting within a particular state to make an accurate prediction.

CHAPTER 6

1. James Bennett, "Politics: The Polls; Use of Daily Election Polls Generates Debate in Press," *New York Times* (October 4, 1996), p. A24.

2. Paul J. Lavrakas and Michael W. Traugott, eds., *Election Polls, the News Media, and Democracy* (New York: Chatham House, 2000), chap. 5 especially.

3. Larry J. Sabato, *Feeding Frenzy: Attack Journalism and American Politics* (Baltimore: Lanahan Publishers, Inc., 2000), p. 57.

4. Albert C. Gunther, "Biased Press or Biased Public: Attitudes Toward Media Coverage of Social Groups," *Public Opinion Quarterly* 56 (summer 1992): 161.

5. Ibid.

6. Telephone interview with Charles Jaco, May 16, 2000.

7. Byron Crawford, "Maybe It's Time to Ask Pollsters for Answers," *Louisville Courier-Journal* (April 13, 1997), p. B1.

8. Telephone interview with Robert J. Rosenthal, April 28, 2000. At the time of this interview Rosenthal had been serving as the *Inquirer's* executive editor for two years, but he had been at the paper for over twenty years.

9. Stephen Ansolabehere, Roy Behr, and Shanto Iyengar, *The Media Game: American Politics in the Television Age* (New York: Macmillan, 1993), chap. 5. These authors conclude that "research on campaign reporting has found that the press is, on the whole, neutral toward the candidates" (p. 64).

10. Quoted in Sabato, *Feeding Frenzy*, p. 58.

11. Ibid.

12. Philip Meyer, "Evaluating the Toolbox," *American Journalism Review* (March 2000), p. 42.

13. Interview with Don Marsh, former distinguished news anchor at the ABC affiliate station in St. Louis for over two decades (March 16, 2000).

14. Ibid.

15. Telephone interview with Charles Jaco, May 16, 2000. Jaco has won many journalism awards, including six National Headliner Awards and two Edward R. Murrow Awards while working for NBC, CNN, CBS, and KMOX radio.

16. Pat Buchanan, CNN's *Crossfire*, November 20, 1998.

17. Jay Rosen, *What Are Journalists For?* (New Haven: Yale University Press, 1999), chap. 1.

18. Telephone interview with Dick Polman, May 15, 2000.

19. Albert E. Gollin, "Polling and the News Media," *Public Opinion Quarterly* 51(2; winter 1987): 88.

20. Ibid., p. 87.

21. Ibid., p. 88.

22. Ibid., p. 89.

23. Interview with Jim Salter, April 26, 2000.

24. Mohamed El-Bendary, "Enough Feel-Good Journalism," *Christian Science Monitor* (November 4, 1999), Opinion section, p. 11.

25. Rosen, *What Are Journalists For?*, especially chap. 1.

26. Michael Kelly quoted in Rosen, *What Are Journalists For?* p. 206.

27. John Leo, "Those Darned Readers: The Gap Between Reporters and the General Public Is Huge," *U.S. News and World Report* (April 24, 2000), p. 16.

28. Alex Beam, "Their Issues Make Us Feel a Bit Civic," *Boston Globe* (October 27, 1999), p. E1.

29. Leo, "Those Darned Readers," p. 16.

30. Rosen, *What Are Journalists For?*, chap. 1.

31. Ibid., p. 69.

32. Ibid.

33. Ibid., p. 70.

34. Ibid.

35. Benjamin Ginsberg, *The Captive Public* (New York: Basic Books, 1988), p. 60.

36. Telephone interview with Cole Campbell, May 4, 2000.

37. Paraphrased by Jay Rose, "Newspapers' Future Depends on Shopping Trends in How People Live," *Bulletin of the American Society of Newspaper Editors* (no date).

38. Rosen, *What Are Journalists For?*, p. 66.

39. John Dewey, *The Public and Its Problems* (New York: Henry Holt, 1927), pp. 166, 203–208.

40. Telephone interview with Cole Campbell, May 4, 2000.

41. Ibid. Interestingly, Campbell is now making the pitch for polls that most traditional journalists make. Traditional journalists don't feel that polls should become the whole story either, but they defend the use of polls for stimulating more interest in their stories. Of course, more interest would likely lead to more story-oriented discussions among citizens.

42. Ibid.

43. Voter turnout reached a modern-day high of about 63% in the 1960 presidential election. Turnout has declined steadily since then, falling just below 50% in the 1996 presidential election and just over 50% in the 2000 presidential election.

44. David Shaw, "The Press as Player," *Columbia Journalism Review* (November-December 1999), p. 73.

45. Ibid.

46. Lavrakas and Traugott, *Election Polls*, chap. 2.

47. Meyer, "Evaluating the Toolbox," p. 42.

48. Ibid.

49. See, for example, V. O. Key, Jr., *Southern Politics* (New York: Alfred A. Knopf, 1949); Duane Lockard, *New England State Politics* (Princeton: Princeton

University Press, 1959); and John Fenton, *Midwest Politics* (New York: Holt, Rinehart & Winston, 1966).

50. Philip Meyer and Deborah Potter, "Hidden Value: Polls and Public Journalism," in Lavrakas and Traugott, *Election Polls*, pp. 135–136.

51. Bennett, "Politics: The Polls," p. A24.

52. Quoted in Lavrakas and Traugott, *Election Polls*, p. 138.

53. Telephone interview with Steve Kraske, May 3, 2000.

54. Interview with Abraham McLaughlin, May 11, 2000.

55. Interview with John Judis, September 26, 2000.

56. Telephone interview with Steve Kraske, May 3, 2000.

57. Ibid.

CHAPTER 7

1. Stephen Budiansky, "Consulting the Oracle: Everyone Loves Polls, But Can You Trust Them," *U.S. News and World Report* (December 4, 1995), p. 52.

2. Carl M. Cannon, "Hooked on Polls," *National Journal* (October 17, 1998), p. 2440.

3. Ibid., p. 2438.

4. Ibid. p. 2438.

5. Ibid., p. 2438.

6. Ibid. p. 2438.

7. James Carney and John F. Dickerson, "Polling for the Perfect Pitch," *Time* (October 9, 2000), p. 59.

8. Cannon, "Hooked on Polls," p. 2438.

9. Ibid.

10. Budiansky, "Consulting the Oracle." p. 52.

11. Quoted in Cannon, "Hooked on Polls," p. 2441.

12. Ibid.

13. Budiansky, "Consulting the Oracle." p. 52.

14. Chris Adams, "Polls' Words Can Sway Answers," *New Orleans Times-Picayune* (January 23, 1994), p. A4.

15. Brian C. Tringali, "Three Trends to Watch in Political Polling," *Campaigns and Elections* (August 1995), p. 20.

16. L. Sandy Maisel, *Parties and Elections in America*, 3rd ed. (New York: Rowman and Littlefield Publishers, 1999), pp. 234–235.

17. Charles W. Roll, Jr., and Albert H. Cantril, *Polls: Their Use and Misuse in Politics* (New York: Basic Books, 1972), p. 17.

18. Unlike demographical traits that can be obtained from the U.S. Census, demographical information learned from polls is obviously very current and particularized and becomes part of the data base, so such information can be cross-tabulated with opinion information.

19. Only a person who has coding experience can appreciate this. Coding open-end questions is an attempt to quantify the qualitative answers or comments by the respondents. This is a real challenge because not only do very few respondents statistically answer open-end questions, but their comments must be interpreted and noted by the interviewers. Some respondents might give elaborate comments, yet the "space is limited" and the interviewers ultimately must decide what brief comment to record.

20. David Maraniss, "Image-Makers Produced Virtual Reality Convention," *Washington Post* (August 17, 1996), p. A1.

21. Herbert Asher, *Polling and the Public: What Every Citizen Should Know* (Washington, D.C.: Congressional Quarterly Press, 1998), p. 115.

22. Ibid., p. 116.

23. Mark Z. Barabak, "Polls Apart: Experts See Study Flaws; Proposes New Way to Gauge Opinion," *San Diego Union-Tribune* (January 26, 1996), p. A11. Also Harriett Smith, "A Community Sounding Board for the Atlanta Area: Getting Involved," *Atlanta Journal and Constitution* (February 5, 1996), p. A11.

24. If any doubt exists, read electoral behavior books such as William H. Flanigan and Nancy H. Zingale, *Political Behavior of the American Electorate*, 9th ed. (Washington, D.C.: Congressional Quarterly Press, 1998), especially chaps. 6–8.

25. Marianne Means, "24% Hold the Key," *Cleveland Plain Dealer* (June 19, 2000), p. B9.

26. Elizabeth Shogren, "Wilder Bows Out of Virginia Race," *Los Angeles Times* (September 16, 1994), p. A18.

27. Of course Wilder, a Democrat running as an Independent, also was pressured to quit the race by the Virginia Democratic Party brass because polls showed that his candidacy was seriously eroding the electoral strength of Robb. The polls proved accurate. When Wilder dropped out, his supporters did go to Robb, and Robb won.

28. In kind contributions are nonmonetary gifts given to candidates, such as free banquet rooms for fund-raisers, free food, free legal services, free transportation, free printing, free labor, and the like, that can greatly reduce campaign costs.

29. Politicians, particularly those holding office, must work with the winners. Consequently, politicians carefully consider the odds of a candidate being able to win. Normally, endorsing losing candidates is bad politics.

30. Paul J. Lavrakas and Michael W. Traugott, eds., *Election Polls, the News Media, and Democracy* (New York: Chatham House, 2000), p. 35.

31. Kenneth F. Warren, "Can a City Slicker Win a Statewide Race?" *St. Louis Post-Dispatch* (March 9, 1999), p. B7.

32. Flanigan and Zingale, *Political Behavior.*

33. Ron Scherer, "Civil Rights May Prove Pivotal for the Fall Races," *Christian Science Monitor* (April 27, 2000), USA: Election section, p. 2.

34. Diana Jean Schemo, "Catholics Minimize Impact of Bush Visit to Bob Jones," *New York Times* (May 2, 2000), p. B5; and Jo Mannies and Ken Leiser, "A Confident Bush Declares in St. Louis: 'I Believe You're Talking to the Next President,'" *St. Louis Post-Dispatch* (March 2, 2000), p. A1.

35. Stephen J. Wayne, *The Road to the White House 2000: The Politics of Presidential Elections* (New York: St. Martin's Press, 2000), pp. 241–255.

36. A humorous story was once told to me by a staffer for Congressman Richard Gephardt. When Gephardt was running for his party's presidential nomination in 1988 in the New Hampshire primary, she was driving some voters to the polls who were designated as "likely Gephardt voters." She suddenly became frustrated, however, when they started talking about voting for Gephardt's opponents. "I was tempted to turn around or drop them at the wrong polling place," she quipped. Obviously, pollsters don't always designate correctly the voters most likely to vote for their candidate.

37. Charles W. Roll, Jr., and Albert H. Cantril, *Polls: Their Use and Misuse in Politics* (New York: Basic Books, 1972), pp. 17–38.

38. Ibid., p. 36.

39. Ibid., p. 18.

40. Ibid., pp. 18–23.

41. Ibid., p. 18.

42. Ibid., pp. 29–33.

43. Ibid., p. 33.

44. Anon., "Political Briefs: Pollsters Form Board for Quality Control," *Boston Globe* (January 7, 2000), p. A9.

45. Cannon, *"Hooked on Polls,"* p. 2438.

46. Lavrakas and Traugott, *Election Polls*, especially chap. 1.

47. E.g., Abraham Lincoln.

48. Seymour Sudman, "The President and the Polls," *Public Opinion Quarterly* 46 (fall 1982): 301–310.

49. Lawrence K. Jacobs and Robert Y. Shapiro, "The Rise of Presidential Polling: The Nixon White House in Historical Perspective," *Public Opinion Quarterly* 59 (spring 1995): 169–191.

50. Ibid.

51. Ibid.

52. Jacobs and Shapiro do an admirable job documenting their argument that Nixon staffers pursued media pollsters Harris and Gallup, commissioning them on occasion to do polls for the White House and on other occasions placing these pollsters in a blatant conflict of interest situation by allowing Nixon's staffers to influence the questions asked in their media polls and how the poll results were reported. See Lawrence R. Jacobs and Robert Y. Shapiro, "Presidential Manipulation of Polls and Public Opinion," *Political Science Quarterly* 110 (winter 1995/1996): 519–538. Recent presidents have not been able to be so influential with media pollsters because there are so many of them and many are

attached to huge media giants (e.g., CBS and CNN). Nonetheless, the Clinton administration was able to communicate regularly with media pollsters in an effort to influence their polling (ibid., footnote 81).

53. Ibid.

54. Jacobs and Shapiro, "The Rise of Presidential Polling," p. 166.

55. Ibid., p. 180.

56. Ibid., p. 193. Also, Cannon, "Hooked on Polls," pp. 2438–2441; Charles Bobington and Bill Miller, "Clinton Halts Execution Until Federal Clemency Policy Is Set," *Washington Post* (July 8, 2000), p. A2.

57. Jacobs and Shapiro, "The Rise of Presidential Polling," pp. 163–195; Jacobs and Shapiro, "Presidential Manipulation," pp. 519–538; Cannon, "Hooked on Polls," pp. 2438–2441; Jeffrey E. Cohen, "The Polls: The Components of Presidential Favorability," *Presidential Studies Quarterly* 30 (March 2000): 169–177.

58. Jacobs and Shapiro, "The Rise of Presidential Polling," pp. 174–175, 190–191. Jacobs and Shapiro studied poll use through 1972, but almost certainly Nixon polled extensively on Watergate.

59. Cannon, "Hooked on Polls," pp. 2438–2441; Budiansky, "Consulting the Oracle."

60. Cannon, "Hooked on Polls," p. 2439.

61. Michael Hill, "Fight Cynicism, McCain Tells Graduates," *Baltimore Sun* (May 28, 1999), p. A3.

62. In the 2000 presidential race, the "official debate commission," wanting to exclude Pat Buchanan and Ralph Nader from the presidential debates, decreed that a candidate must receive at least 15% in the national polls to qualify for inclusion in the debates. This absurdly high arbitrary standard of 15% has the practical effect of preventing any third-party candidate from getting the critical exposure and credibility necessary to mount a serious challenge to the Republican and Democratic candidates. This strikes me as a blatant misuse of polls that undermines the spirit of democratic elections, especially considering the fact that the debate commission consists of only Republicans and Democrats, placing members in an obvious conflict of interest. See Linda Feldman, "How Buchanan Could Hurt Bush's Bid," *Christian Science Monitor* (March 30, 2000), USA section, p. 3.

63. Quoted in Jacobs and Shapiro, "The Rise of Presidential Polling," p. 183.

64. Carney and Dickerson, "Polling for the Perfect Pitch," p. 58.

CHAPTER 8

1. Frank Newport, "Starr's Tenure as Independent Counsel Marked by Strongly Unfavorable Public Opinion," *Gallup News Service* (October 19, 1999), gallup.com/poll/releases/pr991019.asp (2/15/01).

2. Jill Lawrence, "History Has Been Kind to Voters of Conscience," *USA Today* (December 16, 1998), p. A1.

3. Bob Hohler, "House Tries to Hasten Its Inquiry," *Boston Globe* (November 6, 1998), p. A1, quoting Clinton's remark on January 26, 1998.

4. David Maraniss, "First Lady Launches Counterattack," *Washington Post* (January 28, 1998), p. A1.

5. Seventy percent felt Starr should not have released detailed accounts of Clinton's sexual activities with Lewinsky (Gallup Poll, 9/10/98).

6. Molly Moore, "World Weighs the Impact of the Starr Report," *Washington Post* (September 13, 1998), p. A42.

7. Frank Newport, "Americans Agree with House Contention That Clinton Committed Perjury and Obstructed Justice," *Gallup News Service* (January 16, 1999), gallup.com/poll/releases/pr990116asp (2/15/01).

8. Newport, "Starr's Tenure."

9. Reported in Moore, "World Weighs the Impact," p. A42.

10. Richard A. Brody, "The Lewinsky Affair and Popular Support for President Clinton," *Polling Report.com* (November 16, 1998), pollingreport.com/brody.htm (2/15/01).

11. Alison Mitchell, "Testing of a President: The House," *New York Times* (September 18, 1998), p. A23.

12. True, Clinton probably received some boost as a result of giving his State of the Union address.

13. Clinton's jump in his job approval percentage could have been helped by his air strikes against Iraq, but probably not, since the air strikes lasted a very short time, while the impeachment process endured, giving the public plenty of time to dwell on the scandal.

14. Quoted in Katherine M. Skiba, "Instant Polls Don't Tell Whole Story," *Milwaukee Journal Sentinel* (September 15, 1998), News, p. 1.

15. Ibid.

16. Brody, "The Lewinsky Affair."

17. Ibid.

18. Frank Newport, "Clinton Receives Record High Job Approval Rating After Impeachment Vote and Iraq Air Strikes," *Gallup News Service* (December 24, 1998), gallup.com/poll/releases/pr981224.asp (2/15/01).

19. David W. Moore, "Good Times for Clinton the President," *Gallup News Service* (January 23, 1999), gallup.com/poll/releases/pr990123.asp (2/15/01). Around the same time, Clinton received similar ratings for his handling of the economy in other polls (e.g., ABC, 80%; CNN, 79%; NBC, 76%).

20. Ibid.

21. Ibid.

22. Margery Eagan, "Starr-Crossed President Always Comes Out on Top," *Boston Herald* (November 22, 1998), News, p. 4.

23. Seventy-nine percent of the Democrats and 70% of the Independents said it involved an investigation into Clinton's private life, while 90%of the Democrats and 75% of the Independents felt that the investigation into the Lewinsky affair should be dropped.

24. Eagan, "Starr-Crossed President."

25. I'm certain that her rising poll numbers no doubt caused her to first think about running for the U.S. Senate in New York, especially since her poll numbers in "friendly" New York would have been higher than her overall favorability percentage for the nation.

26. An ABC News/*Washington Post* poll (released 12/21/98) found that only 23% of the public felt the Republicans in Congress were "mainly interested in finding out the truth," while 71% believed these Republicans were "mainly interested in hurting Clinton politically."

27. Thirty-seven percent said a "good amount."

28. Jeffrey E. Cohen, "The Polls: The Components of Presidential Favorability," *Presidential Studies Quarterly* 30 (March 2000): 170.

29. Ibid.

30. Ibid., pp. 169–177.

31. If "as a person" were left out and respondents were asked only whether they had a favorable or unfavorable opinion of Clinton, respondents would unlikely confine their thinking to just Clinton "the person" and would likely consider also the job he was doing as president. This might help to explain why Clinton received a 52% favorability rating in a CBS News/*New York Times* poll on December 15, 1998, the same day an ABC News/*Washington Post* poll had him at only 41% favorability.

32. All are ABC News polls, except the December 15, 1998, poll, which is an ABC News/*Washington Post* poll.

33. Brody, "The Lewinsky Affair."

34. Moore, "Good Times for Clinton."

35. Brody, "The Lewinsky Affair."

36. Admittedly, these scores are not impressive, but they are certainly not low.

37. Ibid.

38. Quoted in Mitchell, "Testing of a President."

39. Ibid.

40. Newport, "Starr's Tenure."

41. Ibid.

42. Ibid.

43. Ibid.

44. Of course, Starr seemed to be oblivious to public opinion. The fact that he became so unpopular as a result provides proof positive that public figures who value their public image would be foolish to ignore public perceptions of them in the polls.

45. V. O. Key Jr., *The Responsible Electorate: Rationality in Presidential Voting 1936–1960* (New York: Vintage Books, 1968).

CHAPTER 9

1. Mary McIntosh and Ronald Hinckley, "Challenges to Polling in Eastern Europe," *The Public Perspective* 3 (July/August, 1992): 32.

2. Quoted in David W. Moore, "Exploring American Society: Gallup's Polls: What We've Done and How We've Done It: Six Decades of Gallup Polling: Interviews with Alec Gallup and George Gallup, Jr.," *The Public Perspective* 8 (April 1997/May 1997): 8.

3. Ibid.

4. Humphrey Taylor, "Polling the British Voter," *Marketing Research* 5 (winter 1993): 55.

5. John Maggs, "Not-So-Innocents Abroad," *National Journal* (June 17, 2000), p. 1906.

6. Ibid., p. 1907.

7. Ibid., pp. 1906–1907.

8. Post Express (Lagos), "Nigeria: U.S. Opinion Research Firm for Nigeria," *Africa News* (July 28, 2000), no pagination.

9. James A. Barnes and Peter H. Stone, "Campaign Circuit," *National Journal* (May 22, 1999), p. 1424. Greenberg's track record for pending 1999 campaigns was updated by this author. Greenberg did return home to poll for Al Gore in the 2000 presidential campaign.

10. Ibid., p. 1907.

11. Ibid.

12. Ronald H. Hinckley and Andrew Kohut, "Problems in Survey Research: Polling and Democracy in the Former USSR and Eastern Europe," *The Public Perspective* 4 (September/October 1993): 14.

13. Warren J. Mitofsky, "Public Opinion Abroad: Exit Polling on the Russian Elections," *The Public Perspective* 7 (August/September 1996): 41.

14. McIntosh and Hinckley, "Challenges to Polling," p. 32.

15. The Roper Center for Public Opinion Research, "Japanese Data Archive," www.ropercenter.uconn.edu/JPOLL/home.html (2/15/01).

16. Brian Palmer, "What the Chinese Want," *Fortune* (October 11, 1999), p. 229.

17. Ibid.

18. Interview with Du Yan, "Polling in China," *The Public Perspective* 4 (May/June 1993): 30.

19. Howard Schneider, "Spin Doctors in Iran: Reformists Adopt U.S. Campaign Tactics," *Washington Post* (February 18, 2000), p. A1.

20. Ibid.

21. Interview with Tim Lomperis on September 18, 2000.

22. J. David Kennamer, "The Polling Business: Argentina: Polling in an Emerging Democracy," *The Public Perspective* 6 (October/November 1995): 62.

23. Maggs, "Not-So-Innocents Abroad," pp. 1907–1909.

24. Winston Fletcher, "Why Researchers Are So Jittery: Commentary," *Financial Times* (London) (March 3, 1997), Marketing/Advertising/Media section, p. 16.

25. Ibid.

26. Quoted in Taylor, "Polling the British Voter," p. 55.

27. Nick Sparrow, "The Spiral of Silence," *The Guardian* (London) (October 27, 1999), p. 19.

28. Fletcher, "Why Researchers Are So Jittery," p. 16.

29. Humphrey Taylor, "The Polling Business," *The Public Perspective* 6 (February/March 1995): 3.

30. Ibid.

31. Ibid.

32. Ibid.

33. Alison Smith, "Opinion Polling Faces New Scrutiny," *Financial Times* (London) (March 21, 1997), p. 9.

34. Humphrey Taylor, "Publish Honest, Independent Polls," *The Public Perspective* 9 (February 1998): 89.

35. Interview with John Parker, September 18, 2000.

36. Kennamer, "The Polling Business," p. 62.

37. Ibid.

38. Ibid.

39. Emmanuel Uwalaka, "Conducting Survey Research in an African Country: Suggestions for Other Researchers," in Abdul Karim Banguro, ed., *Research Methodology and African Studies*, vol. 1 (New York: University Press of America, 1994), p. 167.

40. Taylor, "Publish Honest, Independent Polls," p. 89.

41. Ibid.

42. Thomas T. Vogel Jr., "Charges of Vote Fraud Trigger Fears of Unrest in Peru—Opposition Leaders Cry Foul After Tally Is Delayed Again," *Wall Street Journal* (April 12, 2000), p. A18; and Associated Press, "Milosevic Reportedly Rejects Russian Election Mediation Offer," *St. Louis Post-Dispatch* (January 20, 2000), p. A8.

43. Ibid.

44. Ansu-Kyeremeh Kwasi, "The Challenges of Surveying Public Opinion in an Emerging Democracy," *International Journal of Public Opinion Research* 11 (spring 1999): 59.

45. Ibid., p. 61.

46. Ibid., p. 60.

47. Ibid., pp. 63–70.

48. Taylor, "Publish Honest, Independent Polls," p. 89. Although he was citing specific experiences with Mexico, he insisted that "attempts to mislead the public with phony polls and censorships of honest ones are not unique to Mexico."Ellen Carnaghan told me that there is certainly a problem with objective reporting of poll results in Russia too, especially since reporters have not developed, as yet, Western standards of journalistic objectivity. She claims that in the past journalists had no choice but to present the government view. By contrast, now they are often accused of presenting the opinions of whoever owns the media outlet for which they work." Interview with Ellen Carnaghan, September 30, 2000.

49. Interview with James Gibson, September 27, 2000.

50. Interview with Ellen Carnaghan, September 8, 2000.

51. Ellen Carnaghan, "Alienation, Apathy, or Ambivalence? 'Don't Knows' and Democracy in Russia," *Slavic Review* 55 (summer 1996): 362.

52. Interview with Emmanuel Uwalaka, September 8, 2000.

53. McIntosh and Hinckley, "Challenges to Polling," p. 32.

54. Interview with Zogby, September 19, 2000.

55. Interview with Gibson, September 27, 2000.

56. Interview with Uwalaka, September 8, 2000.

57. Kennamer, "The Polling Business," p. 62.

58. Interview with Gibson, September 27, 2000. Nonetheless, he holds that he can conduct reasonably representative surveys in South Africa. He notes that even in the United States, especially in face-to-face surveys, inevitably some groups are underrepresented.

59. McIntosh and Hinckley, "Challenges to Polling," p. 32.

60. Interview with Gibson, September 27, 2000.

61. McIntosh and Hinckley, "Challenges to Polling," p. 32.

62. Interview with Gibson, September 27, 2000.

63. Interview with Uwalaka, September 8, 2000.

64. Interview with Gibson, September 27, 2000. Also, Warren J. Mitofsky, "A Week in the Life of an Exit Pollster," *The Public Perspective* 11 (March 2000): 38.

65. Interview with Uwalaka, September 8, 2000. Also, Mitofsky, "A Week in the Life."

66. Interviews with Gibson (September 27, 2000), Zogby (September 19, 2000), and Uwalaka (September 8, 2000). Also, McIntosh and Hinckley, "Challenges to Polling," p. 32.

67. Du Yan, "Polling in China: Interview with Du Yan," *The Public Perspective* 4 (May/June 1993): 30.

68. Ibid.

69. Ibid.

70. Ibid.

71. Palmer, "What the Chinese Want," p. 229.

72. Du Yan, "Polling in China," p. 30.

73. China Poll and Survey, CPS Results (May 20, 1997), China P & S Home.

74. Palmer, "What the Chinese Want," p. 229.

75. Celinda Lake and Jennifer Sosin, "Public Opinion Polling and the Future of Democracy," *National Civic Review* 87 (spring 1998): 67.

76. Ibid., p. 67.

77. Humphrey Taylor, "From the Field; Opinion in the Mix; Polling, Good Government, and Democracy," *The Public Perspective* 11 (July/August 2000): 33.

78. Ibid.

79. Ibid. It is worth noting that Taylor condemns the democratic countries (e.g., France and Italy) that permit free polling, yet prohibit polling within a few weeks of the election.

80. Kwasi, "The Challenges of Surveying," pp. 59–74.

81. Lynn M. Sanders, "Democratic Politics and Survey Research," *Philosophy of the Social Sciences* 29 (June 1999): 248–280.

82. Kwasi, "The Challenges of Surveying," pp. 59–74.

83. Mitofsky, "Public Opinion Abroad," p. 41.

84. Taylor, "From the Field," p. 33.

85. Ibid.

86. From News Services, "Milosevic Concedes Loss: Milosevic's Concession of Defeat Triggers Huge Street Celebration," *St. Louis Post-Dispatch* (October 7, 2000), p. 5.

CHAPTER 10

1. Frank Newport, "Convention Gain for Democratic Ticket Sustained in Latest Poll: Gore and Bush Remain Tied," *Gallup News Service* (August 29, 2000), www.gallup.com/poll/releases/pr000829.asp (2/15/01).

2. Most late September polls, not shown in Table 10.1, started to show Bush regaining the lead, but Table 10.1 mostly reflects the early to mid-September poll dates so more valid poll comparisons could be made.

3. Some pollsters allocated their undecided voters to the candidates, but if they did not, I used the standard proportionate allocation method to allocate the undecided vote for polling organizations that did not allocate their undecideds so that I could calculate their "prediction error" or the difference between their last poll results ("prediction") and the actual 2000 presidential election results. There are those who criticize the proportionate allocation method, holding that one cannot assume that the undecideds will necessarily go to the candidates in the same proportions as the decided voters. Of course, these critics are right, but allocating the undecideds is not an exact science and such critics do not offer an allocation method that is rooted in a more sensible assumption or is fairer to the candidates. In any event, undecideds must be allocated before an estimated prediction error can validly be calculated. Further, all polling organiza-

tions except Tipp/*Christian Science Monitor* rounded off their poll predictions, yet these predictions are compared to the nearest tenth of one percent of the actual election results. Comparing the rounded percentage makes for a more accurate comparison, but the estimated error could be, within a few tenths of a percent, a little less or greater than the calculated error shown. Overall, since some pollsters would look a little better in their predictions because of their rounding, while others would look a little worse, it would probably amount to a "wash" for the whole table. Regardless of any of these precautionary notes, Table 10.2 conveys with decent precision the accuracy of these thirteen polling firms.

4. These average error margins compare favorably with previous calls in presidential elections, although they are fairly consistent with the average error reported for presidential elections for the past few decades (see Tables 2.2 and 2.3 in Chapter 2). A word of caution: Averages tend to distort the true picture somewhat because just one poll that is way off or right on the mark can distort the overall accuracy of the calls. To me, the better indicator is to count the number of poll predictions that were within a certain error margin range (e.g., ±3%, ±2%, ±1%), as I have done also.

5. Arizona, Hawaii, Mississippi, and West Virginia were excluded. No polls or no recent polls were conducted for these noncompetitive U.S. Senate contests.

6. In most cases the last poll was conducted within a week or a few days before the election, although in some cases the last poll was taken several weeks before the election. No poll was used if it was taken before September. Naturally, polls conducted within a week of the election can be compared more validly and fairly with the actual election results, but earlier polls are used to compare earlier poll results with the ones just before the election. The source for the poll data was NationalJournal.com (poll track, Senate).

7. Interview with John Zogby, September 19, 2000.

8. Some local exit polling may be done for local races, but none for the national media.

9. The Associated Press did not call Florida for Gore or Bush.

10. www.aapor.org/ethics/best.html (2/15/01).

11. Once actual election results start to be merged with the pure exit poll data, the exit poll results, based solely on exit interviewing, cannot be compared to the actual results to test the accuracy of the exit polling itself. The 13,130 figure was taken from www.CNN.com/ELECTION/2000/epols/US/P000.html (2/15/01).

12. Phone conversation with Murray Edelman on November 22, 2000. Edelman was sympathetic with my plight, but was, nonetheless, not in a position to give me the "late afternoon" poll projections that I needed to test VNS's exit polling.

13. The name of the reporter will not be disclosed to protect this person's relationship with VNS.

14. But, to reiterate, I included the latest poll predictions that I could for these major and local polling companies. The reporting dates for these polls are included in Table A.1, so the curious can do the calculations by dates before the election, if they desire. Ironically, however, some polls conducted in September proved more accurate than some conducted just before the election because in many campaigns, if not most, the relative electoral strength for the candidates does not change too much during the course of the campaign. Dramatic shifts do occur in campaigns, but they are uncommon.

CHAPTER 11

1. George Gallup and Saul Rae, *The Pulse of Democracy* (New York: Simon and Schuster, 1940), p. 6.

2. Terry Jones, "Newspapers Often Misunderstand Their Own Polls," *St. Louis Journalism Review* (October 2000), p. 13.

Index